THE GREAT WAR
MYTH AND MEMORY

The Great War

Myth and Memory

Dan Todman

hambledon
continuum

Hambledon Comtinuum
A Continuum imprint

The Tower Building
11 York Road
London, SE1 7NX

80 Maiden Lane
Suite 704
New York, NY 10038

First Published 2005 in hardback

ISBN 1 85285 459 6 (hardback)
ISBN 1 85285 512 6 (paperback)

A description of this book is available from the
British Library and from the Library of Congress.

Typeset by Carnegie Publishing, Lancaster,
and printed in Great Britain by MPG Books, Cornwall.

Contents

Illustrations

Acknowledgements

I am grateful to the BBC for permission to quote from material in its Written Archives Centre; to the Archbishop of Canterbury and the Trustees of the Lambeth Palace Library for permission to quote from the Ramsey Papers; to the Trustees of the Liddell Hart Centre for Military Archives for permission to quote from the Liddell Hart Papers; and to the Trustees of the National Library of Scotland for permission to quote from material held in the Haig Papers. Every effort has been made to locate copyright holders (particularly for material held in the Imperial War Museum and the Brotherton Library, Leeds), but I apologise to anyone whose copyright may inadvertently have been infringed.

The author and publishers are grateful to the following for permission to reproduce illustrations: the Imperial War Museum (plates 1–4, 6, 7, 9); the National Library of Scotland, plate 8; and the Owen Collection, Oxford English Faculty Library, University of Oxford, plate 5.

Introduction

The guns fell silent on the Western Front at 11 a.m. on 11 November 1918. Eighty years after the Armistice, in the autumn of 1998, Britons turned their thoughts back to the First World War. It was a war that few then alive could remember and that even fewer had experienced as adults. Even so, newspapers filled their columns with stories of surviving veterans, accounts of the descendants of dead soldiers travelling back to the battlefields and cemeteries, and reviews of the numerous television programmes, books, plays and exhibitions which had been commissioned to mark the war's anniversary.[1] In one such review, of the Imperial War Museum's exhibition 'The First World War Remembered', the new Poet Laureate, Andrew Motion, suggested that 'memories of the First World War are still endlessly pondered and transformed in the minds of those born long after it ended ... Those guns may have fallen silent eighty years ago, but their echoes neither die nor even fade away'.[2]

That the war continues to play a part in British culture is not surprising. It was a unique event in British history: the mass mobilisation of the population to fight a land war against the main strength of a great power opponent on the European mainland. The effort required affected the life of every Briton at the time, most traumatically through the death of three quarters of a million men. It deserved the epithet 'Great' bestowed upon it by contemporaries. Even if few in 1998 had experienced it at first hand, many had grown up with its echoes resounding in their ears.

Britons in 1998 also shared a clear set of ideas about what the First World War meant and what it had been like, ideas which enabled commentators across the political and social spectrum to discuss the war in shared terms. The war was depicted as a tragedy and a disaster. In 1914 the nations of Europe had stumbled into a struggle that no one really wanted, sparked off by a murder in the Balkans that had little relevance to Britain. In response to their country's call to arms, a generation of eager young Britons joined up to fight a war they didn't understand. They marched off to France and Flanders, leaving behind an idyllic Edwardian age that would never be recaptured. Once there, they fell under the command of a group of incompetent commanders, asinine aristocrats obsessed with cavalry. Safely ensconced miles behind the lines, these generals were unable to grasp the realities of the new style of warfare they were facing. Their men were stuck, for four years, in the most appalling conditions, living in trenches scraped into the ground, surrounded by mud, rats and decaying corpses. Time and again they were thrown forward in ill-conceived assaults that achieved nothing. They were destroyed almost to a man; those who survived going over the top were crippled, went mad, or were shot by their own side for desertion. The war finally ended because of German disintegration at home and the arrival of the Americans. The pitiful survivors who returned to Britain were silenced by the trauma of their experiences – only the words of a tiny band of warrior poets could communicate the truth of what they had been through. Their sacrifices had accomplished nothing. They came home to unemployment and destitution. Worse still, twenty years later another war, spawned from the legacy of the first, ravaged the world again.[3]

This interpretation continues to dominate how Britons think about the First World War in the first decade of the twenty-first century. Almost certainly it shapes how you imagine the war as you read this. This book is about how this version of the war came about and why it remains so powerful.

These beliefs did not become widely shared because they offered the only accurate interpretation of wartime events. In every respect, the war was much more complicated than they suggest. In recent years, historians have argued persuasively against almost every popular cliché of the First World War. It has been pointed out that, although the losses were devastating, their greatest impact was socially and geographically limited. The many emotions other than horror experienced by soldiers in and out of the front line, including comradeship, boredom and even enjoyment, have been recognized. The war is not now seen as a 'fight about nothing', but as a war of ideals, a struggle between aggressive militarism and more or less liberal democracy. It has been acknowledged that British generals were often capable men facing difficult challenges, and that it was under their command that the British army played a major part in the defeat of the Germans in 1918: a great forgotten victory.[4]

None of this has made the slightest difference to what most people actually believe about the First World War. Some readers may have changed their minds about the abilities of generals, or the reasons the war was fought, but the same basic understanding of the war as tragedy and disaster still pervades British culture. In part this is a problem of imaginative inertia: the great human difficulty in jumping from one vision of the world to another. But it is also because of the functions that our shared beliefs about the war fulfil. They have achieved the status of a modern mythology and as such are knitted into the social fabric.

For most people 'history' is not a perfectly remembered set of dates, places and people, let alone a detailed understanding based on exhaustive academic study. Rather, it is a conglomeration of half-remembered facts from school, the occasional reading of books of fact and fiction, references in the media and conversations at the table, the bar or the workplace. Since we live in the same culture and share many of the same sources for our historical beliefs, we hold some of them in common. Even if we realise that they do not fully represent historical events, these shared beliefs are extremely powerful. They enjoy far wider currency than any other sort of understanding of the past; they underpin the historical structure within which we position ourselves and they are held with great certainty. They inform social behaviour, culture, public policy and national, local and personal identity. As the writers of the 1930 satire on school history *1066 and All That* pointed out to their readers: 'History is not what you thought. *It is what you can remember.* All other history defeats itself.'[5] The history you can remember is, if not the only sort that matters, definitely the sort that is held most widely.

In trying to describe this 'history you can remember', this book uses the word 'myth'. Here, a myth is a belief about the past held by an individual but common to a social group. The size of that social group can vary from the nation as a whole, down through towns or districts, to the level of single families. Myths held at different levels of society interact. At the lowest level, although they incorporate national and local myths, they focus on the experiences of family members. One facet of Britons' continuing emotional involvement with the war has been a fascination with what their Dad, Grandad or Great Grandad did in it.

Myths simplify, reducing the complex events of the past to an easily understood set of symbols.[6] Their social function is to ease communication. Rather than explain exactly what occurred each time we refer to a huge historical event like the Great War, we develop myths which sum up what is commonly supposed to have happened and which we can rely on others understanding. 'Myth' is often juxtaposed with 'reality' and used as a synonym for 'lie', but this book avoids such judgements.[7] All historical explanations inevitably simplify the complex nature of the past. Myths in themselves are not a bad thing; they are a necessary part of human society and they can function for good or ill.

Popular myths about the First World War have not remained constant over time. The roots of our current mythology lie in events and opinions held during it, but what we have now was not the only possible version. In 1918, some Britons felt that the war had been a tragedy. For many of them, on an individual emotional level, it was a disaster. Yet even those who had lost loved ones to the war constructed a host of other meanings around it.

The war could mean survival, victory (personal and national), disappoint-
ment, comradeship, unity, sorrow, shared purpose, betrayal, sacrifice,
redefined status, and enjoyment; sometimes all at the same time. It was by
no means certain that it was from these that our modern version of the war
would emerge. How did we get from there to here? Why was it that certain
myths grew stronger and more dominant whilst others disappeared from
view?

Studying how people *thought* in the past is difficult. It is not possible to
conduct a retrospective survey of opinion even amongst those still alive,
since their recollections of how they thought even a short while ago will have
altered over time. What we do have, of course, is the vast quantity of books,
plays, television and radio programmes, memorials, advertisements, films
and ceremonial activities which grew up around the subject of the war. By
exploring how these were produced and received, we can attempt to uncover
the myths which underpinned them.

This book is not a comprehensive catalogue of every representation of the
First World War since 1914. The potential size of such a catalogue would
make its construction impracticable. Instead, it tries to draw on the widest
possible variety of sources and suggest how influential or important they
were. For some books and broadcast media, accurate figures exist for sales
and audience numbers. For others, it has been necessary to use less precise
information, for example the number of times a book was reprinted,
whether it was transferred from hardback to paperback, or how many
times it was subsequently referred to, in order to judge its success and
influence. It is not good enough to record a subjective reaction to a book
or television programme and assume that this is how contemporaries
reacted as well. Historians who do this simply impose their own background
and preconceptions on the past: they commit the sin of psychological
anachronism. Most importantly, this book examines both the production
and reception of these different sources and tries to place them in their
cultural context. Rather than taking a purely chronological approach, it
divides the modern myth of the war up into six constituent smaller myths,
each of which is examined in an individual chapter. The first four are the-
matic: they discuss the genesis of myths about horror, death, generalship
and futility. The final two chapters are about poets and veterans, two key
groups in the shaping and transmission of our modern mythology.

In the course of researching and writing this book, I have built up a wide
variety of debts of gratitude, which I am now glad to repay. For financial
support, I am grateful to the Arts and Humanities Research Council and the
Historial de la Grande Guerre, Peronne, France. Pembroke College,

Cambridge provided a congenial atmosphere to pursue my studies and supported my research trips.

Tony Morris and Martin Sheppard at Hambledon and London have been patient and generous. Martin, in particular, deserves thanks for his insistence that this book should be written so as to make it readable for pleasure. My research benefited greatly from the assistance of librarians and archivists across the country, including those at the Liddell Hart Centre for Military Archives at King's College, the Imperial War Museum, Lambeth Palace Library and the British Library, all in London, the National Library of Scotland, Edinburgh, and the University Library, Cambridge. I am extremely grateful to all of them.

Jay Winter inspired me during the early stages of this project. Peter Martland helped me to see it through to completion as both mentor and friend. Alex Danchev, Mark Connelly, Gary Sheffield, Rob Havers, Peter Hennessy, Keith Surridge and Chris Pugsley have all helped me during its writing, but I owe particular thanks to John Ramsden, who read through the entire work in proof. I am also grateful to my students at the Royal Military Academy Sandhurst and at Queen Mary, University of London, on whom I first tried out many of the ideas in these pages. I never used to believe that academics really meant such thanks: their questions, challenges and enthusiasm have proved me wrong.

My final thanks are personal. My friends have had to live with the First World War for far longer than they deserve. Some have been brave enough to read parts of my work and offer comments. Others have studiously avoided doing so. Nevertheless they have had to deal with its fallout – irascibility, lack of attention and a persistent inability to pass a war memorial without passing comment. Despite this, they have supported and encouraged me: they have therefore made a great contribution to this book. I owe Elton Barker, Michael Booth, Mark Buswell, James Crabtree and Adam Dawson a debt which I look forward to trying to repay.

Their part has been subsidiary, however, to that played by my family. Vic, Penny and Michael Todman made me who I am: it is to them that this book is dedicated.

Mud

There are two photographs of the First World War that everyone has seen. They are used to accompany newspaper reports about the war and its commemoration, to illustrate history books and as stills in television documentaries. The first shows troops walking between waterlogged shell craters on their way from a shattered wood,[1] the second depicts stretcher-bearers struggling to bring in a wounded man.[2] The men in these photographs look disconsolate or desperate. They are smeared with the sodden earth that surrounds them, or literally enmired in it. In the grey tones of the black and white photographs, they can be hard to distinguish from the dead landscape. At the Imperial War Museum Photographic Archive, the first port of call for writers, journalists and television producers seeking images, these are two of the most frequently requested pictures of the First World War. As such, they have come to form a visual shorthand for the British experience in that war.

These are both overwhelmingly pictures of mud. But if it is mud that dominates these images, it is the associations it carries with it that make them so striking. For here mud stands for much more than a mere amalgam of water and soil. It is made up of excrement, dead soldiers and animals, shrapnel, barbed wire and the remnants of poison gas. For all the opportunities it offered to bacteria, surrounding splintered trees and dead men, it seems to be opposed to nature. This mud bears the terrifying potential to engulf the soldiers who struggle within it, to suck them down – spluttering, choking, drowning – and to convert their corpses into yet more mud.

Mud, with all these associations, dominates our understanding of what the First World War was like for those who fought it. We think of the war as being distinctively horrendous, marked out from other conflicts for its participants and for us by its particularly awful nature. If asked to think about the war, we call to mind men trapped in trenches for four years, with only gas or flood bringing relief from rats, launching doomed attacks which left most dead or wounded, before returning home so traumatised by their experiences that they could never bear to speak of them again. 'Mud', therefore, is used here to evoke a broader myth of the horror of the First World War.

Parts of that war were indeed appalling in a way which it still hard to comprehend, even in an age where satellite television brings pictures of mutilated bodies straight into our living rooms. On the Western Front, above all, the unleashing of the full potential of modern industrialised warfare – with its vast quantities of munitions and men – created a new landscape of destruction and death. The killing power of modern weapons forced infantrymen to dig trenches to protect themselves. Commanders' inability to control their forces combined with lack of space to make large-scale manoeuvre extremely difficult. Heavy fighting might therefore take place over the same pieces of ground over prolonged periods. The only sure way through the complicated defensive positions built by both sides was to smash them with artillery fire. Equally, the best way to defend a position against assault was to shell those troops who were attacking it. This fire from both sides killed and wounded the infantrymen below, mutilating them so horrifically that inexperienced troops seeing their bodies believed they must have been desecrated by enemy soldiers. It also tore the ground they were holding to pieces. It created a moonscape of shell craters. The addition of rain to this shattered terrain would turn it swiftly into a morass.

Even when the fighting had finished, the battlefields retained their ability to shock. The writer John Masefield, accustomed to touring the battlefields of Gallipoli and Verdun, reported back to his wife from the aftermath of the Battle of the Somme in the late autumn of 1916:

> We went into a wood, which we will call Chunk-of-Corpse-Wood, for its main features were chunks of corpse, partly human, partly trees. There was a cat eating a man's brain, & such a wreck of war as I never did see, & the wounded coming by, dripping blood on the track, & one walked on blood or rotten flesh, & saw bags of men being carried to the grave. They were shovelling parts of men into blankets.[3]

During combat, the effect on bodies, landscapes and minds was even more horrific. Edwin Campion Vaughan's nightmarish experiences during an attack at St Julieen, outside Ypres, on 27 August 1917 may stand for many:

> Immediately there came the crackle of bullets and mud spattered about me as I ran, crawled and dived into shell-holes, over bodies, sometimes up to the armpits in water, sometimes crawling on my face along a ridge of slimy mud around some crater ... As I neared the gunpits I saw a head rise above a shell-hole, a mouth opened to call something to me, but the tin hat was sent flying and the face fell forward into the mud. Then another head came up and instantly was struck by a bullet. This time the fellow was only grazed and, relieved at receiving a blighty, he jumped out, shaking off a hand that tried to

detain him. He ran back a few yards, then I saw him hit in the leg; he fell and started to crawl, but a third bullet got him and he lay still ...

Exhausted by my efforts, I paused a moment in a shell-hole; in a few seconds I felt myself sinking, and struggle as I might I was sucked down until I was firmly gripped round the waist and still being dragged in. The leg of a corpse was sticking out of the side, and frantically I grabbed it; it wrenched off, and casting it down I pulled in a couple of rifles and yelled to the troops in the gun-pit to throw me more. Laying them flat I wriggled over them and dropped, half dead, into the wrecked gun position ...

Up the road we staggered, shells bursting around us. A man stopped dead in front of me, and exasperated I cursed him and butted him with my knee. Very gently he said 'I'm blind, Sir,' and turned to show me his eyes and nose torn away by a piece of shrapnel. 'Oh God! I'm sorry, sonny,' I said. 'Keep going on the hard part', and left him staggering back in the darkness.[4]

Accounts like this are so awful and so striking that they inevitably leave a huge impression on those who read them. Yet in order to understand them properly it is necessary to try to put them in context. This does not mean dismissing or discarding them: what it does mean is realising that, striking though they are, they do not represent the entirety of the war as it was experienced by men at the time.

One of the most difficult things for us to grasp about the First World War today is its vast size. Its scale, in terms of personnel, geography and logistics, was enormous. It was a war that mobilised almost six and a half million Britons into the armed forces. It stretched far beyond the Western Front – from the Falklands, via Mesopotamia and East Africa, to Tsingtao on the Chinese coast. The financial cost of the war and the huge quantities of munitions it required meant that the domestic population was also crucial to the war effort; a fact the Germans recognised when they shelled and bombed British civilians, as well as attacking the merchant fleet which sustained the British economy. It was a total war, therefore, in the sense that it involved everyone. Whilst its size does not put the war beyond our understanding, it does require us to make a step change from a mode of thought conditioned by conflicts several orders of magnitude smaller.[5] In human terms, the First World War's size meant an enormous variety of different personal experiences for participants. Many different meanings were drawn from those experiences. The war touched the lives of all Britons. For those not involved in combat at first hand, it was not about mud and gore, although it might well be about grief as a result of such horrors. The versions they constructed of the war, also included, amongst other things, different jobs, new government interference in their lives, separation, the finding of shared social purpose and even apathy and disengagement. All these are obscured in our modern understanding by a concentration on the horrors of combat.

Even if we limit our assessment to the Western Front, we can see that these experiences and meanings encompassed more than struggling forward through mud and slime in doomed attacks. Not every soldier served in a front line infantry regiment. The nature of fighting on the Western Front required large numbers of men to serve in the artillery, and to a lesser degree in new arms like tanks and aeroplanes. It also required a very great number of men supporting the effort at the front: moving supplies, guarding lines of communication, training soldiers and administering their lives. Whilst small by modern standards, the ratio of non-combatant to combatant troops grew steadily through the war, not least because of the great increase in the number and variety of munitions employed in attack. From just under a sixth of the army in 1914, it had reached nearly a third by July 1918. These men were absolutely essential to the war effort. The outcomes of the enormous battles of the Western Front were dependent on the supply of shells and of trained and well motivated soldiers. In this vast industrialised war, victory was much less a matter of individual heroism than of the quantity of shells one side could land on the other. Without its bureaucrats, accountants, administrators and dockers, the British Expeditionary Force (BEF) would have been lost. Whilst many of the men thus employed would have seen the impacts of the war on a daily basis and lost friends and relatives to it, their experience of the war was far removed from the popular conception of trenches and relentless mud and guts. Their story has been all but lost by the public and historians and only recently has it become a subject of academic study.[6]

Even in the infantry, no one experienced the most awful aspects of the front all the time. Different parts of the front varied widely in terms of both conditions and activity. Some, like the Ypres Salient in the late autumn of 1917, were fully as awful as popular myth records. Others, even then, were quiet, well ordered and comparatively safe. No unit would expect to be in the front line all the time. Rather, it rotated with its fellow battalions between the front line, the support lines, and being in reserve or at rest. Even if 'rest' often meant arduous manual labour or training, it did imply a greater degree of safety and an improvement in conditions.

In a calculation made in 1929, Charles Carrington worked out that as a junior officer in 1916 he spent less than a third of the year in positions which could be described as 'under fire', either in the front line or in immediate support. A full third was spent within a few hours' march of the front line, close enough to move up to fight if needed. By far the largest proportion of his time, 145 days, was spent away from the front, either resting, at schools of instruction, in hospital, on leave or on the move between these different places. Carrington undertook twelve 'tours' in the trenches that year (out of a total of sixteen by his battalion). He was in action four times: one direct attack, two bombing actions, and once holding the line for another unit's advance. His experience seems typical of many others of his rank: his men would have had leave less regularly and of shorter duration. They might have spent less time under instruction, but they were relatively less likely to have had to assume positions of extreme danger during action.[7]

Probably the most frequently endured experience for most soldiers in the combat arms was not terror or disgust but boredom. A large army, called rapidly into existence, was not by its nature adept at disposing men into roles which they enjoyed or to which they were well suited. It generated a huge amount of bureaucracy and frequent confusion. Soldiers spent a lot of time with their liberties restricted, in dull conditions, being told to hurry up and wait. They did not get to pick and choose their jobs, locations or food. To some, this loss of individual control seemed like a happy result of joining the army. To most it was at best something to be endured. The citizen soldiers who had joined up in 1914 and 1915, motivated by a crusading zeal and certain of their rectitude in fighting a barbarian enemy, were willing to put up with a lot. Inevitably, however, a gulf opened up between their expectations and a humdrum reality that often bred frustration.[8]

On the other hand, many men were able to find compensatory factors in their military service. Most, even if they had been conscripted rather than volunteering (as was commonly the case from 1916), seem to have believed in the rightness of Britain's cause. Working as part of a larger organisation to achieve a result, to take their place in history, gave them a sense of purpose which some found rewarding in itself. In the course of training, fighting and resting together, many forged powerful bonds of comradeship from shared blood, sweat and beers. These bonds – encouraged by the tribal nature of the British regimental system which gave men an immediate source of group identity – served to sustain them through the worst the war had to offer. Laughter, drunkenness and camaraderie were as much a part of the war, for many men, as terror, violence and obedience. This ambiguous attitude to the war was honestly summed up by George Carey and Harold Scott, then teachers, but formerly officers in the Rifle Brigade and the Royal Field Artillery respectively, in a schoolbook on the war they wrote in 1929. The book makes frequent reference to British courage, portrays the High Command positively, and refers to death as the 'noblest climax of this warrior life'. Yet the authors closed the book with a meditation on the war's 'meaning' which focused on other things:

> Mud, monotony and deadly fatigue became the daily portion, varied only by occasional periods of intense fear and less frequent interludes of compara-tive safety and comfort … It is a merciful provision of human nature that memory lets slip the unpleasant and leaves the pleasant uppermost; that for most of the war's survivors the gruesome episodes are overlaid by the recollection of a comfortable billet, a cheerful mess, the smoke-laden atmos-phere of an *estaminet*, the unexpected encounter of a friend, or the bliss of getting into the 'leave train'. It would, indeed, be foolish to pretend that the war had no redeeming features. Though the highest flights of human heroism might be only for the few, the call to serve, whether in the forces, in hospital, canteen, factory, or office, was general and was generally answered with sacrifice. Class barriers were broken down and comrade-ship became a real and unforgettable thing. Yet not one of those who felt the scorch of the war would willingly live through all his or her experiences again.[9]

There were even those who discovered that not only were they good at fighting and killing, but that they could take pleasure in these skills. If we find, in retrospect, some of their accounts bizarre or distasteful, that does not mean that they should be discounted. There were many more who found that, whatever their attitude to violence, they were able and adept sol-diers and leaders. The army gave them responsibility and a sense of place. As the war went on and the British army became more meritocratic in its approach to promotions, it increasingly rewarded those with demonstrated junior leadership abilities, even if its officers remained overwhelmingly middle class. Around 229,000 new commissions were granted during the war, just under half to men who passed through officer cadet battalions after service as private soldiers.[10]

The challenges and achievements of command were rewarding for many men. Billie Neville, newly placed in command of B Company, 1/East Surreys in March 1916, revelled in the trust, loyalty and camaraderie of his men and subordinates:

> The coy. is going very well and I'm no end bucked about it. 220 odd men all to myself. Their meals, clothes, pay and lives too all my responsibility. They are a topping lot, not unlike C coy. I rather won their hearts by paying 'em and sending 'em to Amiens to enjoy themselves. To-day I've been cursing the ones who missed the train home. Bobby Soames has joined us again, and now with Drane and Alcock, we're quite a little party.[11]

It was Neville who won posthumous fame for giving his men footballs to kick over the top and follow towards the German lines on 1 July 1916.

Was the First World War actually more horrific for those who took part than other conflicts? The variety of individual background and experience makes it hard to say. We can look back to accounts of earlier conflicts and find men recording what had sickened them. Descriptions of the siege warfare of the Napoleonic or Crimean Wars contain some of the same grotesque details: mutilated, fragmented bodies, the presence of the dead and dying, and the effects of decomposition. Even to long service professional soldiers, used to a much harder way of life, these things stood out. What was different about the First World War was the scale and duration of its battles and the number and class of British soldiers involved. The destruction on bodies and landscapes wrought by concentrated bombardments created an environment of horrors with a qualitative difference to previous wars. But, as importantly, this destruction was participated in and witnessed, not by a tiny professional army, but by a huge army of citizen soldiers, including numerous well-educated and well-connected men who could record what they saw.

To what degree this devastation was unforeseen or unforeseeable is debatable. The horrendous power of modern weaponry had been visible in the American Civil War and the Russo-Japanese War. It is certainly not the case that the whole of Britain rushed enthusiastically to war in 1914 with the idea that it would be sweet and glorious. There was depression and foreboding as well as enthusiasm. But there was a difference between paying lip-service to the idea that the coming war might be terrible and the experience of it at first hand. The gap between expectation and reality was shocking, even if it was insufficient to persuade the population to stop fighting.

Although it lacked that same shocking quality, the best point of comparison for the horrors of the First World War is its successor. Examining British participation in the Second World War, there are a number of direct similarities with the First. These include the existence of awful conditions to fight in (the Burmese jungle, North-West Europe or the Italian mountains in the winter of 1944–45) and the horrific injuries caused by modern weapons (throughout the war). Descriptions of areas of intense fighting again bear witness to the dreadful impact of modern war. In the aftermath of the Goodwood offensive of 1944, a British officer described the battlefield as:

a scene of utter desolation. I have never seen such bomb craters. Trees were uprooted, roads were impassable. There were bodies in half; crumpled men. A tank lay upside down, another was still burning with a row of feet sticking out

from underneath. In one crater a man's head and shoulders appeared sticking
out from the side. The place stank.[12]

What marked the First World War out for Britain was the length and scale
of her commitment to a land war, the unremitting nature of trench warfare
and the dissonance with previous experience; not what the worst of military
experience had to offer.[13] Taken together, these underlying factors ensured
that the horrors of the war would be written into the heart of its mythology.

Comparing the First and the Second World Wars should lead us to realise
that wars do not have to be represented in popular mythology in terms of
horror. Notwithstanding the fact that some aspects of it were as objectively
'bad' as the First World War, our myths about the Second World War are
overwhelmingly positive, and it is not seen in terms of an abiding and irre-
solvable trauma. Given the horrific conditions of the Western Front, the
scale of the war effort and the differences from Britain's previous wars, it is
not surprising that horror should have become a staple of how the First
World War was represented. But how were divergent wartime reactions
transformed into a myth of war experience that emphasised horror to the
exclusion of all else?

Standing guard over our muddy understanding of the First World War are
two paradoxically juxtaposed figures. On one side is the silent veteran, so
traumatised by his experiences that he is unable to communicate them. This
figure occurs time and again in popular culture and individual memories,
based on a shared familial experience of soldiers who returned home from
the war and spoke about it seldom, if at all. It is easy enough to presume
that what he had seen was too awful to be passed on. Yet on the other side
stands his polar opposite, the soldier writer, poet or dramatist, or more
recently the aged veteran, who did choose to communicate his experiences.
On their testimony is based much of our modern understanding of what the
war was like. Are these figures reconcilable? Who spoke and who remained
silent?

One of the key methodological difficulties of studying how the soldiers
of the First World War felt about its horrors is extrapolating general reactions from individual sources. Historians tend to rely on the most articulate
written sources of personal testimony; but most men did not have the literary skill or inclination to set down what had happened to them in ringing
tones. That in itself tends to distort how we see the front line. In the mid
1970s, the historian Correlli Barnett argued that the British version of the
war was dominated by a group of middle-class poets raised in a rural tradition. Of course these men were shocked by their encounters with the

industrial wasteland of the Western Front. He argued that to the working-class soldiers who made up the bulk of the rank and file, used to industrial accidents, pollution and slums, such conditions were rather less foreign.[14] This argument has to be taken with a pinch of salt. Barnett had a contentious point to back up about the failure of British liberalism and he was not afraid to resort to polemic to bolster it. Not every officer, even those from privileged backgrounds, was shocked by the horrors of the front. Some wrote accounts which deliberately played down such things. Equally, no matter what the failings of Edwardian health and safety, there were differences between pre-war existence and life in the trenches, not least the extremity and persistence of violence and the co-existence with death. The inhabitants of urban Glasgow might regularly have set about each other on sectarian lines, but they did not employ trench mortars, machine guns and flamethrowers.[15] Barnett was correct, however, to warn the historian to be wary before assuming that the experience of the front struck all men the same way, and to be careful about whose version of the trenches was being written. If veterans said nothing, it may simply have been because they found it hard to compose their memories, or were not in the habit of writing them down.

What other reasons were there for veterans to remain silent? The traumatic nature of fighting could sometimes make it difficult to recollect, let alone to construct a narrative that was coherent for the participant, let alone others. Those who experienced combat – that part of wartime life which provided the densest collection of horrors seen and perpetrated – often found it hard to recall precisely. War was full of events that men judged significant to themselves at the time: the first sight of death, the first day of battle, survival. They felt that they ought to remember them. But the combination of stress, adrenalin and trauma meant that precise, sequential recollection could be difficult. The memory was burned deep into the brain, but into a section of it that could be all but impossible to access under normal circumstances. The phenomenon, noted by Adrian Carton de Wiart, of a soldier who could not remember the solo storming of a machine gun position which led to him being recommended for a VC, was only the extreme end of a common experience.[16] The French historian Marc Bloch recalled his first day of combat, 10 September 1914. It was, he wrote, a day that would stay with him forever, but: 'Even so, my recollections ... are not altogether precise. Above all they are poorly articulated, a discontinuous series of images, vivid in themselves but badly arranged like a reel of ... film that showed here and there large gaps and the unintended reversal of certain scenes.'[17] Only by discussion could men quickly compose a coherent story out of what had happened. In the aftermath of battle, many men preferred to escape into sleep, drink or sport instead of rehashing their recent experiences.

During the war, there were obvious reasons for soldiers not to tell their friends and families what was happening to them. Men's letters were read and censored, but more powerful was a self-censorship which was designed to protect those at home from the worries they might have experienced if they had known the dangers that their correspondents were facing. When they returned on leave, most men had such limited time that they concentrated on such pleasures of civilian life as were available to them, rather than spending time talking about the war they had left behind.

Wartime service itself developed a powerful mythic status.[18] A widespread belief at the time that soldiering had set these men apart was self-fulfilling: returning veterans truly did not feel that they could make those who had stayed at home understand them. This was even more the case for those whose wartime experiences did not fit the wider perception of what the war 'should' have been like. From the start of the war, military service was represented in popular culture in terms of action in the front line. If Daddy had spent his war shifting packing cases in Le Havre, he might not want to talk about it not because it was horrific but because it seemed humdrum. Equally under the influence of this myth, listeners might never feel that veterans were telling them the whole truth, no matter what was said. Veterans who did recall the positive aspects of their wartime experiences were presumed to be obscuring what had *really* happened. Communication was a two-way process. Repetition, selection or silence all reinforced the myth and themselves had an effect on what men actually remembered.

There is a human inclination to remember and to rehearse memories for others: we don't just recall, we have to tell. This impulse is even stronger in those who feel themselves to have participated in events that are dramatic, terrible or significant, globally or individually. There is not only an active desire to remember, but for some an inability to forget, which may itself eventually encourage rehearsal. The processes by which memories are laid down, recollected and selected for rehearsal are complex, as will be apparent if you pause to analyse the stories you tell about your own life history. Is that actually what happened? How have you adapted your account, leaving things out or adding them in, in order to make it a better story, to fit with how you see yourself, or to meet the expectations of others?

The raw material for remembering is laid down by experience. Experiences leave memory traces in the brain.[19] Each trace's degree of detail and likelihood of being recollected depends on its density. In turn, its density may depend on its dramatic and autobiographically important nature: participation in war and particularly in combat therefore often leaves a deep trace. Indeed, so great a density may be achieved – as a result of an experience that is particularly traumatic – that recollection may essentially become uncontrolled, either becoming almost impossible, or flooding back despite the will of the individual, perhaps initiated by a similarity of atmosphere or environment. Robert Graves put down his receipt of a post-war pension for nerves to the process of train journey and stressful assessment interview, which in themselves reminded him of the army and exacerbated his symptoms. J. B. Priestley found it, in later life, all but impossible to travel on the London Underground because of a fear of confined spaces deriving from his wartime service.[20] Although memory traces may enjoy remarkable longevity, they are not necessarily available for retrieval undistorted. They meet interference from subsequent experiences, from earlier memories that shape the context in which they are laid down, or from the schemata that individuals apply to their lives.

Memory traces are rendered more accessible by rehearsal. The more individuals retell the narratives which memory and interference have together constructed, the more available they become for future use. Rehearsal of memories is a public act. It is therefore affected by the culture of the social group in which it takes place, its taboos and traditions of expression as well as the myths current within it. Rehearsal highlights certain aspects of a story; necessarily so, because this learning of the key signposts is one of the factors that enables easier future recollection. Yet this highlighting also leads to the emphasis of these aspects, adding a further level of potential distortion. Some elements of the story will fit the myths prevalent in the social group in which rehearsal takes place. These will meet with approval and hence become more likely to repeated and remembered. Others will not and are likely to be unrehearsed and can be forgotten. Where the wider myths are particularly strong, individuals may be encouraged to make additions to the memories they rehearse. Consciously or unconsciously, for a variety of reasons, they may fabricate elements of their rehearsal. In time, these fabrications can come to be held with as much conviction as recollections based on very dense memory traces.

We should also explore more prosaic reasons for veterans' silence. The very process of demobilisation and the return to civilian life could discourage discussion. Soldiers returning from war have often found the dissonance between real and imagined civilian life, the changes that have taken place in their absence, and the removal of the reassuring structures of the military, confusing. The analysis of returning soldiers by a Second World War military psychologist applies equally to their forebears:

> Most men knew that they had a lot to learn, but few were prepared for the problems of emotional adjustment in their very homes, and their own

workplaces, and among their own familiar communities. In fantasy their
civilian life was to be as they left it, with no closing of the emotional ranks
where they fell out, and they felt themselves to be basically unchanged. The
great barriers of unshared experience that grew up in the war years between
them and their families in civilian life could only be half realised ...

The difficulties are often about intangible and uncommunicable deep human
values, and the inability of others, wives and friends, to share a subtle but
important viewpoint makes for distress and growing anger and a belief that
they have forgotten what life is about. Men in such a state are restless, bitter
and irritable at home, and feeling cut off from the very sources of understanding and affection go for long walks or remain silent and morose for long
periods.[21]

The men who fought the First World War also existed in an expressive
culture very different to our own. Unlike modern Britons, they had never
enjoyed the benefits of watching a Martin Bashir interview or a Robert
Kilroy Silk chat show. They felt no need constantly to discuss their emotions and experiences. This selective taciturnity preceded the war:
working-class families at the start of the twentieth century did not expect
fathers or husbands to bring news of work home with them.[22] Indeed, one
mark of a good husband was that he did not bring the problems of the factory home. It was not trauma but habit that prevented some men from
talking about what they had done. Even if they had found aspects of their
service terrifying or awful, why should they want to discuss it? Understandably, many men were eager to get back on with their lives, to find
themselves work in a difficult job market, and to abandon a period which
they viewed, like the poet David Jones, as being 'In Parenthesis'.[23] This did
not mean that these veterans would never rehearse their wartime memories. It did mean that they required specific contexts to feel comfortable so
doing.

Given all these powerful influences towards silence, why was it that
other veterans chose to communicate what they had experienced, both
during the war and after it? More particularly, why were some of them able
to describe some of the horrors they had seen; for it is on their accounts
that our beliefs about the war are based? For some, undoubtedly, there was
a need to set down troubling memories in a bid to exorcise them, to bid,
like Graves, *Goodbye to All That*. But this was by no means the only
reason.

For many of these men, retelling and recording something of what they
had seen was a crucial part of affirming their status as soldiers and as men.
There were details of military service that were striking, which were awful,

but which were not traumatic in the sense that to recall them did damage to the person remembering. Instead, the ability to do so highlighted the distinction of having served. The literary historian Samuel Hynes has used the term 'Battlefield Gothic' to describe these details, recalled, rehearsed and recorded because of their grotesque nature. He suggests that they are a constant of personal accounts of war. War, and particularly combat, is strange and different: men recall the things that make it so, partly because to be able to do so marks them out. They are warriors, who have seen and done what others have not. Asserting that they had been there gave them a sense of identity and of their individual participation in a great historical event.[24] During and after the First World War, in a culture which had come to place increasing emphasis on military participation as a key marker of masculinity and of citizenship, the ability to assert 'I was there' was obviously important for some men.[25] Indeed, the need to do so could overcome a lack of direct experience. In 1915, Captain Martin Hardie, serving on the censor's staff for Third Army, noticed that soldiers:

> consider it their duty – or some of them do – to send home thrilling tales. One writes that a zeppelin has been over their camp, dropping bombs and killing two men (This is pure fiction). Another gay youth writes to a girl ... enclosing a set of postcards 'given to me by a French girl called Rosie (!) who is sweet on me because me and my pals killed 5 huns and rescued her from their clutches'.[26]

There was huge interest in Britain as to what the war in the trenches was actually like, but it was difficult to fit that fascination to soldiers' willingness and ability to recall the details of combat. It was within this context that popular representations of the war and combat were formed before, during and after the Great War.

Despite our tendency to think of Edwardian Britain as looking forward with militaristic enthusiasm to the coming conflict, the idea that war could be awful was present in pre-war British popular culture.[27] Although there were numerous texts which glamorised war in the past and in the present, there were also writers who foresaw a future war with trepidation. They believed that it would bring death and destruction on a terrible scale. Yet both strands of thought tended to present military service in itself as a positive experience: ennobling, exciting and a central part of what it meant to be a man. This construction was strengthened, rather than weakened, as works of popular fiction began to portray combat in more explicitly gory terms from the end of the nineteenth century. It seems likely that audiences were

able to situate even those books which sought to warn them about the ter-
rors of international conflict within a wider 'pleasure culture of war' which
had become well established since the 1850s. In particular, despite considerable popular disdain for the army as a profession, a model of fictional
soldiery had developed in which British officers and men were brave,
muscular Christians, willing to sacrifice themselves in their country's cause
and worth ten of any foe.[28]

Out of this tradition came the first interpretations of the First World
War in terms of horror. From its outset, the British press, both popular
and respectable, focused on the crimes allegedly committed by German
troops against Belgian civilians, in particular the abuse of women and young
children. Accounts of these crimes were not challenged by a government
still dependent on voluntary recruiting, since the appalling behaviour of
German soldiers both formed a powerful rationale for Britain's involvement
in the war and created considerable pressure for civilians to join up. Even
as it offered a basis for recruitment, however, the sort of stories selected
for publication by the press showed that there were less strategically
pragmatic motives at work. Lurid descriptions of rape and murder
brought pornographic titillation onto the breakfast tables of respectable
Britain; horror sold papers as well as encouraging young men to fight.[29]

Popular rhetoric conceived of military service in terms of a fight against
the barbarians who had chosen to unleash the horrors of war. This meant
that more traditional representations of military experience were not immediately shattered by the First World War. On the contrary, the war
strengthened the demand for military-related material, and both journalists
and writers of popular fiction continued to make use of established tropes
of enthusiasm, heroism and gallant sacrifice.[30]

We should not be too quick to write off the creators of these texts as
bombastic duffers persuading innocent youngsters up the line to death.
Official censorship meant that overly graphic depictions of violence might
not reach the public: but as important was a self-censorship based partly
on a more restrictive expressive culture, and partly on a sense of patriotic
obligation. Writing for a country still reliant on voluntary recruitment,
fighting for a cause they believed was just, some journalists felt duty bound
to write positively about the military experience. Not every writer was
ignorant of conditions at the front line: Captain F. S. Brereton, one of
the most prolific and successful writers, had served in the RAMC in the
Boer War and rejoined the army in 1914. He still managed to pump out
twelve novels depicting the war and aimed at the youth market between
1914 and 1919.[31]

The horrific nature of some parts of the fighting was not completely hidden from the Home Front. The mass participation of British men in the army meant that there was considerable curiosity about and emotional commitment with what was happening to them, in particular after the first involvement of the New Army units raised during wartime, from late 1915 on. Local newspapers, subject to less strict official scrutiny than the nationals, often published letters from soldiers detailing the experiences of locally raised battalions, some of which were quite explicit about the terrible fighting in which they had been involved.[32] Soldier writers, like the former navvy Patrick MacGill, published accounts of the fighting based on first-hand experience. MacGill's popular novel *The Great Push*, a barely disguised memoir of his own experiences written as he convalesced after the Battle of Loos, contained descriptions of the battlefield:

> Men and pieces of men were lying all over the place. A leg, an arm, then again a leg, cut off at the hip. A finely formed leg, the latter, gracefully putteed. A dummy leg in a tailor's window could not be more graceful. It might be X; he was an artist in dress, a Beau Brummel in khaki. Fifty yards further along I found the rest of X ...
>
> The harrowing sight was repellent, antagonistic to my mind. The tortured things lying at my feet were symbols of insecurity, ominous reminders of danger from which no discretion could save a man. My soul was barren of pity; fear went down into the innermost parts of me, fear for myself.[33]

Despite his purple prose, MacGill recorded here the destruction of men's bodies, the random nature of death in battle, and the devastating effect of the fear thus created.

The most popular news film of the war, *The Battle of the Somme*, showed some of the landscape and fortifications over which the war was being fought, as well as British and German dead. Twenty million people saw the film in the first weeks of its release. The film concentrated on the scale of the offensive bombardment and presented the battle as a clear British victory, but to an audience unused to such images it was a shocking introduction to what the Western Front looked like, and how men appeared when they returned from combat. At the emotional climax of the film, as British troops went over the top and advanced into the smoke, the piano accompaniment ceased. The dramatic silence was filled with screams from the audience as they saw men fall.[34] An acknowledgement of the awful conditions even began to sneak into works of popular fiction aimed at young men. In Percy Westerman's 1919 novel *A Lively Bit of the Front*, the young New Zealand heroes have their puttees nibbled by rats and smell the dreadful mix of poison gas, high explosive and the dead Germans who have been buried beneath the floor of their trench.[35]

Two things are worthy of note about these wartime representations. The first is the degree to which they were actually able to replicate the experience of soldiers themselves. Whilst there were extremely successful books which concentrated on the raising and training of the volunteer New Armies – for example John Hay Beith's *The First Hundred Thousand* – for most accounts of the war the climax had to come with combat.[36] This was the defining experience that marked war out from civilian life. It was exciting. Yet it was hard to represent: partly because, as we have seen, soldiers themselves might find it hard to recall, but also because of the nature of contemporary technology and warfare. Capturing combat on film was extremely difficult with the unwieldy, hand-cranked cameras of the early twentieth century. The very scenes from *The Battle of the Somme* which caused such great emotion in the audience were, ironically, faked: shot at a trench mortar training school behind the lines. Immediately preceding them, however, was footage of the battlefield on 1 July, a panning shot across a landscape punctuated by occasional shellbursts and distant running figures. The dispersion of men on the modern battlefield, so essential if they were to survive, did not make for good film.[37] The painter John Singer Sargent, visiting the front in 1918 as a war artist, found that the closer he got to the action, the less there was to see: 'the further forward one goes the more scattered and meagre everything is. The nearer to danger, the fewer and more hidden the men – the more dramatic the situation the more it becomes an empty landscape. The Ministry of Information expects an epic – and how can one do an epic without masses of men?'[38] Little wonder, perhaps, that faced with the variety of different personal experiences and the difficulty of representation, many popular authors and artists fell back on tradition.[39]

The second is the meaning that was constructed from these books and images. What we might think of as more 'realistic' depictions of the horrors of war did not cause their audiences to reject conflict. On the contrary, if the initial enthusiasm of the first days of the war disappeared in the course of the attrition of 1916, it was replaced with a conviction that the war should continue to be fought and a resignation that it was going to be a long struggle. The majority of the population remained convinced of the reason for the war: that it was being fought to resist German barbarism. They fitted its horrors into that paradigm. All the pain, suffering and ghastliness of the front merely demonstrated how evil the Germans had been to start the war, and the necessity of continuing it until they were beaten. On the other hand, the atrocities with which the war had started were sidelined as scepticism engendered by the more lurid accounts of the fate of Belgian civilians met with the all too evident suffering of British soldiers. The horror of war as individual experience coexisted uneasily with the rationale of a national war against horror.

The First World War was a cornerstone of British culture throughout the 1920s and 1930s. As Britons memorialised their dead, recorded their experiences and sought to make sense of what had happened to them and their country over the four years of war, an enormous number of different representations of it were produced. These included histories, novels, poems, paintings, plays for stage and radio and feature films as well as a large quantity of memorials, and the formal and informal rituals of remembrance that attached to them. Many of these tried to depict what the soldiers' war had been like. In so doing, they drew on pre-existing models and wartime popular culture as well as on soldiers' own experiences.

With quantity came variety. That not only meant a variety of views about the war, but a variety of reasons for involvement with its remembrance and representation. These could include motivations apparently unconnected with the war itself: the desire for financial profit or political or social aggrandisement. There was no immediate overall agreement about what had happened or what the war had meant. Evidence of the war's impact was all around, but very different meanings could be associated with it. But different views and different motivations were not necessarily exclusive. Instead, they often coexisted.

This is strikingly illustrated by the juxtaposition in the HMV catalogue of new gramophone records released in November 1930. One of the new releases was a recording of a radio play, *Brigade Exchange*, broadcast by the BBC to mark the previous Armistice Day. The play was composed of scraps of overheard conversation from a German military telephone exchange, eventually overwhelmed by an Allied attack. HMV described it as 'a study in realism … the mad hurry, the forced humour, stark tragedy – the hopeless, futile waste of life – the mad, cruel disregard of human happiness – this screaming, tearing, hurtling destruction, the greatest of all crimes, the most horrid and the most terrible creation of human imagination – War'. Immediately below was the advertisement for 'The lighter side of war', a recording based on 'two clever and amusing sketches illustrating the *Cockney Spirit in the War*' before and after a trench raid. That irrepressible Cockney spirit was illustrated on the catalogue's cover, with a grinning Tommy enjoying a post-action cigarette.[40]

The inter-war years saw Britons wanting to remember very different versions of the war. Although none completely obscured the horror and the suffering inflicted by the war, the meanings derived from those experiences varied widely.

In recent years a mass of detailed studies has allowed us to reconstruct the patterns of remembrance, commemoration and memory in the aftermath of the war.[41] The basic elements of public remembrance of the war were constructed relatively swiftly, often arising out of wartime behaviour. By the early 1920s, the key points of national commemoration – mass participation on 11 November, a focus on the Unknown Warrior and the Cenotaph – had become fixed. Throughout the decade, British communities erected memorials to the dead. The new memorials and the rituals which grew up around them used traditional forms and words: few embraced more radical modernist ideas about representation. There was a stress on soldiers' valour, on the value of national solidarity and, in particular, on the redemption of death through sacrifice: they died that we might live. As the decade went on these themes were reinforced through repetition. To discuss the war in public meant acknowledging the country's loss in terms of restrained mourning. There was a heavy social taboo on offending bereaved parents by questioning the validity of their sons' deaths, since there was a presumption that they were comforted by the rhetoric of sacrifice. That rhetoric could include, however, an acknowledgement of the awful conditions of the front line. Indeed, to do so heightened the heroism of those who had given their lives in such circumstances far more effectively than descriptions of military experience in terms of boring drudgery.

Veterans themselves often seem to have felt most comfortable recalling their experiences outside the public sphere, in groups with their former comrades. A large number of ex-servicemen's clubs and associations existed to provide this context, often in an atmosphere of increasing nostalgia. Although these were the Britons who could lay greatest claim to knowing, at first hand, what phrases like 'the horror of war' actually meant, they chose to commemorate other aspects of the wartime experience, including comradeship, laughter and belonging. At a less formal level, these bonds between veterans could become assimilated into wider social rituals, for example in the Lancashire tradition of the communal 'hot-pot supper', in which individuals all brought food to contribute to a group meal. More formally, they could establish rituals of commemoration. For example, the 18th Division Officer's Dining Club met each year to celebrate the anniversary of the unit's founding. Officers of the 1/9 King's Own Yorkshire Light Infantry placed a notice in *The Times* on 1 July each year, commemorating the toast proposed by the adjutant before the Battle of the Somme, 'Gentlemen, when the barrage lifts!' Others could be one off events, for example, the huge turn out of veterans to mourn the death of Earl Haig in January 1928, an occasion which became a trigger for a widespread rehearsal of memories about the war as well as marking the passing of a general who had become associated with veterans' rights.[42]

In other sources from the early 1920s, the depiction of the horror of war was much more explicit. The first successful novels to attempt to make sense of the war were produced in the early 1920s. Works like Gilbert Frankau's *Peter Jackson, Cigar Merchant* – the first post-war novel to sell more than 100,000 copies – were often based on first hand military experience, and did not shy away from depicting its more shocking aspects.[43]

> Suddenly, Peter grew aware of noise. A noise inhuman. The whimper of damned souls. A wail as of enormous wet fingers on an enormous glass: a wail that rose and fell, interminable, unbearable. Suddenly, he was aware whence that wail came.
>
> All along the muddy roadway they lay – the wounded: hundreds of them: thousands: brown blanket shapes: some muttering: some moaning: some singing in delirium: some quite still. The agony of it gripped Peter by the stomach. Vomit rushed to his throat; was choked down again.[44]

Peter Jackson was based on Frankau's own service and contained gory descriptions of his fellow soldiers being blown apart physically and mentally. The meanings which were derived from these experiences, however, were more positive than we might expect. It was possible to make sense of the war by emphasising participants' willingness to undergo such horrors in defence of the nation. Their patriotic sacrifice could be understood in traditional terms. For this reason the early 1920s has been termed the era of the 'popular patriotic war novel'.[45] The horrific nature of trench warfare had not shattered the belief of writers – and, if sales were anything to go by, readers – in the cause for which they had served, or the possibility of constructing higher meanings from their wartime experiences: 'whatever war may have accomplished of good or evil to us other millions whom it caught up in its vortex – to Peter it came like a great clearing storm, terrifying in its violence, unfathomable in its purposes, but bearing him at last, past many rocks of doubt and fear, to safe harbourage, to certainty of body and soul – and better even than these, to love'.[46]

Later in the decade, this popular version was challenged by a different interpretation, in particular following the immense success of Erich Maria Remarque's book *All Quiet on the Western Front*. The novel was an international success in 1929, benefiting from an innovative advertising campaign and the promise of a long-awaited great novel of the Great War. Although widely understood as a literal account, its tone was in fact much more the result of Remarque's post-war career than of his wartime experiences. He blamed what he perceived as his failures on the lasting impact of the war.

All Quiet on the Western Front was noticeably more graphic than many of
the books which had gone before:

> We see men living with their skulls blown open; we see soldiers run with their
> two feet cut off, they stagger on their splintered stumps to the next shell-hole;
> a lance-corporal crawls a mile and a half on his hands dragging his splintered
> knee after him; another goes to the dressing station and over his clasped hands
> bulge his intestines; we see men without mouths, without jaws, without faces;
> we find one man who has held the artery of his arm in his teeth for two hours
> in order not to bleed to death. The sun goes down, night comes, life is at an
> end.[47]

In the host of novels, films and plays that attempted to capitalise on
Remarque's success, the war was perceived through the filter of the post-war
years as an experience which had destroyed even those men who had survived it. The horrific nature of the front line became both a rationale for
post-war difficulties and a powerful argument for society's responsibility to
provide for those who had been through hell in its cause.

As the prospect of a new European war raised its head in the early 1930s,
British pacifists made use of these books to argue against participation in
future conflict. They based their arguments around two beliefs: that technological developments in aerial warfare would see the horrors of the front
line unleashed on the home front, but also – reaching back to wartime rhetoric – that the sacrifice of soldiers who had fought against the barbarity of
war could only be justified by an absence of armed conflict in the future.[48]
In fact, historians have argued that it can be misleading to regard the wave
of writing produced around 1930 as 'anti-war'. Many of the veterans who
produced it continued to discern positive aspects even as they wrote books
describing the war's horrors.[49]

Books which concentrated on the horrors of war without also ascribing
positive meanings to it aroused considerable opposition at the time from
socially and politically conservative commentators. They felt that books like
All Quiet on the Western Front were presenting a false version of the war.
The resultant debate was apparent as a controversy to contemporaries at
the end of the 1920s. Charles Carrington, one of the most persistent British
commentators on the war, was moved to write his first book on his military experiences in reaction to the misrepresentations of popular writing
on the war. It was often possible for critics to find specific inaccuracies in
others' texts, but they objected most fiercely to a concentration on a limited aspect of military experience. They accused war writers of focusing on
'dirt about the war', either out of misplaced pacifism or from commercial
pressure.[50] Cyril Falls, who had served on the Western Front, wrote and

reviewed extensively on the war in the 1920s. He argued that this sort of compression produced an inaccurate impression:

> Every sector becomes a bad one, every working party is shot to pieces; if a man is killed or wounded his brains or his entrails always protrude from his body; no one ever seems to have a rest ... The soldier is represented as a depressed and mournful spectre helplessly wandering about until death brought his miseries to an end.[51]

Writing in even stronger terms, another writer-veteran, Douglas Jerrold, in his pamphlet *The Lie about the War*, accused some of the most successful war books of falsehood in statistical terms: the war had not been as unremittingly awful as their concentration on its horrors implied.[52]

This controversy was based on beliefs which were deeply held, but carried out around books which often continued to reflect the emotional complexities of wartime experience. They were therefore malleable to readers' own interpretation of the war: they found what they were looking for. In this context, the audience's understanding of a text could undercut authorial intention. Robert Graves claimed to be surprised to find his memoir *Goodbye to All That* being reviewed as an anti-war book: he had rather enjoyed aspects of his military service.[53] An even better example is provided by R. C. Sherriff's play *Journey's End*, perhaps the most popular dramatic representation of the First World War in the 1920s and 1930s. Although Sherriff found front-line service in the war difficult to endure, his purpose in writing the play was not anti-war. Instead, he wanted to celebrate the public school ethos he felt had carried the country through its wartime struggle. For all that two of the central characters die during its course, the play is not particularly graphic or bloody, even when compared to others current at the same time. Reviewers of *Journey's End* when it was first performed nevertheless tended to praise it as a realistic depiction of the horror and futility of war. On the other hand, it is clear that many in the audience enjoyed the play because its central characters were recognisably heroic, even if their heroism now lay more in endurance than endeavour. It is difficult to believe that the audience of VC winners for whom a special performance of the play was laid on in 1929 was particularly pacifist.[54] Indeed, in some contexts, *Journey's End* sanctioned nostalgic recreation of wartime camaraderie. One reason for the play's popularity with Canadian amateur dramatic groups in the 1930s was that it allowed ex-soldiers to re-don their uniforms and equipment.[55]

Reviewing *Journey's End* for the second time in 1929, the *Daily Telegraph*'s theatre critic, W. A. Darlington, concluded that it was a good piece, but not a great one. It depicted with great accuracy, he thought, what the war had been *like*. What it did not do – what kept it from greatness in his view – was tell the audience what the war had *meant*.[56] Darlington's distinction is a key one to understanding the development of the representation of the First World War in terms of mud and horror. In the period after the war, such a wide diversity of different experiences existed that it was difficult for Britons to agree on what the war had meant. It was much easier to find common ground in terms of what the war had been like. That the war on the Western Front had been awful was not only an acknowledgement of an aspect of soldiers' experience, or the result of an atavistic fascination with gore; it could also be used to support multiple different meanings.

The point of dispute for critics of the 'war books boom' was not that the war had been horrible: they accepted that it had been. What was at issue was the balance of that horror with other emotions, the capacity of men – specifically British men – to withstand its worst extremities, and the meaning of such endurance. For men like Falls and Jerrold, the war had been the occasion for the reinforcement of traditional values of honour and loyalty as much as about the experience of the battlefield grotesque. Just like many of the writers they criticised, however, their interpretation of the war was bound up with the contemporary context in which they wrote and their anxieties about what a negative view of the war might mean in terms of social cohesion and attitudes to war in the future. The controversy also highlighted a tension between artistic representation and factual accuracy that was to prove an enduring issue in British culture. Even if contemporary critics often acknowledged that the texts they criticised had literary merit, they were angered by the selectivity with which they represented the war. There was – and is – an assumption that a historical event ought to be depicted accurately. But was it possible to represent the variety of military experience accurately? Was it acceptable for artists to compress – or even create – events in order to tell what they saw as the 'truth about the war'? Whose version of the war was truthful in any case?[57]

The cultural ubiquity of the First World War in the 1920s and 1930s had a lasting impact even on those born after its end. Living in a culture where the war was omnipresent, frequently targeted as future bearers of the flame in commemoration and remembrance and often with evidence of the war within their own families, these children were fascinated by the First World War. As one recalled:

> At school many had fathers who had fought in 'the war to end all wars' which ended in 1918, stories were still being written about the battles fought in the Great War. On Armistice Day, which was always a special day at school, we'd

boast about our dads. The Regiments they had been in, the wounds they had received, if we were all to be believed then our village held more heroes than any other. Some of the boasting was justified for more than one still suffered from the effects of Mustard Gas and two of the fathers walked with a limp. Great was the kudos of a child whose father was such a victim.[58]

Higher up the social scale, another remembered the effects of remembrance at his school between the wars:

Some of the most deeply impressive emotional experiences of my boyhood were concerned with the effects of the war ... the number of those killed is almost exactly the same – to within two names – of the school roll in the summer term of 1914. It is as if the whole school ... had been taken out and shot. On a winter evening in my thirteenth year the memorial in their honour was dedicated in the chapel; for six years, Sunday after Sunday, I sat and faced four panels which bore the names of four successive heads of the school, all of whom had been killed in battle before they were twenty-one.[59]

Such rituals offered children a mix of emotions, including fear, pride, disgust, wonder and envy. They also fostered a sense of community and shared identity.[60]

The way individual children thought about the war was inevitably highly coloured by their own family's experience of the war, but there were numerous sources outside the family. Indeed, they grew up in an age when more products were being created specifically for children than ever before. The raising of the school leaving age, the marginalisation of child labour, and a gradual improvement in the quality of life, outside the concentrated areas of industrial depression, all meant that childhood lasted longer and children had time and resources for leisure. This in turn encouraged the growth of industries which catered to their specific leisure wants: specifically children's books, comics and story papers, and radio and film products aimed directly at them.[61]

Many children grew up receiving ambivalent messages about the war. On one level, they learnt that it had been a terrible event, which had put many names on war memorials, scarred men for life, and involved terrible fighting in appalling conditions. On another, they were told that it had been a glorious struggle, involving great heroism and high adventure. They were invited to participate imaginatively in those adventures. They learnt this not only from civilians who had no experience of the real war, but from veterans themselves. Moreover, many of the ways in which children found out about the war engendered feelings of belonging and comradeship – versions of the positive factors which many men had found in it. It is unsurprising, then, that these children developed an abiding fascination with the First World War which would affect attitudes towards it for years to come.

One of the most popular sources which taught children about the war were the serials in the 'boys' papers': weekly print-based comics which were hugely successful with young males.[62] In the years immediately after 1918, the boys' papers did not portray the war. Why this should be the case is unclear, although it is tempting to suggest that it was still seen as a difficult and potentially risky subject. What is apparent is that the decision of the *Champion* to launch the first story set on the Western Front, in 1925, had a major effect. The obvious success of the paper's original story encouraged a number of other papers to begin Great War serials.[63] Magazines also produced memorabilia associated with the war, enclosing albums and collectible cards in the papers that showed scenes from the war, or described features of it.[64]

The form and content of the stories altered over time, reflecting wider changes in the way the war was represented, but the attitudes towards war and violence remained consistent. War stories began very much as versions of the school stories that were the staple of the boys' papers, simply altering the setting to the war rather than a public school. The stories followed the conventions and models of popular adventure fiction of the time, like the works of John Buchan and Dornford Yates and a number of popular children's authors, as well as following in the tradition of writers like G. A. Henty.[65] Some of the writers who contributed these stories had themselves seen service during the war, although this may have been a claim for authenticity made by the papers' editors as much as by the authors themselves.[66]

The boys' papers stories contain some surprisingly grisly details, often relishing descriptions of hand to hand fighting (which occur with great regularity): 'Bullets kicked up the earth in front of Squibs & Co. Others shrieked viciously over their prostrate bodies or ripped their way into yielding flesh'.[67] To begin with, at least, however, these wounds were seldom inflicted on the principal characters themselves. By the later 1920s, the depiction of the horrors of war became much more graphic.

CR-RUMP!
Another dazzling sheet of light, another quaking bang, and the earth heaved and quaked at Vic's running feet. Stones and red hot steel whizzed over his bent head, but on he pounded, to drop beside the two injured Tommies.
One was clutching at a gaping wound in his side. The other was dragging a mangled leg behind him. Vic turned to the third man. His head and shoulders

protruded from the reeking earth. He lay ominously still and his glassy eyes
stared unseeingly at the sky.

Vic moves on: 'Gingerly he straightened up and clambered down into the
pit. Water gushed over his ankles, soaked his puttees – green coloured
water that reeked of death. His boots sank deep into the slime, and standing up to his knees in the stinking water, he groped about him.' He finally
encounters the enemy: 'At the same moment Vic's clubbed rifle lunged
forward. The brass bound butt crashed home in the German's face. There
was a sickening thud and the man collapsed, his body sliding into the
slime.'[68]

As the 1920s moved into the 1930s, some of the authors who made
up the 'war books boom' depicted the war in starker terms of horror.
There was a knock-on effect on the way boys' papers wrote about it as well:
'Jim set his jaw grimly. Modern warfare had its splendid moments … but
in the main it was just fine men being hurled as fodder for the enemy's
guns.'[69] Acknowledgements of the lasting effects of war, effects which
would still have been all too obvious to some readers, also began to creep
in:

> His legs had been bandaged, but the wrappings could not conceal the terrible
> injuries that the shell burst had caused …
> 'It'll take more than a bit of shrapnel to put me out of action. You'll see, I'll
> be back soon. And the next time I have a cut at Johnny Turk it'll be as a full
> blown, properly enlisted soldier.'
> But there Kit was wrong. For him the war was over. Though his badly injured
> limbs eventually healed, he was doomed to walk with a limp for the rest of his
> life.[70]

In spite of visions of the damage caused by modern war, however, the
basic interpretation of the war remained the same: it had been a wonderful adventure. Heroism was not only possible, it was desirable and to be
emulated. This was not a new, modern, ironic view – rather, it harked back
to pre-1914 ways of understanding war. Kit's desire to 'have a cut at Johnny
Turk' and to be a 'proper' soldier is seen as laudable and heroic. It is
juxtaposed unironically with the terrible injuries that have been inflicted
on him.

The inter-war years saw the establishment of lasting conventions about the
ways in which the war should be remembered and represented. In the
process of memorialising the war, Britons composed new versions of what
it had been like and what it had meant. Although there was not, as yet, a

universally shared set of beliefs about the war, opinion did coalesce around certain ideas about how the war had been experienced.

It is possible to argue that it was in the early 1930s, as a result of the 'war books boom', that the memory of the war was monopolised by a small group of highly literate participants, primarily established writers who had served as junior officers, who created the version of the war still dominant today. In the process, they provided a set of scripts by which other veterans could compose their memories of the war.[71] In practice, it was not quite as simple as that. The ten years after 1918 saw a concentration, in popular culture, on the military experience of war, and in particular service in the trenches. Whereas during the war a wide variety of tasks had been portrayed as contributing to the war effort (not least as a rationale for mass mobilisation), post-war culture came to focus on the soldier in the trench as the iconic experience of the real war. Whether accurately or not, such representations had to include descriptions of battlefield gothic in order to affirm their 'realism'. The effect of the more practised and eloquent writers of the war book boom was, at the time, to centre attention ever more firmly on the trenches and encourage a competitive inflation of their horrors. It remained possible to ascribe a range of meanings to the war. As the boys' papers stories of Vic, Jim and Kit make clear, traditional stories of masculine heroism could still be told. In order, however, to appeal to an audience growing accustomed to depictions of the war as horrific, they too had to include the gory details. The writers of the war books boom affected the terms of public discussion long before they dominated its content. Even then, there remained many who rejected interpretations of the war in terms of mud and blood in favour of a nostalgic commemoration of comradeship and social purpose. By their nature, however, such commemorative activities as regimental reunions were private and exclusive events: the emotions they sought to recapture were much harder to pass on to those who had not experienced them than the revulsion engendered by descriptions of the horrors of war.

The influence of the inter-war years was apparent in the reactions of British servicemen and women to the Second World War. Despite the wave of literature which had depicted the war in negative terms at the end of the 1920s, young Britons were not sufficiently deterred to refuse to serve in the Second World War. There was no great wave of anti-war protest in 1939, nor any mass effort to resist conscription. Many men and women entered into military service freely, and some were joyful at their opportunity to emulate their fathers.

Yet beliefs about the First World War did affect the behaviour of soldiers in the Second. Amongst those who joined up of their own accord, applications for what might be termed the 'clean' arms of the services – not just the RAF but the Navy, the artillery and army support services – were higher than those for front-line infantry regiments. Soldiers' mental images of war were based on the preceding conflict. No one wanted to be stuck in the trenches if they could help it:

> We all had these 'Passchendaele' notions about war in those days; it would certainly have shocked Wellington or the Duke of Cambridge or any of the Old Guard if they had been told that one day officers of the British Army at the beginning of a war would be thinking of it more as an affair of mud than of bullets. The prospect of living for years in a dreary ditch was repulsive.[72]

The army itself felt that its soldiers were harder to lead than ever before: they were more likely to question authority, more cynical, and more difficult to motivate. Military commentators at the time and afterwards have put this down to changes in military structures, education and society, and particularly to the experience of an economic depression.[73] To that might be added the effects of an immediate introduction of conscription, and the influence on perception of the army's own mythologisation of the Regular Army of 1914 and its Kitchener reinforcements.

As important, however, was the quantity of second-hand military experience to which the soldiers of 1939 to 1945 had access. The inevitable restrictions and minor irritations of army life had come as a culture shock to many of those who had joined up in 1914, not least because so few Britons at that point had military experience. In the aftermath of the First World War, the military participation ratio (defined as the ratio of men who had seen active military service against the total population) was the highest it had been since the Civil War 275 years before.[74] The sons and nephews of those who had fought in the First World War knew better what to expect.

A mass of military lore had been passed down, either through individual contacts or through works of popular literature. Soldiers in Normandy in 1944 knew not to light three cigarettes from the same match because their fathers had told them that the sniper would spot the first, aim on the second and fire on the third. They told each other stories about the Germans opposite them that they had learnt at their fathers' knees.[75] They would serve willingly enough, but these men had learnt that they should never volunteer, that NCOs and officers could not always be trusted, and that the army wasn't good at empathy and efficiency.[76] One reason that the Army found these men harder to lead was that, although new to soldiering, they had some of the knacks of acting like old sweats.

The personal experience of combat in the Second World War, however, had little effect on the mythic status of its predecessor in young men's minds. Far from feeling that they had gained an insight into what their fathers had been through, the First World War seemed further away. Andrew McKee recalled advancing through Belgium in 1944: 'The incongruity of simply driving across the trench lines which had held our fathers for four years, had brought the decisive, self-centred and selfish reaction, "Thank God I wasn't in that one". The experience of the two generations had been of a totally different order, almost beyond analysis.'[77] Similarly, Gregory Blaxland introduced his book about the 1918 battle of Amiens by writing: 'I was not in fact born until the ink had laid on the Armistice agreement for a month. This as it turned out, was good timing for participation in the second term of World War, and like others of my generation I saw sufficient of it to marvel at the fortitude of those who endured the more intense, more harrowing and infinitely more prolonged fury of the first.'[78]

Such had been the strength of the myths that these men had absorbed as they were growing up that they were unable to consider their fathers' war in the same light as their own. Their presumption was that the first war had been so outstanding in its horror that their own experiences inevitably paled by comparison. The mythic view of the First World War as particularly horrific was therefore bolstered in the 1940s because it was widely used. It defined soldiers to themselves as followers in their fathers' footsteps. It helped them to contextualise and sustain their military service. The First World War was a touchstone for these men – no matter how bad things were, at least there was something that had been worse.[79]

Created out of the experience of participants, emphasised during the 1920s and 1930s and confirmed during the Second World War, how has the myth of the First World War as particularly horrific endured and been passed down to today's Britons? We could argue simply that the same factors which encouraged the myth's popularity before and during the Second World War persisted after it. In a variety of contexts, including the aftermath of another destructive conflict and an atmosphere of continued international violence, it was useful for British popular culture to be able to refer to a model of war as a Bad Thing. At the same time, the prurient interest in second-hand gore which had encouraged the war books boom remained a common cultural feature, encouraging new representations of the battlefield grotesque. But the myth of the war's horror was more than sustained – in the period after 1945 it developed a remarkable momentum and achieved a position of overwhelming cultural dominance. Why did a version of the war which had been controversial when it was first contrived become the only one which was publicly acknowledged?

The 1960s saw a flowering of representations of the First World War in British popular culture. In the period 1959 to 1968, nearly two hundred new books on the war were published in Britain, more than in the previous two decades put together.[80] This was just one aspect of a wave of war literature, plays, films, radio and television programmes.[81] This resurgence in publicly expressed interest in the war was a result of the coincidence of commemorative, commercial, personal and occupational factors. The fiftieth anniversaries of the war obviously provided a stimulus for rehearsing myths and memories. The explosive growth of new popular histories of the war resulted, however, as much from the publishing industry's search for a fresh topic as it realised that the memoirs of the Second World War which had been so popular in the early 1950s were about to run out. Like Remarque's *All Quiet on the Western Front,* the commercial success of Alan Moorehead's *Gallipoli* (1956) and Leon Wolff's *In Flanders Fields* (1958) stimulated other authors to leap aboard the bandwagon. Both these authors and many of their readers came from the generation which had grown up in the aftermath of the First World War. They continued to find the war viscerally fascinating. It was not just the prospect of financial remuneration or historical education that motivated writers and readers, but a burning interest kindled in them by silent fathers, school Armistice ceremonies and playground trading of cigarette cards of soldiers and airplanes.[82] The 1960s also saw considerable activity by veterans of the First World War. As these men retired and began to approach the end of their lives, they had the time and the inclination to reconsider their lives, to pick out the most important events and to attempt to communicate them to a younger generation before it was too late.[83]

Without any doubt, the most popular and most influential production of this period was the BBC television series *The Great War.* Made up of twenty-six forty minute episodes, *The Great War* was a documentary history of the entire war. It consisted of archive footage interspersed with eyewitnesses talking to camera and still photographs. Michael Redgrave was the series narrator, while a number of other eminent actors read quotations from memoirs and diaries. *The Great War* was first broadcast on the new-born BBC 2 from May to November 1964. Even as the final episodes were shown on BBC 2, the whole series was rebroadcast on BBC 1 beginning in October 1964. Shown again ten years later, it has recently been released on video and DVD and rebroadcast once more.

The Great War is one of the most popular series ever produced by the

BBC. An average of just over 17 per cent of the viewing population, or just over eight million people, watched each episode when it appeared on BBC 1. At its most popular – the fourth episode shown on BBC 1 – it achieved an audience of over eleven million. This size of audience was remarkable for a documentary series, and put *The Great War* in a league with BBC favourites of the time like *The Dick Emery Show* and *Z Cars*. Yet the BBC's audience research indicated that viewers were even more impressed with the series than with these staples. When questioned, viewers awarded *The Great War* a 'reaction index' of 82: a rating which ranked the series with FA Cup Finals or Royal Weddings in terms of audience approval.[84]

Despite the huge popularity it enjoyed, however, *The Great War* seemed to inspire great sorrow and heartache. The same reaction research provided plentiful evidence of the audience's perception of the war. As one correspondent put it: 'I find it compulsive and horrifying and of overwhelming tragedy.' Another pointed to 'the horror of trench warfare and the appalling and needless slaughter of young people'. A third argued that: 'This series should be seen by *all* to bring home the horrors of war and the dreadful waste of young manhood.'[85]

The production of the series carried a great weight of hopes and expectations from a variety of sources both within and without the BBC.[86] It was not only designed to form the centrepiece of a range of commemorative programmes broadcast in the summer of 1964,[87] but to provide a piece of 'must-see' programming that would persuade viewers to switch from older sets to newer ones that could receive BBC 2. In the immediate aftermath of its launch, BBC 2 had been subject to a number of criticisms from both within and without the Corporation with regard to its content.[88] The need for *The Great War* to be a success grew proportionately. The series was also being used by the Imperial War Museum in an effort to revive its flagging profile – with the BBC being allowed cheaper than usual access to the museum's stock of film in return for a credit as a co-producer.[89] The expectations attached to the series in this way increased the pressure on those required to produce it, Tony Essex and Gordon Watkins.

Both had previously worked for the BBC flagship current affairs programme *Tonight*. So had many of those they recruited, and their journalistic background undoubtedly influenced their approach and presentation of their material, as well as the frenetic atmosphere which surrounded the creation of the series. In theory, Essex, a former film editor, was to take responsibility for the pictures, whilst Watkins, a former writer for the recently defunct magazine *Picture Post*, looked after the scripts. In practice, Essex was very much the driving force behind the series, with Watkins the insider assigned to hold his hand.

Tony Essex remains an enigmatic figure. An intense and private man, he had worked with *Tonight* as a film editor before leaving to work for the Canadian Broadcasting Corporation. He came back from Toronto to make *The Great War*. His career, his personality and his role in bringing documentary techniques across the Atlantic, in particular the use of rostrum camerawork, deserve a book of their own. It was Essex who, in May 1963, came up with the set of twenty-six programme synopses, covering the whole conflict geographically and chronologically, which were to form the basis of the series almost without alteration. If the breadth of Essex's reading and passion for the subject were impressive, his ability to conceive of and devise such a project was truly remarkable.[90] He also had a clear conception of a new standard of televisual history. In his vision, the series scripts would be written by a prominent but populist historian. Footage and eyewitness accounts would then be cut to fit and support these scripts. Although this has become more or less standard practice for documentary series, at the time it represented a reversal of the normal process, as seen in series like *Time to Remember* or *Victory at Sea*, where the commentary was written to fit the available footage. Essex was justly keen to trumpet the virtues of his approach.[91]

Essex believed that any documentary series should have a 'quest' at the centre of it, and that for *The Great War* this should be 'breakthrough': the search for a way to break the deadlock of the Western Front. Although further influenced in the course of the series by historians who sought to challenge the view of the war as a futile slaughter, Essex's belief in the need for battles of attrition to win a modern industrial war was consistent throughout: 'In the main I think the truth is (and this perhaps could be the moral of the series) there is no cheap, easy or quick way to win *any* war. Today, as ever, this is a point worth making.'[92] If this was a vision firmly grounded in contemporary concerns, it was hardly anti-war per se, nor did it seem likely to emphasise horror gratuitously.

Essex's ideals for the series were soon swamped by the reality of the manic speed with which the series had to be assembled. Precisely because it was so innovative, those involved had seriously underestimated the amount of time it would take to prepare scripts, to interview veterans, to locate, prepare and cut film, and to integrate all of these elements. Work on the series began in earnest in the summer of 1963, preparing for twenty-six broadcasts between May and November 1964. Less than a year was therefore initially allowed for production. As a comparison, the 1996 documentary series *1914–18*, co-produced by the BBC and KCET, took five years to make seven episodes.[93] Working to this hectic schedule left the team with no room for manoeuvre when delays, as was inevitable, occurred. Future

programmes continued to be produced as the first of the series were broadcast, but the initial stockpile of six programmes was rapidly whittled down.
Essex was left begging for a pause halfway through the series to catch up.
In a state of desperation he wrote – fruitlessly – to the head of the *Tonight*
team:

> All our leeway has gone, and, with only Programmes 8, 9 and 11 in hand, the
> three week completion requirements (for opticals, dubbing, negative cutting
> and printing) at present stand at one week.
>
> The risk is appalling, as errors in any of these stages will have to stand, and
> serious errors may in any week knock us off the air.
>
> I am assembling films now with only three weeks to transmission – this
> means that second thoughts are impracticable – inserts of additional material
> to get the show to length are out of the question ... there is no time for refine-
> ment, no time for additional film research – and the films go to their
> completion with material selected and assembled by non-historian me *before*
> *even the script is written ...*
>
> As things stand, my preoccupation is merely getting *something* on the air.[94]

In the end, disaster was averted, and the series broadcast as planned,
but the impact on the form of the later programmes cannot be overstated.
Even though Essex was well informed about the war, and far from left-
wing or radical, his preference as a film editor was for the visually dramatic
rather than the historically accurate.[95] The result was that there was
sometimes a discrepancy between the scripts and footage which tended
to be overly dramatic and concentrate on mud and blood. Alistair Horne,
for example, was surprised to find in relation to his script on Verdun
that

> between the time when I saw this programme and its appearance on the air,
> quite a few alterations were made, which even Gordon Watkins – as one of the
> co-producers – appears to have been unaware of. None of these were substan-
> tial, however; all they did, I thought, was perhaps to overstress the emotional
> conflict – particularly the horror side – of the battle.[96]

There were also problems with the authenticity of the film stock used
in the series. A statement appeared on screen at the beginning of each
episode stating that nearly all the footage used was authentic and that only
a 'very small part of the film used in this series is reconstructed, usually by
Official Photographers two or three days after the events depicted. Material
of this kind is only used where it faithfully reflects the reality, and where
no genuine footage exists.'[97] This was, in fact, untrue. By the standards it
set itself here, *The Great War* misused footage, displacing it chronologically

and geographically, as well as using post-war training and feature films, including *Sergeant York* and *All Quiet on the Western Front*.[98] Very few audience members picked up on these misuses of film. After criticisms from the Imperial War Museum about what it saw as abuses – and developing fury from the Museum's director, Dr Noble Frankland, at what he saw as a betrayal – a researcher was appointed to analyse the percentage of reconstructed footage in each programme, a figure which was announced at the beginning of each broadcast.[99] Other inaccuracies include the appearance of armies of left-handed Germans, the result of reverse printing of film so as to conform to the convention that the Germans should attack right to left (from east to west), and the Allies from left to right. Tellingly, Essex stated that he thought that 'clarity for the masses was more important than accuracy for the few'.[100]

It is not correct, however, to suggest that the audience of *The Great War* simply ignored the narration of the series and reacted viscerally to the images of violence before them. In fact, the audience research reports make clear that viewers were aware of the narration and paid attention to it, although there was often a divergence between the intentions of the writers and the reaction of the audience. The two principal writers for *The Great War* were John Terraine and Correlli Barnett. They worked hard, in different ways, to challenge what they saw as a misplaced British obsession with the horror of the First World War. Pressured by Essex to produce powerful television in a limited amount of production and screen time, both sometimes made use of language which they might in later years have avoided because of its effect on the audience. For example, episode 17, on Passchendaele, contains a reading of Wilfred Owen's 'Dulce et Decorum Est', with the last line translated for the benefit of those whose Latin was not up to the magnitude of the Old Lie. At times Michael Redgrave's solemn tones verge on self-parody: 'Loos: the very name had an air of doom.'[101]

The scripts for *The Great War* did not set out to challenge the existing beliefs of its audience. This was not part of its original intention or remit, nor was there enough time – either on screen or during preparation – to enter into detailed debates. The historians involved do not seem to have suspected the depth of reaction which would be sparked by the images placed before the audience. Tony Essex, on the other hand, was aware of their likely impact, and it seems clear that, with time short, he often chose footage because it would make good television rather than because it was an accurate representation of history. To point out that he did so is not to denigrate his abilities or intentions. He was one of the first to confront a practical issue of television history which continues to trouble its creators.

Controversial debates about great strategic or tactical developments are all
but impossible to represent visually in a way that involves the audience,
because little footage of them exists. In contrast, combat and death are not
only more dramatic but also easier to show. The production process of *The
Great War* therefore emphasised horror not because this was the ultimate
aim of its creators, but as a result of the pressures of expectation, time,
available resources and the nature of the medium.

Visual references to the war as a horrific experience received an enthusiastic reception from the series' audience. In letters to the BBC and in
response to audience research enquiries, viewers repeatedly emphasised how
impressed they were with *The Great War*'s realism. In the words of one
viewer, too young to have fought in either world war: 'I am constantly
amazed by the film as being the visual record of what *actually* happened.'[102]
One explanation for this perception of 'realism' was that contemporary
footage used by the series had been modified so that it ran more smoothly,
producing images without the characteristic jerkiness of much archival film
stock.[103] Another seems to have been that viewers were so struck by the fact
that footage existed at all that they partially suspended their disbelief.[104] The
best explanation for the belief in *The Great War*'s realism was that the series'
representation of the war matched that in the popular imagination, the
audience's 'war-in-the-head'.[105] Its use of feature films from between the
wars – a key source for popular conceptions – may therefore have bolstered,
rather than detracted from, its perceived realism.

Yet others had reservations about the way the war was portrayed. Whilst
many veterans of the First World War greeted the series with enthusiasm,
some felt that it misrepresented their experiences. Oliver Lyttelton, Lord
Chandos, wrote that:

> I admired it greatly, in almost every aspect, as an historical work … Looking
> at the BBC production with the eyes of a regimental officer I had many times
> to exclaim. 'No, it wasn't quite like that.' We, by which I mean both officers
> and men, did not feel quite so doom laden, so utterly disenchanted. We
> thought we were fighting in a worthy cause …[106]

Charles Carrington reacted in a similar way: 'I never meet an "old sweat" …
who accepts or enjoys the figure in which we are now presented, though it
is useless – undignified – to protest. Just smile and make a soldier's wry joke
when you see yourself on the television screen, agonised and woebegone,
trudging from disaster to disaster, knee-deep in moral as well as physical
mud.'[107]

The Great War came at a key moment in the activities and perception
of First World War veterans in British society and culture. It acted as an

important stimulus for the rehearsal of individual memories of the war within families, allowing their perpetuation into the myth kitty of later generations. That the war was still an event in family memory as well as family history is apparent in the degree to which the series' audience still took it personally. Although the Second World War had drawn public interest in the 1950s, its predecessor had not disappeared from popular culture. A base of knowledge and folklore continued to exist and was primed by the resurgence in publicly expressed interest as the fiftieth anniversary of the war's start approached. Many in the audience for *The Great War* sat down to watch with an awareness of their own family's participation. They believed it might offer them a view of what their grandfathers had done. Audience members viewed archival footage as if it was newsreel of contemporary events.

We can tell that this was the case because many viewers believed that they had caught sight of a relative in the series's film stock, and wrote into the BBC to request copies of images of their husbands, brothers, fathers, uncles or grandfathers. Given the scale of British involvement in the war, the comparative paucity of footage and *The Great War*'s frequent displacement or misuse of it, we have to assume that in most cases these viewers had not actually spotted their relatives. Tacit recognition of this came in the BBC's refusal to grant these requests for stills: although the BBC cited copyright difficulties which were undoubtedly present, other archive footage programmes in the 1960s made a habit of providing these images.[108] There is no better illustration of the position the war then held – or of the subsequent change in its status – than this search for recognisable faces in archive footage. Although family history has become a fashionable topic for research and Britons are still keen to seek out their own connections to the war, it is impossible to imagine a modern audience reacting in the same way.

The Great War encouraged the audience to rehearse family myths about the war without challenging their underlying preconceptions. This was an important element in its success. The series's depiction of the horrors of war fitted with its viewers' concept of what the First World War had been like but allowed them to create their own individual stories from it. In fact, its reliance on contemporary images meant that it did not show death and suffering in graphic detail. It is instructive to compare the reception of *The Great War* with that afforded to a feature film released at the same time which offered a much more explicit portrayal of the First World War.

The 1964 film *King and Country*, directed by Joseph Losey, is the fictional story of the trial and execution for desertion of a shell-shocked young British private, Hamp, played by Tom Courtenay. Despite a passionate defence by Captain Hargreaves (Dirk Bogarde) and a recommendation of clemency from the court, the High Command orders that Hamp must be shot at dawn to spur on his comrades.

King and Country's depiction of the Western Front is unremittingly horrible. Rain and mud cover a dead landscape. The artillery barrage is only interrupted by the wail of Larry Adler's mournful harmonica score. Hamp's trial is intercut with scenes of his comrades hunting rats in the carcass of a dead mule. Losey, blacklisted from McCarthy Era Hollywood for his left-wing views, was eager to represent the war in class terms. After the trial, the Colonel tells Hargreaves: 'You lost.' Hargreaves replies: 'We all lost ... We're all bloody murderers.' In the closing scenes of the film, the firing squad fails to dispatch Hamp cleanly, and Hargreaves himself has to deliver the *coup de grâce*. Inserting his revolver in Hamp's mouth, he apologises to him, and blows the back of his head off. The final shots show Hamp's body sinking into the mud as an uninterested staff officer looks on.[109]

For most reviewers, the graphic nature of the film was a cause for praise. As one put it: 'I was forced to admire this film for its steadfast evasion of overstatement and false sentiment. Throughout it maintains its sober hold on unvarnished, unpalatable, but compelling reality.'[110] Yet *King and Country* was an unmitigated disaster at the box office. Forty years later the film is all but forgotten. In the words of a more recent critic: 'It found honour in its own country ... but no profit anywhere.'[111] Losey's gory depiction of the trenches, combined with an overtly political message, put potential audiences off in their droves. Public preconceptions might stress the awfulness of the First World War, but few actually wanted to see that horror up close.

By the fiftieth anniversary of the war's beginning, the myth that it had been a uniquely horrific experience for those who had fought it was well established. It was the default setting for new representations of the war when time was short and pressure high, and it was the 'reality' of the war for many members of the viewing public. But concentrating on horror was not a recipe for commercial success. Just as between the war, some veterans continued to dispute the ascription of negative meanings to their wartime experience. Although the volume of controversy had faded in the previous thirty years, ambiguity about the war remained.

The blend of continuity and change in attitudes to the war was evident in the reception of another dramatic representation of the war, produced more than twenty years after *The Great War* and *King and Country*. In 1986, BBC 1 screened Alan Bleasdale's adaptation of William Allison and John Fairley's book, *The Monocled Mutineer*.[112] The series generated considerable controversy and produced a generational split amongst its viewers, but these phenomena were unrelated to its depiction of the horror of trench warfare. Reactions to the series made clear that many of the issues which had surrounded the representation of the First World War since the 1920s remained unresolved in British popular culture.

Allison and Fairley were journalists. Their book told in sensationalist terms the 'real-life' story of Percy Toplis, a small-time crook and petty criminal. In their version, Toplis joined up, temporarily deserted, returned to the army and was then involved in the organisation of violent disturbances at the Étaples training camp in France in 1917, before escaping back to England. There he was finally hunted down and killed by police in 1920. In fact, although Toplis was in the army during the First World War, there is no evidence that he was anywhere near Étaples when the 'mutiny' there occurred, let alone that he led the disturbances, which were in any case closer to a strike over conditions than a revolutionary overturning of authority. Allison and Fairley used a small selection of evidence, often undisclosed, and their book has no historical rigour.

Bleasdale's adaptation of the book used the story set out by Allison and Fairley as the basis for a drama with a number of political points to make. These were not only international – Bleasdale saw clear parallels between the First World War and the struggle for the Falklands – but domestic. In his words: 'It's the same system has made victims of them whether they're gun fodder or giro fodder.' The accuracy of the original work was unimportant to him. He set out to produce a sophisticated piece of human drama, inevitably influenced by his own political beliefs and what he perceived as fact. He made no pretence that his work was anything more than this.[113] The BBC marketing department, however, presented the series as a depiction of historical reality, laying up a store of trouble for the dramatist and the corporation in the future.[114]

The Monocled Mutineer is remembered to this day for the storm of criticism that broke around it after its depiction of the mutiny at Étaples. It showed British soldiers raping and killing French civilians as they rampaged through the town after breaking out of camp. In a sensational double-page spread on 13 September 1986, the *Daily Mail* described the 'tissue of lies' about Toplis. Others in the right-wing press followed suit.[115]

Its publicity department had painted the BBC into a corner with its portrayal of the series as factually based: it was clear from the historical record that no such sack of Étaples had actually taken place. The Corporation's reaction, as phrased by its Managing Director, Bill Cotton, was at the same time defensive and revealing. Cotton emphasised that the series was part of a tradition of fact influencing fiction, but argued that it also exposed 'the greater truth about the First World War'. In this context, it seemed,

greater truths could be those with no basis in evidence. Whilst not defending such illogicality, it should be noted that it was *The Monocled Mutineer*'s
misfortune to be taken up at a point of issue at the moment when the BBC
needed a new Director General, with elements in the Conservative Government eager to ensure a right-wing appointee to correct what was
perceived as anti-Tory bias. At the same time, the end of the slow summer
season for news left editors keen to fill their pages with any scandal on
offer.[116]

What has been obscured by the memory of this controversy is the
rapturous reception accorded to the series by critics and audiences *before*
the Étaples episode was shown, including by the very papers who would
shortly attempt to tear it to shreds. A large part of this was based on the
series' unflinching portrayal of fighting on the Western Front. The trenches
in *The Monocled Mutineer* remain the muddiest and bloodiest ever
shown on British television. Based on the battles of 1915, every attack is a
disaster and the wrecked battlefields are covered with wounded and
maddened men. The front line is a place of such horror and carnage that
mutiny appears the only reasonable option. This depiction was taken
without exception by reviewers as evidence of the series's realism. As the
Daily Telegraph declared: 'Hindsight turns history into a joke: one of the
sickest jokes of all being the 1914–18 war. How many of us now would volunteer to fight the Kaiser, knowing what we know now about the carnage,
the unimaginative generals, the ranks of brave men ordered forward
through barbed wire and quagmire to throw themselves fruitlessly at
fortified machine-gun positions?'[117] The *Daily Mail* suggested that 'few
will doubt its central charge – that the Great War was an unpardonable
carnage generally officered at a high level by rigid incompetents ... and
that the ordinary soldier was all too often flung to an early and needless
death'.[118]

The BBC's own audience research revealed a generational split in terms
of viewer reaction, but not one based on the depiction of the horror of the
trenches. *The Monocled Mutineer* increased its audience over the course of
its run from 7.9 to 9.7 million viewers, doubtless aided by newspaper reports
of its outrageous nature. The audience reaction index was consistently high.
The audience was evenly distributed by age, sex and class, but there was a
clear difference between those under the age of fifty-five, who generally
thought the series was an honest and accurate depiction of the war, though
they might be shocked by its violence, and those over fifty-five, who reacted
negatively to the depiction of soldiers behaving badly in the course of the
mutiny. Older viewers with their own memories of the Second World War,
and continuing memories of fathers and brothers who had served in its

predecessor, regarded images of them rioting as insulting.[119] That difference
was illustrated in press correspondence at the time. A fifteen-year-old girl
wrote to the *Radio Times* to thank the BBC for bringing into focus 'the
trench battles, the brutality, the horror' in such a 'truthful series'.[120] In contrast, an older viewer wrote to the *Sunday Times* to declare that 'to reclothe
that incredibly brave, patriotic generation in 1980s picket-line clothing is
both shoddy and ineffectual'.[121] Some of the few surviving veterans were
dragged out to argue for both sides, including one who wrote to the BBC's
Points of View to argue that the series was inaccurate because the jokes were
insufficiently dirty.[122]

Fundamentally, however, *The Monocled Mutineer*'s version of the
trenches went unchallenged. The meaning of the war (and in this case the
heroism of British soldiers in particular) was still the subject of dispute, but
its ground had shifted away from the front-line trenches, whose ultimate
horror was indisputable. Yet such a basic tenet of historical understanding
still allowed different interpretations of what events had meant. For Alan
Bleasdale, the suffering of soldiers in the trenches demonstrated the incompetence of the establishment and their willingness to sacrifice the working
class. To older members of his audience, the ability to overcome such suffering demonstrated the heroism and decency of the British soldier. Arguments
about what the war had been like and what it had meant had melded into
each other, but at another level, some of the ambiguities of interwar culture
remained.

These ambiguities can be seen at work in popular novels published
around the same time as *The Monocled Mutineer* was broadcast. In the late
1980s and early 1990s, a host of new works of historical fiction set during the
First World War were produced, sufficient to amount to a second 'war
books boom' and including such well known texts as Sebastian Faulks's
Birdsong, as well as a mass of other, less successful works. These books made
distinctive use of descriptions of trench warfare.

For example, Jane Saunders's heroine learns of conditions in the front line
from the media: 'Those who continued to exist in the daily mire could hardly
be better off than those who died, according to the more hard-hitting news
reports. The conditions of the trenches were said to be filthy and lice-ridden,
the trenches awash with mud and effluent. The winter had been especially
cold and wet, the spring a long time coming.'[123] Emma Stirling's hero cannot help turning his mind back to France: 'To that march along the treeless
road to the trenches ... It had been raining on and off for days. The road
they'd walked was made of wooden planks and on each side as far as the eye
could see there was a swamp of shell-holes filled with water. Each side of the
road had been littered with dead mules in all stages of decay, some green,

some black ... and the smell of decay had stunk to high heaven.' [124] Leaving
aside the glib historical criticisms we could make of these pieces – the unlike-
lihood of any press report being *that* hard-hitting, the attribution to 1915 of
a scene more reminiscent of 1917 – what is important is the role that such
descriptions were fulfilling. They were not a crucial part of the story. The
books containing them concentrated on life on the Home Front: the
trenches are somewhere men go off to or return from but are seldom the
centre of the action. They were not part of impassioned political arguments
about the meaning of the war or denunciations of its awfulness. Most of
these books were traditional both in their structure and in their social politics. They were more interested in soft-focused romance than promoting
pacifism. Instead, these descriptions were functioning as key historical signposts. They let the audience know that they were reading a book about the
First World War. Mud and horror were a requirement, allowing readers
quickly to situate themselves in a shared sense of the past.

The myth of mud and horror clearly changed its status over time. Some cultural analysts would talk about this in terms of a shift from emergence,
through dominance, to universality or hegemony. What they would mean is
that the myth had developed from something that some people thought, to
something that most people thought, to the point where it was what everyone knew. That change was important because it meant that ideas were no
longer challenged. Indeed, for most people, a challenge to such received
opinions only resulted in a strengthening of their beliefs.

We might discuss this shift as a sort of cultural Chinese whispers, where
ideas were altered subtly, almost imperceptibly, over time. It is always easier to use, or modify slightly, an old idea than it is to come up with a
completely new one. Most people did not have the time or inclination to
find out for themselves how their ancestors had thought about the war.
Instead they tended, unsurprisingly, to accept what they were offered,
particularly if it fitted in with their preconceptions about what the past
had been like. This was as true of authors, producers and researchers as it
was for their audiences. In this process of repetition the most dramatic
and easily understood aspects were re-emphasised. More complicated issues
– the alternative understandings, inconsistencies and variations that made
up the experience – moved into the background and disappeared. This repetition and simplification can be seen in the development of a readily
understood symbolic vocabulary of the war, made up of a limited number
of black and white still photographs and the shorter poems of Wilfred Owen
and Siegfried Sassoon, which is used in particular by newspapers and
television. Once formed, such habits were hard to break.

It would be misleading, however, to argue that a gullible public were being fed untruths about the war by a slapdash producers and authors. The people who created television series, dramas or novels usually believed in the same myths that were held more generally. Even if they chose to research their work, they tended to do so in sources which confirmed them in their beliefs. Using these as a basis, they were then under commercial pressure to select their most striking elements to create exciting books, films or documentaries. A drama based on the fourteen days Charles Carrington spent travelling from unit to unit in 1916 might well be fascinating to the historian, but it would be hard to sell to backers. More often, particularly in the case of journalists, it was not necessarily a deliberate selection of the goriest details, but rather the requirements of a deadline, a knowledge of what readers and editors wanted and an unwillingness to challenge established beliefs. In a context where the myth was already so powerful, its inclusion became a prerequisite for acceptance. How else was the audience to locate a historical documentary, drama or novel in its mental map of the past, except by recognising key tropes of time and place? Without mud, it wouldn't be the First World War.

2

Death

The largest British war cemetery in the world is just south of the tiny village of Passchendaele in Belgium. It is called Tyne Cot, because the concrete German pillboxes which confronted attacking troops from Northumberland in 1917 reminded them of cottages in their home county. The fortifications are still there: so are many of the men who tried to take them. Tyne Cot holds nearly twelve thousand graves. At its centre is the original battlefield cemetery: the headstones unevenly spread around a pillbox which was converted into the base for a monumental Cross of Sacrifice. In front and behind them, in more regular ranks, are the graves of those who were brought in from the surrounding desolation after the fighting had finished. Around the back of the cemetery stands a memorial wall, on which are the names of nearly thirty-five thousand soldiers who fell in the Ypres Salient from the start of 1917 until the end of the war and who have no known grave. Some of their bodies were found but were unidentifiable. They are buried in Tyne Cot and other cemeteries, in graves whose headstones read 'A British Soldier Known Unto God'. Others simply disappeared – although to this day their corpses still sometimes come to light when the earth is turned over by ploughing or for construction.

This is a scale of death which is physically hard to take in. The memorial wall has to curl back and forth to fit the names in legibly. Standing with your back to it, the graves in front of you extend beyond your field of vision: you have to turn your head to see all twelve thousand headstones. Visiting Tyne Cot can be an emotionally overwhelming experience: it brings home the immense human cost of the First World War for Great Britain.

It should not be surprising, therefore, that blood partners mud in the modern British mythology of the war. When we think of the war, we conjure up images not only of horrific conditions, but of the horrendous casualties that resulted. We think of families and communities devastated by the loss of their menfolk; of countless village war memorials and their counterparts in the cemeteries and memorials to the missing of the Western Front; of old ladies who did not marry because their fiancés were lost; of legions of men trooping off to war, never to return. Death, it seems certain, touched every family in the land.

It is a prerequisite of modern television programmes and films set during the Great War that they must end with the death of the combatant cast. A recent horror film, *Deathwatch*, set in the trenches, uses the revelation of the death of the entire cast at the start of the film as its twist in the tale. When we watch these dramas, we already know what the end must be. In the words of *Dad's Army*'s Private Fraser (himself a First World War veteran), they're all doomed.

In absolute terms, the war saw a scale of loss that was unprecedented for Britain, and which has never been repeated. The terrible cost of the war underpins many of our other received beliefs about it: the incompetence of the generals whose actions resulted in so many lost lives; the purposelessness of any war with such a butcher's bill; and the miraculous veneration of any veteran who managed to survive the carnage.

In fact, despite the huge bureaucratic effort necessary to mobilise the population of the country for war, definitive figures for the number of war dead remained, for a long while, elusive. The figure, still widely cited, of a million dead was in fact calculated for Britain and her Empire as a whole. For Britain alone, working out the number of dead was complicated by, amongst other factors, wartime disruption to registrars' record-keeping and the difficulty of deciding when to stop counting deaths as war-related. Most writers tended to guess, to repeat others' numbers, or to attempt spurious calculations based on insufficient evidence. Until the 1980s, published estimates ranged anywhere between half a million and 1,200,000. It was only in 1986 that the social historian Jay Winter published an accurate demographic calculation of the number of Britons who had died in military service during the First World War. Whilst still not definitive, Winter's assessment of between 722,785 and 772,000 is generally accepted as the most accurate available.[1]

Since 6,146,574 men served in Britain's armed forces during the First World War, this meant that almost 12 per cent of the men who served died. The bulk of these losses were sustained by the army, in which 5,215,162 men served. Its rate of loss was almost 13 per cent. Working from insurance policy data, Winter was also able to estimate the age structure of these losses. He suggested that just more than half a million men under thirty had been killed. The dead were concentrated amongst younger men: more than one in seven of the adult male population under twenty-five had been killed, compared to one in ten of those between twenty-five and forty, and one in twenty of those over forty. This was clearly a war that was brutally destructive of lives and bodies, and that inflicted heavy casualties amongst young British men in particular. About one in nine households lost a man to the war, and about one in six families lost a member of the immediate family group. A man from about one in every three households was killed, injured or taken prisoner.[2]

Quantifying Britain's war losses is helpful because it gives us some objects for comparison. They show, for example, how comparatively lightly Britain got off. Even relative to the size of her army, Britain lost fewer men than France or Germany. But as Britain also mobilised fewer of her potential soldiers than her allies and enemies, when the degree of mobilisation is taken into account, her relative rate of loss falls even further. For every thousand of the total wartime population, roughly 16 Britons were killed in the war, compared to 30 in Germany, 34 in France and 57 in Serbia.[3]

The figures also show that everyone did not die. Most men came back. Devastating though the war was for young men, taking the country as a whole, a generation was not wiped out. Nor was it the case that wartime deaths had a lasting demographic impact. For two reasons, war losses barely affected longer-term demographic trends. First, the war halted a wave of emigration: before 1914 tens of thousands of young men had been leaving Britain each year, mainly for the Dominions. With such men choosing not to go during and after the war, wartime losses were soon made up. As a result of these men staying put, the war did not create a generation of spinsters, women who *could* not find a man to marry because so many had died in the war. Whilst some may have *chosen* not to find another partner after the death of husband or fiancé, if these women wanted to marry or remarry, as plenty did, there were potential husbands there for them. For many Britons, the war was the healthiest time of their lives. Wartime changes in social policy and behaviour meant better healthcare for many civilians, and in particular better diet and medical attention for their children. It was the poorest Britons who benefited most from wartime increases in wages. Indeed, for those who weren't eligible for military service, the war saw increased life expectancies and standards of living.[4]

But Britons did not compare themselves with their European neighbours, nor did most spend their time calculating the year on year change in their life expectancy. Britain had never fought a great power war on the scale of the First World War. It was never to do so again. The absolute number of dead remains a key constituent of how the war is remembered.

The uniquely high number of casualties that Britain suffered offers an explanation as to *why* death has been such a major constituent of the mythology of the war. It does little, however, to make clear the processes by which this occurred. In the aftermath of the war, there were few Britons who could look back without thinking of the dead, but there were many who were able to construct a version of the war in which death did not play an overwhelming role. How was it that these voices came to be obscured?

Why was it that the Second World War – still a bloody conflict for Britain, if not as deadly as its predecessor – was not mythologised in terms of death? Why is it that subsequent generations have continued to focus so heavily on death in 1914–18 war, to the point where they believe that it was only the lucky ones who came back? As the Conservative MP Keith Simpson, a knowledgeable scholar of the First World War in his own right, put it in the course of a parliamentary debate in 1998: 'I was in the minority; both my grandfathers came back from that war.'[5]

Questioning the myth of universal bereavement is not the same as claiming that the impact of wartime deaths was insignificant. Far from it. But in trying to establish how death came to dominate our understanding of the war, we need to start by acknowledging that, although the First World War killed a lot of Britons, it did not claim the life of every man who served. Indeed, it is possible to suggest that, although so many Britons were killed that everyone knew a man who had died, only for the minority of Britons was that man an immediate relative or a close friend.

The quantitative judgements made above are, of course, completely useless if we do not also use qualitative data to attempt to judge the impact of war deaths. The stark figures should not obscure individual pain and suffering. Depending on geographic area, occupation, social class and rates of volunteering over time, different parts of the country suffered widely different casualty rates. Some social groups – particularly Highland Scots and the aristocracy – sustained much greater losses than others, for instance, Fenland farmers. Famously, some urban areas were devastated because their men had joined up together (in the 'Pals' Battalions' of the New Army), fought together, and died together in the early battles on the Somme.

A host of other networks existed through which Britons, combatant and non-combatant, were brought into contact with death. Wider family members, friends, colleagues, school or university contemporaries and team-mates: these connections and others brought wartime death closer to those whose own families remained unscathed. If the number of those who lost an immediate member of the family was small relative to the total population, the wider circle of those touched by wartime death – those people who would have been invited to a funeral – encompassed the entire population.[6]

For those men who volunteered or were called up, wartime service meant encountering death and mutilation to an unprecedented degree. Whilst some soldiers were shielded by their service in administrative or logistics units, anyone who served close to the action grew accustomed to the sight of violent death. Where trench lines were static but active, front-line soldiers lived with the dead: spotted on old battlefields or in no man's land, laid up against the wall of the trench until they could be buried; encountered, decomposing, as new earthworks were dug; and exhumed, dissected and reinterred by shellfire. Writing to his family in November 1916, Lieutenant Brian Lawrence described his experiences on the Somme: 'The dugout was beastly, and smelt most terrible; it had the stale smell of filthy mud, peculiar to all dugouts, and a little something extra as well. I don't know for certain what it was, but as half a stale Boche fell out of the wall during the night, I might guess.'[7]

Despite Lawrence's jocular tone, the effect of such sights on the soldier's thoughts can be imagined. At the time, Lieutenant Wyn Griffith of 1/15 Royal Welch Fusiliers wrote of

> grim disfigured corpses rotting in the sun, so horrible in their discolour that it called for an act of faith to believe that these were once men, sent to this degradation by their fellow men. One thought ran in and out of the mind like a shuttle in a loom; any one of the thousands of seconds in this July day might reduce Taylor or myself into a travesty of living man, useless lumber best thrown away near some such heap of rubble as Mametz, 'where Ruin calls his brother Death'.[8]

This was not just death in the abstract, or the risk of death occurring to oneself or one's comrades. Those soldiers who survived the frontline had almost without exception experienced the death of close friends, leaders and subordinates at close quarters. Many had also faced, and overcome, the taboo on killing their fellow man. They were acquainted with death in a different way to those who had not served.

It is, however, hard to generalise about soldiers' reactions to death. Young men think that they are invulnerable: here was abundant evidence that this was not the case. Some experiences were, by any measure, traumatic, but it would be misleading to suggest that all soldiers were irreparably scarred. As well as being shocked and scared, many found pleasure and validation in aspects of their wartime service. Withstanding the emotional shocks and horrors of war could be a matter for pride in personal achievement. Not everyone found the dead uniquely repulsive: numerous accounts testify to the fascination that corpses held for soldiers, particularly when they first entered the battle-lines. Whilst social restraints prevented many soldiers from reminiscing too graphically about the dead, the experience of death at close quarters was one of the things that marked soldiers out. It was therefore a point they mentioned when they wrote memoirs or novels. Although some men may have felt guilt at the fact that they had survived while their comrades had died, for others that triumph over death was itself a defining factor in their war experience.

For those left at home whilst their relations went to war, the years 1914–18 were ones of worry, frustration at lack of information, and constant fear of injury or death to those they loved. For a sizeable minority, this fear of death was justified. But the complications of First World War combat and communications meant that the fact of a loved one's death in battle was not immediately conveyed to the bereaved. Men could die in enemy lines, fall out of sight of their own side, be blown so comprehensively to pieces that they disappeared, or hold onto life long enough to be taken into the casualty clearing system before they expired. All too often, therefore, family members had to experience further uncertainty and distress before they were confronted with the incontrovertible fact of their man's death. For some, whose relatives were listed as missing and whose remains were never identified, this uncertainty could go on for years. Barbara Cartland's father was killed in 1918, but it was months before his death was confirmed. Looking back at the end of her life, she remembered:

> those long drawn out days when we waited for the postman, when letters came from friends or comrades of my father saying that they thought he was a prisoner, the speculation that went on and on, day after day, week after week, month after month, as we wondered where he might be, what he was doing, whether he was wounded, whether he was being well treated ...
>
> When the war was over we were sick of it. We couldn't go on living under the dark strain with all these tears and miseries, we couldn't bear all those anniversaries: 'the anniversary of the day that Daddy was missing', 'the anniversary of the day that he was reported killed', 'the anniversary of the day he last came home on leave', 'his birthday' ...[9]

Even when death had been definitely established, the nature of wartime bereavement could be particularly painful. Dead servicemen were not returned to Britain but buried close to where they fell. Most of those left at home had no body to mourn over, no focus for their grief. This absence seems to have hit the parents of dead soldiers particularly hard. Premature death was distressing for all those who were bereaved. Compared to siblings, friends or fiancées, however, older parents had less time or energy to rebuild their lives. The loss of their children struck some parents even more severely because of their generational position in a time of changing practices. Medical and social changes had meant that they had had fewer children than previous generations, with a greater emotional investment in them and a firm belief that their children would not predecease them. The war blew this assumption apart. Meanwhile, developments in mourning ritual and religious belief, in particular a trend for less public display of grief, had eliminated some of the mechanisms through which these parents might have sought consolation. Some desperately reached back for traditions of a certainty in the afterlife or the tenets of spiritualism.[10] The devastation suffered by Rudyard Kipling and Sir Arthur Conan Doyle after their sons' deaths has been described on numerous occasions.[11] Another example comes from the experience of Harry Lauder, the popular Scottish singer, whose only child John was killed at the end of 1916, serving with 1/8 Argyll and Sutherland Highlanders in France. Lauder was distraught:

> I felt that for me everything had come to an end with the reading of that dire message. It seemed to me that for me the board of life was black and blank. For me there was no past and there could be no future. Everything had been swept away, erased, by one sweep of the hand of a cruel fate. Oh, there was a past though! ... I clutched at every memory, as if I must grasp them and make sure of them, lest they be taken from me as the hope of seeing him again that the telegram had forever snatched away.[12]

For many poorer parents, the loss of a child was a practical disaster as well as an emotional one. For those who had depended on their offspring's time and money as they themselves grew older, that child's death meant the loss of any provision for their old age. The government's provision of pensions, not just for disabled soldiers and widows but also for the dependent parents of soldiers killed in battle, acknowledged the loss of this financial security in the service of the country.

The ways in which wartime deaths affected Britons were varied. Many soldiers were marked by the experience of death at first hand, but few were devastated by it – most continued to function and many found compensatory factors in wartime service. Some took pride in their wartime survival. Fear, anxiety and the bereavement of others had been a commonplace wartime experience. The death of their children in war left some parents distraught and inconsolable.

The influence of all these factors was apparent even on the very first Armistice Day. Britons reacted to the news of peace with widely different behaviour, depending on location, role and personal experience. On the Western Front, even if the end of the war had become foreseeable, its precise moment was not: numerous units began 11 November either preparing for combat or in contact with the enemy.[13] For those soldiers who were engaged in combat up until 11.00 a.m., there was often not the energy or the means to engage in raucous celebration. As Sergeant Robert Cude wrote in his diary: 'I should have preferred to be in London today, I guess that there is high jinks there, we cannot get a drink to celebrate today except a good issue of Rum!'[14]

Servicemen who were behind the front line, or at home, and had access to alcohol, fireworks and women, were better able to demonstrate their joy,

and also keen to mark Britain's victory and the end of the war.[15] They were
joined in their celebrations by many civilians. The release of tension borne
during four years of war resulted in some bacchanalian scenes, particularly
amongst the young. If the euphoria of the initial celebrations faded, it did
not completely disappear as the months passed. Photographs of the numerous public parades held to mark the return of troops after November 1918
show large crowds enthusiastically waving flags and cheering their returning
heroes.

But there were others, both servicemen and civilians, who did not feel
able to indulge in party-going, for a variety of reasons. Celebration seemed
to mock their dead loved ones, or they judged the release of emotion too
grotesque, or their war experience, individual and collective, remained too
problematic.

Four of the twelve children of Sussex schoolmaster Robert Saunders
served in the armed forces. All survived the war unscathed. But Saunders's
diary of November 1918 suggests the ways that death could affect those
whose own families were untouched:

> I think most people feel that some time must elapse before we can properly
> celebrate peace, our feelings have been too much harassed and our sympathies
> too often called forth, for the losses of our friends and neighbours. As I look
> back over the last 4 ½ years I can see so many tragedies in families I know well,
> & I can see so many of my old boys who are dead or wounded, or dying of
> consumption & recall them as boys at school where I used to urge on them the
> duty of patriotism, so that at present, it doesn't seem right that those who have
> escaped shall give themselves up to Joy days.[16]

These issues – the inconsolable grief of those who had lost close relatives,
the desire of some soldiers to celebrate their survival, a more general sadness
at the loss of life, and the concern of those who had escaped personal
bereavement for the emotional needs of those who had not – would all
continue to influence commemoration of the war into the early 1920s.

The form of that commemoration came largely from below: it was based
on the interaction of the expressed and perceived desires of the population
at large, rather than officially imposed. This process is well shown in the
building of the Cenotaph, the monument to the war dead that stands in
Whitehall today. The first version of the Cenotaph was intended as a temporary construction. It was created, out of plaster, cloth and wood, to play
a part in the Peace Day parade of 19 July 1919. The Cenotaph's original purpose was to incorporate the dead in a celebration of military victory. The
armed forces were to march through the streets of London, saluting the
King and being cheered by the crowds: it was considered necessary to

represent those who had fought and not returned. The Cenotaph was meant, however, as a subsidiary component of the main event, whose focus was on military achievement.[17]

Public reaction to the Cenotaph completely undercut official intentions. The crowds at the monument were such that the parade route had to be changed so that troops could march around them. After the parade had finished, the Cenotaph became a centre for mourning and commemoration, laden with wreaths brought from all over the country. These wreaths continued to be laid in the weeks and months after the parade, so that it was only when the temporary monument began to disintegrate that the Office of Works was able to justify its removal. The government had to respond to calls to replace the temporary monument with a permanent version.

This stone Cenotaph was unveiled on 11 November 1920. On the same day, in an elaborate ceremony, the coffin containing the remains of the Unknown Warrior was borne through the streets of London and interred in Westminster Abbey. Taken at random from a number of unidentified bodies selected on the Western Front, the symbolic purpose of the Unknown Warrior was to act as a representative body for all those which had not been returned. This body at least would be honoured; given full military ceremonials and buried amongst the greatest in the land. Initial plans gave little space in these ceremonies for ex-servicemen, let alone for the bereaved, but press outrage at the lack of consideration being paid to distraught parents resulted in a swift reconsideration: both MPs and Lords gave up the places they had been allotted to the mothers of dead soldiers. In subsequent days, before the grave was filled in, the Abbey and the Cenotaph became the centre of a vast pilgrimage. Some one and a quarter million Britons filed past the open grave. It was clear that for many of those who visited the remains were not unknown – they came with the belief or hope that it was their soldier who lay in the Abbey. The level of emotion amongst the crowds was extremely high – shrieks permeated the Silence at 11 o'clock – the pain of wartime loss was clearly still raw.[18]

The early 1920s saw the rituals at the centre of Armistice Day become established.[19] At eleven o'clock on 11 November, the country was silenced for two minutes as workers downed tools, cars, buses and trains stopped, and Britons emerged onto the streets to gather, bow their heads, and remember the dead. The Poppy Fund, established by Earl Haig and the British Legion as a means of raising money for disabled soldiers, became the most popular way of demonstrating participation in remembrance of the dead and care for the wounded. On the Sunday nearest to 11 November, there were also parades and services based around the war memorials that had been erected in towns and villages across the country. On these were named the dead. Organised at the local level of parish, council or county, these memorials continue to hold a place in the built landscape of the country.

Huge crowds attended these weekend ceremonies and the two minutes silence was universally honoured. Not everyone had lost someone, but, given the general sorrow at wartime losses, the high emotional intensity and the emphasis placed on national unity and redemption in these ceremonies, taking part seemed natural and necessary to many Britons. It was easy for those, like Robert Saunders, who were saddened by the loss of life, even though they had not lost someone close to them, and who were concerned to respect the bereaved, to become bound into such displays of mourning. Indeed, given the reports of violence offered by crowds to those who broke the silence, non-participation must have appeared not only difficult but dangerous.

There were those, however, who continued to view the anniversary of the Armistice as an opportunity for a celebration, as well as, or rather than, for mourning. Celebration did not preclude respectful participation in rituals of remembrance, but it did mean a different understanding of the wider mean-ing of Armistice Day. Large numbers of ex-soldiers gathered, often on the evening of 11 November, to mark their survival, to recreate the camaraderie and social release of the war, and to remember their comrades in a way that matched their understanding of what the war had meant. Large London hotels offered, in the early 1920s, the opportunity to attend Armistice Balls. These socially exclusive events were often marked by riotous behaviour, drunkenness and excess. Away from the metropolis, less public celebrations took place elsewhere as well, sometimes as fund-raising events for local war memorials. It is easy to understand a desire, as ex-servicemen faced up to the realities of post-war life, to attempt to experience once more those aspects of the war that seemed, at least in retrospect, positive. Marking the war as a significant event in veterans' lives led, easily enough, to gathering together to drink and renew wartime bonds.[20]

These veterans were not alone in their desire to think of Armistice Day in terms that went beyond death and sorrow. When the Cabinet discussed the building of a permanent Cenotaph, some of its members felt uneasy about constructing a memorial to the war that so specifically connoted death and mourning. Even so soon after the war, they perceived a tension between marking Britain's victory and mourning her dead, with the risk that the latter might obscure the former. The King's proclamation that insti-tuted the two minutes' silence at 11.00 a.m. on 11 November made it clear that the two requirements should coexist. The silence was intended to allow the population to 'perpetuate the memory of the Great Deliverance' *and* 'of those who laid down their lives to achieve it'. The committee that arranged the 1921 ceremony at the Cenotaph was insistent that Armistice Day should not be a day of national grief. The chairman of the committee, Lord Curzon, emphasised his belief that 'in this and subsequent years, the 11th November would not be a day of mourning but would be the commemoration of a great day in the country's history'.[21]

Armistice Day in the early 1920s should be seen, therefore, as a multi-faceted event. It involved sadness, celebration and solidarity, and extended beyond the two minutes silence at eleven o'clock on 11 November. Yet by the end of the decade, the public rituals and behaviour of Armistice Day had become much more codified, consistent and regulated. The celebration of national or personal victory had lost ground, in favour of a restrained mourning of the dead, which emphasised the validation of their deaths in terms of redemptive sacrifice: they died that we might live. 11 November was became seen as a day of national unification in mourning. There was no room for drunkenness. The solemnity of the occasion was all-encompassing and extended beyond 11 November to regulate behaviour surrounding the day itself. How was it that alternative versions of commemoration – whether from veterans or from the state – were abandoned?

The historian Adrian Gregory has described the ways in which the ex-servicemen's celebrations were criticised in the mid 1920s, on the grounds that they were disrespectful to two communities. First, during an economic slump that had seen so many former soldiers reduced to poverty or destitution, ostentatious London parties were deemed offensive, particularly when it was suggested that many of those celebrating around 11 November had not, in fact, done their bit. Those who had stayed behind and profited from the war should definitely not be drinking whilst others, who had laid their lives on the line, were starving in the streets. These criticisms represented both the justified anger of some poor ex-soldiers and the realities of increased class tension and militancy in the aftermath of the Russian Revolution.

Even more effective in restricting these celebrations was the suggestion that they were offensive to the bereaved. Contributing to a debate that began over the use of the Albert Hall for huge Armistice Balls, and developed to consider all such revels, the Revd Dick Sheppard asked readers of *The Times*:

Is it dreadfully old-fashioned to be shocked at the announcement again this year that a great Victory Ball is to be held at the Albert Hall on Armistice night? ... Dancing is frequently the obvious and fitting form of grateful commemorating a glad event, but a fancy dress ball on a vast scale as a tribute to

the Great Deliverance which followed on from the unspeakable agony of
1914–1918 seems to me not so much irreligious as indecent.[22]

The complaint was that drunken excess in celebration of the end of the war
not only disrespected the dead but also upset those whose sons and husbands had not returned. Celebrations of survival disturbed their mourning;
worse, they mocked their loss.

This was not an issue that was quickly resolved. Indeed, the subject of
appropriate behaviour on Armistice Day became a topic for media debate,
with the *Daily Express* defending veterans' right to enjoy themselves against
the *Daily Mail*'s campaign to restrain them on behalf of the bereaved. The
letters received by newspapers made it clear that a variety of different ways
of marking 11 November remained. There were those, like this letter writer,
for whom commemoration of the dead and celebration of victory were not
incompatible: 'Many people regard Armistice Day as one of universal
thanksgiving. One ventures to think the fallen are like-minded. They were
not melancholy people, and many of us celebrate as they did when home
on leave. The great silence at 11 is the most poignant vital moment of the
day, but afterwards cannot gratitude express itself fully through happiness
and good cheer?'[23] This letter, with its use of the present tense to describe
the dead and its vision of the First World War as a hard-won victory, is
distinctively of the 1920s. Clearly – although their interests were suppos-
edly being considered – not all bereaved Britons wanted mourning to
dominate all other aspects of Armistice Day. But it was the idea of causing
offence to bereaved non-combatants which had most social influence.
Notwithstanding these divergent voices, then, a concern for propriety and a
widespread belief in the moral obligation to pay respect meant that hotels
and restaurants cancelled Armistice Balls.

What were veterans to do to mark Armistice Day? In fact, it was often
those social conservatives who criticised revelry on Armistice Night who also
greatly valued wartime comradeship and feared its mobilisation for political
radicalism. They recognised, therefore, that some alternative was necessary.
In place of drunkenness and excess, and picking up on newspaper suggestions, Sheppard proffered what was to become the Festival of Remembrance:
a gathering of veterans in the Albert Hall which would recreate the camaraderie of the war years by singing the more respectable wartime songs
together – 'Keep the Homes Fires Burning', 'Sister Susie', 'I Want to Go
Home' and 'Abide With Me'. Beginning on Armisticetide – the night before
11 November – 1927, and supported by the *Daily Express*, the Festival of
Remembrance swiftly proved popular with the public and with those veterans who attended. Other ex-servicemen, who wanted a more boisterous

celebration, were forced to modify their public behaviour. By the late 1920s, a pattern that emphasised remembrance and national rededication, rather than celebration, was set.[24]

The result of this was not to exclude former soldiers from Armistice commemoration altogether. Festivals of Remembrance were put on throughout the country, and the BBC broadcast of the Albert Hall event was one of its most popular programmes. Many still attended commemorative ceremonies – particularly on the Sunday closest to 11 November, when it was easier for working men to gather during the day. Most still felt an obligation to remember their mates, or to act as a reminder of the past to younger generations. There were good associational reasons for the British Legion to encourage attendance at such events – they demonstrated its organisational prowess and degree of support – but in truth only a small minority of veterans were ever active members of the Legion.[25]

That veterans could be coerced in this way was indicative of their lack of unitary identity and the diversity of their understandings of their war. For every veteran who wanted to celebrate victory on 11 November, there was another who was happy to participate in any form of remembrance, and two or three more who would respect the silence but were otherwise not too bothered. British veterans did not usually act cohesively in the political sphere during the inter-war years, in contrast to their counterparts in France and Germany. The variety of ways in which they interpreted and reacted to their wartime experiences meant that public ceremony was dominated by the need to satisfy the perceived emotional needs of the bereaved.[26]

As the rhetoric of Armistice Day became increasingly focused solely on death and mourning, some veterans felt unable to participate. The solemn rituals did not fit with their memories of the war, either because they sanitised death, or because they concentrated too heavily upon it. One former officer stopped taking part in Armistice Day in the 1920s because, he wrote, it felt 'too much like attending one's own funeral'.[27] In other cases, soldiers found it difficult to locate their specific traumatic losses within the framework of Armistice Day. There were individual anniversaries to be marked. Harry Patch's Lewis gun team was all but wiped out during the Third Ypres campaign: an incident never assimilated into national forms of remembrance. 'That day, 22 September 1917 – that is my Remembrance Day, not Armistice Day ... I'm always very, very quiet on that day and I don't want anyone talking to me really ... I shall always remember it. I shall never forget the three I lost.'[28]

If Patch found it difficult to relocate his loss to 11 November, why should it have been any easier for others who were bereaved? Reading the 'In

Memoriam' section of *The Times* from the inter-war years makes it clear
that individual anniversaries of death remained of vital importance to those
left behind. This might point us towards an analysis of how remembrance
was structured. It would be a mistake to see the regulation of the wilder
excesses of Armistice Day celebration as part of a wider victory for the
wishes of the bereaved. Rather, it represented a far more complex process of
compromise and social control.

Many parents from all social backgrounds attempted to involve themselves in commemorating the war dead. Some undoubtedly found the
rituals and memorials associated with annual remembrance consoling.[29] Yet
for others, whether any form of mourning actually ameliorated their grief
is open to question. During the war, the bereaved father Harry Lauder was
more able than most to participate in potentially consolatory activities. As
a popular celebrity, he aided the war effort by singing for soldiers in France
and Flanders, and by making propaganda trips to American and Canada,
where his popularity equalled that in Great Britain. Whilst in France he was
able to visit his son John's grave and retrieve his Highland bonnet and a
scrap of tartan.[30] He sustained himself with his faith in God, the afterlife
and a belief that his son's death had been glorious and in a just cause.[31]
Yet none of this assuaged his sorrow. He abandoned his Scottish home
because it held too many memories of John: 'There were his photographs,
his guns, his fishing rods, his horse, his billiard cues, his books, his
music! ... I tell you we cried ourselves to sleep every night.' His first
thoughts when he received his knighthood in 1919 were that he 'would willingly, aye, with great joy, have bartered the whole lot for one smile from
John, one shake of his hand, to hear him say "Dad, old man!" once more'.
Writing his memoirs nine years after the war, Lauder confessed that: 'I have
been consumed by a restlessness which has kept far in the background all
thoughts of settling down to the quieter life I had been looking forward to
before and during the war. The loss of John completely altered his mother's
life and mine ... there were too many sad memories for us to feel happy
for more than a few days at a time.'[32]

Official forms of remembrance and commemoration did not always work
for the bereaved. Given the obvious continuing grief of parents in particular, and the apparent concern for their welfare, it might in theory have
been easy for them to mobilise public support to influence the mourning
of their sons. In reality, parents were not a large or cohesive enough group
to exert political influence. In 1926, the state was paying pensions to 327,
355 dependants of dead soldiers.[33] Whilst this was a large group, it was
not significant in terms of political power when their wishes went against
government policy.

We can see this when we look at the issue of what should happen to the bodies of the dead. A firm decision had been taken during the war that the dead would be buried in cemeteries close to where they fell, and that (although some personalisation of the inscription would take place) the basic pattern of the Imperial War Graves Commission headstone should be fixed in terms of size and shape. This was based both on aesthetics and a desire to uphold the idea of a national sacrifice without regard to fame or fortune. Men had served and died together and they should not be marked out in their immortal rest. Some relatives found comfort in the burial of their menfolk where they had died, with their comrades, overseas, unified in death by their apparently identical headstones, but at least as many wanted a far more explicit and individual recognition of what their men had given up. Some wanted the remains of their husbands or sons returned home for private burial. If this were not possible, they and others would have liked the right to erect their own individual grave markers in Imperial War Graves Commission cemeteries, distinguishing their grave from those around them, just as they would have done at home. In the demands for these rites, we can see an understandable desire to reach back to traditional forms of mourning and commemorating the dead. There was also a desire for agency: for the opportunity to act individually to commemorate the dead and to take control of remembrance. None was allowed, despite the considerable distress caused as a result.[34]

Similarly, in 1921, the War Office ended the option of military funerals for those who had returned home but died of their war wounds. It had proved too popular, it was difficult to ascertain whether war wounds were the cause of death and, at a time of military cutbacks, it was too expensive.[35] For individual families, however, this represented a denial of their sacrifice. Again, although some of the bereaved plainly were comforted by the attention shown to them on Armistice Day, for others 11 November represented either a cruel stirring up of emotions they tried to keep under control, or the hypocrisy of a nation willing to forget the dead for the rest of the year. Their grief was too specific and enduring to be entirely subsumed into the rhetoric of official remembrance.

By the late 1920s most Britons did not think about the dead every day. Emotions still ran high on Armistice Day, but the burden of death had proved wider than it was deep. Rather, whether they chose to articulate it or not, they wanted to get on with their lives. As early as 1923, the decline in the proportion of the crowd dressed in mourning on 11 November was noted in the press.[36] Britons – bereaved or not – had not stopped caring about the dead. But the socially appropriate period of mourning for those who were not immediate relatives had come to an end. Most, however, remained conscious of and respectful for the sorrow of a smaller group. Since they were unwilling or unable to mourn the dead continuously, but still believed that it was right to honour them and their relatives, the solution was to fix on a single day of commemoration. Interested groups and individuals would still choose their own special occasions to remember, but only on one day would mass participation be expected. If the focus for remembrance as a nation was to be a single day, it was even more important that the occasion should be regulated and sanctified.

For many, particularly those who found solace in its rituals, Armistice Day retained power and significance throughout their lives. By the 1930s, however, the grief for more distant acquaintances and relatives that had brought so many within the emotional circle of Armistice Day immediately after the war had faded. A younger generation had grown up which, although it was still fascinated by the war, could not remember wartime sacrifices and community as well as its elders. Commemoration was being carried out in a changed international and domestic economic context. Increasingly, other themes crept into Armistice Day, including a sense of disillusionment, a mistrust of politicians, and the fear of another European conflict.[37]

All these factors meant that there were changes in the language and behaviour which surrounded 11 November. It became, in prospect, something that you did for others, not yourself: a social obligation rather than an emotional necessity. As a woman of twenty-five responded to a Mass-Observation Surveyor: 'Oh it's a good thing, I didn't lose anyone myself, but it's right that we should shed a tear for those that did.' The day itself retained its emotional power. The tacit, or not so tacit, emotional coercion exerted by those who had participated or lost someone to the war continued to encourage mass participation. Most Mass-Observation participants expressed dislike or disapproval of the idea of Armistice Day in advance – but in practice nearly all participated in the Silence when eleven o'clock came.[38]

By 1939, Britain had an annual ceremony to mark the war, with an emphasis on death, mourning and redemptive sacrifice, participated in by the bulk of the population, at least partly in sympathy for the perceived needs of the bereaved. That sympathy itself influenced how the war could be remembered. Excessive celebration was not just tactless, it was offensive. Instead, the emphasis had to be on restrained mourning. Memorialised in this way, the dead were *the* recurring presence in a representation of the war that – at least in public – placed less and less emphasis on Britain's survival and victory as the fruits of success seemed less sweet through the inter-war years.

Events during the 1940s affected the remembrance of the First World War in a number of ways. In practical terms, the Second World War disrupted annual Armistice Day ceremonies. Such large-scale public gatherings were dangerous in wartime, and the maroons and sirens that had signalled the two minutes silence were being put to other uses. This disruption hardly meant that the dead were forgotten, but it did reduce their prominence in public life. Nevertheless, there were unofficial pilgrimages to the Cenotaph and the grave of the Unknown Soldier in 1943 and 1944.[39]

At the end of the Second World War the government decided that, ceremonially, the dead would be remembered together. Most communities chose to add the names of the newly dead to existing war memorials, rather than building new ones. The day of commemoration, was renamed – for Remembrance in general, not one Armistice in particular – and moved to the Sunday nearest 11 November. This reduced the disruptive impact of the two minutes silence. No longer was there the stunning moment when cars, trains and factories halted in the middle of the working day. It may actually have increased attendance at formal remembrance ceremonies, however, since it meant that working men and women could afford the time to attend them.

The decision to incorporate the two groups of dead in one ceremony can be understood in a number of ways. A generation of Britons that was different in outlook and attitudes from its predecessor thirty years earlier wanted to invest its efforts in projects of greater utility: hospitals, playing fields and village halls rather than lumps of stone. The country that had produced a Labour landslide in 1945 had been fighting to create a more tangibly beneficial world. Improving the community was the best memorial to the dead. On a practical level, most communities had a war memorial at their centre by 1939 in any case, with space to add the smaller number of Second World War dead. Adding those names seemed likely to assure them of the same veneration their predecessors had received.

Demographic change during the 1940s altered the make-up of the community of the bereaved. The parents of dead soldiers from the First World War, whose perceived wishes had done so much to shape behaviour in the 1920s and 1930s, reached the end of their own lives and began quickly to die out. This change in population had an effect on what could be said publicly about that war. The parents of soldiers dead in the Second World War, though no less grief-stricken, were at least perhaps better prepared by their own earlier experience of a total war: they had access to a template for reactions to and remembrance of death in war.

The community of the newly bereaved was much smaller in 1945 than it had been for the previous war. Britain had simply suffered fewer deaths. There were undoubtedly those who would have wanted their son's sacrifice marked out by a new monument – but they had even less influence than before. The Second World War itself had an effect on how

central death was to the mythology of its predecessor. Once again, Britain
was involved in a struggle for survival; on this occasion a struggle that came
very close to disaster. Yet, because of the nature of the war, she suffered
many fewer casualties. The expulsion of British troops from mainland
Europe in 1940 and the length and ferocity of the conflict between Soviet
Russia and Nazi Germany meant that, unlike a generation before, Britain
did not take the leading role in land warfare against the bulk of her opponent's armed forces. As numerous military historians have pointed out, the
loss rate for the British army in individual actions in the Second World War
was often not much different from that of twenty years before:

> what is markedly different is the scale of its commitment. At El Alamein, the
> eleven British divisions of the Eighth Army faced four weak German divisions
> and a further eight Italian divisions of varying strength and quality, at a time
> when 171 German and other Axis divisions were operating on the Eastern
> Front. The BEF of 1914–1918 deployed at its peak up to sixty-six divisions, in
> five armies, with a total manpower sometimes over two million. During the
> German offensives of March-April 1918 the British armies engaged a total of
> 109 German divisions, and ninety-nine divisions during the final offensive
> from August 1918 to the Armistice.[40]

It was not that the defeat of Nazi Germany did not require *someone* to suffer
very heavy casualties. Huge attrition of the enemy's resources of personnel
and equipment was in the nature of modern total war. Such destruction
could not be achieved without enormous human losses on both sides. But
from 1941 to 1945 this attrition occurred on the Eastern Front. Britain was
spared the major commitment she had been forced to make in the First
World War. Those British units who were involved in prolonged fighting
against well positioned and battle-hardened defenders suffered rates of loss
as heavy or heavier than their predecessors.[41]

Britain suffered about 360,000 dead in the Second World War. Approximately 270,000 came from the armed forces and about 30,000 from the
merchant marine. At least 60,000 civilians were killed by enemy bombing.[42]
Terrible though these losses were, they were only around half of those who
died in the First World War. They were also divided more evenly than before
across age groups and between civilians and soldiers. Not least because of
changes in conscription and allocation of men, Britain did not suffer the sort
of disaster that befell individual communities after the Somme, with very
high rates of casualties inflicted on men from one locality on a single day.

In retrospect, the end of the Second World War might seem the moment for
a change of course in the remembrance of the dead of the First World War.

Britain had won a second victory over its European enemies in the space of thirty years. Many of those who had fought in the First World War had come back to serve their country once more in 1939. As the numbers of bereaved parents – whose perceived needs had been so important between the wars – fell, was there not an opportunity for the representation of the war to change? Might those veterans who had chosen to dance, rather than mourn, on Armistice Night now come to the fore in the remembrance of the war? Why was it that death continued to overwhelm victory in the popular conception of the First World War?

One explanation is simply the long-lasting effect of wartime death on those who experienced it. Some grieving relatives never recovered. For others, the misery of bereavement could re-emerge as the salient fact of a life viewed in retrospect. Philip Orr has written of the way his own family was marked by his great-uncle's death. Orr describes his

> childhood fascination with the sepia portrait of my great uncle John, in army uniform, which hung on the shadowy landing of the staircase in my grandmother's house. I knew only that he had gone missing during the latter part of the First World War and that for several months his mother had waited in anticipation as each train pulled into the village railway station, until she finally obtained news that he had been killed a few months before the armistice ...
>
> A measure of the impact of that death is the fact that, over sixty years later, when my grandmother ... was an elderly and dying woman, she did not recall more recent bereavements but increasingly thought of her long dead brother and cried for him as if he had died only yesterday.[43]

In contexts like these, where the impact of wartime bereavement was still so apparent, it was unsurprising that death dominated family myths of the First World War.

Through the 1940s and 1950s, the generation of bereaved parents whose grief had been so influential between the wars became almost extinct. There remained, however, large numbers of adults who had experienced the impact of wartime death at first hand as children and who remained marked by it. Their continued interest would see death elevated to a place of prominence in the mythology of the First World War during the 1960s.

Charles Chilton was one of them. Chilton's father was killed in action just after his son was born, in 1918. His mother died shortly afterwards. Chilton was brought up by his grandmother in circumstances of extreme poverty. Although his father was lionised, no one knew of his wartime activities or the manner of his death. He was a mythical figure; but myths about his actual service were lacking. Nevertheless, Chilton attended Armistice Day parades and laid wreaths at the Cenotaph wearing his father's medals.

After leaving school, Chilton got a job working as a messenger boy at the BBC in 1932. One of his jobs was to make deliveries to the 'Addressing Department', from where the *Radio Times* was sent out direct to its customers. This department was staffed by facially disfigured veterans, men who could not work with others because of the disturbing nature of their wounds. One of Chilton's jobs was to fetch them lunch – they did not care to eat in public. Both Chilton and these broken-faced men shared a conviction that they had been employed and were being looked after because the Director General of the BBC, Sir John (later Lord) Reith, was himself a facially scarred veteran. He would look after his own.[44] Whether this was actually Reith's intention or not is unimportant: a belief in his patronage was strongly held. The shared traumas resulting from conflict formed strong emotional bonds.[45]

Chilton was a signatory of the Peace Pledge, a nationwide movement in the early 1930s whose members pledged not to fight in a future war, and he took his promise seriously. He spent the first part of the Second World War as a conscientious objector, fire-watching at the BBC, but then was convinced to renounce his views and serve in the RAF. After that he returned to the BBC, working on the successful science fiction radio series *Journey into Space*. His experience of the aftermath of the war remained at most a passive influence on his life, although one *Journey into Space* storyline did feature a friendly and wise alien who was too hideously disfigured to reveal himself. Yet Chilton was drawn back to the war by his grandmother's continuing grief:

> In 1958 I was on holiday in France. At the request of my grandmother I visited Arras in order to photograph the grave of my father (her son) who had been killed in that area in 1918. I had no idea that there were so many soldiers' cemeteries around Arras. When at last I discovered my father's official memorial it was to find that he had no known grave [instead he was commemorated on the Arras monument to the missing].
>
> What could possibly have happened to a man that rendered his burial impossible? What horror could possibly have taken place that rendered the burial of 35,942 men impossible and all in one relatively small area?[46]

Fascinated by his experience, in 1961 Chilton prepared *The Long Long Trail*, a radio programme for the Home Service based on music from the First World War, contrasting the songs of soldiers on the Western Front with those sung on the Home Front. The programme attracted a considerable audience and a very favourable response from listeners. It was subsequently rebroadcast twice, with the popular entertainer Bud Flanagan, himself a First World War veteran, narrating and adding some anecdotes from his own experiences. The emphasis of *The Long Long Trail* was on the valour, humour and endurance of the ordinary front-line soldier: 'In spite of mud, blood, hell and high water they smiled – and carried on.'[47]

One of those listeners was the theatrical producer Gerry Raffles, consort to Joan Littlewood, one of the founders of the East London based Theatre Workshop group. They took up the concept created by Chilton and developed it into the 'musical entertainment' *Oh What a Lovely War*, one of the best known dramas of the First World War, first performed in 1963. In the process they emphasised a radical political perspective only implicit in Chilton's approach; although he remained involved, a host of other influences affected its form and content. One particularly striking feature of the production of *Oh What a Lovely War* was the use of statistics of death to back up the play's argument about the war.

Theatre Workshop made use of an electronic message board, positioned above the actors at the back of the stage, to highlight the 'facts' of the war. At different points, amongst other pieces of information, this newspanel told the audience: 'NOVEMBER ... SOMME BATTLE ENDS ... TOTAL LOSS 1,332,000 MEN ... GAIN NIL.', 'SEPT 20 ... MENIN ROAD ... BRITISH LOSS 22,000 MEN GAIN 800 YARDS ... SPET 25 ... POLYGON WOOD ... BRITISH LOSS 17,000 MEN GAIN 1,000 YARDS' and 'THE WAR TO END ALL WARS ... TOTAL KILLED TEN MILLION ... WOUNDED TWENTY ONE MILLION ... MISSING SEVEN MILLION.'[48]

Leaving aside the accuracy of these figures, their shifting between the losses of both sides and one alone, and the utility of the ratio of men killed to ground gained as a measure of military success in this context, what is worthy of note is the reaction of some members of the audience. These figures, after all, stick in the mind, with or without the ability to make sense of them. The *Daily Mail* reviewer of the play was deeply moved by 'the fact, never so clearly stated, that ten million men had died in unimaginable squalor for Kitchener's pointing finger, for a few yards of worthless mud, for patriotic lies, for the vanity of bad commanders'.[49] The degree to which the millions of German, French and Russian conscripts who died were motivated by Kitchener's finger is questionable: this writer had confused the total figures for all combatants in the war with those for Britain alone. That he could do so was significant: even during the worst days of the war itself, it would have been difficult to believe that nearly a quarter of the country's entire population had died. Notwithstanding the continuing importance of the war to many Britons in the 1960s, the status of wartime death had begun to shift. It was becoming a historical 'fact' rather than a lived experience. In this context, what the statistics represented was not a strictly accurate counting of the dead, but the knowledge that the war had been particularly bloody.

This changing emotional connection to the war was apparent when the musical entertainment was made into a film, produced in 1968 and released the following year. The film version, *Oh! What a Lovely War,* was adapted by Len Deighton and Charles Chilton, directed by Richard Attenborough, and starred many of the leading lights of British cinema.[50] In the process many of the play's more extreme political attitudes were toned down. Whilst satire remained, the political passion had faded. It was replaced by grief. The contemporary critic Margaret Hinxman suggested that, in contrast to the play, the film was 'moved not so much by a cynical outrage than by a desperate sadness'.[51] This was most clearly obvious in the film's closing shot.

In the final scenes of the film, Jack Smith, the last of the central characters to survive, takes part in an attack as the Armistice is being signed. Following a guide tape through the smoke, he eventually emerges, in silence, onto the Sussex Downs. There his dead brothers are reclining on the grass around the women who have survived them. It is clear that Jack too has died. Unaware of their ghostly presence, the women are eating a picnic. Jack's daughter breaks the silence by asking 'What did Daddy do in the war?' To the sound of the wartime parody 'They didn't believe me', the Smith men transform into white crosses. The camera continually pulls back to reveal that the women are wandering in a seemingly endless field of crosses.[52]

There was not a dry critical eye in the house. 'We are left with a sense of wasted lives, a feeling of impenetrable sadness, of unassuagable grief', wrote Philip French.[53] 'The impression it leaves is still too profound and too personal adequately to describe', were the words of another reviewer.[54] This shot was more striking than any radio or stage scene could have been because of its sheer scale. It involved the screwing into the chalk downland of some 15,000 crosses, more grave markers than are in any single British cemetery on the Western Front.[55] It remains extremely powerful.

Yet it was also significant of a shift in the implied standpoint of the audience. The stage production sought to involve the audience, inviting them to sing along. The play ends with no hint that the war itself ever came to a conclusion. In contrast, the film views the war as history. The Armistice is signed and the dead are buried, even if the sorrow continues. Attenborough made much use of subverted symbols of remembrance to make his point. Poppies – symbols of the remembered dead – become precursors of death in the film, handed to those who are about to die. Jack Smith's return home at the end of the film takes place in exactly two minutes of silence.[56] For all that it makes use of a comforting nostalgia, the film of *Oh! What a Lovely*

War is about imagining the war as a past event rather than participating in it. It is a film created by and for the generation that followed the war. Their own familial experience and their participation in inter-war school culture had inscribed death upon them as children: for all that they retained affection for the past, their vision of the war was bound up with death.

If there was a human legacy that continued to emphasise death in representations of the war, there was also a structural influence. In the inter-war years, the war had become bound up with the concept of death in the national mythology. This association of event and myth meant that, by the 1960s, anyone wanting to represent the former naturally made use of the latter. In this way the myth was not only reinforced but became self-perpetuating, accepted uncritically by subsequent generations as accurately representing the reality.

We can see this process at work in the creation of the title sequence of the BBC series *The Great War*. Its most striking image was of a mournful British soldiers sitting in a trench, apparently surrounded by his dead comrades:

FADE UP VISION AND SOUND

1. OPENING SHOT: CU silhouetted cross inscribed 'In Memory'.

2. Pulls back to reveal silhouette of soldier.

3. Tracks down, down, down over images of the dead strewn over battlefields.

4. And comes to rest on a skeleton of a soldier still in his uniform at the bottom of a trench.

5. Pans across left into adjoining trench with a British soldier sitting left of frame against the trench wall, surrounded by his dead comrades.

6. Starts track into his haunted face and eyes.

7. CU haunted face and eyes.[57]

Whilst it is apparent that this sequence is not a single shot, but rather a selection of different photographs, it is not immediately obvious that the final image, in which the soldier appears, is in fact a montage of a number of other images. Although the soldier appears to be in a corpse-filled trench, he was in fact cut from an original photograph which showed him surrounded by his very much alive, and much more cheerful, comrades.

This collaged image struck a resonant chord with the audience, who wrote in to the BBC in their hundreds to ask for a picture of him. Postcards of him were sent out across the country: he was transformed into a dismal pin-up. The language used to request these postcards was consistent in its high level of emotion: 'It is one of the best "anti-war" pictures I have ever seen ...', 'My uncle, now dead, suffered greatly during the First World War and the picture reminds me of the futility of total war'. 'I am thirteen and agree entirely with the girl who said "he means more to me than the Beatles".'[58]

When the collaging which had produced the image was revealed, Tony Essex responded to a viewer's criticism by explaining the rationale behind it:

> The opening sequence was designed to take us back in time, from the cross, which could be any memorial any time, via the survivor standing over the grave, down to the *long-dead* skeleton, over to the *recently* dead in the trench, and across to the '*not-yet-dead*' soldier with tragic face at the end of the sequence. To achieve this simple thought, the 'not-yet-dead' soldier has indeed been taken from another photo and placed in this more suitable setting.[59]

Attempting to introduce his audience to, and engage them with, the First World War as a topic, Essex made use of a symbolic rhetoric that was principally concerned with death. The decision was natural enough: not only did the series specifically aim at creating a memorial, but also, since it was concerned with the war, death was one of the audience's (and indeed the creators') principal expectations.

This process of repetition and reinforcement is still apparent in the way the First World War is represented today. It is perhaps most clearly apparent in the use of the statistics of death. As with *Oh What a Lovely War*, these figures can be used to attract the audience's attention, to make a point, or to try to ground a specific aesthetic representation in wider experience. There is not, in this context, necessarily a pressure to be accurate with figures or to explain their relevance.

Two recent examples highlight the way that numbers continue to be simplified for dramatic effect. The first comes from a programme on royal gardeners in late 2003. Contemplating the fate of Edwardian gardeners, Alan Titchmarsh described, with emotion, the impact of the First World War on Britain: 'millions died'.[60] The second comes from the opening, in November 2003, of the Australian War Memorial in London. Media reports of the event made much of the fact, doubtless released by an embassy press official, that the Australian forces suffered the heaviest rate of casualties of any nation in the First World War.[61] It is the case that the Australian Expeditionary Force suffered heavier deaths per thousand soldiers than its imperial allies – largely because the Australians relied on British logistics and artillery units, so that most of their soldiers served in combatant rather than support roles. The rate of loss in the Australian army was, however, still lower than that in the French or German. Moreover, if we compare deaths per thousand of the eligible male population, then only Canada and Japan suffered a lighter rate of loss than Australia, which had a comparatively low rate of mobilisation. No matter what the measure, the loss rates of any other country are dwarfed by those of Serbia, which lost just under a quarter of its male population aged fifteen to forty-nine in the period 1914–18.[62]

Demanding accuracy in all such circumstances would be the mark of academic pedantry carried to the level of complete divorce from reality. These throwaway lines have an implication, however, for the way we think – or rather fail to think – about the First World War. Presented out of context, and appreciated without personal connection, these figures have lost their meaning. They no longer represent specific deaths, but rather the concept of mass death. To represent that idea, any figure becomes plausible: the larger the better if one wants to attract attention. The precise enumeration of the dead – a matter of considerable concern in the years immediately after the war – is no longer of relevance.

This morbid revelling in mass fatality can itself seem rather disturbing. Writing about post-war remembrance, the writer Geoff Dyer has asked:

> was there not, amidst all this grief, a faint shudder or shiver of excitement at the unimaginable vastness of it all? The war had set all kinds of records in terms of scale: the greatest bombardments ever seen, the biggest guns, shells and mines, the biggest mobilization, the greatest loss of life ('the million dead'). Was there not a faint glow of pride, an unavoidable undertow of semantic approval, in terming the war 'Great'?[63]

This amazement with vast catastrophe – in which we stare at an historical event like ghoulish passers-by at a car crash – has inevitably changed its character over time. The first generation to grow to adulthood in the twentieth century without experiencing a total war was nevertheless tightly aware of the war as a cataclysmic event through its personal and cultural legacies. Their distance from that event encouraged a range of emotions in younger Britons: a never-to-be-fulfilled curiosity, perhaps even a romanticising of the war, and a respect, and a sort of envy of those who had taken part.

Dyer's suggestion about the 'unavoidable undertow of semantic approval' of writing about the number of deaths, and the Australian Embassy's emphasis on superlative wartime casualties, suggests that there are other elements to our continuing fascination with death. Looking back on a century that seems particularly full of violence and tragedy, do we perhaps want a violent, tragic event in our own past? Is this a way to seek entry to a global community of suffering? Certainly some powerful writers on the war, like

Pat Barker and Robert Kee, have felt able to write of it in terms of a British holocaust. Such an interpretation is based on a misunderstanding of both historical events; but that it is considered at all is indicative of a bizarre aspiration to misery.[64]

If the precise enumeration of total dead has become irrelevant, individual deaths are still important to modern Britons. Enquiries to the Commonwealth War Graves Commission about dead men have undergone a rapid rise in the last twenty-five years. In 1978, the Commission received around 2000 enquiries from the public about graves from both world wars. By 1988, that had risen to 21,000 letters and phone calls a year. In 1998, 50,000 requests for information were received, 35,000 relating specifically to the First World War.[65] Whilst the numbers of First World War veterans attending Remembrance Day parades has inevitably continued to decline, their place has been taken by associations commemorating an interest or a link to the war; perhaps most strikingly, the participation in the Cenotaph march past of 'Shot at Dawn' campaigners. The number of visits to battlefield cemeteries by British tourists is increasing. Many come to search for a specific name or grave. Attendance at the nightly ceremony at the Menin Gate at Ypres – where the names are inscribed of those who fell during the first part of the war in the Salient and whose bodies were never identified – is sometimes so great as to force people away from the memorial itself.

Given that a generational fracture has taken place – that nearly all those who experienced the First World War as adults are now dead, and that we are starting to lose the generation that grew up in its aftermath – how can we explain this continuing fascination with individual deaths? Underlying it was a desire to establish a family connection with the war. One factor in this was the survival of individual family stories about death in war of the sort described by Philip Orr. The narrative of the unreturning son, lover or husband fits, after all, into a much longer tradition of story telling and was thus likely to be remembered and retold. The boom in family history over the last twenty-five years has often been the occasion to explore such stories. The scale of wartime death offered a means for any Briton who was interested – whether or not their family had preserved a mythology of bereavement – a chance to participate in the national heritage. The bureaucratisation of death makes it much easier to search the names of the dead than the living. Now that the CWGC database of 'Soldiers Died' is online, it is spectacularly easy to type your surname in and find a dead soldier namesake. Indeed, this is what children who are going to visit war cemeteries on school trips are encouraged to do. Even though, as has been stressed, most families did not lose an immediate relative, it is likely that the majority of modern Britons will be able to find a soldier who shares their surname or their mother's maiden name.

Of course, this only represents an electronic version of what, for many, has long been instinctual behaviour when looking at war memorials: to search the lists to see if our own name is present. Confronted with the vast scale of death in the First World War, it is only natural to seek a personal, individual method of comprehension. But there is also, for some, an illicit thrill in the accident of historic survival. The journalist Christopher Moore examined the war memorial in his home town for the space where his grandfather's name might have been: 'I placed my fingers between the lines and touched the dizzying possibility of my own non-existence. If Walter's name had been there, I would not ...'[66]

For some, it is a natural step from locating a relation who died in the war to visiting their grave. The closeness of Western Front cemeteries makes it easy to follow up a link with the past with a personal visit. What to do when you get there can be more problematic. The immediate families of dead soldiers behave, when visiting their graves, in similar ways to pilgrims visiting religious shrines. The most obvious point of comparison is the wave of cathartic release that sweeps over these parties of pilgrims after they have seen – and significantly touched – the memorials to their sons, husbands, brothers or fathers.[67] In contrast, more modern visitors to the graveyards of the First World War often seemed confused as to what their emotional reaction should be. For all that they had located their visit to the battlefield around the existence of this familial link, any established emotional connection was missing. Paul Barker, visiting the grave of his great uncle in Belgium, was unsure about how to behave:

> Both Sally and I find it strange to be here. After all, Edmund Ashworth is someone we have never met, only heard about and seen in a photograph. We know almost nothing about his life or his death. I feel an odd mixture of abstraction and overwhelming sadness. I don't think it relates directly to Edmund Ashworth. It is the emotion produced by the cemetery on this cold, clear, inappropriately beautiful day. We take snapshots, feeling like out of place tourists (we get edgy about which shots to take and how many). We make sure that the snapshots show only his grave and the cemetery. We don't want pictures of ourselves. It would be wrong. This isn't a seaside outing.[68]

This can be directly contrasted with the behaviour of widows of Second World War servicemen on the trips organised by the British Legion studied by the anthropologist Tony Walter. On these tours, specifically termed pilgrimages, the guides encouraged widows to take photographs of themselves with gravestones, so that they could prove they had been there. These women were mourning a specific, remembered individual: their grief was of a different character to that of more distant relations. It is hard to mobilise emotion on behalf of a relative one has never known. As Walter notes: 'family historians do not go so far as to say – as do widows – that now their life is complete and they can die in peace.'[69]

Death works both as a powerful symbol to interest people in the First World War and also as a mechanism to discover more about familial participation in it. The concern to locate family casualties does not result from a sense of grief inherited, in some way, from previous generations. Rather, the First World War has become a key element in a 'heritage culture' in which Britons seek to establish an emotional engagement with the past. Why are they so keen to do so? One popular explanation centres on the dislocation of identity attendant on the modern world. The rapid pace of change has removed individuals from the countries, communities and social backgrounds in which their parents existed and they were raised. That rapid change has also made them instinctively wary of predicting the future: if things have already altered so much, who can say how much further they will change? The world seems more and more uncertain. Facing these challenges, people work harder to seek stability and an affirmation of identity in the past. An imaginative connection with past people or events – particularly with members of our own families – allows us to tell ourselves powerful stories about who we are and to reinforce our sense of self.

Another explanation focuses on the possibilities held out by modern consumer culture. A culture of home ownership and consumer durables meant the generation born at the end of the nineteenth century had artefacts to leave, and somewhere to leave them. These artefacts remain to stimulate interest in the past long after their owners are gone.[70] Meanwhile, many in the expanded middle class have experienced rising levels of disposable income and leisure time over the past fifty years. This has given them the time and the money to think about where they came from and how they got here. Such interest quickly spawned a host of businesses keen to pander to their interests with battlefield tours, museum exhibits and research guides.

These points relate to Western culture more generally, but we can see their influence coinciding with regard to modern Britain and the First World War. They can help us to understand the continuing fascination with death and the war. For many British families, the First World War is where 'history' begins, both because it has slipped beyond the edge of living memory and because some artefacts and records – in particular photographs and personal diaries – have remained to back up the myths.[71] In the aftermath of 11 September 2001, the journalist Charlotte Moore wrote about a black tin trunk, belonging to her great uncle Gillachrist, passed down through her family, and containing his effects, which were returned to the family after he was killed at Ypres in 1914. She found it impossible to throw these arte-facts away: 'They give me a sense of the great uncle no living member of my family ever met; the younger son who loved birds and couldn't spell very well. And because I have this sense, I understand that the Great War was something that happened to real people and had ineradicable effects on their families and the nations to which they belonged.'[72]

Participation, success and sacrifice in war also play a key part in con-firming national and local identity. The end of Empire has encouraged Britons to look to other spheres for their identity and engage – comfortably or otherwise – with different national roles. The regional affiliation of British regiments makes them, of course, an ideal research topic for those who wish to bolster their feelings of local identity.[73] Alternatively, for those – particularly those Englishmen – concerned by their country's engagement with Europe, the notions of sacrifice and ultimate success in combat were a source both of national pride and an oppositional alternative to ever-closer union. Christopher Moore (no relation of Charlotte) found that the search for his grandfather's story brought him back to 'the Anglo-Saxon virtues which had prevailed on the Western Front. Honour. Justice. Wherever I might go in the wide world, I was rooted in the heart of England.'[74]

The process by which this re-engagement with the past takes place has been made much easier by the release by British governments of historical data into the public sphere. As a result, the service records of soldiers and officers from 1914–18 that survived German bombing in the Second World War have been made available at the Public Record Office, now the National Archive, rather than being held by the Ministry of Defence. They are now available to all, rather than only to those who could prove a familial link and were willing to pay a fee. Similarly, developments in technology have made the search for dead ancestors in particular much simpler. The com-pilation of databases onto CD-ROMS and the Internet has made it much easier to locate relevant data. Searching for a family member in the CWGC's list of 'Soldiers Died' is no longer a matter of locating a multi–volume work in a reference library and leafing through page after page of notes. Visit www.cwgc.org.uk, type in a name, and receive an almost instantaneous answer. This is clearly a popular pastime: when the site was first opened in November 1998, it received 55,000 hits a day.[75]

Whatever we think of its rationale, the way it was fought or its outcome, it is hard to see the colossal casualty lists of the First World War as anything other than a tragedy. The sheer scale of that tragedy ensured that death would play a major part in how Britons thought about the war at the time and after. Yet the emphasis placed on death was not inevitable or unchanging. It emerged as a result of the changing context within which the war was commemorated. The scale of death created a tense interrelation between general and specific loss which was distinct and influential. The commemoration of the dead was formed out of the perceived need to respect the bereavement of a minority, even when those who were bereaved actually found it difficult to locate their specific death in the broader mass. More recently, the primacy of death in modern representations of the war has led individuals to seek out their own imaginative connection to the war through its long list of fatalities. The emotional links thus established – even when they are half-formed or confusing – have ensured a continued passionate engagement in controversies over how these men died.

3

Donkeys

Field Marshal Earl Haig died on 29 January 1928. Haig had been Commander-in-Chief of the British Expeditionary Force in France and Flanders from 1916 to 1918. He had led the army through the notorious - battles at the Somme and Passchendaele. In the years after the war he avoided further military appointments, but had acted as the head of the principal ex-servicemen's organisation, the British Legion, after its formation in 1921.

Haig's coffin lay in state in London and Edinburgh before being carried north for a private burial close to his ancestral home of Bemersyde. These obsequies were the occasion for widespread mourning. Huge queues of people formed outside Westminster Hall and St Giles' Cathedral before passing silently before the Field Marshal's coffin. Hundreds of thousands crowded the streets of London and Edinburgh to watch the funeral procession. Across the country, services of commemoration were held to mourn Haig's passing. The size and sorrow of the crowds were striking. Their sadness, as evinced in letters of condolence to Lady Haig, was heartfelt. As one former soldier wrote to her: 'I feel the passing of the General as though it were my own father, he was a friend to us and treated the private soldier like a human being, and made one proud to serve him in all matters.'[1] Arguably as many Britons came to pay a final tribute to Haig as turned out for Sir Winston Churchill thirty-seven years later. If crowds are any measure of national mourning, the British felt worse about losing Sir Douglas Haig than they did about losing Princess Diana.

To Britons today, contemporary reactions to Haig's death seem extraordinary. It is impossible to imagine a modern ceremony to venerate Haig's memory receiving any support, let alone the enormous crowds of 1928. Our popular image of the British generals of the First World War is as a group of heartless aristocratic bunglers. Haig and his fellow generals are widely seen as 'butchers' and 'donkeys'.[2] They are the villains of the war, the enemies most likely to account for the unfortunate private soldier with idiotic plans based on their incomprehension of modern warfare. Writing on the eightieth anniversary of the war's end, Max Hastings summed up this view in the *Evening Standard* (in the process confusing the Haig's first name with that of his predecessor, Sir John French):

> Let us start with *foie gras*. And then, perhaps, a *pièce de boeuf à l'os*, as we think of Thiepval and Ypres, of Messines and Vimy, of men dying in thousands and hundreds of thousands upon those muddy wastelands which bulk so absurdly small upon even the largest map ...
>
>   You still do not care for champagne? The men who presided for four years over this greatest of military disasters had no such qualms. For here, between 1916 and 1918, was the headquarters of Field Marshal Sir John Haig, Commander-in-Chief of the British Army, who like most of his fellow generals dined nightly off china and crystal upon the finest fare that Montreuil could provide, even as his men ate a last supper of bully beef and biscuit with plum and apple jam before they climbed over the top for the first and so often the last time, in all those years of futile assault upon the German lines.[3]

This was not the work of a radical left-winger keen to make a point about the victimisation of the working class, but the comments of an established journalist who had made a considerable reputation through his time as a war correspondent and writer of military history. His vitriolic criticism of the generals stands in stark contrast to attitudes seventy years earlier. Public perceptions of British generalship had changed dramatically over the course of the twentieth century. How accurate were these perceptions, and when and why did they change?

To assess the performance of Britain's generals during the First World War, it is necessary to grasp four fundamental points: the realities of Britain's strategic position; the technological context of the war; its totality; and the means Britain had with which to fight. For all that the violation of Belgian neutrality provided a justification, the reason Britain went to war in 1914 was to prevent a hostile hegemonic power gaining control of continental Europe and in particular the Channel Ports. This was a traditional element of her foreign policy: Britain and her Empire were dependent on a sea-borne trade that would be threatened by any such power. To stop Germany successfully in 1914, Britain had to make sure that France resisted the onslaught on the Western Front. Although Britain's main strength lay with her navy, therefore, she immediately committed her tiny army to the support of France. It did not matter how strong Britain's fleet was: if France fell and Germany gained control of her industrial resources and sea ports, Britain was finished as a great power.[4]

From the outset, therefore, Britain was locked into fighting a war of alliance. She had always to consider the needs and wishes of her most important ally, France. The British Expeditionary Force in France, whilst it remained under London's control, could only function in cooperation with the French army. In late summer and autumn 1914, the German army occupied a large chunk of north-western France, including much of the country's industrial resources and plant as well as a significant portion of the population. Its advance brought it as close to Paris as Canterbury is to London. The German offensive was unable to knock France out of the war, but it did establish them in a position of power. There was only one way to make the Germans leave French and Belgian territory on terms that would be acceptable to French politicians and people: to force them out.[5]

The problem with attacking the German forces in France and Belgium was that technological developments in the nineteenth century had favoured the defence. The introduction of accurate, quick-firing field artillery, magazine rifles with smokeless cartridges and machine guns provided armies with devastating quantities of firepower. Barbed wire slowed down assaults, exposing them to this fire. Railways and motor transport could be used to move large quantities of men, munitions and stores up to the front. Some of the impact of these new weapons systems had become apparent in wars in the fifty years before 1914: the American Civil War, the Franco-Prussian War and the Russo-Japanese War. Studying these wars, the generals of all the Great Powers had seen evidence that modern wars killed and wounded large numbers of men, but also that victory had gone to the side that had been able to press home its attacks notwithstanding those casualties. They therefore placed a heavy emphasis on the importance of high morale and persistence in the attack. They were mistaken, but they were trying to deduce solutions from the evidence available to them.[6]

In fact, given the improvements in weapons technology that had taken place in the two decades before the war, and the close concentration of troops within Western Europe, such emphases were disastrous, as became abundantly obvious to all sides in the early years of the war. As troops dug trenches to protect themselves from enemy fire, defensive positions became increasingly complex and impenetrable by infantry relying on *élan* alone. Rather than the war of manoeuvre that many expected, necessarily swift because of the scale of casualties, a deadlock resulted.[7]

At the tactical level, the first challenge facing attacking troops in this situation was how to break into their opponent's trench lines without being destroyed by their fire. Despite the technological advantages enjoyed by the defence, it was possible to do this, given the right combination of forces and circumstances. Determined, well-trained infantry, launching an assault close behind a concentrated artillery bombardment, could catch their opponents still stunned in their defences. Throughout the First World War, all sides experimented with variations on this theme. Notwithstanding improvements in defensive techniques, all became increasingly, if not consistently, adept at breaking into their opponents' position.

Such attacks required vast quantities of munitions and men. Even then success could not be assured. This was where the attackers' technological disadvantage became most apparent. The technology of firepower had improved radically before the First World War, but the technology of communication and mechanisation had not. Communication in battle relied on telegraph or telephone wires, visual signalling, runners or carrier pigeons, or the human voice. Fixed wires and flesh were all too vulnerable to the hurricane of defensive shellfire that fell as soon as an attack started. Once troops had gone over the top it could be all but impossible to communicate with them, to discover whether they were enjoying success or failure, and to find out whether they needed support, supply or reinforcement.[8]

The huge bombardments of shells that were necessary to neutralise an opponent's trenches tore up the ground around them, making movement difficult. Even where attacking troops were successful and could inform their commanders that this was the case, supplies, reinforcements and the guns that would enable a further advance had to reach them across this shell-shattered landscape. Meanwhile, the defender could seal any breach in his lines, or organise a counter-attack, by using the roads and railways that lay further back in his territory, unaffected by the bombardment. It was extremely hard for commanders to convert tactical success – the break-in to the first line of an opponent's trenches – into operational success – breaking through numerous lines, shattering the deadlock of trench warfare, and moving into the green fields beyond.[9]

All sides experimented with technological solutions to this deadlock, including the use of gas, flame-throwers, lighter machine guns, aeroplanes and tanks. Some of these developments made it easier or less costly to break into the enemy's ever-widening defensive belt. But they did not miraculously solve the wider impasse that had been created. By their nature, they were in their technological infancy. Each such development by attackers led swiftly to counter-measures by the defence.

The tank, pioneered by the British, is an excellent example. First World War tanks were slow, mechanically unreliable and difficult to control. Conditions for the crews who operated them – hot, suffocating, all but blinding – were appalling. Moreover, they were vulnerable to direct artillery fire and wide ditches or boggy ground. As the Germans realised the threat tanks posed, they introduced a host of such counter-measures into their defensive schemes. Tanks became a useful component in British attacks, but they were never a war-winning weapon on their own.[10]

Was there another way? Given this deadlock on the Western Front, it was tempting to seek other options to defeat the Central Powers. Since the war, commentators have desperately sought for other options that should have been pursued to avoid the huge casualties of the Western Front. From the start of the war, the British navy had blockaded German merchant traffic in an effort to prevent Germany receiving vital resources. The blockade aimed to starve Germany into submission. By itself, however, it was insufficient. Given the large amount of productive territory that the Germans had been able to capture from France and Russia in the first years of the war, it would take a long time to affect the German population seriously enough to prevent the prosecution of the war, if it was to work at all. Another solution was necessary.

An option that appeared attractive, both at the time and since, was to attack the Central Powers somewhere other than on the Western Front, with the dual intentions of reducing that alliance one by one and finding a different route to attack Germany itself. The geographical position of the Central Powers, however, gave them an advantage in countering any such attack. The alliance of Germany, Austro-Hungary and Turkey enjoyed interior lines of communication and contiguous land borders. It was therefore easier for them to move troops to any threatened spot than it was for the Allies, with exterior lines of communication, to launch and supply any such attack. In any case, the areas over which such alternative attacks could be launched tended to favour the defence, either by their distance from the centre (as in the Sinai Desert), or the broken nature of the terrain (the hills of Gallipoli or Salonika). There was no soft underbelly to the Central Powers in the First World War.[11]

In any case, the Entente's principal opponent was Germany. The surest way to defeat Germany was to destroy her principal military strength, her land army. The quickest way to do this was to engage it where it was already heavily committed, close to Britain, on the Western Front. Destroying the German army had to be the main aim of the Allies: attempts to win the war that did not recognise this reality represented diversions of effort that only prolonged the conflict. Attacking the Germans on the Western Front was also, of course, emotionally attractive to the French, understandably eager to drive the foreign invaders out of their country and rescue their countrymen from the Prussian yoke.[12]

Examining the whole of the First and Second World Wars, rather than just Britain's part in each, a fundamental of modern total war between industrialised great powers becomes apparent: they are not normally won

swiftly by brilliant manoeuvres but by the grinding destruction of the
enemy's material and morale. Sustaining such total wars required huge
emotional as well as physical resources. If either side, in either war, had been
less committed to the causes they espoused, conflict would have ended
sooner: the casualty rates would have been too much to bear. As it was, their
morale and material were both sufficient to sustain long periods of terrible
warfare. We have to see this too as a result of developments in the nineteenth century. These had affected not only the industry and technology of
war, but its social and cultural aspects as well. In the course of the nineteenth century, the populations of European countries had not only
expanded dramatically but had also developed strong senses of national
identity. Over the same period, states had acquired the bureaucratic and
communications technology to mobilise these populations culturally and
militarily.[13]

How well positioned was Britain in 1914 to participate in this total modern war? The pre-war British army was highly professional, extremely well
trained, and had learnt its lessons from the Boer War twelve years previously. As a result, it placed heavy emphasis on skilled rifle-handling and
individual decision-making, wore khaki uniforms that blended into the
landscape and fought in extended lines rather than dense-packed ranks. Its
cavalrymen could fight as well dismounted as mounted, and relied on their
horses as much for mobility as for shock in the charge. Although, like the
society from which it came, the army was socially stratified, fiercely hierarchical and built on patronage, the range of challenges that it faced in its
imperial duties meant that its officers were widely experienced, pragmatic
in approach and generally open to innovation. Tactically, the British Expeditionary Force of 1914 was probably the best equipped of any army to take
part in the battles of the Western Front, as its performance in action that
year demonstrates.[14]

In terms of manpower, logistics, command experience and doctrine, on
the other hand, Britain was profoundly ill equipped for a modern total war.
The pre-war British army was tiny compared to its French and German
counterparts. Designed for its imperial role, it did not have the vast reserves
of conscripts maintained by other European nations. Britain's armies had
too few heavy guns, and too few shells to fire from them. This was a new
type of warfare for soldiers who had spent their professional lives on imperial duties, carried out on an unprecedented scale. None of the generals in
the field with whom Britain started the war had commanded more than a
division on active service or on manoeuvres. The General Staff – that part
of the officer corps responsible for the organisation, administration and supply of the army – was still in its infancy. In learning how to fight this new

type of war, the ad hoc culture of the pre-war army was not necessarily an advantage. 'Making do' kept the army in the field but did not create the sort of systematic solutions that were needed for warfare on this scale. The army's abhorrence of rigidly imposed doctrine (a function of its variety of pre-war responsibilities) worked against the most effective innovations being noticed and widely disseminated and practised. Professional officers' reliance on patronage made it difficult for them to disagree with, or criticise, their seniors.[15]

Within this straitjacket of circumstances, how did British generals perform? On the Western Front, 1914 saw the small British Expeditionary Force help the French to withstand the German onslaught. In the process it was all but destroyed. Like their French and German counterparts, British officers struggled with the novelty of the war they were fighting. The Expeditionary Force's commander, Sir John French, demonstrated a worrying tendency for vacillation and a preference for preserving his army over cooperating with his allies. There were deep-lying tensions between French and the commander of II Corps, Sir Horace Smith-Dorrien, which at one point risked the existence of the army. On the other hand, British officers at all levels succeeded in maintaining the army's cohesion as it conducted a dangerous retreat and repeatedly demonstrated an ability to hold off greatly superior numbers of German troops.[16]

The year 1915 saw rebuilding and adaptation, but also confusion and catastrophe. The Expeditionary Force expanded dramatically, absorbing reservists, territorials and the first elements of the New Armies – the units formed from the volunteers who had flocked to recruiting offices in 1914. To support its French ally, the BEF launched a number of offensives, some of which enjoyed initial success – as at Neuve Chapelle in March 1915; others were ignominious failures – as at Aubers and Festubert in May. None succeeded in making major gains; all resulted in heavy casualties without seriously damaging the Germans. Throughout the year the British were hamstrung by their lack of artillery shells; the result of a munitions industry left to its own devices by a government that was reluctant to take too much control of British businesses. Batteries were continually rationed as to the number of shells a day they could fire. Efforts to make up for the lack of artillery with other weapons – notably the use of gas at Loos at the end of September – were less than successful. Loos also demonstrated the difficulty in coordinating troops in the topographical and technological conditions of the Western Front. British generals struggled to deal with a war fought on a scale and with an intensity they had not foreseen. Out of any year, the generals of 1915 probably match most closely the modern myth.[17] Yet, for all their difficulties, they were not cowards:

1915 saw such heavy casualties amongst staff officers that they had to be ordered to stay out of the front line.[18] The worst command mistake of the year – the mishandling of the reserves at Loos, which resulted in the slaughter of two New Army divisions – resulted in Sir John French being replaced by his senior army commander, Sir Douglas Haig, at the beginning of 1916. Haig was to become the iconic general of the First World War.[19]

If 1915 had seen an old army struggling with a new way of warfare, 1916 saw new troops having to deal with the same problems. The year was dominated for Britain by the enormous battle on the Somme, in which the New Armies were used en masse for the first time. Confusion over the planning of the battle between Haig and his junior commander, Sir Henry Rawlinson, the inexperience of some New Army units, a widespread lack of trust of these citizen soldiers by regular generals, a continuing lack of reliable shells of the right calibre and charge to destroy enemy trenches: all these factors contributed to the disaster on 1 July on the Somme, where, notoriously, 20,000 British soldiers were killed and 40,000 wounded in a single day. But the Somme battle went on for another five months after 1 July, during which time those same citizen soldiers who had suffered so heavily as the battle opened achieved some notable successes against their opponents. On 14 July, just two weeks after the devastating losses of the first day, the same army launched a surprise night attack against the German lines that resulted in significant advances. British commanders and units were learning on the job. Command and control difficulties nevertheless continued to make it difficult to exploit successes when they occurred. The Somme did not come close to achieving the major gains of territory Haig had aimed for, and his excessive optimism led to its being continued even as ground conditions deteriorated, but its result was to inflict very heavy casualties on German forces (not least because of their policy of constant counter-attacks to regain lost ground).[20]

The skills which the British Expeditionary Force had learned on the Somme were practised and honed over the winter of 1916–17. Over the same time, the army benefited, for the first time, from an adequate supply of heavy artillery. Improvements in ranging, together with a reorganised system of supply and logistics which kept them supplied with high explosive shells, made the expanded indirect fire arm even more effective. Throughout 1917, the BEF repeatedly demonstrated an ability to fight successful 'break-in' battles through a combination of carefully planned and highly destructive artillery bombardments and barrages, aggressive and flexible infantry tactics, and the use of new technology, in particular the tank.[21] Four problems remained. First, following the mutinies that removed the French armies from offensive operations in the summer of 1917, the British had to take principal responsibility for fighting the bulk of the German army for the first time in the war. Secondly, given the technological and tactical factors identified above, even highly organised and successful battles still cost the British heavy casualties. Thirdly, it remained as difficult as ever to coordinate a response to events that fell outside the planned battle. Fourthly, it was unclear how these improvements in British fighting power should be put to best use. Was it better to fight a succession of minor 'bite and hold' battles that never aimed at achieving greater success, but only at gaining small quantities of territory whilst inflicting heavy casualties on the Germans, or should there continue to be higher operational aims, including aspirations towards a major geographical advance? Was it worth risking higher casualties by attempting attacks at a higher tempo, without the high degree of planning, limited aims and slower pace that would ensure success?[22]

This lack of clarity contributed to the command problems evident during the Third Battle of Ypres, which has become known to us by the name of its final struggle over the village of Passchendaele. Just like the Somme, although Third Ypres has been remembered in terms of disaster, a more detailed study of a long campaign shows a mixture of success and failure. Again, the battle inflicted heavy suffering and casualties on the Germans as well as the British, notably during a series of battles fought by Plumer in the early autumn. Such successes, combined with a desire to see his troops on higher ground for the winter, encouraged Haig to drive the battle onwards, even as ground conditions again deteriorated to the point where men and guns sank into the mire.[23] The story of Haig's Chief of Staff, General Kiggell, crying, in the mud at Passchendaele, 'Did we really send men to fight in this?', is almost certainly apocryphal, but it encapsulates a view, held at the time, that the High Command had lost touch with the realities of soldiers' lives.[24] Haig had good military reasons for continuing the battle, to enable his men to spend the winter in command of the Passchendaele Ridge rather than under its observation, but in so doing he came close to permanently damaging the morale of his men. The offensive did not achieve its principal initial objective, breaking through the German lines to threaten the crucial rail junction at Roulers.[25]

In 1918 the Germans launched their first large-scale assault on the Allies since their attack on the French at Verdun in early 1916. Attacking British and French forces who were worn out, overstretched and unused to defensive warfare, the Germans achieved substantial territorial gains in the spring of 1918. The Allied armies did not break. As the Germans attacked, they too suffered the realities of the offensive in the First World War: disruption and confusion because of poor command and control, occasional disaster, and always heavy casualties to the attacking troops. The German tactics of concentrating their best men in stormtrooper units to head the assault meant that the cream of their army was rapidly skimmed off. The attack slowed as the summer approached, at which point the Allied armies, reinforced by significant numbers of Americans for the first time, began their counter-attack.[26]

It was here that the British Expeditionary Force came into its own. Despite the reverses it had suffered earlier in the year, and the fact that many of its men were now young conscripts or veterans wounded two or three times, it took the pre-eminent role in these counter-attacks. In the process, it combined the skills and technology that it had developed at every level since 1914 – infantry tactics of fire and movement that are still the basis of modern doctrine, efficient and reliable staff work, devastating artillery fire, tanks employed en masse, aircraft, armoured cars, and even the cavalry, who seized the opportunity to work as mobile exploitation troops for almost the first time on the Western Front.[27] In a series of assaults through the summer and autumn of 1918, the Germans were driven back. The morale of their men and their commanders cracked. One reason for that collapse of morale was that the German army had suffered so heavily in holding off British offensives in 1916 and 1917. It is hard to argue that the destruction of German manpower was ever Haig's principal aim at the beginning of the great battles of the middle years of the war. Nevertheless, in the course of pushing for more definite – if ultimately unattainable – geographical objectives, his army had helped to inflict such damage that the Germans could not carry on. It was military defeat in the field, not civilian uprisings at home, which forced the Germans to surrender.[28] The BEF played the immediate main role in inflicting that defeat. Between them, the French, American and Belgian armies took 196,700 prisoners and 3775 guns between 18 July 1918 and the end of the war. Despite being much smaller than the combined forces of its allies, the BEF alone took 188,700 prisoners and 2840 guns over the same period. It was the greatest military victory in Britain's history and we cannot deny the generals their part in it.[29]

That is not to say that they were perfect. It has become fashionable amongst military historians to speak of a 'learning curve', in which the British army as a whole gradually adapted itself to a new form of warfare. The risk, however, is that this implies a steady learning process carried out consistently throughout the army. It can obscure the degree to which mistakes were made as a result of inability or incompetence, rather than lack of experience. There were a number of cases where British commanders were clearly at fault. At a more junior level, we can point to clear cases of apparent overpromotion and repeated failures of comprehension. Although the metaphor is less neat, it is better to picture the development of the army as being composed of a series of individual learning processes that included plateaus, backward steps and peaks at an insufficient level, as well as great leaps forward. Overall, however, the fighting power of the army improved significantly.[30]

Few issues in modern British military history have inspired so much writing as the quality of generalship in the First World War. For much of the twentieth century, studies of the generals tended to be biographically based: they examined the personal qualities of the High Command in an effort to divine their abilities. Much passion was expended on whether they were nice or nasty men.[31] This sort of history as *Blind Date* makes a fundamental mistake about the nature of command – whether these men are personally sympathetic to later generations bears little relationship to whether they were good commanders at the time. More recent military history has tended to avoid such debates, moving on to look at the structures and processes of command and the context within which it operated.

Nonetheless, the twenty-first century mind struggles with some of their attitudes and behaviour. Haig, in particular, strikes many of those who study him as unsympathetic: monosyllabic, convinced of his own destiny and the Lord's favour, seemingly hard-hearted to the fate of his men. Yet he appreciated from the start where Britain's main effort would have to be, and seems to have grown to understand how his army's effort could be most effectively applied, as demonstrated by his concern with small unit tactics from the end of 1917 onwards.[32] Whilst it may have appeared that he did not care about British casualties, this is hard to square with his evident hard work for ex-servicemen after the war. Officers invest time, energy and emotion in creating their organisations. Unlike all other leaders and managers, however, they have to be willing to destroy what they have created in an instant if circumstances demand it. No general who cared too much about the lives of his soldiers could function in the attritional warfare of the Western Front. This was one of the reasons that French proved an ineffective commander and had to be replaced.

The final test of any commander should not be whether he is a good man in terms of personality or morals, nor whether he makes bold manoeuvres that look impressive on maps. It should surely be whether he wins or loses with the minimum possible losses to his own side. Haig scores highly on the first part of that test, less well on the second, but given the context in which he had to operate, not as badly as we might think. He deserves more credit than the myth of High Command stupidity allows.

That Haig had led the army to victory, and that he continued to care for his men after the war was over, were the two points that seem to have counted most with people at the time. In fact it is difficult to say with accuracy to what degree ordinary soldiers recognised or held opinions about senior officers. The evidence of memoirs, diaries and letters suggests that junior officers were aware of their superiors up to the rank of brigadier, whilst those in the ranks were much more interested in the abilities of their platoon or company commander. This was a pressing issue for them because on a day-to-day level, the quality and length of their wartime lives very obviously depended on it. The British army was intensely tribal, in the sense that it rapidly developed strong regimental loyalties amongst its men, but this also encouraged them not to look far beyond the boundaries of their own battalion. Even in memoirs of the war that might be expected to be critical of the most senior officers – such as the works of Sassoon and Graves – there are actually remarkably few references to their competence or personality. It is possible to find contemporary diaries and letters in which junior officers express both positive and negative opinions about Haig or French, but they are rare, and there seems no preponderance either for or against.[33]

The scale of the war, the frequently rapid turnover of men, and the limitations of contemporary information technology made it hard for all commanders to make themselves known to all their men. It was extremely difficult even for those in charge of divisions – let alone those who commanded corps, armies or an Expeditionary Force – to fulfil all their command responsibilities and make themselves physically apparent to all the troops under their command.[34] It seems likely that the majority of troops would have known who French and Haig were, if only from newspaper reports. They would therefore have been more recognisable, at least in name terms, than most army or corps commanders.[35] Yet whether this meant that most privates at the time held an opinion about their abilities or personality is another matter. They were simply too distant and godlike to call forth any opinion from most soldiers, who had much more immediate things to worry about. As Charles Wilson, Lord Moran, who served in the BEF as a Medical Officer, wrote of Haig: 'we in France knew nothing of this man until he was explained to us after the war.'[36]

This did not mean, of course, that front-line soldiers did not have opinions about those who they thought worked in unfair safety, who offered what seemed like needless bureaucratic complications or who brought trouble in the shape of orders or inspections. Since time immemorial, fighting soldiers have felt an antipathy for those who do not share their risks but tell them what to do. In *Henry IV Part One*, that fearless frontline soldier Hotspur tells the King of a meeting with his envoy:

> Fresh as a bridegroom, and his chin new reaped
> Show'd like a stubble-land at harvest time.
> He was perfumed like a milliner.

Hotspur's reaction is the enraged bafflement of the combatant disturbed by the administrator:

> I then, all smarting with my wounds being cold,
> To be so pestered with a popinjay,
> Out of my grief and my impatience
> Answered neglectingly, I know not what,
> He should, or he should not, for he made me mad.[37]

That this anger at those removed from the realities of the front line could be felt by all those 'at the sharp end', officers and men alike, is illustrated by the comment of Rowland Feilding – then the officer commanding 1/15 Londons – in a letter to his wife in August 1918. Commenting on his new Brigadier, Feilding remarked: 'I never met a more companionable man. There is nothing whatever of the Staff Officer about him. In fact, though he himself has to wear red tabs as a Brigadier General, he has a saying that "once a man has put on red tabs it is only a matter of time before he becomes a *******", which is view not uncommonly held in the fighting line'.[38]

Some such criticisms of the Staff arose from a – very understandable – inability to see the bigger picture, or from the bureaucracy that was essential to the equipping of an army for modern total war. One staff officer wrote after the war that such criticisms were not 'of course, founded on any mental process, or it would be deeply interesting to investigate how these gentlemen came to think that ammunition and supplies could arrive fortuitously, or a concentration of troops or tanks could "just happen"'.[39] Infant bureaucracies tend, by their nature, to be inefficient and staff officers to risk becoming divorced from the realities of regimental life. By 1918 such criticisms were unjustified; in that year the Staff's ability to coordinate troops and supplies played a major part in the army's survival and eventual triumph.

However strong the army's distaste for the gilded lilies of the Staff, it does not seem to have led to criticism of the overall commander. Haig particularly endeared himself to those he commanded through his apparent steadfastness and resolve in March 1918, when it appeared that the last German offensive of the war might be successful. On 11 April that year he issued what has become known as his 'Backs to the Wall' Order of the Day. It had an effect on the army comparable to that of Churchill's 'We shall fight them on the beaches' speech on Britain in 1940:

> Many amongst us are now tired. To these I would say that Victory will belong to the side which holds out the longest. The French army is moving rapidly and in great force to our support.
>
> There is no course given to us but to fight it out. Every position must be held to the last man: there must be no retirement. With our backs to the wall and believing in the justice of our cause each one of us must fight on to the end. The safety of our homes and the Freedom of Mankind alike depend on each one of us at this critical moment.[40]

Vera Brittain, no friend of generals, testified to the effect of this order on her as she served as a VAD in France:

> Although, since that date, the publication of official 'revelations' has stripped from the Haig myth much of its glory, I have never been able to visualise Lord Haig as the colossal blunderer, the self-deceived optimist, of the Somme massacre of 1916. I can think of him only as the author of that special order, for after I read it I knew that I should go on, whether I could or not. There was a braver spirit in the hospital that afternoon, and though we only referred briefly and brusquely to Haig's message, each one of us had made up our mind that, though enemy airmen blew up our huts and the Germans advanced on us from Abbeville, so long as wounded men remained in Étaples there would be no retirement.[41]

Since both used newspapers as a source of information about generals, Haig was probably as familiar to civilians as he was to most soldiers. The publicity that he received from the print media was not always positive, but most journalists patriotically restrained their most serious criticisms until after the war's end. Much of the wartime press coverage was favourable, to the point where Prime Minister Lloyd George suspected Haig of running a press campaign for his own advancement, but as the press barons were absorbed into government at the end of 1917, their newspapers began to reflect the attitudes of politicians rather than soldiers. (It is at this point that we can see the beginnings of a conflict between the generals and press magnates like Beaverbrook that would influence subsequent representations.)[42] Haig was lauded by the press and the public for his part in Britain's victory, with his London house becoming a site of celebrations into the night of 11 November 1918. This celebrity may, however, have been muted because it was shared with the Allied Generalissimo, Foch; because of an awareness of the heavy casualties that had been incurred; and because of the unexpected swiftness of the end of the war. Although his name was well known, Haig made little impact on popular culture as a heroic figure in the mould of Gordon, Scott or Kitchener. Unlike these men, Haig did not become a subject for popular memorabilia in the form of busts, pictures and children's stories.[43]

Given the huge numbers of casualties Britain had suffered, it should not surprise us that there was interest in and controversy over how well the war was being fought both before and after 1918. The replacement of Sir John French as commander of the BEF with Haig at the end of 1915 certainly implied that some generals were more competent than others. Politicians and generals struggled to maintain their personal power and fight the war in the way they thought best: the use both sides made of the media meant that these struggles escaped into the public sphere. During the war, public controversies over the supply of shells and men to the Western Front led to the replacement of organisations, bureaucrats and commanders.

Whilst many journalists felt a patriotic duty not to criticise the country's leaders in time of war, British culture was not blindly militaristic or deferential to the status of officers. Britain's two great military efforts of the nineteenth century, the wars in the Crimea (1854–56) and South Africa (1898–1902), had seen repeated disasters as generals struggled to deal with the organisation, supply and leadership of unaccustomedly large bodies of men in unfamiliar surroundings. Their failures had attracted widespread press criticism. The Crimean War, in particular, had seen lengthy discussion at home of the inadequacies of an officer class made up of junior aristocrats who were more concerned with good form and their own well-being than with the welfare of their men. These criticisms can be interpreted as part of a much wider movement in which the burgeoning Victorian middle class – obsessed with professionalism and efficiency – took on an aristocracy which still maintained its hold on many offices of state and of the military. The famous *Times* editorial which did much to bring down the Aberdeen government in the middle of the Crimean War could, with dates removed, be read as applying to the generals of the First World War:

> We say, on the evidence of every letter that has been received in this country ... that the noblest army England ever sent from these shores has been sacrificed to the grossest mismanagement. Incompetency, lethargy, aristocratic hauteur, official indifference, favour, routine, perverseness and stupidity reign, revel and riot ... We say it with the utmost reluctance, – no one sees or hears anything of the Commander-in-Chief ... If the staff itself made up for the invisibility of the commander, we should not complain ... But unfortunately, the staff is said to consist of young gentlemen whose honour and courage nobody can doubt,

but who are devoid of experience, without much sympathy for the distresses of such inferior beings as regimental officers and privates, and disposed to treat the gravest affairs with a dangerous *nonchalance*.[44]

Whatever its roots and its validity, the idea of the staff officer as upper-class bungler was well established before 1914, even if it sat in uneasy coexistence with a set of more heroic images of the regimental officer as imperial hero.

Debates about the recognition of achievement and the responsibility for failure did not finish in 1918. Shortly after the First World War's conclusion, numerous accounts were published that sought to exonerate their authors or identify the guilty. By the mid 1920s, a number of leading generals, such as Sir John French, Sir Ian Hamilton and Sir William Robertson, had published their own accounts of the war. The disagreements over strategy in 1917 and 1918 between Haig and Robertson and the Prime Minister, David Lloyd George, continued to be picked over. One reason for this was that the political battles that had divided the Liberal Party during the conflict had survived into the post-war world. If, as some argued, Lloyd George had been responsible for prolonging the war by his meddling in strategic matters, this was a powerful stick to beat him with as the Liberal Party struggled with its identity after 1918.[45]

Questions about the quality of British leadership therefore very quickly became a staple of post-war writing. Haig himself did not participate publicly in these debates, seemingly on the basis that to do so would not have befitted an officer and a gentleman. In fact, as David French has shown, he was active behind the scenes in efforts to defend his reputation from attack. One example was the publication of J. Boraston and G. Dewar's *Sir Douglas Haig's Command* in 1922.[46] Boraston had been Haig's private secretary and the two-volume work presented a version of the war in terms of necessary battles, planned attrition and ultimate victory.

It was never likely that wartime politicians would allow these debates to fizzle out without having the last word. Instead, a war of words had been initiated which would pitch the generals against two of the most articulate and vituperative British politicians of the twentieth century, Winston Churchill and David Lloyd George. *The* non-fiction publishing success of the inter-war years, Winston Churchill's *The World Crisis*, (1923–31) presented a less than sympathetic version of Haig in its third volume. Churchill's praise was damning in its faintness:

> He had fulfilled with exceptional credit every requirement to which the pre-war British military hierarchy attached importance ... The military profession

reposed in him a confidence which the various fortunes, disappointments and miscalculations attendant upon three years of war on the greatest scale left absolutely unshaken. The esteem of his military colleagues found a healthy counterpart in his own self-confidence ... He was as sure of himself at the head of the British army as a country gentleman on the soil which his ancestors had trod for generations, and to whose cultivation he owed his life. But the Great War owned no master; no one was equal to its vast and novel issues; no human hand controlled its hurricanes, no eye could pierce its whirlwind dustclouds.[47]

As a former Cabinet minister with responsibility for one of the most disastrous projects of the war, the debacle at Gallipoli, Churchill had good reason for portraying the war as beyond the control of any one man. Since one method for Churchill to vindicate himself was to point to his own innovation as an outspoken supporter of the tank in its early stages, it was also in his interest to represent the generals as unimaginative and unaccepting of modern technology.

Yet Churchill was also motivated by a genuine fascination with the historical events with which he had been involved. To this he added not only his remarkable rhetorical skills, but also a fierce analytical intelligence that encouraged him to seek the truth about the number of casualties and the effectiveness of attrition. Overall his comments on Haig were moderate and avoided overt criticism. Churchill had in fact sent preliminary drafts of the book for Haig's consideration.[48] They were returned with minimal alterations. Haig viewed Churchill's comments as balanced and was content to leave the final word on his abilities to longer-term history judgements. This may have been made easier by the fact that Churchill's criticisms of the High Command were not always aimed personally at Haig. At the time, the *Daily Herald* suggested that Churchill was 'almost unrestricted in his admiration' for Haig.[49] The extracts from *The World Crisis* that were published in *The Times* focused on key events of the war rather than apportioning blame, but specifically absolved Haig from responsibility for the disaster on the Somme.[50] On the other hand, a different reviewer remarked that:

> Taken as a whole Mr Churchill's account of the last two and half years of the War constitutes a tremendous indictment of the Higher Command of the Allies ... Of Sir Douglas Haig he has many good things to say, but he does not conceal his profound conviction that if General Headquarters in France had possessed a scrap of enterprise, had ceased to oppose every new idea, had grasped the superiority of tanks over cavalry, had been less spendthrift in their use of 'cannon fodder' the War might have been ended a year or two earlier and millions of lives saved. All this we now know to be true but Mr Churchill

is in the fortunate position of being able to show ... that as early as the spring
of 1916 he had realised the fundamental fallacy of the famous doctrine of
'attrition' so beloved of Haig and Robertson and the French General Staff.[51]

Churchill therefore set many of the terms for the debates which would rage
around Haig's reputation for the rest of the century.

When Haig died, obituarists were moved to consider his military
achievements. Few were able to discern in him the evidence of military
genius. Writing in the *Daily Mirror* the day after Haig's death, Sir Frederick
Maurice declared that 'His was that spirit of British doggedness, which
whatever it may lack of facile brilliancy, wins through in the end'.[52] Similarly, the editor of the *Daily Sketch* noted that 'if Britain did not possess the
superman for whom the occasion called, it was fortunate in being able to
supply the next best thing – a loyal and capable soldier'.[53] Haig's post-war
work for veterans had endeared him to the country as a whole and to the ex-
servicemen's community in particular. It was this, as well as the attraction
of any state funeral connected to the war for those who had never been able
to bury their relatives, that helps to explain the scale of the mourning
crowds in 1928. As the *Daily Sketch* concluded, 'The best thing Earl Haig ever
did was done after the war. He devoted himself heart and soul to the men
who were broken in the King's service. He never forgot.'[54]

On the other hand, in the left-wing *Daily Herald's* obituary we can see the
seeds of a class-based approach to the judgement of Haig's military abilities:
'He was more than an officer in the Old Army; he was of the military caste.
From Clifton and Oxford he passed into the cavalry and never in later life
was he able to shake off the cavalry mentality. He has been described as a
' "great lieutenant but a faulty commander" '.[55] The *Herald* had, in 1924, criticised the British Legion as the 'fascisti' of 'Haig's White Guard': it saw
Haig's work with the Legion as the formation of a politically conservative
paramilitary body that would act against the workers' interests.[56] It is a
measure of Haig's post-war popularity, however, that even the *Herald's*
obituary offered a positive assessment of the Field Marshal's life as a whole.[57]

Doubtless these obituaries were affected by a desire not to speak ill of the
dead, but even so they recognised that there was an ongoing controversy
over British generalship. In Haig's case, any such prohibition did not last
long. The obituaries also confirmed the trend towards an argument carried
out in terms of personality and heroic traditions. The case for or against
Haig was based on whether he had been a good or a bad man and how he
fitted into previous models of great generalship: was he an Alexander, a
Marlborough, a Napoleon or a Wellington? These two measures were the
standards by which he was to be judged during the inter-war period.

An influential example was Basil Liddell Hart's *The Real War*. Published in 1930, this was the first popular single-volume survey of the course of the war. Liddell Hart had served three short tours with the BEF on the Western Front in 1915 and 1916, being wounded or falling ill on each occasion. He claimed authority from his military experience, but he did not, therefore, experience the 'learning curve' undergone by other volunteer soldiers. Liddell Hart was to become one of the best known military analysts of the middle part of the twentieth century, but he was always to maintain an interest in the war in which he had won his spurs. Convalescing from wounds received on the Somme, Liddell Hart wrote a pamphlet about his experiences in which he idolised Haig's achievements. After the war, his view changed. He came to abhor entrenchments and static warfare as a result of his own wartime experiences. Liddell Hart also believed in a military genius that, through the brilliance of its manoeuvres, could surpass its historical context – that there were 'Great Captains' who, put into any military situation at any time, would instinctively understand it and see clearly a cheap path to victory. He therefore came increasingly to believe that the generals of the First World War had missed an opportunity to win by imaginative use of technology or manoeuvre. It is these views that permeate *The Real War*. Liddell Hart was in fact always capable of offering a balanced and sophisticated assessment of Haig, but the popularity of his book was to set the terms of debate over the First World War for years to come.[58]

Liddell Hart also happily associated himself with projects that were more explicitly condemnatory of the High Command. The most famous was David Lloyd George's *War Memoirs*, to which he acted as military adviser. Lloyd George's continued political activities meant that he came to his memoirs later than other participants in the war. To his writing he brought an excellent team of advisers and contacts, and a prodigious work rate, but also a store of vendettas and perceived slights stocked up from the war and a reading of other accounts. Lloyd George also had a bitingly sarcastic rhetorical style that fitted well with the new style in political biography that had developed with the work of Lytton Strachey and Margot Asquith after 1918.[59]

Vindicating himself meant vilifying others. Lloyd George focused in particular on the Third Ypres campaign as an example of the generals learning nothing, conniving against politicians, and inflicting massive casualties on their own troops to no tactical or strategic purpose. Whilst he blamed the entire High Command, he reserved specific ire for Haig; in part because he felt his own role in final victory had been denigrated by the celebration of the Field Marshal.[60]

Such powerful assaults from such a well-known figure attracted a large readership for the *War Memoirs* when they were published between 1933 and

1936. Assisted by advance serialisation in the *Daily Telegraph*, all the volumes became best sellers on their release, with the cheaper edition selling over a hundred thousand copies of each volume by May 1938.[61] They also attracted considerable opposition. Violent personal letters to the author included the suggestion that he was a 'foul, treacherous, loathsome, Welsh reptile' who should 'burn in Hell fires for ever, and that right soon'.[62] The British Legion also worked hard to counter Lloyd George's assault on a man they had come to regard as their patron saint. Even if they were not roused to such fury, many readers were aware enough of Lloyd George's reputation to take his accusations with a pinch of salt. His memoirs played, however, a crucial role in confirming Haig and his personality as a key topic in discussion of the First World War, and in establishing some of the most vivid criticisms of the military.

A second project to which Liddell Hart offered advice was C. S. Forester's novel *The General*, published in 1936. *The General* is a description of the career of Herbert Curzon, a dutiful but stupid and unimaginative cavalry officer. Having become a hero by mistake during the Boer War, Curzon leads his regiment of lancers to France in 1914. By his bravery and by the huge casualties suffered by his men, he rises rapidly to the rank of general in command of a corps. Faced with a form of warfare to which he is unused, Curzon and his fellow commanders simply demand more soldiers and bigger guns to smash their way through:

> In some ways it was like the debate of a group of savages as to how to extract a screw from a piece of wood. Accustomed only to nails, they had made one effort to pull out the screw by main force, and now that it had failed they were devising methods of applying more force still, of obtaining more efficient pincers, of using levers and fulcrums so that more men could bring their strength to bear.[63]

Curzon leads his men through the bloodbath at the Somme to that at Third Ypres, where 'Under his direction and those of his colleagues the British Army used up its strength in wild struggles like those of a buffalo caught in a net, or a madman in a straitjacket, rather than submit to what seemed like the sole alternative, which was to do nothing'.[64] When the Germans attack in spring 1918, Curzon's frontline disintegrates and he rides out to rally his troops and meet his death in battle. Instead he is seriously wounded, and condemned to spend the rest of his life beneath a rug in a bathchair at Bournemouth.

Forester said that *The General* was his favourite book, and that Curzon was 'the prototype First World War officer, unbending, inflexible and ignorant of the technology which ... made the heroic cavalry charge ... and the infantry charge … equally obsolete'.[65] Although it is hard to ascertain a specific model for Curzon, his cavalry background and his marriage into the aristocracy are plainly reminiscent of Sir Douglas Haig.

The book is based on a profound misunderstanding of the war, in that it assumes there was somehow a technological alternative to slaughter on the Western Front. Attractive though the metaphor of the savages and the screw is, it is misleading. The book is nonetheless a very good read and acute in many of its observations of military life and culture, despite the fact that Forester had been excluded from military service on the basis of a weak heart. Its picture of Curzon is not without sympathy. He is brave, or at least so unimaginative that he can perform deeds other see as brave without a second thought. He cares deeply for the welfare of his men and fights alongside them when necessary. He is assailed by traumatic memories of his own front-line experiences, which he forces back because he has to carry on. He is in many ways an admirable figure. *The General* is at least half in love with the character it condemns. Forester's work reflected the ambiguity many Britons still felt towards the men who had led them through the First World War. Curzon embodied both concerns over the amateurishness of British officers and respect for a set of what were seen as traditionally manly virtues: restraint, bravery, responsibility for self.

In 1937, nine years after his death, a statue of Haig was unveiled in White-hall. Although there had been immediate agreement in 1928 that Haig should be commemorated, the statue's creation had been dogged by controversy. Contrary to what we might expect, the debate was not over *whether* Haig should be commemorated, but *how*. Like commemorative bodies all over Britain in the interwar years, those deciding on the statue had to balance the need to create a lasting piece of public sculpture with the artistic fashions of the time and the demands of grieving relatives. The result – with the Field Marshal seated on a rather stolid charger – was judged insufficiently realistic by many of his family and friends.[66]

A year later, Liddell Hart, considering Haig's reputation in his book *Through the Fog of War*, felt that public representations more generally failed to capture the real man:

> The figure of Haig has become enfolded in a dual legend – one might describe it as a 'Jekyll and Hyde' legend. On the one hand there has grown the conventional picture of a great commander – far-sighted, profound in reflection, quick of decision, unshakeable in resolution, moved solely by a sense of duty. On the other hand, there is the picture of a soldier moulded to a different yet not less popular pattern – short-sighted, dull, slow, obstinate and callous. This also follows a convention of popular caricature. It has left Haig a wooden

effigy, at which the man in the streets shrugs his shoulders ... Is there any way of reconciling such contrasting pictures, and of discovering the real form which lies hidden underneath them?[67]

Liddell Hart's comments were perceptive. By the end of the 1930s, the British generals of the First World War, and particularly Sir Douglas Haig, had been subject to prolonged criticism, to the point where for some they had become figures of mockery. This criticism came from three sources. The first was an abhorrence of the scale of British casualties and an incomprehension of how this could have occurred if leaders had been doing their job. The second was the assessment of the generals on two different sets of established standards – either in terms of the traditional military virtues of heroism, compassion, inspirational leadership, or in terms of a long-running British debate about 'the officer class'. The third was the ongoing debate about military competence created by generals and politicians, both of whom were eager to shift the blame for those casualties away from themselves.

A competing vision still existed in which great commanders had won a famous victory. Those who condemned the generals were still forced to recognise the reality of their eventual success. Assaults on Haig's reputation resulted in violent rebukes from those who kept the sacred flame of his memory burning strongly.

Authors, critics and reader worked with a knowledge of both these versions of the generals. They were aware that this was a debate with two sides, even if they felt no responsibility to take a balanced position on it. The inter-war years had initially seen an enormous range of different interpretations of Britain's war experience. Certain versions of the war gained ground over others as the period went on, but ambivalence and ambiguity remained. A range of opinions continued to exist. It remained to be seen how the two effigies identified by Liddell Hart would fare as Britain moved through a second world war.

The Second World War was a crucial event in the developing and establishing the mythology of the First. It was naturally an occasion for using ideas about a previous conflict. The expectations of the men who went off to fight in 1939 had been formed by the popular culture of the inter-war years: they expected mud and trenches. The very rapid German defeat of France and the expulsion of the British army from mainland Europe in 1940 were surprising to those who had expected a prolonged slogging match. The desire to seek an explanation for this defeat, combined with pre-war ideas about national character, encouraged a belief that the Germans had won through the employment of better technology in an unstoppable new form of war, *blitzkrieg*. The failure of Britain and France could be put down to their military elites' inability to comprehend and utilise this new technology properly. Such arguments could, of course, make reference to existing ideas about generals' incompetence when it came to innovation in a previous conflict and key into a longer-running belief in military ineptitude.

An interpretation of German success that stressed their greater modernity was, in fact, based on a widespread misunderstanding of what had actually occurred in 1940. German success in France was helped by good tactical leadership and the use of airpower to support advancing troops. But it was dependant on a failure of will and morale amongst French politicians and generals, poor strategic planning, and a great deal of luck. When used against opponents with greater cohesion and leadership, or when countered by a well organised defence in depth, the limits of such technological and tactical innovation as the Germans had achieved were revealed. Tanks, aircraft and radios made it possible to exploit an enemy's weaknesses more swiftly, but battles against determined, well dug-in opponents were still matters of high bloodshed and slow progress.[68]

In these circumstances, one way to win battles whilst limiting infantry casualties was to make careful, well planned advances supported by overwhelming artillery fire. These were the tactics adopted by successful British generals as Field Marshal Bernard Montgomery. Even so, such battles were far from bloodless. The iconic British battles of the Second World War – El Alamein and Normandy – bore a resemblance to the way the British had fought in 1918. That we can see such similarities should not surprise us. Generals who had learned their trade as staff officers with the most successful units on the Western Front – Montgomery is a case in point – employed these methods in an effort to ensure victory. Similarly, the problems caused by the need to expand rapidly a small professional army – the necessary employment of those with outdated military experience as a stopgap measure, the inadequacies of equipment designed to meet imperial demands – were constants of the British experience of both world wars.[69] Churchill, an inveterate imbiber of the myths he helped create, was concerned on each occasion that such slugging battles would generate the same casualty lists as the First World War, an effort he felt would be nationally – as well as politically – unsustainable.[70] The key difference was that in this second war, once the enemy was broken, the pursuit could be much faster and more devastating.

The generals of the Second World War, were, however, often conscious of their media images, and were certainly aware that their predecessors' tactics had been the subject of debate, They therefore worked harder to make sure that they appeared in a more favourable light. Many were aware of the PR demands of a total war. In strategic terms, British generals in the Second World War faced a different task from their predecessors, since the bulk of the fighting to destroy the German army was taking place on the Eastern Front rather than in the West.[71] They also had to cope with less challenging technological developments, enjoyed a generally more positive interaction with politicians and were able to refer back to an example of how things should not be done and appear more competent in comparison.[72] That these developments had an effect on the memory of the Great War generals is apparent in a letter written by Doria Haig to her brother, Dawyck, in 1949 regarding plans to publish the papers of their father, Field Marshal Earl Haig:

> I suppose that there are many reasons to publish this book: 1. To exonerate Daddy as a general; 2. To dispel this idea of him as a man, that he was stupid, obstinate, unimaginative, ruthless, lacking in humour and humanity but hard, in fact the lowest sort of Colonel Blimp; 3. Practical purposes are rather ruled out. There has been a bigger war since when people said we mustn't make the same stupid mistakes as last time (nine times out of ten referring to Daddy and Passchendaele) ...[73]

The newspaper cartoon character Colonel Blimp had been created in 1934 by the artist David Low to exemplify the stupidity of the reactionary right. Blimp – bald, walrus-moustached and indignant – would emerge from the Turkish bath at his London club to impart plainly self-contradictory *bon mots* to Low and his readers. He was the archetypal upper-class officer in decay. The cartoonist abandoned the character before the start of the Second World War, but he was revitalised in the 1943 film *The Life and Death of Colonel Blimp*, produced by Michael Powell and Emeric Pressburger.[74] The film starred Roger Livesey as Major General Clive Wynne-Candy. It begins in 1943, with Wynne-Candy commanding the Home Guard in an exercise against the regular army. An eager young regular lieutenant, Spud Wilson, launches a pre-emptive strike by racing to London and captures Wynne-Candy, in a Turkish bath, six hours before the exercise is due to begin.

Wynne-Candy's career is then narrated in flashback. We see him, as a young lieutenant, travel to Berlin before the First World War in an effort to counter the anti-British propaganda reported by an English governess, Edith Hunter (Deborah Kerr). His unsubtle approach almost causes a riot, and Wynne-Candy fights a duel against a German officer, Theodore Kretschmar-Schuldorff (Anton Walbrook) after he insults the German army. Wynne-Candy wins, but then falls through a window. He and Theo end up in the same hospital and become friends. Theo marries Edith, Wynne-Candy's secret love.

We next meet Wynne-Candy at the end of the First World War, when he is an acting Brigadier General on the Western Front. He sees the British victory as a triumph for traditional soldiering, declaring that 'Clean fighting, honest soldiering have won the day'. This is undercut by a scene in which a German prisoner is interrogated. Wynne-Candy's gentlemanly approach fails, but after he leaves a South African officer employs more brutal methods which enjoy success. Although the film sets its First World War scenes around the Allied victory, it is made plain that Wynne-Candy has been confused by a modern war, which has in fact been won by the ruthlessness and efficiency of his Dominion and American allies. Exhausted, Wynne-Candy visits a hospital where he meets and marries a young nurse, Barbara Wynne (Kerr again), who reminds him of Edith. Back home in Britain, Wynne-Candy finds Theo as a prisoner of war: his kindness cannot placate Theo's bitterness at Germany's defeat.

By the time the Second World War breaks out, both men have been widowed and Theo has arrived in Britain as a refugee from Nazi persecution. He finds sanctuary with Wynne-Candy. He, in turn, has come back from retirement to rejoin the regular army as a Major General, but is out of touch with the new way of warfare. His attitude, that it is better to fight fair and lose than to fight dirty and win, is deemed inappropriate. Wynne-Candy retires again from the regular army but finds fulfilment commanding the Home Guard, up until the point where he is captured by Spud. He manages, however, to see something of his younger self in the lieutenant and forgives him. Spud, encouraged by his girlfriend, Wynne-Candy's driver 'Johnny' Cannon (Kerr yet again), also finds something to respect in his adversary. The film ends with Wynne-Candy saluting a march past of Spud's regiment.

Assisted by the suggestion that Churchill and the War Office had attempted to ban the film, out of fear of its subversive nature and its suggestion that there were 'good Germans', *Colonel Blimp* was a commercial success when first released. It was the second most popular British-made film of 1943, and the fourth most popular film overall. Its success may, however, suggest wartime hunger for quality technicolour entertainment rather than an overriding fascination with the life of Blimp.[75] Unlike his cartoon predecessor, Powell and Pressburger's Blimp is not entirely unsympathetic. Like *The General*'s Sir Herbert Curzon, Clive Wynne-Candy is a man of honour. He is brave. He believes in fair play. He is courteous to foreigners and to women and he is capable of great love. He cares passionately for his country. Nevertheless, the film offers a stark and striking contrast between Wynne-Candy's traditional values and the 'new' army which was fighting the war in 1943, most obviously in the opening scenes when his torpor, confusion and rage that the rules of engagement have been broken make a vivid contrast to the speed and dynamism of Wilson's assault.

In so doing, *Colonel Blimp* shows us how the First World War was reconsidered in the light of the Second. The disasters of the first years of the Second World War were understood in Britain in terms of German efficiency and modernity versus Allied tradition and incompetence. Adopting new technology and new methods of war seemed to be the only way to win. Those who wanted to stress the need for Britain's armed forces to revitalise themselves – to seek modernity rather than tradition – could tap into the myth of aristocratic military incompetence which predated the First World War.

In making use of this myth, however, there was a natural tendency to turn back to the previous conflict. By emphasising the criticisms of the generals which were already current in the 1920s and 1930s, it was possible to fit them into this model of an outdated officer class whose modes of behaviour would have to be abandoned if victory was to be achieved. This rejection of First World War generalship was doubly attractive: it not only offered an easy explanation of Britain's failures from 1940 to 1942, but also held out the promise that the grinding battles of 1916–18 would not be repeated.

Ambiguities remained, however, as *Colonel Blimp* also makes clear. The problem was that the ideal of British heroism embodied by the caricatured officer – amateurism, effortless insouciance, courage beyond the bounds of military sense – continued to be influential, not least since many of the men who fought the Second World War internalised and copied it. Baffling, infuriating, sometimes wasteful as they were, these standards of behaviour were also personally impressive to those who experienced them. They were not totally mistaken. Successful wars require careful organisation, planning and management. But they also require young men to do things that are foolish and unreasonable: being the first to stand up under fire, charging the enemy head on, taking extreme risks to move the battle forward. This sort of junior leadership – what we might call the 'useful fool' approach – was something that the old aristocracy, and those who sought to emulate them, were extremely good at: certainly much better than they were at logistics or the operational art. With the weight of cultural expectation behind them, they continued to carry out their traditional role, even as they were mocked for it.

The poet Keith Douglas, a junior officer in an armoured regiment in the Western Desert, captured both the studiously amateurish bravery of some of his colleagues and the way in which they were caught at a moment of cultural change, in his poem 'Sportsmen':

> How then can I live amongst this gentle
> obsolescent breed of heroes, and not weep?
> Unicorns, almost. For they are fading into two legends
> in which their stupidity and chivalry are celebrated;
> the fool and the hero will be immortals.[76]

The dual myth of the British officer as hero and idiot went back well beyond 1939, and indeed beyond 1914. It was to underpin many representations of the Second World War at the time and afterwards, from *In Which We Serve* to *A Bridge Too Far*.[77] In the years after 1945, however, as military experience and the last remnants of a deferential culture disappeared, the mix of nostalgia and condemnation with which officers in general had been regarded began to fade.

The late 1940s and early 1950s saw public interest unsurprisingly focused on the Second World War. As paper rationing was relaxed, there was a boom in the publication of popular military histories and memoirs, telling the story of the Second World War to those who had lived through it. Debates over the conduct of the First World War were sidelined. Interest in the earlier war was briefly aroused by the publication of the final volume of the British Official History of the Western Front in 1948, and of an edited selection of the Haig's papers by Robert Blake in 1952, but the public controversies thus generated did not last long.[78]

At the end of the 1950s, the public's interest in war as a topic for popular history seemed undiminished, but the stock of unexploited memoirs, campaigns and battles from the Second World War was growing low. Publishers therefore began to encourage authors to look back to a previous conflict as a source for their works. One of those who sought a new field for popular history in the First World War was a writer in his early thirties, Alan Clark.

Clark's book on the British army in 1915, *The Donkeys*, was published in 1961. It remains a popular source on the war: in particular, many of the anecdotes that Clark retailed have been taken up by subsequent authors and have entered into folklore. Perhaps the best known is the book's title and epitaph, taken from the supposed comment of the German General Hoffman that the British soldiers fought like lions but were led by donkeys.

The book has two main strands. A series of chapters describe the battles of 1915: Aubers Ridge, Neuve Chappelle and Loos. Basing his work largely on the *Official History*, Clark recounted the events of these battles in a narrative style. Interspersed with these chapters were others focusing on the

British High Command. These are polemical attacks on the principal British generals, with a highly sarcastic tone. Clark's criticisms were particularly aimed at Sir Douglas Haig, who was depicted as incompetent, venal, obsessed by status and out of touch with the realities of modern war. Haig was seemingly condemned out of his own mouth with a series of quotations from his diary and letters. Clark in fact repeatedly took quotations out of context or omitted key phrases. This was most obvious when he implied that Haig was more concerned with George V's fall from his horse during a visit to France than with the fate of his army.[79] Similarly with the book's title: the *bon mot* about lions and donkeys dates originally from the Franco-Prussian War rather than the First World War. There is no evidence that it was reused at the time about the British army.[80]

Why did Clark, the son of a member of the British cultural establishment, educated by way of Eton, Oxford and the Life Guards, produce a book that was so damning of British generalship? In the preface to *The Donkeys*, he suggested that he had been moved to commemorate a forgotten year by reading the 1915 diary of an officer in the Leinster Regiment. He argued that for his generation (he was born in 1928), the First World War was 'as remote as the Crimean, its causes and its personnel obscure and disreputable. I have tried to put down simply, factually, tediously even, what happened to those men in one year, 1915. Because in print they have no memorial.'[81]

Clark's claim to speak for a whole generation for whom the war was distant and all but forgotten is not completely plausible. His lack of familial connection to the war may have made it seem far off to him, but there are plentiful examples of Britons born at the same time who grew up obsessed by the war, including such influential writers as John Keegan (born 1930), Martin Middlebrook (born 1932) and Lyn Macdonald (born 1934). Examining British popular culture between the wars, even into the 1930s, we have to suggest that, if he felt this way, Clark was the exception rather than the rule.

We can be similarly critical of his suggestion that he was motivated by the Leinsters officer's diary to commemorate a forgotten generation. This source plainly did affect Clark – he included a section of it as an appendix – but he had been seeking to write a book on a wider First World War topic before he encountered it. As he explained to Basil Liddell Hart in 1958, his original plan had been to write on the Ypres Salient from 1914 to 1917, but his thunder had been stolen by the publication of Leon Wolff's *In Flanders Fields*, dealing with the same subject. Clark wrote to Liddell Hart to ask about using his extensive archives to locate and research another First World War topic.[82]

Liddell Hart had a complicated relationship with the genesis of *The*

Donkeys. He obviously formed a great friendship with Clark – he was godfather to Clark's first son – and looked on him, as he put it, as 'the great white hope' of young British military historians. Subsequent commentators have therefore tended to ascribe the opinions and errors in *The Donkeys* to Liddell Hart. Much though he enjoyed *The Donkeys'* polemical style, however, he was infuriated by Clark's sloppy attitude towards facts and accuracy, and repeatedly informed both the author and his publisher of changes that ought to be made.[83] The Haig estate also demanded a series of corrections to the proofs of the book, which Clark carried out to the letter but not the spirit, retaining the book's sarcastic tone.

Clark's motivation was financial and professional. His intention was to earn his living as a writer. He had already published a novel set around the Stock Exchange, but this was not sufficiently well received to ensure his future. Branching out into popular military history, he needed to create a work that would be a success and ensure his future. He was, therefore, looking to produce a book that would attract attention. Later, Clark wrote to the historian and editor of Haig's papers, Robert Blake, who had criticised his poor use of the evidence:

> Privately, all I can say to you is this. I came to this subject absolutely fresh. I was not alive at the time. I have no familial or political axe to grind, and such personal instincts as I have are right wing and authoritarian. But, after three years work I came to the conclusion that, quite honestly, Douglas Haig was a pretty bad egg, and I use the diaries to support that contention.[84]

It is apparent, in fact, that from his first visit to the Liddell Hart files at the end of 1958, at the very beginning of his research, Clark sought evidence with which to condemn Haig. This was less a case of three years' careful research and weighing of the evidence than of spotting a gap in the market. The book's title is a good example: Clark had decided to use *The Donkeys* early in 1959 but was certain it was from an earlier conflict (he thought it might be the Peninsular War). He wrote to Liddell Hart, who confirmed that it pre-dated the First World War. Clark used it anyway.[85]

The Donkeys was written in haste, but also in genuine anger at what Clark perceived as the venality and stupidity with which the war was fought. If there is a year to get angry at the performance of British leaders in the First World War it is 1915, when the demands of the war exposed every fault of the pre-war army. But the book should be seen as the first venture by a young writer more concerned by telling a good story and selling plenty of books than with taking pains over the evidence.

Re-reading the book in 1961 as it made its way to publication, Clark confided in Liddell Hart: 'I still like parts of the book, but on reading it in

print for the first time it seems horribly *young* and *polemical.* I am afraid
it will get some really vicious reviews, although I've laid on a few friendly
ones as well and with any luck the Beaver will lend his support.'[86] Max
Aitken, Lord Beaverbrook, to whom Clark referred here, was the press
baron who owned the *Express* group of newspapers, but was also a one-
time political ally of Lloyd George. He had a long-term involvement in
denigrating the generals of the First World War that went back to 1918. In
turn, professional soldiers of both wars roundly detested him. Beaverbrook
wrote to Clark praising the book and advising him not to worry about, or
respond to, hostile comment, but his publishers remained nervous about
the reception the book would receive: 'Hutchinson's are still very uneasy
about the book, they don't know whether it will cause a lot of indignation,
or be ignored, or be a success.'[87]

Initial reviews seemed to bear out the publisher's fears. Many reviewers in broadsheets and periodicals criticised Clark heavily for his lax
approach to his sources. Bernard Fergusson accused him in the *Telegraph*
of 'monkeying with the evidence'. A. J. P. Taylor, in the *Observer*, suggested
that 'this book is valueless as a serious contribution to history. It lacks
understanding and sympathy, it disregards the most elementary rules of historical scholarship ... A reader who goes back to the sources – say to Haig's
diaries – and examines how they are used in this book, will discover that
Mr Clark has twisted the sense time and again: suppressed the limiting
phrase, added a slant of his own'. Michael Howard pointed out that: 'As
"entertainment" this book is good value. As history it is worthless. Like
other contemporary works on the First World War it accepts unquestion-
ably [*sic*] a popular stereotype of brave British lives being squandered by
stupid generals'.[88]

The exceptions to these criticisms were the papers owned by Beaverbrook.
These portrayed Clark as the gallant young historian setting out to fight the
legion of establishment defenders of Haig. Clark remarked in an interview
with the *Daily Express* that 'there is still a whole group of people who try to
keep his reputation intact'.[89] He also wrote a preparatory puff-piece in the
Evening Standard setting out his strident views on Haig.

If Clark's motivation in writing *The Donkeys* was financial and professional, he undoubtedly succeeded. The book proved that he could turn out
exciting, entertaining military history that would receive copious publicity
and enjoy healthy sales: both much more important to publishers and agents
than historical accuracy. For his next books, on the Second World War, *The
Fall of Crete* and *Barbarossa*, Clark not only received very large advances but
negotiated well-remunerated serialisation deals.[90]

What does the production and reception of *The Donkeys* tell us about perceptions of the First World War in Britain at the beginning of the 1960s? Clearly there was still controversy about how good or bad British generals had been. As Paul Johnson wrote in the *New Statesman* review: 'It seems a pity that, even after forty years, we cannot get objective books about the First World War.'[91] But – as Beaverbrook personified – this was part of a fight that had been conducted since the war itself, not a completely new departure. Clark's criticisms of the generals – that they were foolish, strategically and tactically blind and corrupt – were not created from scratch. Instead, they were an elaboration of beliefs that had long been present in British popular culture. Seldom, however, had they been expressed so crudely or so viciously.

On the other hand, for all that reviewers thought this was an old debate, it still aroused anger from the establishment. The portrayal of Clark as a radical shaking up the old order was not entirely false. Criticising Haig was still a way to *épater le bourgeoisie* – perhaps particularly for Clark, who had been a student of Hugh Trevor-Roper, Haig's son-in-law, whilst at Oxford. In this sense, Michael Howard was surely right to suggest that *The Donkeys* was entertainment rather than history.

Reviewing *The Donkeys*, some commentators speculated that interest in the First World War had been stimulated by fears of another global conflict. The *Economist* wrote that: 'Today, military thinking appears to have run into another impasse, created by the development of nuclear weapons and offering an even more terrible butcher's bill. It may therefore seem worth going back to discover what went wrong and why.'[92]

In fact, of course, Clark's research had no such underpinning in a desire for contemporary relevance. Interest in what this part of the past could teach the present was, however, clearly apparent in one work that took up and further popularised Clark's denigration of the generals: the stage entertainment *Oh What a Lovely War*. The musical was developed out of Charles Chilton's radio play *The Long Long Trail* by Gerry Raffles and Joan Littlewood's Theatre Workshop company. Littlewood and Raffles, with the assistance of the Labour MP and editor of *Tribune*, Raymond Fletcher and Chilton himself, transformed the radio play into the basis of a stage production that was first performed at the Theatre Royal, Stratford, on 19 March 1963.

The eventual form of that production was Littlewood's idea: a show put on by a band of pierrots, with the stylisations of the music hall added to Chilton's more realistic script. In the transformation from radio to stage, the play became more ardent in the expression of its left-wing views, with the importation of scenes designed to stress the callous incompetence of the High Command and the ruling classes. The result was also affected by

Littlewood's own directorial style. Although ultimately extremely autocratic, this attempted to involve the actors more fully in the play by encouraging a collective development of the script through research and improvisation by the whole cast. To this end the actors read a number of autobiographical and historical works about the war. These included popular histories like *The Donkeys* and Barbara Tuchman's *August 1914* as well as older texts such as Churchill's *The World Crisis*.[93] The cast were also lectured by their 'historical adviser', Fletcher, with a version of the war, as he put it, 'one part me, one part Liddell Hart, the rest Lenin'.[94] The process of improvisation and alteration was far from complete when the play appeared before the public: indeed, a key concept was that the play would change over time as it was performed. The script now available for *Oh! What a Lovely War* was produced by transcribing a performance after the play had moved to the West End and become more established in its form.[95]

For both Littlewood and Fletcher there were striking political and contemporary reasons for presenting their material as they did. Littlewood was keen to recast history from the perspective of the common man:

> the story of us – the victims, the people, the underprivileged – has not been told before. We've heard the poets speak – and we admire them – and we've had *Journey's End*, and we know about the sacrifice of the people who supported the system. But what about our fathers, who went as their dupes? I know I have been accused by some critics of having an anti-officer bias. But the officers have had their day. They've had their theatre. They've had their poetry. They've had their culture long enough.[96]

Her intention was to make this representation of the war dramatic and didactic from an extremely left-wing perspective. For this reason she rejected scripts which offered a realistic depiction of life in the trenches. The result is a black and white picture in which officers at all levels are stupid, callous cowards, while their men are sardonic heroes. The debunking of officers' culture is cruel, ahistoric and funny:

> WILSON: With regard to that, sir, do you think I ought to organise an interpreter?
> FRENCH: Don't be ridiculous Wilson; the essential problem at the moment is that we must have the utmost secrecy.[97]
>
> ...
>
> COMMANDING OFFICER: I know you've had it pretty hard the last few days, bombs, shells and snipers; we haven't escaped scot-free at Staff either, I can tell you. Anyway, we're all here – well, not all of us, of course; and that gas of ours was pretty nasty – damned wind changing.[98]

...

HAIG: The loss of, say, another 30,000 men may lead to really great results.[99]

It is not solely British generals who are lampooned, however, although they do come in for the heaviest fire. No establishment figure – be he Kaiser or arms manufacturer – escapes criticism.[100] Littlewood was motivated not only by a fierce class hatred of the establishment, but also by the contemporary international situation. She intended the play to act as a warning about how easy it was for idiotic rulers to allow their countries to slide into conflict by accident: a powerful lesson in the context of the Cuban missile crisis and developing American involvement in Vietnam.

Oh What a Lovely War reached a large audience. For an innovative play, it was remarkably popular. It reached far more people than those who came to see it during its run at Stratford and then on the Aldwych. *Oh What a Lovely War* enjoyed several international tours and was also produced by many English repertory theatres during the 1960s, six in 1965 alone.[101] The play also led to court cases about attribution and copyright which received substantial press coverage.[102] The BBC acquired the rights to broadcast a radio adaptation of the play, which was broadcast on the Home Service in 1964.[103] *Oh What a Lovely War* was also widely reviewed, on television and radio as well as in numerous papers and magazines. In the years since it was first produced it has become a favourite of the local and amateur theatre, and in 1998 was revived by the National Theatre. It can therefore be seen as a key milestone on the path to British hatred of the donkey-like generals of the First World War.

Seeing the context in which *Oh What a Lovely War* was first performed, it is tempting to ascribe the attitudes it struck and its success to the growth of anti-establishment and anti-war movements in the 1960s. We all know what the 1960s were like: a decade of free (or at least freer) love, artistic experimentation, anti-war feeling and protest against the nuclear arms race and American involvement in Vietnam, social mobility and the debunking of an established order. This feeling of new liberation is often summed up with Philip Larkin's famous poem 'Annus Mirabilis': 'Sexual intercourse began/In nineteen sixty-three'.[104] If *Oh What a Lovely War* is seen as part of this wild decade, we can argue that the modern, negative view of the First World War was born out of the play's appropriation of it for a new political and social agenda.[105]

Such an interpretation is misleading. As with any myth, this version of the 1960s contains some roots in fact. But it is also reductive and in some areas simply mistaken. The period saw important changes in British society and culture, but their duration and genuine effect on the majority of lives are not as easy to describe and locate as the myth of 1960s suggests. One problem in writing about it is that the decade was heavily mythologised even as it was going on: there was a widespread perception of change, but when questioned more closely about it, most would acknowledge that it was change happening to someone else. Those who quote Larkin tend to forget that his poem is about observation, not participation. In the next line of his poem, seldom quoted, he informs readers that the beginning of sexual inter-course came 'just too late for me'. If you think you can remember the mythical 1960s, you probably weren't there.[106]

Instead, the changes which took place in Britain at this time were more complex and less complete than a concentration on the counter-culture suggests. The most important and consistent development across the country was a boom in modern consumer society, based on an increase in wages for the youngest workers and the availability of cheap consumer durables and hire purchase agreements with which to pay for them. This meant a change in the quality of life and assumptions of prosperity in the future that was experienced across the country. Moreover, it gave young people the freedom to begin to break away from traditional social hierarchies. In most cases, however, this break was far from dramatic: it meant greater social mobility rather than the wholesale breakdown of society itself. It coin-cided with the arrival into adult life of the first generation to experience the benefits of the post-war expansion of education and a longer term change in the culture of deference and attitudes to authority (a change at least partly the result of the First World War). Yet neither of these resulted in a revolution. On the contrary, given the upheavals of the first half of the twentieth century, it is remarkable how effectively the structures of British society were maintained.

In legal terms, the 1960s did see Britain became more liberal. A series of acts reformed the laws on abortion, censorship, homosexuality, divorce and the death penalty. Whether these permitted and encouraged changes in atti-tudes, or themselves reflected changes in social practice that had already occurred, is still a matter of debate. The combination of new legal freedoms with medical developments, in particular the availability of effec-tive antibiotics and the contraceptive pill, might have seemed to promise sexual revolution, but the number of those actually experiencing dramatic changes in their lifestyle was relatively small.[107] As a recent historian has pointed out rather wistfully, changes were more in professed attitudes than in practice: 'London may have invented the mini-skirt, yet there were no live sex shows, gay bath houses, or singles bars as were found in Amsterdam, Copenhagen, San Francisco or New York.'[108] For those outside a very limited metropolitan circle, the swinging element of the Sixties remained a matter for speculation rather than personal experience.

The success of the show *Beyond the Fringe*, the launch of magazine *Private Eye*, and the broadcast by the BBC of *That Was The Week That Was* all seem to indicate the birth of a new, cynical satiricism. But both had their roots in a strand of undergraduate review humour which went back well beyond 1939. Public satire of organs of state did not spring new-minted into view in 1960 – although it had a very different tone, the Second World War radio series *It's That Man Again*, better known as *ITMA*, based itself on mockery of government bureaucracy. Given that the key figures within *Beyond the Fringe* and *TW3* came from within its bosom, how much threat they posed to the established order can be questioned. Both Peter Cook and Willy Rushton, devastating impersonators of the Prime Minister Harold Macmillan, confessed their affection for him – as Rushton put it: 'I should hope so too: I voted for him'. It is possible to argue that allowing itself to be mocked was a survival strategy for a crumbling social order: a strategy which, at least in the short term, was successful.[109]

The 1960s are now often thought of in terms of exciting new forms of artistic expression. We should pause, however, before assuming that the outermost extremes of art represented what the majority of Britons bought and enjoyed. In 1968, that much fabled year of radical unrest, number ones in the British charts included Des O'Connor's 'Anyone Who Had a Heart' and The Seekers' 'I'll Never Find Another You' and 'The Party's Over Now'.[110] These were not indicators of musical or popular revolt, but of the more staid tastes still shared by the bulk of the population. Changing boundaries of what could be said and done in public did offer artists greater freedom of expression, but Britain in the 1960s was always more Cliff Richard than Rolling Stones.

There was profound change as Britain emerged from the shadow of the Second World War. It took place, however, over more than a single decade. Few changes were as radical or as unambiguous as they have subsequently come to be seen. For most Britons, the advent of anything approaching a mythical Sixties came at the very end of the 1960s and the beginning of the 1970s.[111] During the early 1960s, certainly, they retained many of the values, patterns of behaviour and view of the world that they had held during the 1950s and before. We can see *Oh What a Lovely War* as a product of the period from which it came, but we need to move beyond a concentration on sex, drugs and rock and roll in understanding its reception.

Littlewood herself embodied many of the aspects of the mythical Sixties, but the audience which came to see *Oh What a Lovely War* was not necessarily the one she would have wanted. Theatre Workshop's stated intention was to provide plays for those who were normally excluded from mainstream theatre: the working class. In this they were at times remark- ably successful, but by 1963 it was apparent that the Theatre Royal Stratford was being kept open by the support of those regular theatregoers who were willing to travel out from the West End. Howard Goorney, actor and chron- icler of Theatre Workshop, remarked that 'Stratford tube station was a very busy place during the runs of our most successful productions'. Ewan MacColl, one of the Workshop's founder members, believed that *Oh What a Lovely War* represented a betrayal of the company's aspirations, because 'The wrong kind of good write-ups from the critics produced a situation where you couldn't get near the Theatre Royal for Bentleys and Mercedes, with the result that working class people in the area felt "This is not for us"'.[112] This view was also apparent in the *Daily Telegraph*'s inverted commas: 'The air of excitement was there once more and the Rolls-Royces were back in the street. The "workers"' theatre returned to full strength at the Theatre Royal, Stratford, last night'.[113] The audience for the play became, if anything, more traditional after *Oh What a Lovely War* moved to Wyndham's Theatre in the West End. A significant part of the audience for the play's first year of performance in both venues was probably middle aged and middle class.

Two things are striking about the reviews of *Oh What a Lovely War*. First, very few reviewers perceived the performance as an objective representa- tion of historical truth. The audience for Theatre Workshop's productions were not unsophisticated: the company was known to be experimental, left wing and controversial. Much though the programme notes stressed that 'Everything spoken during this evening either happened or was said, sung or written during 1914–18', many in the audience were critical of what they were watching on historical grounds.[114] The *Guardian*'s reviewer noted that *Oh What a Lovely War* was 'as unfair as any powerful cartoon'.[115] The *Sunday Telegraph* remarked on the 'monumental crudity' of the play's attack on the officer class.[116] The *Observer* sought out A. J. P. Taylor and Basil Liddell Hart in the first night audience, who both emphasised, perhaps sur- prisingly, that the play was too severe on Haig. 'Haig wasn't as stupid as he's painted here', declared Taylor.[117]

It is doubtful, therefore, whether the play's original audience came to it as *tabulae rasae*. Instead, many arrived with prior knowledge of the First World War. A debunking view of the commanders of the war had hardly originated with the 'instant histories' cited by the creators of *Oh What a Lovely War*. Reviews of *The Donkeys* made it plain that there was a widespread awareness of a continuing debate surrounding the generals' reputation. This remained a disputed history. At the time,

Oh What a Lovely War was criticised for its hackneyed view of General Staff incompetence:

> the familiar view of the 1914–18 war as a criminally wasteful adventure in which the stoic courage of the common soldiers was equalled only by the sanctimonious incompetence of their commanders and the blind jingoism of the civilians. This approach is hardly likely to send audiences storming out of the theatre: the war is a sitting target for anyone who wants to deliver a bludgeoning social criticism without giving offence.[118]

'I should perhaps have fewer reservations if Theatre Workshop's target had not been so heavily pitted with other men's arrows', remarked the *Sunday Telegraph*.[119]

If older audience members had reservations about *Oh What a Lovely War*'s caricatures, they approved wholeheartedly of its songs. But these in themselves were less important than the emotions which they inspired. This is the second point to be made about audience reaction to *Oh! What a Lovely War*. Reviewers did not comment on the aesthetic qualities of the tunes and ditties the play contained: instead, time and time again, they described the emotional impact of the songs. 'Sentimentality', remarked one, 'is the effective centre of *Oh What a Lovely War*.'[120] The *Sunday Times* commented 'this immensely brisk charade gives nostalgia a top-dressing of belated anti-establishment respectability'.[121] 'One shouldn't go to *Oh! What a Lovely War* in search of clever acting', said the critic Roger Gellert, 'but to honour the doomed gallantry of those songs in that context.'[122] An older reviewer suggested that:

> For those who fought in that war and were lucky enough to survive it, this show conjures up memories that are not all painful. To hear the songs we sang – even though the younger generation doesn't know how to sing them – is to catch again a whiff of that wry, disillusioned, humorous resignation with which our armies faced trench life.[123]

At least part of the audience was interpreting the *Oh What a Lovely War* in a way which was essentially nostalgic. For some, this was sufficient to offset any offence caused by the politicised caricatures. Such emotional reactions were encouraged by the photographs, showing themes from the war, that were beamed onto the backdrop of the stage. These came from three volumes published in the 1930s: Sir Ernest Swinton's *Twenty Years After*, Sir John Hammerton's more sensationalist *World War, 1914–1918*, and *I Was There: Undying Memories of 1914–18*. These books had been brought out as weekly part-works. Bought in large numbers, they were one of the ways that those who had not experienced the war learned how it had looked.[124]

The way the creators of *Oh What a Lovely War* reacted to the wave of nostalgia they had unleashed is unclear. They seem to have been aware of the potential impact of the songs. Littlewood, in her own memoirs, wrote that 'Those songs took me back to childhood – red, white and blue bunting, photos of dead soldiers in silver frames, medals in a forgotten drawer, and that look as family and friends sang the songs of eventide – God, how I loathed those songs'.[125] Introducing a new edition of *Oh What a Lovely War* published in 2000, both Littlewood and Victor Spinetti, a member of the original cast, emphasised that their initial reaction to Chilton's radio play had been that it was overly sentimental and nostalgic. Particular ire focused on the presentation of the songs by the BBC Choir. They stressed that the cast of *Oh What a Lovely War* aimed for a more 'authentic' approach.[126] Murray Melvin, another original performer, spoke thirty years later of his emotional reaction when a family in the audience presented him with a royal souvenir box which had belonged to their father, killed in the war. 'It's one of my greatest treasures; they said that it was the first time some sort of justice had been done to that lot, the wonderful clowns. Such humour and wit came out of the suffering.' Littlewood made her actors play against these feelings, telling them, 'Stop falling in love with it; it's not a sentimental subject. And don't ever mention a poppy in a corner of a foreign field, where there's likely to be some poor bugger screaming to death'.[127]

It could be argued that Littlewood and Raffles played up to the air of nostalgia they had, unwittingly, created:

> When I saw it in Stratford Victor Spinetti made the closing speech, which went something like 'The war game is being played all over the world, by all ages, there's a pack for all the family. It's been going on for a long time and its still going on. Goodnight.' This cynical speech, which followed the charge of the French soldiers, was quite frightening and left you crying your heart out. When I saw it again, in the West End, I was shocked by the change of ending. After Victor's speech the whole cast came on singing 'Oh What a Lovely War' followed by a reprise of the songs. All frightfully happy and guaranteed to send the audience home happy. I think it was George Sewell who said 'The Management didn't take kindly to a down ending'. As far as I knew, Joan and Gerry were the Management.[128]

The critic David Pryce-Jones noticed this when he reviewed the play for a second time, as it closed its run at the Aldwych: 'Showbiz has crept in to bespangle the poor relation from Stratford East, and make it more polite, and I fear that the latter audiences imagined themselves back in the days of the good old musical shows, wishing the girls were rather more gaiety.'[129]

Nostalgia for the comradeship of the war did not mean that it was impossible to criticise the generals. Grumbling about the Staff was, after all, one of the things that united front-line troops. It was nostalgia, however, rather than politicised caricature, that attracted many in the audience to the play. Pointing out these more complex reactions to *Oh! What a Lovely War* is not to suggest that attitudes to authority, hereditary privilege and the establishment remained constant over the twentieth century. Over that long duration, changes clearly did take place in public and private attitudes and behaviour. A culture of deference to authority declined, even if it did not disappear completely. Changing views of the British High Command clearly fitted into this broader development. It is unhelpful, however, to perceive an all-encompassing and total shift in attitudes in the 1960s. Such an interpretation obscures the continued co-existence of competing or contradictory beliefs about the war, and the degree to which the quality of British generals continued to be disputed.

The emotion and personal involvement that continued to characterise this debate continued into the 1960s is provided by the production of the 1964 BBC TV series *The Great War*. The series employed two historians whose interpretations of British generalship were widely different. Basil Liddell Hart became Consultant Historian to the series. Although his focus of interest had moved away from the First World War, his involvement with the production of popular histories in the early 1960s had strengthened his belief in the need to fight back against those who were trying to bolster Haig's reputation. Liddell Hart had reacted in fury when his contributions to a radio programme marking the centenary of Haig's birth in 1961 had been, as he saw it, misused – edited so as to remove all trace of criticism:

> It was an oily stream of adulation mixed with trivialities ... it merely showed the BBC playing its part in the British 'Establishment' as purveyors of gloss and promoters of the complacency that has led to repeated disasters. I have never felt more incline to vomit, and to emigrate, than after listening to this BBC effusion.[130]

John Terraine, the principal scriptwriter for *The Great War*, was no less passionate in his beliefs, but held almost precisely the opposite position to Liddell Hart. Like Charles Chilton, Terraine was a member of that generation which had grown up after the First World War and been heavily marked by its effects. His veteran father's early death left Terraine to grow up in a house where the war was ever present but never discussed.[131] His first school prize was a volume of heroic tales from the war called *The Crown of Honour*, its stated purpose being 'to influence the new generation which is growing up since the war ... to impress upon it more vividly an adequate conception of the heroism, self-sacrifice and indomitable courage of those who played their part so greatly in those unforgettable years'.[132] Terraine's subsequent passionate engagement with the war can be traced back to this childhood fascination.

From 1944 to 1963, Terraine worked for the BBC, recording and organising radio programmes.[133] From the early 1960s, he began to write books in which he set forth his own interpretation of Britain's First World War. In a series of volumes, starting with the 1960 *Mons: Retreat to Victory*, Terraine put forward the achievements of the British army. He developed a position that focused on the enormous casualties and limited movement of the war as a function of the technological and social developments of the nineteenth century. In 1963, he published his magnum opus, the biography *Douglas Haig: The Educated Soldier*. The book enabled him to move away from the BBC to act as a freelance historian. It argued for Haig's abilities as Commander-in-Chief, particularly his realisation that the war could only be won by defeating the German army on the Western Front. The biography aroused Liddell Hart's opposition and he circulated a briefing sheet to a number of reviewers in an effort to counter its arguments. Although Terraine's view has subsequently come to be seen as over-deterministic and too heavily based on published sources, but his work continues to underpin much of the modern military history of the war, including the interpretation put forward at the start of this chapter.

It was always likely that there would be trouble between Terraine and Liddell Hart over the episode of *The Great War* that dealt with the Battle of the Somme. This had been one of the few battles of the war that Liddell Hart had actually participated in: he retained a fierce and disputatious interest in it. Terraine saw the programme as an opportunity to present an interpretation of the battle that got away from an obsession with the horrendous British casualties of 1 July 1916 and instead concentrated on the need to destroy the manpower of the German armies, and the inexperienced New Armies' success in so doing. As he wrote to Tony Essex, the series producer:

> for fifty years the Battle of the Somme has produced more emotion and misconception than almost any other event ... It is for us to consider carefully whether we wish to perpetuate this cliché or offer something fresh ...
>
> This bloody parochial nation of ours can *never* see beyond the end of its toffee nose; it's about time to tell them that the Germans were there too, busily losing the War. That's what the Somme was about. The absolute bloodiness of it was not so special: plenty more of that about, for all and sundry.[134]

This was not merely a matter of divergent academic interpretations:

1. British stretcher-bearers in the mud during the Third Battle of Ypres, autumn 1917. This photograph has become an iconic image of the horror of the Western Front. (*IWM Q5935*)

2. Royal Irish Rifles rations party, Somme, 1 July 1916. Note the range of expressions and attitudes. (*IWM Q1*)

3. The seated figure in the middle was cropped from this photograph and used with images of dead soldiers to form the title sequence of the 1964 BBC TV series *The Great War*. One viewer wrote: 'He means more to me than the Beatles'. (*IWM Q1*)

4. Men of the Royal Fusiliers celebrate the capture of Thiepval, Somme, 26 September 1916. The war confronted those who experienced it with a range of emotions, including pride and comradeship as well as horror and despair. (*IWM Q1398*)

5. Second Lieutenant Wilfred Owen in the uniform of the Manchester Regiment, June 1916. Owen has become the best known trench poet, but his work does not necessarily reflect how every soldier thought about the war. (*Owen Collection, Oxford English Faculty Library*)

6. Women at a Birmingham aircraft factory, September 1918. These workers seem to be enjoying the opportunity of wartime employment, but photographs like this were often composed specifically to attract women into the factories. (*IWM Q 28186*)

7. King George V at the unveiling of the Cenotaph in Whitehall, London, 11 November 1920. The monument became the focus of national mourning in the 1920s. (*IWM Q 31488*)

8. Field-Marshal Earl Haig inspects Glasgow Cub Scouts, *c.* 1925. Haig's work for the British Legion made him a popular figure in the post-war period. (*NLS Acc 3155/234*)

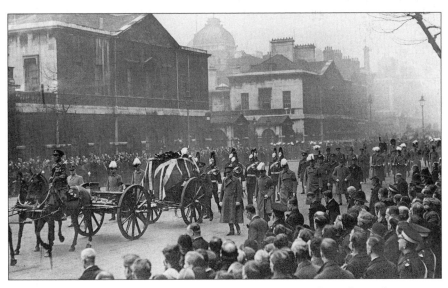

9. Haig's funeral procession, London, 3 February 1928. Throughout the country, Britons mourned the death of a man who, though controversial, was not yet seen as a 'donkey'. (*IWM Q 46457*)

10. First World War veterans play football near the Thiepval Memorial after the ceremony commemorating the fiftieth anniversary of the Battle of the Somme, July 1966. In the 1960s, veterans were still vigorous and healthy enough to try to influence the way the war was remembered.

Liddell Hart took Terraine's comments on the need for the New Armies to learn their job as a personal affront. He argued that Terraine had absolved Haig from responsibility by accepting a post facto explanation of the battle in terms of attrition rather than attempted breakthrough. In fact, Liddell Hart's criticisms were valid: Terraine's script did gloss over the mistakes made by British generals and the failures of command and control.[135] Liddell Hart may also have been angered by a feeling that he had been sidelined in the production of the series, employed more for the kudos of his name than for the value of his opinion. This was a result of the frantic speed with which the series was produced, which left little time for additional reading of scripts and semantic fine-tuning.

Tony Essex moved Terraine away from an academic exposition of Allied strategy and difficulty towards a more atmospheric presentation, but it was Terraine's version that triumphed in the script for the broadcast programme.[136] Enraged, Liddell Hart resigned from the series in the most public way possible, writing an article for the *Sunday Telegraph* and a letter to *The Times*. His resignation provoked press comment, although Essex and Terraine successfully avoided being dragged into a slanging match, but did little to affect the popularity of the series with the general public. They continued to watch in huge numbers. Few seem to have paid close attention to the points the script was making. Whilst some veterans felt offence, as Liddell Hart had done, at the criticism of the citizen soldiers of the New Armies, the bulk of the audience focused on the awfulness of the battle and the terrible losses. They tended not to comment directly on the abilities of the High Command, but rather to react emotionally to 'the horrors of war and the dreadful waste of young manhood'.[137] The power of the myths of mud and death overcame an effort to rescue the reputation of the generals.

Notwithstanding the power of these myths, and the strength of feeling on both sides of the resignation debate, this episode demonstrated how, even fifty years after the war, different interpretations of generalship and the war were still in existence. The subject of the High Command aroused dispute, but these arguments had been ongoing for so long that it was acceptable – even expected – that different opinions would be offered. Indeed, the wonder of this argument was that both sides in it could present themselves as iconoclastic crusaders against the weight of received opinion. That this was possible demonstrates that, although the myth of generals' incompetence enjoyed wide popularity, it was not yet universally accepted. Positive interpretations could sometimes still seem to hold the upper hand.

It was in the twenty years after the 1960s that the representation of its generals as donkeys became so dominant that it stopped being disputed.

We can see this shift if we compare the reaction to dramatic representations of officers in the 1980s to those in the 1960s. For example, in 1986 the BBC screened *The Monocled Mutineer*, written by Alan Bleasdale. Another left-wing writer, Bleasdale had long been interested in the First World War as a result of his family's involvement. His grandfather had died after being wounded and taken prisoner in 1917. As he put it, 'I feel personally about the First World War. We've still got the last letter from my grandfather, who was killed in it three months before my father was born, asking for the kid to be called George if it was a boy. He knew he wasn't coming back'. He responded quickly to the BBC's suggestion that he should adapt the book, and once engaged on the project exerted considerable pressure to make sure that series was properly funded and produced.[138]

Initial critical reaction to the series was extremely favourable, in particular to the depiction of trench warfare and its effects. Over the course of the series as a whole, class distinctions were not painted in such black and white terms as in *Oh What a Lovely War*, but the blame for the conditions and the suffering was clearly placed:

8. EXT. GAS BAY
[*We see a soldier checking the direction of the wind,
using a stick held in the air with a rag on it*]

SOLDIER: It's too windy, Sarge.
[*Brings stick down*]
OFFICER [*Out of vision*]: I said '*Carry on, Sergeant!*'
SOLDIER [*to himself*]: ... soddin' hell ...
TOPLIS: There's bastards up there who are supposed to know what they're doin' – they've been trained for years for all this – we're just the crowd. But any fool in the crowd can see – the artillery never broke enough of the wire, so what idiot gave the order to go over the top?[139]

There might seem to be clear parallels between *The Monocled Mutineer* and *Oh What a Lovely War*. Bleasdale shared some of Littlewood's political stance, and was just as keen to use events in the First World War to make contemporary political points; in his case about unemployment, urban unrest and the Falklands War. *The Monocled Mutineer* also makes use of First World War songs and music hall jokes at key moments in a style that recalls its predecessor.[140] A more detailed examination of audience reaction makes it clear, however, that there had been a profound change in the way dramas about the war were received in the twenty-three years since the initial production of *Oh What a Lovely War*. The subsequent furore over the depiction of the Étaples mutiny so dominates modern recollections of *The*

Monocled Mutineer that it is worth restressing the degree to which the opening episodes were greeted with acclaim as an accurate representation of the reality of trench warfare and the incompetence of the High Command.

Reviewers from all newspapers greeted this version of the war as a muddy, bloody mess, organised by asinine officers, with great enthusiasm. The *Daily Mail* declared: 'the Great War was an unpardonable carnage generally officered at a high level by rigid incompetents (lions led by donkeys) and ... the ordinary soldier was all too often flung to an early and needless death'.[141] Bleasdale was using the myth of generals' incompetence for political effect, but his efforts were largely negated because that myth had become accepted fact. By 1986, this was no longer perceived as a politicised interpretation: few were outraged by this part of Bleasdale's argument because they already 'knew' it to be correct. Ironically, the 1980s would see the first stirrings of a revisionist history that would seek to rescue the generals – but this was to have almost no impact on popular belief.

What had happened in the space of twenty years to move the 'donkeys' version of British military history to the point where it was indisputable? In the absence of widespread military experience, it may have been that the British public were more willing to accept caricatures of officers' incompetence uncritically. As the more controversial works of the 1960s were reincorporated into new dramas, novels and histories in the 1980s, they gained the status of fact rather than opinion. More important than this sheer weight of repetition, however, was the disappearance of those Britons who had sustained popular debate over the generals' reputation.

Up to the 1960s, each anniversary of the war saw the letters pages of British broadsheets taken over by veterans arguing over how well they had been led. Most veterans had not held such strong beliefs during the war; nonetheless, they could use their experiences to back up arguments for and against the generals. Veterans' groups tended to foster positive representations of the High Command. The British Legion had particular reason to commemorate their founder, Earl Haig, but veterans' associations in general encouraged loyalty through their celebration of wartime camaraderie and social unity.

In the 1970s, the number of veterans left alive rapidly diminished. This changed both how veterans participated in popular discussion of the war and what they had to say. They no longer had the numbers or the vitality to influence popular culture. This may account for a seeming increase in old soldiers who were willing publicly to criticise their former commanders. Some of these men had always held these views; others had altered their opinions over time. As veterans grew older and died, the networks in which they had sustained debates about the generals went with them. Without a context which encouraged the rehearsal and reinforcement of alternative views, surviving veterans were increasingly vulnerable to the myths of incompetence which were established amongst their descendants. By its nature, the way veterans' associations had remembered the war was complex and exclusive. It could not easily be passed on to a younger generation of Britons, who shared a very different set of experiences, attitudes and expectations. The specific circumstances in which *The Monocled Mutineer* was broadcast, however, meant that a production that was perceived as politically oriented was liable to much greater criticism than had been the case in the 1960s. The polarisation of British politics in the intervening years, and the spectre of violence in the streets and on the picket line, meant that elements on the Right were far less willing to accept such dogmatic drama as interesting in itself.[142]

The most influential representation of the donkeys in the 1980s, however, was the BBC TV comedy series *Blackadder Goes Forth*. Regularly inflicting lunatic orders on Captain Blackadder was General Sir Anthony Hogwhistle Melchett, played by Stephen Fry. A clear line of descent can be drawn from the generals of *Oh! What a Lovely War* to those in *Blackadder Goes Forth*. Since Fry has claimed *The Life and Death of Colonel Blimp* as one of his favourite films, it may be that earlier influences were also at work.[143] Melchett is a savage buffoon, eager to send his men over the top to certain death:

MELCHETT: Now, Field Marshal Haig has formulated a brilliant tactical plan to ensure final victory in the field.
BLACKADDER: Would this brilliant plan involve us climbing over the top of our trenches and walking slowly towards the enemy?
DARLING: How did you know that Blackadder? It's classified information.
BLACKADDER: It's the same plan we used last time sir. And the seventeen times before that.
They all move over to the desk.

MELCHETT: E-e-exactly! And that's what's so brilliant about it. It will catch the watchful Hun totally off guard. Doing exactly what we've done eighteen times before will be the last thing they expect us to do this time. There is, however, one problem.
BLACKADDER: That everyone always gets slaughtered in the first ten seconds?
MELCHETT: Exactly. Field Marshal Haig is concerned that this may be depressing the men a tadge, so he's looking for a way to cheer the men up.
BLACKADDER: His resignation and suicide seem the obvious answer.[144]

In the celebrated final episode, Blackadder, desperate to escape a doomed final advance, rings up General Haig, who owes him a favour from a pre-war colonial campaign. Haig, played by Geoffrey Palmer, is seen contemplating toy soldiers laid out on a model battlefield. As Blackadder speaks to him, he knocks them over, sweeps them up with a dustpan and brush, and flings them over his shoulder. His advice to Blackadder, needless to say, is utterly useless.[145]

Military historians sometimes need to recognise more clearly that laughter is a crucial tradition in British efforts to understand the First World War. We cannot be too po-faced about the caricatures of *Blackadder Goes Forth*, however much they make us bristle. They can also be used to demonstrate just how far attitudes had changed. Sixty years previously, such a savage attack on the generals would have inspired outraged objection. Even twenty-six years before, such a representation would have been disputed. In 1989 they were unchallenged: any unease the audience felt was at the incongruity of laughing at doomed men in such horrific circumstances, not at mocking the leaders who had won the war.

Just how well the donkeys myth had become embedded in British popular culture was made clear by the reaction to a 1996 programme that offered a more positive assessment of Haig. *Timewatch – Douglas Haig: The Unknown Soldier*, produced by Helen Bettinson, was an impressive example of a piece of military historiography on the screen: a detailed, accurate and balanced representation of the Field Marshal's career that has aged extremely well.

The Unknown Soldier sought to interact explicitly with existing myths about the First World War. It included excerpts from *Blackadder Goes Forth* to illustrate the received wisdoms about Haig, as well as footage of his burial to show how views of him had changed over time. Whereas in previous documentaries many of the debates between historians took place behind the scenes, affecting the broadcast version but not apparent to the lay viewer, *The Unknown Soldier* put these debates at its heart. The historians involved appeared on screen as opposed 'talking heads', inter-cut with maps, diagrams and archive footage. The programme achieved relatively high audience figures for a one-off documentary – some three and a half million viewers – and was reviewed in every national newspaper the following day.[146]

The critical reaction was generally positive but puzzled. Despite the high production standards of the programme, highlighting and questioning myths that had become so established were offensive to many reviewers. The well-argued views of eminent historians – views that have grown in popularity since 1996 – met with little acceptance. Sean Day Lewis saw the point of the programme but was unconvinced: 'Haig apologists presumably mean

that the dour, uncommunicative Scotsman will be given credit for learning
the hard way that mass attack on a wide front was not the best way
through ... I am sorry, I cannot buy the new line'.[147] Thomas Sutcliffe, in
wondering about historians' motives, pointed out just how entrenched
myths about Haig were: 'Who, after all, would make a name or a reputation
by arguing that General Haig was a blinkered fool, detached from the suffering of his men and incompetent in his tactics?' He too was unpersuaded:
'Forty miles behind the line, or even eighty years after the slaughter, Haig's
stubborn persistence in attack might look heroic. From the less lofty
perspective of the trenches it still looks like criminal incompetence'.[148]
To criticise from the point of view of the trenches was a remarkable
appropriation of a veteran's viewpoint.

From opposite sides of the political spectrum, reviewers in both the
Guardian and the *Daily Mail* were strongly critical of the programme in
terms which more emotional than historically accurate. The former wondered about 'Those men for whom the odds of death in battle were about
evens. Those men who, if they survived, were all but certain to be scarred
mentally or physically ... the costs of Haig's slow learning lay on the fields
of Flanders'.[149] The *Mail,* whilst offended at the use of the Unknown Soldier's name to describe Haig, was even more annoyed that 'In the week of
the eightieth anniversary of the Battle of the Somme, with the brave old survivors (all are at least ninety-five years old) visiting the battlefield probably
for the last time, little effort was made to salute their sacrifice and lift our
hearts'.[150] The files of viewers' letters to the BBC have not yet been opened,
but this was clearly a topic which inspired a great deal of emotion: it led to
the military historian Gary Sheffield receiving hate mail for his role as a
defender of Haig.[151]

The novelty of prolonged involvement in a modern war and the specific
technological context of the First World War both meant that British generals' performance did not match traditional models of successful military
leadership. No one could talk of Alexander in 1918, let alone of Hercules.
Nonetheless, during and immediately after the war many Britons did recognise that a military victory had been won and credited Haig with its
achievement, through persistence if not through brilliance. Others, however,
reacted to the scale of casualties and the absence of swift victories by questioning their leaders' competence. In the memoirs written between the wars,
disputes raged about who, if anyone, had been at fault. Taking part in this
controversy, Churchill and Lloyd George were able to put forward a highly
articulate view which stressed the generals' inability to deal with the massive
catastrophe which faced them. Both men believed strongly in what they

wrote, but it also had the convenient side effect of diverting attention from their own involvement and errors.

By the later 1930s and 1940s, criticism of the generals became part of a wider discussion of the relationship between tradition and modernity. German successes in the first part of the Second World War could be taken to show that traditional hierarchies and behaviour had failed in the face of aggressive modern technology. As the country mobilised to fight its second total war, Britons told themselves that they would have to do things differently this time.

In the years after 1945, this interpretation was easily developed into a more radical analysis, which suggested that British failure in the First World War was the fault of the traditional ruling class. It was bad enough that the upper classes had preferred others to do the fighting for them; but, worse, they had then managed the war incompetently. This version of events had an obvious attraction to the political Left, but it was not limited to them. It was also espoused by the more radical Right, whose attitudes were to underpin Thatcherism in the 1980s. They would have been loathe to admit it, but this interpretation of aristocratic incompetence made unnatural bedfellows of Joan Littlewood, Alan Clark, Corelli Barnett and Alan Bleasdale.

In the 1970s and 1980s, however, the myth of military incompetence established a separate existence in the public sphere. In popular culture, it was no longer at the centre of a prolonged debate. Instead, it enjoyed the currency of fact. As responses to *The Monocled Mutineer* and *Douglas Haig: The Unknown Soldier* show, it became acceptable to make almost any accusation against the generals of the First World War, except to argue that they might have been good at their jobs. Such a suggestion aroused howls of anger from all sides.

The establishment of the 'donkeys' myth as a widely accepted fact can be put down to three factors. First, it offered an easily understood explanation for a unique event. Britons continued to look back in shocked fascination at the scale of loss in the First World. When they did so, it was much easier to blame someone for the huge casualty lists than to make the mental leap to horrified understanding of the results of involvement in a total war. This temptation was only strengthened after the Second World War seemed to offer an alternative version of a similar war with much lighter casualties. The generals were the natural people to blame: not only had they been in charge, but, because of the ways Britain had fought her wars in the nineteenth century, a caricature of incompetent officers already existed in popular culture.

Secondly, the myth remained useful throughout the twentieth century. Britain did not undergo complete social, political or economic revolution as an immediate result of either world war. The result was that many of the tensions embodied in the concept of 'lions led by donkeys' continued to be discussed. It was still relevant to talk about the disasters which would follow from a failure to remain at the cutting edge of technology, the utility of established class structures, or the relationship between amateurism and professionalism. The mythical view of the First World War could be used to exemplify each of these problems. The result was that it remained current in popular culture and was reinforced by repetition.

Thirdly and finally, a demographic shift took place which changed Britons' relationship to the war. Veterans had profoundly disagreed with each other about the quality of their leaders, but they had maintained an environment of debate. It was as veterans vanished that the 'donkeys' myth became universally accepted as the true interpretation of the First World War. Its dominance represented the triumph of a version which, whilst it was used in complex ways, simplified the past into an easily comprehensible form and keyed into deeper myths about relationships between leaders and led. This simplification was aided by the growing chronological distance between Britons and the war. Simultaneously, a widely recognised set of mutually understood myths made the war an attractive setting for literature, drama and documentaries, maintaining its position in British popular culture.

4

Futility

Writing an online review of Sebastian Faulk's First World War novel *Birdsong* for the website bookshop Amazon in January 2000, a reader from London declared that 'with this war nearly a century ago it's not a bad time to stop and think back on this extraordinary, foolish, disastrous, ultimately unnecessary war'. Another reviewer suggested that *Birdsong* was 'a book that should be read by every politician on this planet as a testimony to the pointlessness of War'.[1] Pointless, foolish, unnecessary – these readers were summing up a commonplace view of the First World War as a futile conflict.

A seemingly simple word in fact covers a complex tangle of different beliefs, many tied into the myths that we have already considered. When we call the First World War 'futile', we are making a judgement, whether we articulate it or not, of costs and results. Considering the appalling conditions in which men fought and the huge numbers of deaths, we are bound to ask whether the end justified the means. The word gets applied to the way the war was fought as well as the war as a whole. Attacks that cost many soldiers their lives but gained little ground must have been worthless, perhaps unsurprisingly if those in command were idiotic butchers. If the war brought so few positive results, we can go further, to suggest that the decision to take part in it was either mistaken, unduly influenced by those who would benefit, or was not in fact taken at all. Perhaps the war was entered into because nobody could think of anything else, or because the war machine, once started, could not be stopped. These cost-benefit judgements are, of course, highly subjective. They also differ depending on the level at which we look. On what basis can we dare to compare the gains and losses of a country with those of an individual? This tension between national and individual interests and the terrible scale of losses has always underpinned thoughts about the futility of the war. As the First World War has receded into history and personal contact with it has been lost, it has become increasingly easy to judge the war futile. But this judgement has not been all-encompassing in the sense that the dead have been dismissed. In terms of national rhetoric and family connections, it remains difficult for Britons to deny all meaning to wartime death. Instead, the perceived futility of their cause has come to mark the bravery of those who fought.

Britain went to and stayed at war because her leaders and people believed strongly that she should. Wars take place not only because policy makers ordain that they should, but because populations either support them, or oppose them insufficiently strongly. If this is the case for all conflicts, it is even more so for the enormous efforts of modern total war. Plainly they thought they were fighting for *something*.

We might look first at the decision by the ruling elite to go to war. Contrary to conspiracy theories put forward at the time and since, most historians would now accept that the war was not fought for the purposes of capitalist profits or imperial rivalries, that it was started by accident or entered into through the restrictive, compelling alliances formed by the secretive old diplomacy. Capitalists generally prefer the stable, open markets which flourish in peacetime. The nations of Europe had demonstrated their ability to come to colonial compromises. Whatever the confusion of communication or the restrictions imposed by railway timetables, nations always had the option of holding back, of not going to war. They did so because they believed it was in their interest, not because they were compelled to do so by the limitations of technology. Similarly, alliances reflected a nation's perceptions of its strategic interests and concerns. They were subject to change as the international situation developed. If war did not fit those interests, they would not abide by the alliance; as indeed, Italy did not when it chose not to accompany the Central Powers to war in 1914.[2]

British ministers in 1914 went to war to maintain the balance of power in Europe. It was in Britain's interests then, as it had been for centuries, to prevent a single hegemonic power dominating the whole mainland of Europe, and in particular the Channel Ports that could be used to threaten invasion. For all that the German violation of Belgian neutrality provided a reason to go to war that would allow the Cabinet and the country to act in unity, it was the fear of German domination that lay at the heart of Britain's decision to join the war.[3]

Were Britain's leaders right to feel this way? If Britain had not joined the war in 1914 and Germany had won, would she have attempted to take control of the European mainland in the style of Napoleon, as they feared? It is difficult to predict with certainty because it might have depended on the circumstances in which victory was achieved. While some historians, following the work of Fritz Fischer in the 1960s, have come to see Germany as launching a war of deliberate aggression with wide-ranging territorial objectives, others have disputed the degree to which these aims can be imputed from the beginning of hostilities. At the very least, it seems likely that a Germany victorious in 1914 would have imposed a customs union on its neighbours over which it would have exercised primary control for its own benefit. It might have taken on a more direct rule over areas of the Low Countries, Eastern Europe and the border regions with France.[4]

Would this have been such a bad thing? In the short term, it might not have mattered to the British; certainly there were no immediate German plans for an invasion of their homeland. In the longer term, cut off from the European economies that were her main trading partners, her economy would have been strangled. Furthermore, Germany, a country whose elite had chosen war – with all the huge risks it entailed – as an option of policy to get what it wanted, would have found its actions fully justified. Economically and militarily strengthened by her control of a European customs union devoted to her own economic primacy, would that elite have held back from further conflicts in the future? What would this have meant when Germany's aims at the global level – particularly her aspirations to empire – seemed destined to bring her into dispute with Britain? Had she stayed aloof in 1914, it is likely that Britain would have found herself, in the medium term, alone and facing a stronger and no less dangerous opponent.[5]

Did that matter? Was the British way of life in 1914 worth preserving? In recent years, historians have come to represent the First World War as it was understood by contemporaries: as a struggle of ideologies between liberal democracy on the one hand and autocratic militarism on the other.[6] This is not about making value judgements between different modes of government so much as attempting to understand how people saw the war at the time. No country that was allied with Tsarist Russia could really claim to be fundamentally opposed to autocracy. Britain in 1914 was a long way from full democracy. Even by the standards of the time, a voting system that excluded 40 per cent of the adult male population, as Britain's did, placed it some way down the European democratic league table. British society was rigidly hierarchical, contained appalling levels of inequality, and offered minimal welfare assistance to its poorest citizens. In contrast, German democracy, though younger, offered the vote to more of its male citizens and as a result had a junior house of representatives dominated by Social Democrats. Germany had a much better welfare and educational system than Britain; in the war that was to come, German soldiers were repeatedly to remark on how stupid and ill-informed British prisoners were. By modern standards both countries were shockingly racist, although Britain at least made a pretence of running its imperial relations on broadly liberal principles. No matter what their separate starting points, liberal tendencies in both countries were to suffer as a result of the strains and emotional tensions of total war: both countries became increasingly restrictive and socially conservative over the four years from 1914.

Yet there were important differences. Britain actively espoused the principles of liberal democracy: it was widely assumed by 1914 that further changes to the franchise could not be far off – indeed, had it not been for the violence of the Suffragette movement, such changes might already have been in place. The British state was democratically accountable in a way that the German state was not, for the Reichstag had relatively little control over the conduct of affairs, with real power concentrated in the hands of a small group of unelected figures around the Kaiser. It was this group that was willing to accept war; that took the risks that transformed the unstable international situation of the years before 1914 into a world war. They embodied a militaristic attitude that gave primacy to the use of force and which, whilst it was not all-encompassing, permeated much of pre-war German society. In contrast, many British politicians regarded their country's much smaller armed forces with trepidation or disdain. There was, in this, the basis for a war of ideologies.[7]

It was this militaristic tendency that saw German troops advance into Belgium in 1914 with a deliberate policy of carrying out atrocities against civilians in the event of them offering resistance. The German army was worried, after its experiences in the Franco-Prussian War of 1870–71, at the prospect of facing a prolonged guerrilla war against the civilians of a country whose armies had been defeated. Such a conflict was confusing to fight, not least since the enemy did not wear a uniform, extremely difficult to win and domestically unpopular. To forestall a recurrence in 1914, German soldiers were warned of the possibility of such attacks and allowed to respond to them by carrying out deliberate acts of terror to cow the population. The taking, and if necessary the shooting, of hostages was seen as the quickest way to avoid a long struggle against *francs-tireurs*, as they were known. Their heads full of the prospect of such opposition, inexperienced German troops marched into Belgium and France in 1914. They promptly faced resistance from both the Belgian regular and territorial army (identified by their hats and armbands) and uniformed French cavalry patrols. There is no firm evidence that Belgian civilians took any part in actions against the Germans. The range of modern weapons, however, meant that in practice it was often impossible to spot the source of gunfire. Many German soldiers took this as proof that the threat they had been warned about had materialised. Rumours of Belgian *franc-tireurs* ran rife through the invading armies. The result was a series of violent incidents in which Belgian and French civilians were rounded up and shot. Although they often arose from the terror and inexperience of men new to battle, these were not just the actions of soldiers out of control of their officers: German atrocities were a matter of policy, not just panic. Whilst they did

not violate nuns, cut off children's hands or spit babies with their bayo-
nets, as later propagandists would suggest, they did murder somewhere
between 3000 and 5000 civilians, and destroy three major towns including
the historic university library of Louvain.[8]

These atrocities – or rather, exaggerated reports of their nature and
extent – helped to inflame British public opinion. Even though most
Britons had not greeted the approach or outbreak of war with wild enthusiasm, many were willing to join up when it appeared that the regular army
might be defeated and Prussian barbarism unleashed on Britain. Looking
back on a century marked with appalling atrocities, we may not feel that
the German crimes were so great in their extent, but that its to apply a
retrospective judgement. At the time, Britons saw the war in terms of a
struggle of good and evil. As the war went on, their emotions would
regularly be re-inflamed by further examples of German militarism. Some
of these were fabricated by a media keen to play up to popular conceptions and support the government. Others were based firmly in fact.
Repeatedly, the German armed forces committed acts which, whilst
many may have been legal under the terms they set themselves, demonstrated a savage disregard for liberal tenets. The shelling of civilians in
British seaside towns, the execution of Edith Cavell, the spoliation of occupied areas of France and Belgium, unrestricted U-boat warfare, not to
mention the bombing of British cities, all seemed to offer evidence of
German frightfulness.

It is also worth questioning how great the differences between Britain
and Germany actually were. Britain's naval blockade of Germany targeted
civilians because it prevented the importation of vital foodstuffs. Close to
a million German civilians may have been the victims of blockade-related
death. This form of atrocity was, however, much less visible outside
Germany itself. Deliberate acts of terror were not the exclusive preserve of
the Germans. Given the performance of elements in the British army in
South Africa, India and Ireland in the years around the First World War,
it is difficult to claim categorically that the British would not have acted in
a similar way to the Germans if it had been them invading Belgium in 1914.
But that was the point: since Britain was not trying to gain a position of
dominance in Europe by force of arms, her troops were not in the position to exercise the power of life and death over enemy civilians caught in
the combat zone.[9]

If we accept that there were justifications which underlay British participation in the war – both morally and geopolitically – it may start to look
less futile. Even if we do not, we have to recognise and offer some respect
to contemporary views that the war was justified, and to look beyond an

interpretation that suggests that the population was somehow duped into fighting a war it didn't understand.

Was the war fought in a futile fashion? The static nature of the Western Front can tempt us with a seemingly clear ratio of yards gained for lives lost. In these terms almost every attack was futile. We have to resist the temptation to apply a standard of measurement which is inappropriate. The context in which the battles were fought meant that decisive territorial advances – for all that generals sought them out – were never likely. In these circumstances, it was better for commanders to aim at the destruction of the enemy's manpower and matériel as a means of winning the war than to concentrate on moving his forces to a point where they would persuade the enemy to stop fighting: to seek attrition rather than manoeuvre.[10]

The problem with analysing the success of Britain's strategy of attrition is primarily one of definition. As the military historian David French has shown, it was a word with multiple shades of meaning even at the time, used and understood in different ways by participants in the same negotiations.[11] On occasion it was deliberately misused: mobilised by generals to persuade their political masters that the war was winnable in the near future. For different men at different times, attrition could mean the wearing out of the enemy to force the commitment of his reserves, thus allowing a decisive battle; or the conduct of limited offensives in such a way as to maximise German casualties; or the killing of sufficient Germans to prevent them launching a major assault; or the destruction of so much of the enemy army that it could not be rebuilt. It was also used as a post-facto justification to suggest that offensives which had not reached their geographical objectives had still achieved some success.

If we indulge in a sort of grisly combat accountancy, and define attrition as the attempt to kill more of the enemy than your own side loses in each engagement, or as the effort to kill so many Germans that their numbers could not be made up from new recruits coming of age, we can question whether these aims were ever actually achieved. Figures for casualties on both sides on the Western Front have been the subject for fierce debate. Any army involved in huge battles like the Somme or Third Ypres inevitably suffered very heavy losses. In most actions, however, the Allies lost more men simply because they were doing the attacking. It appears unlikely that they were ever killing so many Germans that their numbers could not be made up. It has been argued that Allied losses were in fact so high in proportion to those of the Central Powers that it was the former who were being brought closer to defeat.[12]

To judge attrition only in these terms is rather to miss the point. British strategy had to take account of a number of factors besides killing Germans in the short term: not least the need to ensure that their allies stayed in the war as long as possible. That objective could sometimes override the need to minimise British losses. Although British commanders set themselves false measures of the damage they were doing to the German army, they were doing damage nonetheless. Whether this was their primary aim or not, it was what they achieved by 1918. The immediate precursor to their final success was the heavy losses the Germans suffered when they took the offensive in the spring of that year. But the collapse of German morale in the summer would not have taken place without the suffering inflicted on them over the previous two years. A simple comparison of casualty rates and their projection into the future does not necessarily help us to understand the realities of victory and defeat on the ground. Allied casualty rates shot up, of course, in later 1918 as they began to attack. In the long term, these rates would have been unsustainable; but this was irrelevant – in the short term, the continued Allied advance forced the Germans to sue for peace.

What of that peace? Did the war achieve anything, or did it just pave the way for a second round of conflict twenty years later? We can answer yes to both questions. It is certainly possible, although not necessarily useful, to see the roots of the 1939–45 conflict in Europe in the settlement reached at Versailles in 1919. It would be rather surprising if we could not see the impact of a total war in Europe playing itself out over succeeding decades. We can also criticise some aspects of the Versailles treaty, as has been done since it was signed. The result of compromise between the widely differing aims of the Entente alliance, its objectives were ill thought out and its clauses inadequately supported. That does not mean we can use a misconstructed or mismanaged peace settlement to suggest that the war that preceded it was futile. The First World War stopped the German threat that had erupted in 1914. Perhaps that was enough. The Britons who had gone to war in 1914–18 had achieved their objective.[13]

During and after the war, most people did not go through this lengthy process of academic dissection and nitpicking over its roots and purposes. Yet the war, by its nature, persistently presented them with occasions to reassess whether it was worthwhile. Individual deaths – the loss of friends, comrades and relatives – were obviously points at which the balance could suddenly tip. National or ideological justifications for war could not meet the pain of individual sacrifice. Moments like these caused some of the most famous rejections of the war. It was the death of friends and loved ones that famously influenced Siegfried Sassoon, then a captain on the Western Front, to issue his declaration against the war, which read in part:

> I am a soldier, convinced that I am acting on behalf of soldiers. I believe that this war, upon which I entered as a war of defence and liberation, has now become a war of aggression and conquest. I believe that the purposes for which I and my fellow soldiers entered upon this war should have been so clearly stated as to have made it impossible to change them, and that, had this been done, the objects which actuated us would now be attainable by negotiation.
>
> I have seen and endured the suffering of the troops, and I can no longer be a party to prolong these sufferings for ends which I believe to be evil and unjust.[14]

Yet the author of this passionate statement was to return to the front the following year, to lead and fight again. Sassoon was not alone in feeling this disillusionment over war aims and purposes. The eponymous character of H. G. Wells's 1916 novel *Mr Britling Sees It Through*, who had started the war with high hopes and whose son serves in the trenches, declares in September 1915: 'It is now a war like any other of the mobbing, many-aimed cataclysms that have shattered empires and devastated the world; it is a war without point, a war that has lost its soul.'[15]

Uncertainty or disillusion was not the same as rejection. We need to recognise that, for many Britons, the factors that had motivated them to support the war in 1914 were sufficient to withstand the emotional shocks of four years of conflict. The heavy losses on the Somme and at Passchendaele were a reason for pessimism over the length of the war, but also for resolution on the need to continue. British hatred of German barbarism, created by sensational press reports in the early days of the war, did not cease as a result of their experiences: if anything it was heightened. The historian of men and trauma, Joanna Bourke, has quoted the distressed words of a shell-shocked soldier, written in a nurse's day book, to illustrate a point about psychological injury. In another reading, however, what is remarkable about these words is his attitude towards the enemy:

> showers of lead flying about & big shells its an unearthly sight to see them drop in amongst human beings. The cries are terrible, I escaped being hit but ... got buried once that caused me to fits ... & trip to France is nice but not when the murderers are killing anyone children included and destroys Churches. May the Lord put an unholy curse on them for ever & ever. The sights cannot be explained in writing. Writing is not my line. No fighting either. For they that wants to let them fight because I will never like it no no never.[16]

The trauma suffered by Private Lucas and his personal aversion to further combat come across in his writing. So too does his anger at the men whose murders and desecrations led to him going to France. It is hard to imagine that, at the time he wrote, Lucas saw his own service in terms of benefits outweighing costs, but he certainly seems to have felt that war against the Germans was justified.

Bereavement could itself be a powerful reason for continued support of the war. Since the dead had gone to serve their country in a just cause, to lose faith in the struggle would be to betray them. This is the principal emotion behind John McCrae's popular poem 'In Flanders Fields', albeit that it is encapsulated in a final verse which is now seldom quoted:

> Take up our quarrel with the foe:
> To you from failing hands we throw
> The torch; be yours to hold it high.
> If ye break faith with us who die
> We shall not sleep, though poppies grow
> In Flanders fields.[17]

The notion of the dead having sacrificed themselves in a worthy cause was to be an enduring one.

As the realities of the post-war world hit home, it was natural for Britons to ask why they had entered the war and what, if anything, they had gained. The negative effects of the war were abundantly obvious, as the combination of demobilised wounded soldiers and economic hardship left homeless ex-servicemen on street corners. The tangible benefits, for most, were much less apparent. The scale of British losses made it hard to describe war in terms of a hoped for, necessary national cleansing, as had been possible before 1914. Even those men and women who had found fulfilment or enjoyment in their duties and their identity as part of a greater machine struggled to make sense of what they had done. Looking back at the war, Britons drew their own conclusions about what it had meant. Personal experience during and after the war, political orientation, location and audience could all affect whether they thought it had all been worthwhile or not.

Throughout the 1920s and 1930s it is possible to find examples of Britons questioning the war's purpose, rationale or results, or expressing the heartfelt belief that all war was wasteful or useless. At the dedication of the war memorial outpatients' department at the hospital in Ilford, in 1923, the mayor of West Ham, Will Thorne, declared that the war 'was a wicked waste of money and a wicked waste of life, and if people only had the common sense they ought to have, the millions spent on building armaments would be devoted to social purposes and bettering the conditions of the workers'.[18] Thorne was a socialist who had supported the war whilst it was being fought, and had lost a son at Passchendaele. In the post-war context of the opening of a utilitarian war memorial, he was able to use a representation of the war as a waste to reinforce his political views and status.

The economic slump that followed the war was a harsh introduction to the post-war world. By 1921, 11 per cent of the British workforce was unemployed. Three years later, the figure remained above 7 per cent.[19] Although job levels improved in the later 1920s, the impact of the Great Depression meant that in the years after 1930 unemployment rose once again to 15 per cent.[20] According to one contemporary survey, 58 per cent of those unemployed were former soldiers.[21] Unsurprisingly, many veterans wondered whether the four years of their lives they had given up in the service of their country had been worthwhile when they found themselves penniless and hungry. The high ideals that had underpinned participation in the war had raised unattainable expectations for what would be achieved in its aftermath. Notoriously, the promise of 'homes fit for heroes' did not seem to have been fulfilled for many returning servicemen. Such reassessments were encouraged by the revelation in the 1920s of the discords amongst senior leaders, as well as the post-war writings of journalists such as Philip Gibbs, who renounced his romanticised wartime reports in ringing tones.[22] There was widespread interest in the causes of the war, and a growing willingness to ascribe its causes to influences other than the national interest and a popular eagerness to fight. Should not the blame really be attached to secret or incompetent diplomacy, or to shadowy cabals of capitalists who would benefit from the war?

In his 1933 comic novel *England, Their England*, A. G. Macdonell describes the visit of his hero, Donald Cameron, to a sleepy English village. Donald goes into the local pub, filled with the village elders. Discussing the changes that the war has brought about, they argue that the war has done none of them any good. Donald tries to suggest the importance of treaties, Belgium and national honour. One of the ancients, Mr Stillaway, replies:

> 'But can you tell me, sir, what national honour does for me? I've worked on the land all my life, and the least I've ever earned is four-and-six a week and the most is twenty-nine shillings. It isn't a fortune, either of them. In 1914 a man comes down to the green here, and he makes a speech about just that national honour that you've been talking about. Mind you, sir, in 1914 the nation and all its honour was giving me twenty-two shillings a week and I was working seventy-four hours a week for it. But I had to give three sons and eight grandsons to fight for the national honour. Eleven of them. And three were killed and two lost legs. And what good did that do to them or to me or Mr Davis here, or Mr Darley? Cost of living is higher. Beer is more expensive and

so is tobacco. And my grandsons, the ones that weren't killed, can't get work. And all that for what you call national honour.'[23]

Macdonell, like Donald, had fought in the war. He later stood as a Liberal candidate. His book neither condones nor dismisses Mr Stillaway's opinion. Donald can find no answer to him, but the impact of these words is then undercut by Mr Darley's immediate suggestion that Britain should have been fighting the French ('never any use to us') instead. What is powerfully put forward in the passage above is a body of thought that the bargain had not been fulfilled: that the huge wartime sacrifices of the nation had warranted social improvements that had not occurred. These were arguments which acquired a new resonance as it appeared more likely that Britain might have to enter into another European war in the mid 1930s.

In practice, however, it could be difficult to describe the most recent conflict as 'futile' in public. Simultaneously with this questioning of the war's purpose, there had grown a powerful rhetoric that explained it in terms of sacrifice and redemption. The First World War resulted in a vast quantity of commemoration based around monuments and rituals, from the makeshift roadside shrines which grew up during the war through to the more permanent and elaborate memorials that were erected in the 1920s. Neither imposed from above nor created individually in isolation, memorials involved an interaction of national, communal and individual attempts to give meaning to wartime death.[24]

It was often in the very process of involvement with the design and creation of these monuments, and the ceremonies around them, that individuals found an expression for their bereavement. They tended to work, however, from a set of concepts of design and wording held in common. Across the country, local war memorials interpreted the war in traditional terms of national identity, loyalty, bravery and personal sacrifice in the service of justice, liberty and dignity. They ascribed a positive meaning to the war. Death in the cause of liberty and future generations was not in vain. For example, the walled Garden of Remembrance at Todmorden, in Yorkshire, commemorates the dead with a fountain sculpted in 1924 by Gilbert Bayes. The wall behind it holds the inscription:

THESE ARE THEY WHO BEING PEACEABLE CITIZENS OF TODMORDEN, AT THE CALL OF KING AND COUNTRY AND IN DEFENCE OF THEIR NATIVE LAND, LEFT ALL THAT WAS DEAR TO THEM, ENDURED HARDSHIP, FACED DANGER AND FINALLY PASSED OUT OF SIGHT OF MAN BY THE PATH OF DUTY AND SELF-SACRIFICE, GIVING UP THEIR OWN LIVES THAT OTHERS MIGHT LIVE IN FREEDOM.

More simply, the Reigate and Redhill memorial featured a figure on a granite plinth inscribed: 'COURAGE, HONOUR and SELF-SACRIFICE'.[25]

These memorials elicited a powerful emotional reaction from those who took part in commemoration, whether or not they personally had lost relatives. Post-war ceremonies did not necessarily include everybody, but they did attract at least passive participation from most Britons. They were a significant means by which a younger generation were educated in what the war had meant. The commonly expressed idea, that young Britons owed a debt of loyalty to the men who had sacrificed their lives for the liberty of future generations, bound them together in a concept of duty and responsibility.

There were, of course, many who were able to contest this rhetoric of remembrance: who believed that deaths had been in vain, soldiers deceived and effort wasted. That they did not do so more publicly or dramatically can be explained by the powerful taboo exerted by those presumed to be the key beneficiaries of remembrance; the bereaved parents of dead soldiers. There was a strong cultural tradition of respect for the emotional needs of this group. Many of them did, indeed, seem to derive comfort from the idea that their sons' deaths had been meaningful. It would have been cruel to deny them that belief. In the words of the *Ilford Recorder* of November 1928: 'Our hearts go out to those who are now going down the hill of life, without the comfort and support of those they loved and tended from birth.'[26] The vicar of St Andrew's, Bethnal Green, pointed out that: 'Armistice Day has many tender memories for the passing generation; many of our mothers and fathers look back to the children who gave their lives at the call of their country's need.'[27] When, on Armistice Night 1921, the Revd G. A. Studdert Kennedy described the war as 'futile' in a public meeting in Westminster Hall, he was rebuked by the next speaker, the Revd Dick Sheppard, for the offence that he might have caused to bereaved relatives. He hoped 'that no mother who had lost a son or wife her husband would go home with the impression as he feared they might that those lives had been given in vain'.[28] Sheppard was also one of those who led the campaign against frivolous Armisticetide parties in the mid 1920s. He was later to become a major figure in the pacifist movement in the 1930s, when he argued that, to validate soldiers' deaths, it was necessary to struggle against war in the future. Like many others, he worked to construct a meaning for wartime death. The rhetorical framework erected around remembrance was intended to act as a consolation to those bereaved by the war.

Alongside war memorials and ceremonies that honoured and validated death in battle, books, plays, newspapers and comics ascribed positive meaning to the war and continued to represent it in terms of a justified struggle against barbaric opponents. Boys' papers left their readers in little doubt about the justifications for fighting a heroic war. R. C. Sherriff's play *Journey's End*, Ernest Raymond's very successful book *Tell England*, and the films of both, explicitly depicted the war in terms of Christian redemptive sacrifice and made use of traditional visions of heroism.[29] This was not the pious preaching of those who had taken advantage of soldiers' sacrifices to stay at home in safety: Sherriff and Raymond had each served in the front line.

Tell England's hero, Edgar Doe, dies at the end of the book, fatally wounded whilst storming a Turkish gun position on the Gallipoli peninsula that has killed his friends. The book's narrator, Ray, discusses with the padre, Monty, the validity of Doe's death:

> 'There's no beauty in death and burial and corruption.' I said.
> 'Yes, there is, even in them. There's beauty in thinking that the same material which goes to make these earthy hills and that still water should have been shaped into a graceful body, and lit with the divine spark that was Edgar Doe. There's beauty in thinking that, when the unconquerable spark has escaped away, the material is returned to the earth, where it urges its life, also an unconquerable thing; into grass and flowers. It's harmonious – it's beautiful.'[30]

This comforting vision of death redeemed by time and nature was extremely popular in Britain between the wars. *Tell England* remained constantly in print until the 1940s and had sold 300,000 copies by 1939.[31] But it represented the extreme end of the spectrum. For many other writers, the desire not to offend the bereaved did not prevent a continued questioning of what the war had actually achieved. Because 'futility' could cover a variety of topics, it was perfectly possible to use the word 'futile' about one aspect of the war whilst not applying it to another. Here once again we encounter the range of views about the war which was so typical of Britain in the 1920s and 1930s. Carey and Scott, the veteran schoolmasters who wrote a school textbook on the war, clearly believed in the valour of British soldiers but could not bring themselves to argue that the achievements of the Somme had been worth the cost: 'The military result seems utterly lacking in proportion. It weighs hardly at all against the expense of the heroic spirit of the nation, the blood of its best youth, the tears of their beloved.'[32] Grief was persistent.

In their books about the war, both Churchill and Lloyd George were harshly critical of what they described as a strategy of attrition. Churchill went to great lengths to research the comparative figures for casualties in order to prove that attrition was militarily futile because it killed more Britons than Germans. But neither disputed the need for the war: on the contrary, both continued to believe that the war as a whole had been necessary and fought in a worthy cause against a barbaric enemy. No matter what criticisms they launched against those who had arranged, organised or managed the war, neither was willing to declare that deaths in battle had been futile. The language used by both about the dead depicted them in terms of traditional heroism. Indeed, it was almost a prerequisite for criticism of the war's management to emphasise the bravery and dignity of those who had died; their sacrifice could not be robbed of meaning.[33]

This public version of the war, formed by the mid 1920s, that redeemed death by stressing self-sacrifice and purpose, was extremely strong. Subsequent influences would see it developed, but it would not disappear. The international uncertainties of the 1930s, and growing fear of another European conflict, encouraged a pacifist element in British thought. Particularly in the early 1930s, when the threats that might be posed to Britain were still largely theoretical, a number of bodies expressed pacifist sentiments – including the famous 1933 Oxford Union resolution that 'This house will in no circumstances fight for its King and Country'. A well-organised campaign encouraged Britons to take part in the Peace Pledge: declaring that they would not fight in a future war. Millions signed the Pledge. A great deal of the support which they received seems to have resulted from the precise terms in which pacifism was represented, in particular to the middle classes, and the lack of a specific threat to Britain. It was easy – indeed, it was natural, fifteen years after the First World War – to express a hatred of war in general. To what degree this represented a complete rejection of war is, however, open to question. As the specific threat from Germany grew clearer in the later 1930s, Britons seem to have become resigned to the fact that they would have to fight again.

The pacifist movements of the 1930s depicted war as a wasteful exercise that solved nothing. The discussions attendant on the growth of popular pacifism in the mid 1930s were often predicated on the basis that the war to end all wars had not only failed in its objective, but had been so wasteful that it must never be repeated again. As the emotional furore of the war weakened, it became easier to represent it as a tragic accident that had gone against the human instincts of its participants. As school textbook written in 1936 for eleven year olds suggested: 'In all countries men who fought did not want to kill each other; they were caught up in something bigger than their private wishes ... In all countries men long that peace may not again be broken.'[34] Here was a vision of futility used as a warning to a younger generation.

Yet even the most ardent pacifists were reluctant to deny the war any meaning at all.[35] Examining the Mass-Observation participants' reactions to

Armistice Day in the 1930s, in particular their continuing concern for the need to respect those who had lost loved ones, it is easy to understand why. Instead, pacifists revalidated death in battle on their own terms: men had sacrificed their lives in an effort to prevent future wars. As early as 1932, a *Times* correspondent commented on changing attitudes to Armistice Day. Some, he thought, would 'more cynically declare that we have learned by this time that the Great War was a great blunder, and the less said about it the better'. Older readers, he suggested, would think more kindly of soldiers, 'recalling ... much that was done bravely and unselfishly'. But he emphasised that remembrance of the war included a contemporary relevance for a younger generation:

> For them also Armistice Day has its significance, even if it be only a grim warning of the futility of war and of the diplomacy that is selfish and seeks only material advantage.
>
> All those young lives with their promise of service and happiness sacrificed, and mankind not saved, are not wasted if they set the feet of their successors upon the way of peace.[36]

The historian of culture and of war Mark Connelly has suggested that the Second World War provided the British people with a 'yardstick of futility' against which to judge the First. Compared to its predecessor it was more clearly fought in a good cause against a dreadful enemy, to counter a direct threat to the British Isles.[37] After 1945 – and particularly following the public revelation of the Holocaust and Japanese mistreatment of prisoners of war – it was certainly the case that the Second World War was easily portrayed as, in A. J. P. Taylor's phrase, a 'noble crusade'.[38] The comparison worked both ways, however, particularly during the war, as the British used the earlier conflict to understand and to justify their experiences. In the process, they rehearsed a set of beliefs about what the First World War had been like and what it had meant. The effect was to emphasise its futility.[39]

In his poem 'To a Conscript of 1940', Herbert Read, a veteran of the First World War, instructed a later generation of soldiers in the lessons his had learned.

> We think we gave in vain. The world was not renewed.
> There was hope in the homestead and violence in the streets
> But the old world was restored and we returned
> To the dreary field and workshop and the immemorial feud
>
> Of rich and poor. Our victory was our defeat.
> Power was retained where power had been misused

> And youth was left to sweep away
> The ashes that the fires had strewn beneath our feet.[40]

Read's conclusion – that service, however inglorious or unproductive, might in any case be necessary and honourable – was not one which had much emotional appeal or which could be used to mobilise the population into uniform or munitions factories. Much more powerful was the belief that this time things must be different. Ernest Bevin, Minister of Labour, cried when, whilst he was watching troops getting ready to embark for D-Day, someone shouted out: 'Ernie, when we have done this job for you, are we going back on the dole?' They did not: with the model of post-1918 Britain in their minds, the one thing the 1945 government was not going to do was allow widespread unemployment or deprivation.[41]

The dark days of 1940 and the long slog that followed forced the British government and people to make frequent recourse to a set of myths about their national past. Some of these had been built up over the *longue durée*: that Britain was at its best as an underdog, that she would win through in the end, and that she was best off without the burden of untrustworthy foreign allies. But others had a conceptual basis in the more recent past. There were two great myths which helped to mobilise the British population: first, that the war was a unifying experience, being fought by the people, for the people, and that, as a result, it would have a transformative effect; secondly, that social change would have to result from popular participation in total war.[42] Such myths required an opposition to give them full effect. Popular notions of the aftermath of the First World War, in particular the betrayal of soldiers' sacrifice by the economic deprivations of the 1920s and 1930s, helped Britons to define the results they expected from this second conflict. The cry of 'Never Again', so resonant to that wartime generation, was not just about the need to avoid another devastating war.[43] Rather, it encapsulated a belief that the effort of a previous war had been wasted and that this time things would change. Whether or not these myths accurately reflected the results of the First World War or the degree of social unity and change resulting from the Second was less important than the motivational role they fulfilled. Nevertheless, one of the effects of their use seems to have been to strengthen the idea that the First World War had been futile. The use of this negative myth for a positive purpose has gone largely uncommented on by historians of the First World War. They have been so focused on the need to disprove the 'futility' myth – to demonstrate that the First World War was worthwhile – that they have missed the degree to which the subsequent employment of the myth is itself of interest.

In a different context, the end of the 1950s and the 1960s saw British popular culture making recourse to these underlying myths once more. Reviews of Alan Clark's *The Donkeys* in 1961 suggested that analysing military incompetence in 1915 was worthwhile because of what it could teach the modern world about the dangers of nuclear holocaust. In constructing the stage version of *Oh What a Lovely War*, Joan Littlewood's preoccupation was less the spirit of war past than that of the war yet to come. Much though parts of the play might concentrate on the experience of men in war, this particular war had been selected for another reason: 'the whole business – the accidents, the chaos, the small minority who were really for it – seems to be more like what we are trying to avoid now than the last war ...'[44] Given the background to the play's production, in particular the Cuban missile crisis and developing American involvement in Vietnam, it could be argued that references to the approach of a new war had a special power. This emphasis – the play as warning – is apparent several times in the script:

> KAISER: War is unthinkable. It is out of the question.
> FRENCHMAN: It would upset the balance of power.
> BRITAIN: It would mean ruin of the world, undoubtedly.
> FRENCHMAN: Besides, our alliances make us secure.
> KAISER: But if you threaten us, we have the supreme deterrent, which we will not hesitate to use ...
> MC: Ssh ... secret.[45]

The programme drove the point home:

> In 1960 an American Military Research Team fed all the facts of World War One into the computers they use to plan World War Three. They reached the conclusion that the 1914–18 war was impossible and couldn't have happened. There could not have been so many blunders nor so many casualties.
> Will there be a computer left to analyse World War Three ?[46]

Littlewood was reviving a set of myths which went back to the political and moral rejection of the war in the 1930s, even if she expressed them in much more brutal terms.

A. J. P. Taylor liked the play so much that he dedicated his *Illustrated History of the First World War* to Littlewood. Taylor had grown up during the war at a Quaker school. He had been sent there because of his mother's revulsion at the treatment of her brother, a conscientious objector. Having established himself as a leading historian of nineteenth-century Europe, by 1963 he was already revelling in the role of historical maverick, lecturing to the masses on television and radio and in newspapers, attracting the disdain and envy of his colleagues in equal measure.[47]

Hired that year to churn out a few words to accompany a volume of photographs produced by the publisher George Rainbird, Taylor not only took the project seriously, but insisted on composing the captions for the illustrations as well.[48] The result was the *Illustrated History of the First World War*, a unique work which combines a tone of sharp cynicism with a highly readable style. Taylor can be criticised for his sometimes sweeping judgement in areas in which he was not a specialist, as well as occasional lapses of accuracy, but his provocative approach did not preclude efforts at balanced judgements on events and personalities. Concise but not corrupted, Taylor's work was a model of history not just popular but popularising. His captions to the photographs are the icing on the cynical cake. Taylor proved incapable of restraining his wit with regard to photos of Sir John French leaving the War Office at a run ('in training for the retreat from Mons'), or the philandering Prime Minister inspecting factory workers in 1917 ('Lloyd George casts an expert eye over munitions girls').[49] This palpable lack of deference itself seems to mark a departure from previous historical representations of the war.

In the *Illustrated History* Taylor frequently describes the war in terms of purposelessness and futility:

> No one asked what the war was about. The Germans had started the war in order to win; the Allies fought so as not to lose. Of course the French hoped to recover Alsace and Lorraine; the British were determined to liberate Belgium. But these were not enough in themselves; they were the symbols of victory, not the reason why it was being pursued.

'Winning the war was the end in itself.' Third Ypres had been 'the blindest slaughter of a blind war'. Yet hidden in the closing pages was his judgement that the war had useful results, not least the temporary halting of militant German expansionism. And whilst he condemned the generals, he also pointed out that their failings were common across the combatants and argued that politicians, as well as generals, were to blame. Taylor's righteous anger and phrasemaking ability may, however, have got the better of his historical analysis, not only in his writing but in the understanding of his audience.[50]

Taylor's work is infuriating to those with a detailed knowledge of the events of the First World War because it operates at two levels. There is a deeper undercurrent of historical understanding which is expressed in more superficial terms. Many of Taylor's opinions are highly debatable contentions – but he expresses them with the confidence of fact. The qualifying statements that a more painstaking – and less readable – historian would have wanted to insert are absent.

Perhaps unsurprisingly, given his passionate involvement with the Campaign for Nuclear Disarmament (CND), Taylor used the First World War as an object lesson in the failure of deterrence and the shortsightedness of wartime leaders. He had been trying out these ideas in print for a number of years. In a series of articles for the *Observer* on the outbreak of war, published in 1958, he had argued that deterrence simply did not work. 'The statesmen of Europe, with one accord, accepted the theory of "the deterrent": the more strongly and firmly they threatened, the more likely they were to preserve the peace and get their own way.'[51] He was less expert on the events of the war itself, and sought Basil Liddell Hart's help in correcting his manuscript. Liddell Hart removed some but not all of the errors of fact contained in the book.[52]

Rather like Liddell Hart's *The Real War* in 1930, Taylor had a heavy influence upon subsequent attitudes to the war because he had produced a popular, readable, single-volume history of the war at a point of public interest. The *Illustrated History* sold well from its publication and has a claim to be the single most widely read historical book on the war.[53] It has exerted further influence on public attitudes as a result of its use as an authoritative source of information and opinions for subsequent works of popular history and fiction. Since both are easily accessible, it has often been used in conjunction with Liddell Hart's book as one of two authoritative sources of opinion on the war, as in Norman Dixon's famous work on generals' blunders, *On the Psychology of Military Incompetence*.[54] Unsurprisingly, despite the two men's differences of opinion, for example over the primacy of the Western Front, the two books' contentions about the High Command and the futility of the military effort on the Western Front seem to back each other up. The quotation from Taylor used by Dixon as an epigraph for his chapter on the First World War recalls Churchill or Forester on the incomprehension of the generals: 'The opposing lines congealed, grew solid. The generals on both sides stared at these impotently and without understanding. They went on staring for nearly four years.'[55]

Referring to such sources should highlight for us the degree to which Taylor's book represented a reworking of texts produced between the wars, rather than a piece of original research. It was this sense of familiarity that allowed Paul Johnson, reviewing the *Illustrated History* for the *New Statesman*, to offer the downbeat assessment that 'Mr Taylor's essay is a fairly conventional summary of contemporary attitudes towards the Great War'.[56]

Other reviewers were more enthusiastic, but it is worth taking Johnson's comment at face value and attempting to investigate further what some of those contemporary attitudes were. One way to do so is to examine the research undertaken by the Church of England when it considered rewriting the Remembrance Day service in the 1960s. That the service might need to be changed to keep it relevant to a younger generation of Britons had been a persistent worry for the Church since the 1950s, but firm action was only initiated in the latter half of the 1960s. The Archbishop of Canterbury's Private Secretary, Robert Beloe, asked the advice of leading media figures, including Cecil King, chairman of the IPC, which owned the *Sun* and the *Daily Mirror*, and Kenneth Adam of the BBC. Their responses paint a picture of a generational divide with regard to the First World War. King's

> immediate reaction was that he knew what the young of this country thought and wanted, sixteen million of them read the *Daily Mirror*. They are not interested in past wars except as mistakes of their forebears. They are not, therefore, in any way penitent and they are not particularly anxious to dedicate themselves. The thing which hangs over their consciousness, or subconsciousness, is the atom bomb and the possibility that this country may be an atomic desert any week. They would, therefore, be interested to some extent in peace.[57]

The BBC painted a slightly different picture:

> it was to be noted that the curiously jumbled Remembrance Day programme in the Albert Hall, which was televised annually, was among the most popular programmes on the television to the continuing surprise of the BBC. The size of the audience on 12th November, 1966 between 7 and 8 pm was 12½ million, or 25% of the population, and between 8 and 9 pm 12 million, or 24% of the population. The 'reaction index' was 75. They reckoned that a reaction of 65 was extremely favourable so this was an especially favourable reaction. He agreed that people under the age of thirty were not in the least interested in the Cenotaph Service or other commemorations of those who died in the two wars.[58]

It certainly appeared to many at the time that the young had lost touch with the 'meaning' of remembrance. Yet this was a relative judgement. In response to encouragement from the Church of England, the *Times* commissioned a survey of young people aged nine to thirty in Birmingham and Solihull in early November 1967. The newspaper reported that fewer than half considered Remembrance Day worthwhile, and some of those who did qualified their answers with statements like: 'It is a monument to human folly, but it is rather glorifying it' or 'It serves to remind us of the horrors of war, but far from discouraging military attitudes, it has a tendency to eulogise the dead as having died "for a worthwhile cause" whereas all they died for was to serve as a monument to mass incalculable folly'. Those who answered with comments such as: 'They died so that we can live in freedom and this is something that cannot be forgotten' may have been referring to the Second rather than the First World War.

Looking at the results of the survey more closely, however, we can see a complex situation. Questioned about their recognition of names from the two world wars, 27 per cent of those questioned could identify the Battle of Mons, 45 per cent the Red Baron, 48 per cent the Battle of the Somme, 21 per cent Douglas Haig and 34 per cent the Battle of Jutland. In contrast, from the Second World War, only 14 per cent identified Goebbels, 55 per cent Rommel, 39 per cent Tobruk, 20 per cent Arnhem and 67 per cent a Hurricane fighter. Bearing in mind that nearly fifty years had passed since the First World War and only twenty since the Second, this does not seem to be evidence that the earlier conflict was being forgotten. Similarly, 47 per cent of those questioned thought that Remembrance Day was 'a touching and worthwhile occasion', and only 12 per cent of answers contained a strong anti-war element.[59]

At the time, the Church faced considerable inertia from the Home Office and Buckingham Palace – both crucial constituents in any change to such ceremonies – on the basis that neither was willing to risk offending survivors and bereaved relatives of the First World War (a matter close to home, since the Queen Mother had lost a brother to the war).[60] The changes to the Remembrance ceremony, when they came, were minor – the removal of six hymns judged too nationalistic or triumphalist and their replacement with others that emphasised peace and brotherhood. In fact, any change at local ceremonies remained at the discretion of those conducting the ceremony.[61]

The 1960s saw the reuse of myths that had first appeared between the wars, together with evidence of a generational divide in attitudes towards the First World War, but it is hard to interpret the decade as one purely of new departures in the understanding of the war in terms of futility. Strong undercurrents from previous discourse remained in place: there was at least as much continuity as change. What the period did see was a change in expression, with many more Britons now being willing to say publicly, without qualification, that the war as a whole, rather than the military effort alone, had been futile. This was exemplified by audience reactions to the BBC's 1964 *The Great War* series: 'the horror of trench warfare and the appalling and needless slaughter of innocent people'; 'This series should be seen by *all* to bring home the horrors of war and the dreadful waste of young manhood'.[62]

What were the reasons behind this shift in expression? One explanation may be that public attitudes had changed as a result of intervening events and experiences. Just as with the development of the image of generals as donkeys, so with regard to futility, texts from the 1960s have become seen as crucial points in the development of contemporary myths of the First World War. They are seen as symptomatic of the development of a widespread anti-war movement, resulting from revulsion at the losses of two world wars, the beaming of images from conflicts around the globe into Britain's domestic TV sets and a widespread fear of nuclear holocaust, represented in radical new ways by a liberal media elite.

The Second World War undoubtedly affected the attitudes to war of those who experienced it at first hand. It introduced British civilians to the damage that could be inflicted by modern weapons to a far greater degree than had occurred in the First World War. The inhabitants of blitzed towns were well qualified to argue against war. Yet few at the time or since made reference to the losses of the Second World War as an example of futile sacrifice. When some Britons once again wanted to make those arguments therefore – as they did in the 1960s as the Cold War developed and seemed to run the risk of turning hot – it should not surprise us that they looked back fifty years to the First World War.

The impact of the two great conflicts of the time – the Cold War and its hot sub-variant in Vietnam – is hard to judge. CND had enjoyed considerable support in the late 1950s, but by the early 1960s it was falling apart in a mixture of failed hopes and internal wrangles.[63] Far from increasing its strength, the Cuban missile crisis of 1962 seems to have marked CND's temporary demise, until its resurrection in the 1980s. It made two points clear: that nuclear war was not the inevitable result of a confrontation between the superpowers, but also that Britain's influence on any such situation was limited.

This resignation to impotence did not, of course, preclude a fear of nuclear obliteration; an underlying concern that lay at the back of many British minds throughout the period. Even if this fear was only brought to the forefront of their thoughts at times of international tension or public controversy, the existence of nuclear weapons made it abundantly clear to most Britons that involvement in a future global conflict would indeed be futile: what benefits could match the cost of domestic destruction?[64] The existence of atomic and then nuclear weapons did affect any discussion about the utility of a future global war, but we need to be careful about assuming that it universally affected attitudes towards previous conflicts.

In contrast to an interpretation that emphasises anti-war protest, we can examine the degree to which Britons accepted that a nuclear war might occur and trained to fight it. The Civil Defence Corps – which was intended to provide expanded fire, police, rescue and medical services in the event of another global conflict – began recruiting at the end of 1949. Within a year it numbered over 61,000 men and women. By 1960, 360,000 Britons were members of the Corps – far more than involved themselves with anti-nuclear demonstrations. Although the Corps' numbers were thereafter rapidly reduced, this was a result of government cutbacks, based on the recognition of how ineffective any such measures would actually be, rather than any lack of popular enthusiasm. The commitment required of Civil Defence Corps members was only a few hours a month and their motivations varied; but their numbers imply that the great popular reaction to nuclear weapons, at least initially, was preparation for war not pacifism.[65]

The Vietnam War resulted in shocking images in newspapers and on television, but in the end it was a conflict far away in which Britain was not directly involved. It is remarkably difficult to find any comparisons being made between the Vietnam War and previous conflicts at this time. The war inspired protests, it is true, but only by members of a metropolitan elite who cannot be judged as representative of wider opinion. In contrast to the Cold War, Vietnam excited fewer immediate comparisons with the First World War. The involvement of British servicemen in the conflicts of decolonisation and the end of national service may have affected how war was talked about at the time: but no detailed study of these phenomena in this context has been undertaken.[66]

Did new radicalism in art encourage the production of anti-war texts? Again, it is necessary to reconsider how culturally radical the 1960s actually were. Changes in what could be publicly represented offered artists greater freedom of expression, but there was no guarantee that their audience would react positively. The film *How I Won the War*, released in 1967, aimed to show the futility of war through an exercise in Brechtian alienation, but as Richard Lester, its director, noted: 'One has learned over the years that Brechtian alienation is a euphemism for audiences' backs seen disappearing down a street.'[67]

In contrast, we can point to a host of examples from popular culture in the 1960s that seem to suggest a continued interest in traditional themes of adventure, violence and heroism. The top box office performers of the 1960s were the James Bond films *Dr No, From Russia With Love, Goldfinger, Thunderball* and *You Only Live Twice*. Bond as played by Sean Connery was a development in the heroic ideal, to include a distinct element of thuggishness, but his popularity was hardly evidence of a turn away from violence carried out in the name of the state.[68] 1960 saw the launch of a comic for boys, *Victor*, whose main story each week was based on the true story of a British soldier's medal-winning heroism in conflicts earlier that century. There was little room for irony or anti-war sentiment here. *Victor*'s popularity saw it published for more than thirty years, introducing whole generations of boys to the idea that war was a heroic adventure. Although later, in the 1970s, more graphically violent comics did feature First World War soldiers who had to fight against staff officers as well as Germans, the Great War heroes who appeared in *Victor* had no thought of disobedience or mutiny.[69]

One explanation for the continuing belief in more traditional representations of valour and sacrifice in war, and a rejection – at least implicitly – of more extreme expressions of the war's futility, may have been the continuing part played by wartime victories in British national identity. As the pace of Britain's imperial decline quickened, so did challenges to Britons' well-established conception of themselves as 'Top Nation'. Yet there was room to bolster a threatened sense of national grandeur through reminders of the part Britons had played in preserving democracy and fighting dictatorship. If popular conceptions of this role naturally centred on Britain's 'Finest Hour' in 1940, this did not completely obscure memories of the part she had played twenty years earlier. It was, after all, *two* world wars that partnered her one world cup in popular memory.

More important in shaping the tone of discussions about the futility of the First World War in the 1960s was the disappearance of that generation of bereaved parents whose presence had exercised such a restraining influence in the 1920s and 1930s. Whilst they were alive, critical statements about the war could not be too harsh, lest they further distress this group. It is possible to gain an indication of their numbers through the figures produced by the Ministry of Pensions for payments to the dependent parents of ex-servicemen. These figures show a dramatic slump in the numbers of this generation in the period just after the Second World War. Simply, they had reached an age where they started to die in very large numbers.[70] The extinction of this group removed a key limiting factor on the terms in which the First World War could be discussed. Opinions that had been held in private before might now be expressed more openly. Those who sought publicity through an open and extremist condemnation of the war or its management no longer needed to restrain their venom.

One of the most convincing pieces of evidence for the effect of this generational shift is an absence. The consistent discussion of the need to avoid offending bereaved parents, so influential between the wars, disappears from the popular cultural record. The new texts produced in the 1960s did not rely for their success on a wholesale acceptance of their interpretation; the reception of *Oh What a Lovely War* makes it plain that audiences were capable of rewriting the script of a play to fit their own preconceptions in any case. These works did depend on not causing such widespread offence that they were publicly censured or banned. The ease with which it could now be suggested that the war had been utterly meaningless distinguished the period from the mid 1950s onwards from that which had preceded it.

Negative myths about the war gained in strength throughout the 1970s and 1980s through a mixture of utility and repetition. The ratcheting up of Cold

War tension led to the revival of CND and other forms of anti-nuclear protest. There was a fresh need for an example of the futility of war – a need filled by the portrayal of the First World War over the previous twenty years. Even if Taylor's *Illustrated History* and *Oh What a Lovely War* were not representative of attitudes at the time they were published, they came to dominate subsequent opinion because of their ubiquity. At the same time, however, Britons retained many of the ambiguous attitudes which they had exhibited over the previous seventy years towards the dead, and towards the lessons that should be drawn from the war. As an example of that, we can turn to the final episode of the 1989 BBC TV comedy series *Blackadder Goes Forth*.

Blackadder makes a clear case for the futility of the war on the Western Front. The primary aim of offensives is 'to move General Haig's drinks cabinet six inches closer to Berlin'. The war is also pointless for those fighting it, because they cannot understand why it began:

BALDRICK: I heard it started when some chap called Archie Duke shot an ostrich because he was hungry.

BLACKADDER: I think you mean it started when the Arch-Duke of Austro-Hungary got shot.

BALDRICK: No – there was definitely an ostrich involved.

BLACKADDER: Well, possibly. But the real reason for the whole thing was that it was just too much effort not to have a war.[71]

There follows an explanation of the rival blocs of world powers and the failure of deterrence straight out of *Oh What a Lovely War*.

At the end of the episode in which this discussion takes place, the last in the series, occurs a final scene which in 2000 was voted amongst the ten most popular television moments of all time.[72] With their plans for escape having failed, the cast, with the exception of General Melchett, gather together in the trench before going over the top for the big push and certain death. The guns fall silent. Has the war ended? Temporarily they seem ready to celebrate the miraculous end of 'The Great War, 1914–1917', before Blackadder points out that in fact: 'The guns have stopped because we are about to attack. Not even our generals are mad enough to shell their own men. They feel it's more sporting to let the Germans do it.' Ignoring a last chance to feign injury and escape, the company heads over the top:

Blackadder blows his whistle. There is a roar of voices – everyone leaps up the ladders. As they rise above the sandbags they are met by thunderous machine gun fire.

Blackadder, Baldrick, George and Darling run on, brandishing their handguns.
They will not get far.
Silence falls. Our soldiers fade away. No Man's Land turns slowly into a peaceful
field of poppies. The only sound is that of a bird, singing sweetly.[73]

As the *Sun* leader put it the next day: 'The last shot ... was so poignant that
if you cried it was no surprise.'[74] The *Sunday Times* reviewer said that Elton
and Curtis's ending was not only poignant but 'with Remembrance Day so
close, it was properly responsible'.[75] In a much related anecdote, Geoffrey
Elton, Regius Professor of History at Cambridge and Ben Elton's uncle,
wrote to him when the series began, to suggest the First World War was not
a suitable subject for satire. The final episode, apparently, made him take it
all back: his nephew had been respectful enough in his treatment of the
dead.[76]

The unanimous celebration of this scene has hidden the degree to which
it undermines the subversive and cynical approach of the rest of the series.
The main characters, even the previously villainous and cowardly staff officer, are brought together for the assault. The attack, and the presumed death
of the heroes, is less than graphic: they disappear, to be transformed by the
passage of time into a traditional symbol of remembrance, a field of poppies.
This is a vision of death redeemed by nature and time which fits with that in
Ernest Raymond's *Tell England*, published sixty-seven years before.

Even as *Blackadder Goes Forth* was broadcast for the first time, wider
developments were under way that would revitalise remembrance of
the First World War and demonstrate the continuing ambiguity over the
meaning of the war. A campaign by the British Legion to renew public recognition of Remembrance Sunday and revive poppy sales, memorably fronted
by the Spice Girls, combined with the growth of associations based around
the study of the First World War and developed into a campaign to reintroduce the two minutes' silence on 11 November itself. This move benefited
from the increased interest in family history and the war. Britons were
encouraged to think about their family connections to the war, and a growing number of them actually sought out such links. Over the same period, a
boom in the publication of new novels set during the war brought it back
into the forefront of popular culture in a fashion unseen since the 1960s.

Many of these works took it for granted that the war had been futile. For
example, Pat Barker's 1995 Booker Prize winning novel, *The Ghost Road*,
closes in the last days of the First World War. James Hallett, a young, ide-
alistic officer, who has argued that his country is fighting a just and
necessary war, has had half his head shot away. He lies dying in a London
hospital, his family gathered round him. In the last moments of his life, his

mangled mouth begins to whisper, then to shout, 'Shotvarfet, shotvarfet'. His doctor, William Rivers, interprets for the family: 'He's saying, "It's not worth it.' Hallett's fellow patients begin to cry out too, echoing his words, until 'Rivers was aware of a pressure building in his own throat as that single cry from the patients went on and on. He could not afterwards be sure that he had succeeded in keeping silent, or whether he too had joined in.' This scene, coinciding as it does with the death in action of the book's hero, Billy Prior, forms the emotional climax of the book.[77]

At the same time, however, the Cold War context that had made arguments about the failure of deterrence seem so relevant had disappeared. Arguably, deterrence had succeeded: there had been no Third World War. Meanwhile, the rediscovery of familial links to the war led individuals to reformulate emotional connections to the war. These made them reluctant to invalidate their ancestors' contribution. On a tour to the battlefields, the commentator Vitali Vitaliev overheard 'Ron, a robust, elderly man with misty blue eyes ... telling the only American on the tour: "We British are not militaristic. We have simply come here to honour our sacrifice."'[78] Many of the readers of the novel *Birdsong* attributed their enjoyment of the book to the way it made them think about their ancestors' 'sacrifice'.[79] Even Niall Ferguson, a historian who has argued that British participation in the First World War was mistaken, writes in the introduction to his book *The Pity of War*: 'That my grandfather fought on the Western Front was, and still is, a strange source of pride. If I try to analyse that pride, I suppose it has to do with the fact that the First World War was the worst thing the people of my country have ever had to endure.'[80]

As Ron's comments suggest, this renewed interest and changed context led to a reversion to an established vocabulary of remembrance based around redemptive sacrifice. In an editorial on the same day, the *Sunday Telegraph* declared: 'Remembrance is more than a ritual, a polite annual genuflection to the dead. It is part of the moral fibre of our society, marking the continuities between past sacrifice and present freedoms.'[81] For some on the political right, these continuities were particularly important.

The tensions that could result from this rediscovery of the validity of sacrifice were apparent in critical reactions to the 1996 BBC-KCET documentary series *1914–18* produced by Blaine Blaggett and Jay Winter This was the first series to tackle the First World War in its entirety since the BBC's *The Great War* thirty-two years before.[82] It shared many of the same hallmarks: a co-production with the Imperial War Museum, a classical soundtrack, a massive list of archival sources of authentic film, a pantheon of acting stars to narrate and speak the lines of dead participants, and off-air squabbles between the historians involved. Again, the series had a memorial intention, with the BBC offering a special study pack on 'Remembering' for viewers to send off for after the initial episodes.[83]

The series attracted fierce critical comment from some reviewers opposed to its politics as well as its production. The television critic A. A. Gill wrote:

> What a puny, sick, ill-disciplined, gutless shower BBC2's *1914–18* turned out to be. American money and sensibility have made this the social services war, the group therapy to end all group therapy ... Presumably we'll be getting the pivotal role of ethnic minorities, the differently abled, and those with eating disorders and dyslexia in future programmes. This is the Great War as remembered by Oprah Winfrey.[84]

Similarly, Correlli Barnett in the *Spectator* bemoaned the fact that:

> the series as a whole is content uncritically to trot out yet again the downbeat view about the war cherished by the 'progressive' intelligentsia ever since the 1920s ... Casualties, grief and hardship are emphasised at the expense of patriotic enthusiasm, belief in a righteous cause, and popular resilience and humour ...
>
> The apparent anchor-man of these talking heads is a Dr Jay Winter of Pembroke College, Cambridge, honking away in academic's American. I have to say that by the end of the series I was so maddened by the cocksureness of his expression and pronouncements that I longed to hang one on his hooter.[85]

It did not necessarily represent the attitude of the majority of viewers, but the vehemence of this outburst was remarkable. In part, this anger was based on a deliberate incomprehension of the approach and structure of the series. Blaggett and Winter aimed to create a new style of documentary based on the cultural history of the war. This was the result of a turn towards cultural history in the study of the First World War that had been gathering strength since the mid-1970s. As explained in their introduction to the book which accompanied the series:

> Here cultural history means the exploration of hopes and dreams, the ideas and aspirations, the exhilaration and the despair both of those remote from power and of those who led them ... Whereas diplomacy, political conflict and military events have long been a staple of historical presentations of the war, they have never been presented to the general public as cultural phenomena, encoded with rich and complex images, languages and cultural forms.[86]

In terms of style, *1914–18* followed on from the documentary series *The Civil War* produced in the United States by Ken Burns for the Public Broadcasting Service (PBS), which told the story of the American Civil War in similar terms, making use of both the stories of individual participants and the voices of famous actors. *1914–18* was structured around seven themes, which also broadly encapsulated the chronological progression of the war: 'Explosion', 'Stalemate', 'Total War', 'Slaughter', 'Mutiny', 'Collapse' and 'Legacy'. The episode titles, in particular the uncompromising 'Slaughter', also summarised Winter and Blaggett's own attitude towards the war. There was a coherent logic here, and an ability to conceive of the war in televisual terms which was as striking as Tony Essex's. The concentration on individual experience and representation of war was an extremely effective tool for involving an audience.

Yet there were profound disadvantages to this approach as well. Following the lines of the established cultural history of the war meant that some elements of the war – the campaigns in Italy, the Balkans and Africa – were all but absent. For a lay audience this made the series hard to follow; for example, a sudden mention of the Battle of Caporetto when Italy had previously gone unmentioned was frankly confusing. Winter and Blaggett's work was perhaps better suited to the broader spaces of a book than the tight confines of a television programme. In the volume published to accompany the series, there is space, in the chapter on 'Mutiny', for a detailed discussion of the variety of forms of shell shock and the ubiquity of breakdown as an eventual response to the appalling conditions imposed by industrialised warfare. This occurs before a consideration of the particular cases of Sassoon and Owen. The programme, with less time and eager to engage its audience, rushes straight on to Owen's suffering in the mud.[87]

Barnett was wrong, however, to suggest that the pessimistic tone arose solely from a continuation from the 'intelligentsia' of the 1920s. Rather, it was the result of taking a standpoint at the end of the twentieth century, looking back on a period which was seen to have involved an unprecedented degree of human suffering, and seeing at its opening the Great War. *1914–18* was book-ended by assertions that the First World War was the starting point for an awful period in human history. As the narrator put it in the opening moments: 'the lost generation. Nine million people killed during four years of world war during which people, lands and nations were changed forever. The years 1914–18 set the violent twentieth century in motion.'[88] Indeed, the series title for broadcast in the United States, rejected by the BBC, was *The Great War and the Making of the Twentieth Century*. Such an approach grew from the personal and familial experiences of those involved in the growth of the cultural history approach to the First World War. It is not an approach that has found much favour in Britain, where prevailing myths about some of the intervening events – most obviously the Second World War – have been predominantly positive.

This approach might be considered ahistoric, but it has a certain logic. If

the twentieth century is considered in terms of napalm, poison gas, industrialised slaughter, extremism and genocide (as opposed to antiseptics,
plastic surgery, the welfare state and the triumph of liberal democracy), and
the initial examples of all these are found in the First World War, then it
might be considered reasonable to posit that war as the starting point of a
terrible era.

Unlike its predecessors, *1914–18* allowed no hint of romanticism or meaning to the war. When it said futile, it meant it. Previous programmes had
shared a common mythical vocabulary of the war as a muddy, bloody mess.
They had spoken of it in terms of mismanagement, carnage and futility.
But they had still allowed the viewer leeway for allowing the war some
meaning; a coherent narrative with a part for a hero, normally played by
the long-suffering infantryman. In contrast, *1914–18* offered no such escape
route. The war had not only been futile and wasteful; worse, it had begun
the worst of all possible centuries. This absence – indeed, refusal – of any
comforting vision of the war's validity was what so offended reviewers.
Gill explicitly contrasted the series with the commemorations at the Cenotaph on Remembrance Sunday: he suggested that the latter offered an
example that the BBC did sometimes still know how to behave. In his view,
representations of the war had a duty to honour the dead.

In fact, the version of *1914–18* which reached British screens was probably
less negative than it might have been. That an episode should be entitled
'Slaughter' caused controversy which went as far as the BBC Board of
Governors, still twitchy from the aftermath of *The Monocled Mutineer.* Winter stuck to his guns and the title remained. The Imperial War Museum
insisted on the involvement of its own historian, Peter Simkins, in the production process. Simkins is a proud defender of the reputation of the British
Expeditionary Force and its generals. The series's occasional discussions of
– predominantly British – strategic and tactical development do rather seem
to have been shoehorned in to appease restless military historians. The BBC
demanded several alterations of the KCET version before transmission,
mainly based on lowering the emotional tone of the programme.

These changes almost certainly lessened the impact of the series. It is possible to imagine a more partisan, polemic *1914–18*, which would have
attracted the same criticism but appeared more coherent. These debates may
also account for the eventual decision to broadcast this 'prestige' series at
7 p.m. on a Monday evening on BBC 2: hardly a primetime slot. Perhaps as
a result, audience share was disappointing.[89]

Both Gill's and Barnett's reviews also highlight the way in which *The Great
War* itself had become mythologised as the ultimate in televisual representation of the First World War. Whilst the 1960s series *The Great War* was a

remarkable achievement in many ways, it suffered from several severe faults: not least its occasionally melodramatic depiction of the war. It had elicited responses from its audience emphasising the war's futility. Yet Gill remembered it as 'brilliant' and spent some time describing his frustration at being unable to obtain a copy.[90] Barnett was, of course, one of the principal scriptwriters for the 1964 series. It is interesting to compare his reaction to 1914–18 with that of veterans like Lord Chandos and Charles Carrington to *The Great War*. The two are almost identical, with the exception that the veterans were too gentlemanly to offer fisticuffs.

This 'heritaging' of texts produced in the 1960s was even more apparent when, in 1998, *Oh What a Lovely War* was revived as a national production for the first time in thirty-five years. Whilst many reviewers remarked in passing on the futility of the war, this was hardly the focus of attention. The nostalgia for the camaraderie of the war that had been felt by some of the play's original audience had been replaced by nostalgia for the heady days of the mythical Sixties. 'I well recall', wrote the *Financial Times* critic, 'the impact simply of hearing about this show during my 1960s childhood.'[91] The *Guardian* critic, Michael Billington, suggested that the original production 'was not just theatre history but a show that, as A. J.P. Taylor wrote, changed for ever popular perceptions of the war and the myth of military competence'. Billington confessed that: '*Oh! What a Lovely War* itself has also become part of theatrical legend: for someone of my generation, present experience is overlaid by past memories, as one recalls the unforgettable sight and sound of Victor Spinetti, Brian Murphy, Murray Melvin and Avis Bunnage in the original cast.'[92] In a profile in the *Daily Telegraph*, the director Fiona Laird made it clear that her production was intended as 'a tribute to Littlewood and her unique place in British theatre'.[93] The feeling that the play had passed into history was perhaps best summed up during the Salisbury Festival, when the touring company performed the play in Tidworth and Bulford Garrison, an army camp of some 4000 soldiers. The camp's deputy commandant was quite content: 'I think soldiers today will see the work chiefly as an item of historical interest.' he said, 'It's a first class play, but also a reflection of the times in which it was written.'[94] In the heritaging of texts like *Oh! What a Lovely War* and *The Great War* we can see the creation of a new set of meanings surrounding their representations of futility and the First World War in which beliefs about the 1960s and their impact on the present day coincide with those about the war. The myths are themselves becoming mythologised.

A paradox existed at the heart of British attitudes towards the futility of the First World War. No war that killed so many people could easily be judged worthwhile. Yet the very scale of the casualties limited the degree to which the purpose of the war could be publicly debated. Instead there arose a rhetoric of remembrance designed to console the bereaved – or at least to ease the conscience of those who had not lost their loved ones. The 'big words' thus employed – 'sacrifice', 'redemption' and 'glory' – exercised a long-term effect on the way Britons talked about the war. The passing of the generation of bereaved parents, whilst it opened up the boundaries of publicly permissible expression about the war, did not change the national vocabulary. Words like 'sacrifice' continued to be used about the war dead, even as increasing numbers of Britons came to believe that the war itself had lacked purpose. That they did so was at least partially the result of texts produced in the 1960s, when the subject of failed deterrence seemed particularly relevant in the context of the Cold War. Such views were never, however, as homogeneous as those about the stupidity of British generals. Not only were they less permanently useful, but worse, they threatened the heroic status that individual soldiers continued to hold as Britons looked increasingly back into their national and familial past.

5

Poets

Tucked away somewhere in the loft of my parents' house are some yellowing sheets of paper with the emotive story of a First World War battle. They describe the horror, the suffering and the terrible tragedy of the loss of young life.

Yet they are not the last remnants of some scribbled trench diary. Instead, they are a more recent addition to the Todman family archive: the story I wrote for my GCSE English literature class in response to the poems of Wilfred Owen and Siegfried Sassoon. Like most Britons, literature was at the heart of my first encounters with the Great War. In this case, myth and means of transmission come together, for so central has poetry become to how we interpret the war that its existence has been subsumed into the wider mythology. As *Blackadder*'s Captain Flasheart puts it when he sums up the horror of the war: 'the mud, the blood, the *endless* poetry'.[1]

The war encouraged a vast range of literary reactions, from before its outbreak, in the host of invasion stories and imaginings of future wars that haunted the pre-war mind, via the poems of combatants, through to the present day in the writing of novelists imagining their forefathers' experiences.

Writing about the war was an immediate response to it. That writing took many forms, including private letters, journalistic accounts, diaries, memoirs and novels. But one of the things that marks out the First World War is the enormous quantity of poetry that was written whilst it was going on. Some historians have attempted the mammoth task of counting this literary output. The historian Catherine Reilly has identified 2225 poets published in Britain between 1914 and 1918. These were just the visible tip of an enormous iceberg: far, far more was written privately. From the Laureate down, Britons produced a vast wave of verse of varying standard.[2] In part, this constant writing can be understood as Britons' attempts to work out their reaction to a war which repeatedly posed them with new, and frequently difficult, experiences. That this compulsive expression took the form it did was the result of the educational, commercial, cultural and technological developments of the nineteenth century. These meant that many Britons were primed to respond to major events in the first thirty years of the twentieth century by writing verse for public or private consumption.[3]

Whilst the population of Great Britain was still shockingly undereducated by the standards of some of its competitors, mass literacy of a sort had been achieved by the turn of the century. Writing by hand was the principal means of communication across long distance. Many Britons, therefore, became practised in written self-expression. Along with mass literacy had come a market for printed works which placed them alongside a host of other diversions in popular culture. The anthologies of poetry produced as part of this market provided models of a means of expression for the reader. The middle classes were educated to regard poetry not just as an acceptable pastime, but as a natural response to dramatic events. It is hard to take completely seriously Paul Fussell's suggestion that every soldier went to war with a volume of verse in his knapsack. Many of the slum dwellers who made up the bulk of the regular army's recruits would have found a use for these books which was more intimate than literary. Nonetheless, the influx of volunteers and conscripts with an element of education meant there was a significant proportion of the wartime army who instinctively turned to writing to record their experiences. Equally, there were many on the Home Front whose first reaction to the shocks of war was to write about them. To this extent, it should not surprise us that it is remembered as a literary war.[4]

If it were possible to take the vast quantity of writing produced by servicemen and civilians as a whole, published and unpublished, it would reflect the range and ambiguity of attitudes towards the war that we have already encountered.[5] The involvement of the entire population in a total war produced a wide range of responses that differed hugely in content, approach and form. The shock of war inspired or forced some writers to choose new means of expression, abandoning previous structures and beliefs. Others reacted by falling back on what they knew well, producing texts in traditional form which emphasised familiar versions of war as an occasion of heroism, love of country and self-sacrifice.

For example, the poem printed by *Punch* to mark Haig's dispatch on the capture of Messines Ridge in 1917 celebrated the traditionally manly aspects of his character:

> Steadfast and calm, unmoved by blame or praise,
> By local checks or Fortune's strange caprices
> You dedicate laborious nights and days
> To shattering the Hun machine to pieces;
> And howsoe'er the battle sways
> The Army's trust in your command increases;
> Patient in preparation, swift in deed,
> We find in you the leader that we need.[6]

Strangely, this stolid verse does not seem to have made it into subsequent anthologies.

The great bulk of this material has not, of course, come down to us. Some of it was neither well written nor popular. Much was not intended for publication. Privately expressed, it was by its nature ephemeral. Other examples were hugely popular at the time but have since disappeared from the canon of war literature. For example, John Oxenham was by some distance the most successful British poet of the war years, his works striking a chord with hundreds of thousands of readers. To the modern reader, Oxenham's work can seem gushing, twee or contrived, but his comforting vision of the war expressed within a Christian framework seems to have found an eager readership and his slim volumes had sold over seven and a half million copies by 1918. Their popularity did not endure, however, and as popular literary fashion changed they vanished. Ninety years after the war's beginning, Oxenham is all but forgotten.[7]

The writing did not stop when the guns did. The inclination to respond to the stimulus of the war by writing about it continued into the post-war world. Around four hundred 'war novels' were published in the 1920s and 1930s.[8] Again, what is most visible to us in retrospect is a limited section even of the published work, let alone the mass of private written responses to the war which have continued to be produced down to the present day. In contrast to the war years, however, the predominant form of the subsequent period has been prose – albeit sometimes prose written by poets or with their work at its foundation.

Academic and later popular attention has tended to focus on the literature produced during the so-called 'war-books boom' of the late 1920s and early 1930s. This period saw the publication of many of the novels and memoirs which remain at the heart of the modern British mythology of the First World War, including Siegfried Sassoon's *Memoirs of George Sherston*, Robert Graves' *Goodbye to All That* and Edmund Blunden's *Undertones of War*. Produced ten years after the war, they can be seen as personal attempts to create coherent stories out of their authors' wartime and post-war experiences. Graves, in particular, was part of a publishing phenomenon which followed on from the international success of *All Quiet on the Western Front*. Reviewers at the time agreed that these texts depicted the war in negative terms: they disagreed on how far that depiction accurately represented the meaning of the war. Individual readers' reactions were varied and depended on their own background and experience. The reception afforded these books was not always that intended by their authors: Robert Graves was surprised to find his heavily fictionalised memoir hailed as anti-war. He had been proud of his war service and had written his book not to decry the

war's horrors but to make enough money to avoid bankruptcy. Numerous
other authors attempted, like Graves, to jump on the bandwagon by selling
their fictionalised accounts of the war. The degree to which such accounts
emphasised the horrors of the front was enough to prompt a backlash from
more conservative commentators, who disagreed with their interpretation
of the war in terms of moral as well as physical desolation.[9]

Recently, historians of literature have pointed out that a concentration on
the 'war-books boom' has obscured the production of a host of other texts
in the years immediately after 1918. In this period, a large number of British
writers used the war as a setting for popular fiction. Their interpretations of
the war varied, but readers bought those texts which portrayed it as worthwhile nationally and individually. Some of these novels, such as Gilbert
Frankau's *Peter Jackson, Cigar Merchant* (1919) or Wilfred Ewart's *Way of
Revelation* (1920), enjoyed considerable success. They did not necessarily
deny the horror or frustration of war. Even so, they were popular. Again, we
come back to a difference between what the war had been like and what
its meaning had been. *Peter Jackson* in particular is starkly realistic in its
depiction of wartime incompetence and suffering, but the optimistic moral
it draws is one of validation. Their style was very much of its time, but the
message they conveyed had longer-term appeal, even if Ewart's melodramatic tone confined *Way of Revelation*'s popularity to the early 1920s. In the
same genre, but far more restrained, was Ernest Raymond's naive story of
schoolboys gone to war, *Tell England*, which in contrast remained in print
from its first publication in 1922 until after the Second World War.

After at least ten years of steady production, there was, by the early 1930s,
a glut of war literature. The war books boom had laid itself open to satire.
In 1933, Archie Macdonell began *England, Their England* by making it clear
to his audience that although the book began in wartime:

> From Chapter 2 to the end there will be no terrific descriptions of the effect of
> a chlorine gas cloud upon a party of nuns in a bombarded nunnery, or pages
> and pages about the torturing remorse of the sensitive young subaltern who
> has broken his word to his father ... by spending the night with a mademoi-
> selle from Armentières. There will be no streams of consciousness, chapters
> long, in the best style of Bloomsbury, describing minutely the sensations of a
> man who has been caught in a heavy-howitzer barrage while taking a nap in
> the local mortuary ...
>
> And, finally, there are going to be no long passages in exquisite cadences and
> rhythms, shoved in just to show that I am just as good as Ruskin or any of
> them, about the quietness of life in billets in comparison with life during a
> trench mortar bombardment ... and so on and so on and so on.

In a word, after this first chapter there will be, to borrow the name of an ardent society of left-wing pacifists, No More War.[10]

Whilst the 1930s did see a steady trickle of novels and memoirs, the need to pick over the war in literary form had been temporarily sated. This trend was strengthened by the outbreak of the Second World War, which led not only to the introduction of paper rationing but put many readers off the idea of reading about another conflict. Practical restrictions met emotional ones, and the most popular books, plays and films were escapist. Understandably, those whose loved ones were about to go into battle did not want to read about the trenches of a previous war. As one respondent to a Mass-Observation survey explained:

> I read now more than I ever did. My boy's away in the Middle East, and I don't get out much, I expect that's the reason. I like light fiction best, of the family type, and I prefer them to have a happy ending, even if it is highly improbable. There's enough tragedy in real life to want to read about, and that's one of the reasons I *never* read a war book.[11]

Young soldiers preferred the distractions of violent American-style crime fiction: James Hadley Chase's *No Orchids for Miss Blandish* was the wartime best-seller with sales in excess of half a million.[12] There were exceptions where the myths of the First World War could be adapted for service in the Second. RAF pilots in 1940 rushed to find copies of V. M. Yeates's memoir of the First World War in the air, *Winged Victory*. His depiction of flyers as valiant knights engaged in duels against similar opponents, separated from the filth of the war below, appealed strongly to the self-conception of his military descendants, who also appreciated the immediacy with which he wrote about air combat.[13]

Perhaps surprisingly, there was no great wave of new prose writing to meet the upsurge in interest in the First World War in the 1960s.[14] Instead, the 1960s saw the republication of many of the books that had first seen the light of day thirty years before. The revitalisation of the works of Graves, Sassoon and Blunden was helped by the fact that all three were still alive as the 1960s began. The dominance of these books from an earlier age may have seemed an insurmountable barrier to younger authors. The 1960s were also a key moment in the creation of the canon of war poetry which has come down to the present day. The publication of anthologies of war poetry to meet the fiftieth anniversary entailed a process of selection and organisation which foregrounded the work of some poets whilst obscuring others. The publicity afforded by the anniversary in 1964 and the arrival of First World War poetry on the O and A level examination syllabus ensured these anthologies sufficient initial success to secure a position in popular culture. The poets were afforded special status amongst the commemoration of the war. As the *Times Literary Supplement* reviewer of Brian Gardner's anthology *Up the Line to Death* remarked: 'It is doubtful whether even the photographs of the *Sunday Times* supplements or the film records of the BBC's long series can recall the hell more vividly than can the reportage of the poets who lived through it.'[15] *Up the Line to Death*, first published in 1964, remains in print and is a staple of school and university libraries, its sections on Sassoon and Owen particularly well-thumbed and annotated. It was in this period that Wilfred Owen's poems first achieved widespread popularity.

These books formed a key constituent for one of the most influential works on the literature of the war, Paul Fussell's 1975 *The Great War and Modern Memory*. Fussell's book has now, indeed, taken its place alongside the volumes of poetry and memoirs as an essential introductory text on the war. Fussell was an American professor of English literature who had seen service as an infantry subaltern with the US army in Western Europe in the Second World War. He produced a study of war literature with two main arguments. Heavily influenced by the work of the literary theorist Northrop Frye, he argued that the experience of the First World War had played a key part in the development of an ironic mode of expression that was a distinctive feature of 'modern' literature. As opposed to previous writings, in which the central characters had been superhuman, or at least human, in their understanding and ability to influence events, 'modern' writing had at its core characters who had less understanding of their circumstances than its readers. Secondly Fussell suggested that the ways of writing about war established by British writers during the First World War had formed the basis for all subsequent literary representations of conflict in the UK and the US.

The Great War and Modern Memory was evocatively titled (for all that there is actually very little thought about what 'memory' in this context might consist of) and provocatively written.[16] Fussell's approach to much of the writing on the war was original. He was, for example, the first analyst to treat Graves' *Goodbye to All That* as a work of dramatic confection rather than a strictly accurate memoir.[17] He wrote with an evident passion, deriving from his own experience of combat and the military and contemporary anger at America's involvement in Vietnam. As a work of literary theory, *The Great War and Modern Memory* may be judged a success, although Frye's work has fallen out of favour. As a work of history – cultural, social or military – it is seriously flawed.

Even by the standards of the mid 1970s, Fussell was spectacularly ignorant of the military history of the war.[18] Convinced by his own service that high commands existed only to feed soldiers useless orders ('chickenshit', as he termed it in a later work) and purposely sacrifice their lives, he transferred his attitudes direct to an earlier conflict. He believed that his interpretation of the way that a small number of soldiers chose to represent the war accurately reflected the experience of the army as a whole. Rather than conduct wider research, he simply expressed his own prejudices in the most violently sarcastic way.[19] In terms of cultural history, Fussell came to his subject with a strict theoretical framework and then selected texts which supported his case. He therefore blinded himself to the variety of different literary reactions to the war, which included not only a striving for new modes of expression but also a falling back onto reassuring traditions. The war produced a range of responses across the spectra of form, content and attitude: Fussell's work gives no indication that this was the case.[20] Although he subsequently made much of his extensive research in the archives of the Imperial War Museum, such work plays little part in the argument of the book. Fussell selected the words of less famous writers only where they fitted his case. *The Great War and Modern Memory* is, in other words, a work of polemic rather than analysis and has to be treated as such.

Fussell has subsequently protested – with some justification – that it is unfair to judge his work in these terms. He wrote as a literary professor, not as an historian. But his work is read as history and he himself clearly continues to believe that, whatever inaccuracies are pointed out in *The Great War and Modern Memory*, he was portraying a deeper truth about war and military experience beyond the comprehension of military historians.[21] Many of those who read his work would agree. Fussell's book keyed into many of the negative myths of the war which were achieving dominance in British popular culture by 1975. This is why it has been so easy for readers to accept it as a work of history rather than of literature.

The Great War and Modern Memory highlights the problems of using literature as the basis for historical understanding. Potentially, literature is an extremely useful source. It can demonstrate the ways in which individuals understood what was happening to them. A work that carries the force of lived experience can help the scholar empathise with the human beings involved in historical events. Developing an awareness of and sensitivity to the similarities and differences of attitudes and behaviour across the ages is a crucial part of the historian's craft.

In using works of literature we have, however, to be constantly aware that these are representations of an individual's reaction to events. As a result, they may tell us as much or more about the individual as they do about the event. We cannot assume that because a work has aesthetic merit it is necessarily representative of wider experiences or reactions. Inevitably, the form and content of such works is shaped by the context in which they are produced: like any historical source, we need to bear in mind when, where, why and by whom a work of literature was created.

In addition, we have to be careful not to allow our own subjective reading of the poem, novel or memoir, which is shaped by the context in which we are reading it, to overwhelm our effort to use it as a piece of evidence. Since we are used to judging such works by our own reaction to them, there is a temptation to ascribe our reaction to all readers and to assume that our understanding is the one intended by the author. If we do not take care, all we do is to project our own beliefs back uncritically on the past. One of the roles of a historian is to unpick a thread of narrative from the tangled net of the past – but such story-telling should follow a careful weighing of the evidence, not precede it.

The Great War and Modern Memory both reflected popular myths of the war at the time it was written, and reinforced them by giving them academic approval. As a result, it was rapidly absorbed into the literary tradition of the war.[22] As such, it became a key source for the next great upsurge of writing. In the late 1980s and early 1990s, a new wave of prose fiction was produced, set during the war but written by those who had not experienced it. The bulk of these books were ephemeral popular literature: romances, adventure and detective stories. Yet they also included more self-consciously literary works (such as William Boyd's *The New Confessions*), and others which were both popular and critically successful, such as Pat Barker's *Regeneration* trilogy, the final part of which won the 1995 Booker Prize. The most successful was undoubtedly Sebastian Faulks's *Birdsong*, with sales of a million and a half in paperback. What these novels shared was a set of recurrent themes and images which summed up the First World War for writers and readers: poets, men shot at dawn, horror, death, waste. Since they were seeking a setting in the past that was easily understandable to their readers, rather than to educate or inform them, these books unsurprisingly reflected the dominant myths of the culture that produced them. In repeating them, of course, they reinforced their power.

In terms of popular culture, the literary history of the war is one not only of production but also of concentration. Notwithstanding the large number of poets and authors who have written on the war in the ninety years since it began, in practice most Britons know the names and the work of just a few. Their works are the ones read at school as part of GCSEs, quoted in television documentaries and newspaper editorials and referred to by subsequent authors. The core is formed by the poems of Rupert Brooke, Siegfried Sassoon and Wilfred Owen. If they appear together, these men's poems are usually arranged in that order: we know Brooke as a marker of pre-war innocence before the disillusion, cynicism and sorrow of those who experienced more of the war.

One measure of the strength of these poets' influence is that way in which their phrasing has entered the language we use to describe the war. A bibliography of the First World War can read like a list of Owen and Sassoon's best-remembered lines: *The Pity of War, Strange Meeting, They Called it Passchendaele, Up the Line to Death*. Even in this select group, it is Owen who stands out as the symbol of war poetry in British popular culture: the 'Known Poet' to match the 'Unknown Warrior'.[23]

How did Owen come to achieve this position of pre-eminence? He was not always as widely known as he is now, nor was his rise by any means inevitable. It was hardly the case that he was typical of the army in his experiences, attitudes or reactions to the war. A rather priggish young man, whose mother had inculcated in him a strong dislike of 'dirt', moral and physical, Owen overcame an initial reluctance to serve and joined up in 1915. He came from a lower middle-class background which, though hardly as comfortable as that of his fellow officer-poets Brooke or Sassoon, was at a remove from the industrial poverty experienced by most of his men. On his arrival on the Western Front, Owen seems to have found it hard to integrate himself fully amongst the officers of his first battalion. In part, this was because he did not match the pre-war regulars' model of officer material. It was also because he was, by his nature, something of a lone wolf, who was unable to adapt his behaviour to match his social setting. It may have been this absence of a support network that meant that, when he displayed the symptoms of shell shock, he was sent home with his commanding officer's suggestion of cowardice lingering over him. After treatment (during which time he famously met Sassoon), he returned to the front in time for the fighting of summer 1918. Here, determined to prove himself and undergoing a personal and poetic transformation, he won the Military Cross by capturing a German machine gun nest and turning the weapon on its previous owners, before dying leading his men in an attempted crossing of the Sambre-Oise Canal in October.[24]

Even by the standards of a period that caused confusion in the heads and hearts of many Britons, Owen's attitude towards the war was complicated. He did not join up immediately on the outbreak of war, but after he had already seen the effects of war on the bodies of wounded French soldiers. At some levels, military service seems to have appealed to him because it offered him the chance for a new start in life and made him a member of an exclusive brotherhood. Owen is now often discussed in terms of his homosexuality, but it is not necessarily helpful to classify him by modern measures of modern sexual identity. It seems clear that he was physically attracted to men, but how he might have defined this to himself is harder to say. This aspect of his sexuality was problematic both on a personal level, and on a social and cultural one, in a country in which homosexuality was illegal and despised. The army legitimated male love in the form of comradeship and the paternalistic relationship of officers and men. More particularly, war appealed to Owen because he had already bound himself up in a rhetoric of redemption through suffering.[25]

At the same time, the physical damage war wrought on the bodies of his fellow officers and men pained Owen very deeply. As his letters to his mother make clear, he initially found the conditions in which he was supposed to function in the army distasteful. He then experienced traumatic combat. The apparent inability of some at home to grasp what their menfolk were doing on the Western Front aroused his anger. The effect of his war experience was to distance him further from a society from which he had already felt separated and aloof. Little wonder, perhaps, that caught in the midst of these different emotions, he referred to himself as 'a conscientious objector with a very seared conscience'.[26] To appreciate Owen's work, we need to endeavour to understand this mixture of different feelings, which goes far beyond the simplistic anti-war message often read into his poems.

When he died, in the penultimate month of the war in 1918, Owen was all but unknown as a poet. Few of his poems had been published; most were not even finished. Yet, before he died, Owen had had the good fortune briefly to come into contact with others who were sufficiently impressed and well connected to ensure that his poems did not disappear completely. In 1920, the first very limited collection of his work was published in a volume ostensibly edited by his fellow soldier poet, Siegfried Sassoon. In fact Sassoon left the majority of the work to his co-editor, Edith Sitwell.[27] The book was not widely distributed. There were only 730 copies in the original impression, and a second impression of 700 copies had yet to be fully bound by 1929. By the same point, in comparison, the collected works of Rupert Brooke had sold some 300,000 copies.[28] Edmund Blunden edited a second, fuller edition of Owen's work which was published in 1931. Figures for its print run are not available, but anecdotal evidence from contemporary memoirs suggests that this version reached a larger audience, including a substantial proportion of the intellectual elite. They seem, for example, to have influenced the work of the Second World War poet Keith Douglas, perhaps during his time as an undergraduate in the 1930s. Blunden's volume was, however, reprinted only once in the fifteen years after its first publication. Owen's work was far from universally popular even amongst those who had read it. Famously, Owen was one of those war poets who

W. B. Yeats refused to include in the 1936 *Oxford Book of Modern Verse* on the basis that 'passive suffering' was 'not a theme for poetry'.[29]

It was only in the years after the Second World War that Owen's popularity began to increase. Blunden's edition of Owen's poems was reprinted in 1946, 1949, 1951, 1955, 1960, 1961 and 1963. In that year they were republished in a new edition by Cecil Day Lewis. That new edition was reprinted eleven times in the next ten years, four times in hardback and seven in paperback. Indeed, the 1960s saw a dramatic increase in the attention paid to Owen. His poems were the basis for Benjamin Britten's *War Requiem* in 1961, the centrepiece of two best-selling anthologies in 1963 and 1964, released on a spoken word record in 1968, and became a regular element in radio and television documentaries (most notably in *The Great War*).

From the 1960s to the present day, Owen's status as the celebrity poet of the First World War has only grown stronger. By the 1980s, Owen could be described without controversy as the 'outstanding English poet of the First World War'.[30] He has been placed at the heart of televisual and radio representations of the war, honoured by the erection of plaques and memorials in his home town and close to where he fell, his poems recited by generations of schoolchildren and his life story incorporated, explicitly or otherwise, in contemporary novels and poems. Owen has become a remarkable symbol of the modern myths of the war, the button to push if television producers or novelists want the audience to reorientate themselves swiftly towards thinking about the First World War. The battle in which Owen died was one of the crucial victories of the last months of the war. It demonstrated not only British tactical developments and military flexibility, but also the remarkable determination of units made up predominantly of conscripts and men who had already been wounded and returned to combat, to close with the enemy, notwithstanding the strength of his defensive positions, and drive him back towards Germany. That the Battle of the Sambre-Oise Canal should now be remembered, if at all, for Owen's death, bears out the military historian Gary Sheffield's contention that the First World War is Britain's 'forgotten victory'.[31]

There are two explanations for the domination by a single poet's life and work of the British mythology of the war. The first concentrates on the survival of Owen's poetry, when it might so easily have vanished, given its half-finished nature and his early death. The second examines the process by which it rose, after the Second World War, to a position of such prominence.

The support of fellow wartime poets was crucial to the survival and revivification of Owen's work. Sassoon repeatedly emphasised Owen's status, but it was Edmund Blunden who did most to ensure that Owen's poems were known and accessible. Blunden seems to have become convinced of

Owen's stature during the 1920s, not only because of his work's quality, but because it could be fitted in with his own developing reaction to the war in terms of a shift from initial enthusiasm to resigned disillusion. His work went beyond editing the first full collection of Owen's work. As an influential figure in English literary circles before and after the Second World War (he taught English at Oxford and wrote for the *Times Literary Supplement*), Blunden introduced younger writers to Owen's work and pushed for its republication. Through the 1960s, he continued to involve himself in the developing literary mythology of the First World War. He provided advice to those, like Brian Gardner and D. S. R. Welland, who were anthologising or studying the war poets. As a First World War poet who had not only survived but was easily approachable, Blunden was an early port of call for such writers. As such he was able to exercise a substantial influence on their interpretations.[32]

Blunden's support ensured that Owen's poetry remained publicly available, but it was not enough to ensure its popularity. We tend to accept now that Owen's poems had intrinsic literary quality, but, as Yeats's reaction suggests, this was open to dispute. In any case, literary quality is no firm predictor of survival and success, even if Owen's mysticism and pararhyme fitted better with poetic fashion in the 1940s and 1950s than previously. More study needs to be done on reactions to Owen before the Second World War, but it seems likely that his work simply did not fit the prevalent public mood in the 1920s when, as the success of Brooke's poems demonstrates, the tastes of the poetry reading public were for more traditional forms and representations. As we have seen, inter-war attitudes towards the earlier conflict were ambiguous. For all that Owen's poems might have appealed to those who believed in the horror of war and were saddened by its results, they left little room for pride in a job well done or a belief in national or personal validation. His recurrent theme of the division between generations and the sorrow of war may have been more attractive in the 1930s. But by the point at which Blunden's new edition of Owen's work was published, the book-buying public may well have satiated its desire for texts set during war.

In the aftermath of the Second World War there was a new attractiveness in Owen's emphasis on the tragedy of war. The bombing of civilians – an experience much more easily definable in terms of passive victimhood – was one of the defining features of the second conflict. Reviewing Day Lewis's edition of Owen's collected poems in 1963, Philip Larkin remarked that: 'in the end Owen's war is not Sassoon's war but all war; not particular suffering but all suffering, not particular waste but all waste. If his verse did not cease to be valid in 1918, it is because these things continued, and the necessity for compassion with them.'[33] Another critic of the same volume suggested that: 'The respect that falls to Owen is not only for his poetry but also in part for the "rightness" of his attitude towards the war in terms of our present-day view of it.'[34]

In this context, Owen's prominence was assisted by two factors. First, he had a good background story. His death, at the head of his men, in one of the last battles of the war, with the news arriving in Shrewsbury as the bells pealed to announce the Armistice, formed a memorable mix of pathos and romance. Death in battle was the true mark of the warrior poet. As the First World War came increasingly to be seen in terms of tragedy, so this tale enjoyed a better and better fit with the story of the conflict as a whole, as demonstrated in its use as the opening anecdote for the 1996 BBC KCET television documentary series, *1914–18*.

Secondly, for all that Owen's poems make reference to poison gas, dugouts and artillery bombardment, they are much less specifically rooted in a description of trench warfare than, for example, Sassoon's. Owen's efforts to transcend the context of the trenches in poems such as 'Anthem for Doomed Youth' and 'Strange Meeting' made his work more easily applicable to subsequent conflicts, or to war in general. The reader does not require specific knowledge of the First World War to draw out a layer of meaning based on Owen's horror at the mutilation and death of young men.

This was apparent in the use made by Benjamin Britten of Owen's work in his *War Requiem*.[35] The piece intermingles Owen's poetry with the words of the Latin mass. Britten had grown up feeling the influence of the First World War. When Lowestoft was attacked by Zeppelins in 1916, the Brittens and their baby boy had to shelter in a cellar: he would later claim that the first sound he could remember was a wartime explosion. A veteran with the MC taught Britten at school. Yet the *Requiem* came out of more immediate international and personal tragedy. Having originally contemplated a requiem after the destruction of Hiroshima, Britten eventually composed it for the rededication, in 1962, of Coventry Cathedral, destroyed by German bombing twenty-two years before. He dedicated it to four of his friends, of whom three had died in the war, whilst the fourth – to whom Britten has been linked romantically – had survived only to commit suicide on his wedding night in 1959.[36] In Britten's own words: 'It is a full scale Requiem Mass ... (in memory of those of all nations who died in the last war) ... These magnificent poems, full of the hate of destruction, are a kind of commentary on this mess.'[37]

The cultural historian Jay Winter has suggested that the *War Requiem* is as much a meditation on the First World War as the Second.[38] Britten's own motivation, his description of the piece, and its structure – Owen's words are sung by three soloists, those of the mass by two choirs – seem to undermine this interpretation. Owen's poems are enlisted to comment on the awfulness of the Second World War. Critics of the first performance were stimulated to note the horror of war in general, but did not discuss the First World War in particular.[39]

The *Requiem* is unashamedly highbrow. It is a complicated and pro-longed piece. Listening to all of it can be a challenging experience. Despite those restrictions, it swiftly acquired a substantial audience within a context that did overlay Britten's work with a discussion of Owen and the First World War. Two years after its first performance, the BBC included the *Requiem* amongst its programmes to mark the fiftieth anniversary of the war 'by popular demand', and paired it with a discussion of Owen's life by Cecil Day-Lewis that stressed: 'It took the horrifying degradation of the battlefield, the futility and shame of it all, to forge the supreme artist.' The BBC published copies of the words for audience members to purchase.[40] In contrast to *Oh What a Lovely War*, it seems unlikely that listeners wanted to sing along with Britten. Rather, they were interested in reading the poems, in themselves much more accessible than the music.

The transmission of what was still, in the early 1960s, a comparatively 'highbrow' interest into popular culture took place largely through the educational system. With Owen's poems used in the teaching of both English and History, it was in the classroom that the bulk of the population encountered them for the first time. It is relatively easy to track the arrival of these poems as potential subjects of study through examination papers and the publication of new textbooks. It is much harder, however, to follow how often or in what fashion they were actually taught, particularly before the introduction of the National Curriculum in the early 1990s. It is possible to suggest the lessons teachers tried to impart – which may differ widely from what students in fact learned – but wider generalisations must remain speculative.

From the 1960s onwards, Owen's poems began to appear on English Literature examination papers, first for A and then for O levels. Combined with an expansion in the numbers of those taking GCEs, beyond the traditional preserves of private and grammar schools, this widened the number of those exposed to Owen's poetry at an early age. By the late 1980s his work had achieved a remarkable ubiquity – with 'Dulce et Decorum Est' being almost the only poem that it could be guaranteed every schoolchild had come into contact with. More recently, although Owen has not been a set text for English Literature under the National Curriculum, he is on the exemplar list of post 1900 (from 1996, post 1914) poets regarded as suitable for teaching purposes, and his poems remain a popular choice for Year 9 (thirteen to fourteen year olds) study.[41]

Owen's popularity with English teachers was based, at least in part, on practical reasons. The best known of his poems are short enough to be considered in the space of a single lesson. They raise interesting points of technique and style. The immediacy of some of Owen's work made it easy to involve children in the poems themselves: poison gas and moral denunciation always being more likely to fascinate unruly teenagers than natural beauty and emotional confusion.

Some commentators have suggested that another reason for the popularity of Owen's poems in the English classroom was that they could be used to elicit the 'correct' reactions to war: that it was stupid, wasteful and futile.[42] One teacher who taught war poetry in secondary schools from the 1960s to the late 1980s argued in retrospect that: 'perhaps the most serious weakness in the way poetry is sometimes taught is the misuse, even abuse, of it for the purpose of teaching pacifism in general or attempting to direct pupils' responses to more recent, completely unrelated conflicts'.[43] As an example we might take the volume of poetry produced privately by students at St John's College, Southsea, in the late 1970s. Their teacher introduced a class of thirteen- and fourteen-year-old boys to the poetry of the First World War: 'The poems of Wilfred Owen and Siegfried Sassoon seemed to make a great impression on them – something for which I had hoped – so in order to test their sensibilities to such poetry, and to give their imaginations full reign ... I asked the boys to prepare their own "war poems".'[44] The resulting works reveal identification with the soldier poets – most are written in the first person, the prevalence of negative perceptions of war – death and madness are the dominant themes – and the influence of Owen in terms of style and subject.[45] Alun Epps's poem, 'Over the Top' was one of many that displayed this influence:

> Far away, distant gun shots worried their minds.
> Their legs grew cold with waiting
> And terror gripped their hopes.
> They stood, chained in their trenches,
> Waiting for nothing.
>
> Suddenly there came an order;
> 'Over the top, lads', a voice shouted
> And young and frightened men
> Climbed up the mud walls.
> Bang, bang! bellowed the bloodthirsty bombshells
> And many fell.
>
> Sad and sorry screaming shattered the sordid scene
> And mud became red

The day is done,
The ground is taken,
But what of the cost of young lives gone forever?
And mothers standing alone and forsaken?[46]

The extent to which this poem has been shaped by Owen's poetry is clear; indeed, some of the individual poems that the student has read can be identified. What is also apparent is the considerable degree of emotional involvement with the subject. That his teacher selected this poem for publication makes it clear that Epps's response was the 'correct' one. Whatever young Alan thought about the First World War before he entered the English classroom, he left it with a clear set of ideas about what the war had been like: muddy, bloody and wasteful.[47]

We have to be wary, however, about what students were actually learning, whatever were the didactic intentions of their teachers. British popular culture continued to place considerable value on soldiers and military heroism. Children still played with toy soldiers, read war comics and tried to question their parents and grandparents about wars gone by. Unsurprisingly then, their reactions to war poems were sometimes more complex than their teachers might have intended. The journalist Christopher Moore, remembering his first encounter with the war, recalled that:

It began in a classroom ... We were reading the War Poets for O-Level. For the first time in my inky, football-crazed life I was about to be knocked sideways by a work of art: 'Dulce et Decorum Est' by Wilfred Owen. As we read the words aloud, my boy's store of feelings overflowed without warning. It had to be stopped. I choked on the injustice. That night I read all the War Poets in the textbook and learned 'Dulce et Decorum Est' by heart.

I identified with Owen's gassed Englishmen to the extent of an overwhelming pity, but I was also jealous that I had been denied a chance to suffer with them. I was old enough for irony, but the physical impact of Owen's words went deeper. His gassed men had died for me in a straight swap, their future for mine. Death by German phosgene did not diminish them. If England was worth fighting for, then 'Dulce et Decorum Est' could not be a lie.[48]

Moore is obviously indulging in some personal myth-making here, but his writing should warn us to be careful of assuming that children learn what they are taught.

The use of Owen's poems was not restricted to the English classroom. Increasingly, his work also appeared in history teaching, although the use in which it was put could be similar. The First World War appeared on history examination papers for the first time in the 1960s, but questions tended to focus on historical events and personalities rather than experiences. For example, in 1963 one exam board asked O level students to: 'Explain the importance of two of the following in World War I: (a) the British Expeditionary Force; (b) the Gallipoli campaign; (c) the Battle of Jutland; (d) Lawrence of Arabia.' In response, history textbooks produced at the time tended to focus on getting students to remember names and dates; in doing so they often combined heroic myths of British valour and endurance with an overall depiction of the war in terms of horror and death. Anecdotal evidence suggests that most history teachers did not take the opportunity to study such recent events, preferring to concentrate on more traditional subjects such as the Plantagenets, Tudors and Stuarts.

The use of poetry to teach the First World War occurred at least a decade later in the History than in the English classroom. It reflected a wider shift in which history teaching came to focus more on the modern period and on an understanding of the individual's historical experience, rather than the memorising of dates and kings. This was part of a change in the topics deemed worthy of study within the academic community. It was also part of a development in the nature of history teaching itself. Teachers became more mobile over the course of their careers, and were increasingly better trained in educational theory and practice. As a result, however, they developed less subject specialism. It may have been that the teachers produced in the 1970s were more confident in their status as educators than as historians.[49]

Taken together, these changes made some history teachers keener to offer their students sources that would enable them to empathise with individuals than to assess those sources objectively. Better to offer children a simple narrative of the past that they would grasp and encourage them to emote than to risk revealing to them the complexities and confusions of history. There was also, as we have seen, a clear and uncontroversial set of myths about the war by the 1970s: a commonly agreed version that could be passed on to the young. It should be pointed out that the most imaginative history teachers, or those who had a specific interest in the First World War, sought different ways to involve their classes, or taught the war in more detail. For the majority of history teachers without that specific interest, however, there was little reason to question the repetition of simplistic myths about the war.

This seems to have encouraged the use of poetry in the history classroom, a use further spurred on in the case of the First World War by the fact that some poets offered the 'right' message and the opportunity for a cross-curricular project with the English department. A textbook first published in 1973, but which was used to teach me about the First World War in the 1980s, suggested that 'The bitterness and disillusionment came in the poems written by the true poets who found themselves in uniform'. Owen's poems 'conveyed with disturbing clarity the ugliness and outrage of war'. [50] If poets were those who really told the 'truth' about the war, then evidently they were the essential historical source.

This approach reached its nadir in the mid to late 1990s. In 1994, Fines and Hopkins published a guide to *Teaching for Attainment Target One in National Curriculum History (Using a First World War Project)*. This was based on experience of teaching a Year Eight (twelve-year-old) class for about eight weeks. One feature of the project, proudly quoted by the authors, was the poetry the children had been encouraged to write after exposure to a range of poets including Owen. One unidentified child produced the following:

War is Hell

War is hell I'm destined for death
The only music I've got to hear is the melody of the machine gun
and the bass playing of the bombs.
The constant destruction
And for this the only consolation is a smoke and a chat with
friends.[51]

An article in the history teacher's professional journal, *Teaching History*, in 1999 suggested that reading and writing poetry was the ideal way to teach children about the First World War. The author argued that:

When pupils are enthused, they will observe source material in more detail, they will strive to include in their writing their background knowledge of events and contemporary terminology. They will try to avoid anachronism. And they will remember and understand. Knowing in their hearts and remembering vividly the horrors of trench warfare, they will understand Chamberlain's desire for appeasement. They will be able to develop as historians.[52]

She cited examples from her class's work, including a poem by a boy called Matthew:

Days of Glory

'Over the top!' the officer calls,
'Cha-a-a-arge!'
Man by man the regiment falls,
Like a tidal wave falling and slowing,
And slowing and falling.

The repetitive sound of machine gun fire
Blitzes through like a schoolboy's choir.
Then there is silence,
Until the cry of pain can be heard,
Time and time again.[53]

Here is the modern mythology of the First World War laid out in poetic form: horror, death, futility. Owen's model has been followed to the point of absurdity (what does 'blitzing through like a schoolboy's choir' actually mean?). Pupils were extremely good at regurgitating the war poetry they had been force-fed; a tendency reinforced by the selection of 'good' works their teachers then made for publication. Children had undoubtedly learnt lessons about the war in terms of horror and onomatopoeia, but what was understood about the experience of soldiers other than Owen can be questioned.[54] The point here is not that writing poems about history and attempting to empathise with individuals in the past is in itself invalid, but that in this case it did not offer a helpful vision of the very different ways in which Britons experienced the war. Rather, it encouraged an ahistoric imposition of modern beliefs and attitudes onto the past without an objective assessment of the evidence.

Owen's poetry came to play such a dominant role in popular mythology through a combination of fortune, structural factors and potential malleability. His death offered an attractive mix of romance, tragedy and heroism. His association with other poets who survived the war meant that he had influential advocates who ensured that his work did not fade into obscurity, as it could so easily have done in the 1920s. Whilst poetry and war remained important elements in British culture, the forms Owen chose – relatively short poems which aimed to communicate primary emotions – turned out to be useful to television producers and classroom teachers. An Owen poem could bookend an episode or be dealt with in an hour. Most did not require extensive elaboration or footnoting to enable the lay reader to create a meaning, as would, for example, David Jones' epic poem *In Parenthesis.*

It is in that layer of created meanings that Owen's popularity can be best explained. In the period after the Second World War, his poems continued to seem relevant not only because of their preference for mystic imagery over specific detail, but also because they discussed the experience of war in terms of suffering and victimhood. This fitted the British domestic experience of the Second World War much better than poetry that emphasised the moral ambiguities of fighting and killing. Owen was, and is, a poet for non-combatants. If this helps to account for the growth in publication of his poems immediately after 1945, his longer-term popularity was based on another set of created meanings. As we have seen, the depiction of the First World War in strongly negative terms – as the worst of all possible wars – grew much stronger during the 1960s. It is easy to read Owen's poems as evidence of the horror and awfulness of the First World War, and this is how they have been used in schools since the late 1960s. If some have seen them as containing a simple message – war is bad – which it is appropriate to inculcate in the young, others have used them because they seem to be such an effective way to communicate the 'facts' about the First World War. In this way, Owen's poetry became a staple of the History as well as the English classroom (a fate that is currently being shared by the last episode of *Blackadder Goes Forth*). There is a malleability here that is reminiscent of the initial reception of *Oh What a Lovely War*. For a poem, a play or a television series to become popular and influential, a key element is not how accurately it depicts the war in historical terms, but rather how easily others can use it to bolster their own preconceptions. Since this reinforcement is taken as proof, a tradition is established that such works communicate 'the truth' about war – whereas in fact they convey much more about the author and audience.

One of the reasons that Owen was seen to be 'truthful' was that he experienced the war at first hand. The meanings others constructed from his poetry were validated by their knowledge of his experience. Yet in the last thirty years, the war has become a subject and a setting for contemporary novels, some of them extremely successful. Generations with no experience of the war are writing and reading about it. Why do they choose to revisit the First World War?

We can try to explain the popularity of the First World War in contemporary novels in practical terms. Recent years have seen a explosion in popular fiction of all kinds – there are simply more novels being published overall. Changes in the publishing industry modernised its approach to production and sales. A series of buyouts and mergers concentrated publishing power in fewer hands and incorporated the industry into popular media empires. More sophisticated marketing and positioning allowed the sale of more books, in turn encouraging the publication of more fiction, but also the demand for bestsellers. As in previous generations, publishers were quick to follow a profitable trend. Sebastian Faulks's novel *Birdsong*, which tells in parallel two stories – one of the war in the tunnels under the trenches fought by its hero, Stephen Wraysford, and the the other of his grand-daughter's discovery of his wartime experiences through his diaries in the 1970s – was a surprise word of mouth success. Its dominance of the bestseller lists encouraged publishers to cry out for similar novels to throw on the bandwagon.[55]

The imagined past became more attractive as a setting in popular culture more generally during the 1980s. In this respect, historical novels were just one aspect of a much larger growth in the 'heritage' industry; other examples of which included the celebrations surrounding the raising of the Tudor ship *Mary Rose* in 1982, the popularity of films set in the past, like Merchant Ivory's *Room with a View*, and the development of numerous 'heritage' centres, at which the public was encouraged to experience the past, rather than to examine it through the glass panels of museum cases. This 'heritage boom' continued through the late 1990s and certain aspects of it – particularly the popularity of television history documentaries – show little sign of abating. As a result the historical novel, from the Victorian period a staple of the English literary canon, became a successful form of expression and an acceptable setting for a wide variety of different literary genres.

An explanation put forward by commentators at the time was that this wave of writing resulted from a long-lived trauma:

> What we are witnessing here is something more than a literary fad – it is nothing less than what Stephen Wraysford, the young narrator of *Birdsong*, calls the 'long perspective of forgiveness', a process through which the past painfully works itself out in subsequent generations.[56]

Faulks himself, in the sequel to *Birdsong*, *Charlotte Gray*, wrote of the passing down of traumatic memory between generations; in this case, a direct transmission through a quasi-religious laying on of hands.[57]

How seriously we take this idea depends on the degree to which we think of the First World War as an experience which traumatised all those who went through it. As we have seen, this is a version of the war which has enjoyed greater strength in recent years than it did at the time. Indeed, the concept of lingering and destructive traumatic memory, in the guise of post-traumatic stress disorder, has only really been developed since the 1970s.[58] It is easy to see the emotional advantages of a literary interpretation that allows a generation which has never experienced total war to believe that it is somehow connected to a key historical event, and even to believe that it can share in its forefathers' 'victimhood'. It is rather harder to see how that younger generation can have a 'memory' of an event in which it did not participate. We might do better to investigate the desire to appropriate grandparents' or great-grandparents' experience than to suggest cod-psychological processes for this invented phenomenon.

On the other hand, it is possible to discern family links between some authors and the First World War. For example, Susan Hill described her first encounter with the war in the introduction to the 1984 reprint of her novel *Strange Meeting*. As a child she would visit her maternal grandmother and her sister. They were two of nine children, with one brother:

> cherished and idolised by them all, of course. When he was eighteen, he went to war – the Great War, as they called it, the 1914–18 War. On his nineteenth birthday, he was killed, like so many other thousands of young men, at the Battle of the Somme.
>
> I don't think the family was ever the same again.
>
> They had a photograph of him in his uniform, and I used to take it down and look at it. He had such a young face, even I could see that, as a child, he was not much more than a child himself. His ears stuck out, I remember, and his hair was cut very, very short under his cap. His Christian name was Sidney, and the family surname was Owen. It is a coincidence of course, but the long arm of *that*, as they say, is long one, and I am believer in these small signs and symbols, as important parts of one's life.[59]

It was the poet Owen, however, not Hill's relative, who had the clearest influence on her work in terms of style and content: *Strange Meeting* took its title from Owen's poem and focused on the developing love between two British officers.

Two male writers of adventure stories set in the First World War included episodes from their own fathers' experiences. Douglas Reeman remembered his father's reminiscences as he wrote *The Horizon*:

> It was long ago in the Sixties ... that my late father really began to talk of his own experiences at Gallipoli and on the Somme. As a boy I had sometimes listened to him speaking about them to his close friends, who had shared the nightmare of trench warfare, but he never mentioned them directly to me ... in his own way he passed some of his experiences to me, and for that I am grateful.[60]

John Harris's father saw service on the Somme and claimed to have witnessed one of the last charges made in action by a regiment of British cavalry: this episode is the climax of Harris's 1983 work *Blunted Lance*.[61] In a similar fashion, Julia Hamilton's *The Idle Hill of Summer* had its inspiration in the wartime experiences of her ancestor, Ralph Gerard Alexander Hamilton.[62]

The author whose family connection attracted most attention from contemporary commentators was Pat Barker. Her grandmother's second husband, William Dunne, had been a batman to Lord Lascelles during the war. After being bayoneted during an assault, he had been left out on the battlefield for twelve hours before being rescued. He retained a two-inch scar on his stomach, into which his grandchild was sometimes encouraged to put her hand.[63] Here was a visceral connection to the war, a powerful ritual of family memory that could be seen as the basis for her writing about the war.

Barker herself has been scathing of those who make facile causal links. 'To me it's a story that has a built in yuck factor – golden haired girl slips her hand inside the Christ-like wound of her dear grandpa – which unless you're Tolstoy you can't overcome. In fact, seeing my grandfather's balls when he was getting washed probably made a much greater impression on me.'[64] An examination of her other works, *Union Street, Blow Your House Down, The Century's Daughter* and *The Man Who Wasn't There,* seems to indicate interests closely related to her own experiences which were carried over into the *Regeneration* trilogy.[65] Barker grew up unaware of her father's identity – although her mother maintained the convenient fiction that he had been a bomber pilot killed in the Second World War. When her mother married another man, she was effectively abandoned to the care of her grandparents. Her books' themes include the social position of working-class women in the north of England, the lasting effects of trauma and the human potential for violence.

On the other hand, the *Regeneration* trilogy has a recurring image of characters examining each other's scars. Dunne's confusion in his declining years, the return of his wartime memories to haunt him, is revisited in her later novel *Another World.* Barker chose to write about the First, rather than the Second, World War. And in her acceptance speech for the Booker Prize, she paid tribute to Dunne: 'He was the one who made me interested in the war. He was cheerful, wily, very short-sighted, tight with money and a life-long Tory who never questioned whether the war was just or not. In my work, of course, I constantly pose that question.'[66]

For some authors, then, a familial connection with the war did serve as a source of information and inspiration in their writing. Fascinating though these examples are, knowledge of a family link to the war does not seem to have acted as a trigger for writing specifically in the 1990s. Hill's book was first published in 1971; Reeman and Harris had, by the 1990s, been writing about the war for thirty years. This was a slow trickle of authors writing about something that interested them, not the bursting of a dam of pent-up inherited trauma.[67]

Few of those who bought these new novels seem to have had prior knowledge of their families' experience of the war. Readers of the most successful of these new books, *Birdsong,* described their encounter with the novel for Amazon in terms of a discovery of the First World War. This was attended by considerable emotion: 'I still think about *Birdsong* and it is two years since I read the book. I read many books and *Birdsong* will always be remembered by me as the book that brought me an understanding of a time in history that before I couldn't identify with.'[68]

> How many other people of my age (thirty-eight) simply view WW1 was being stuck in trenches firing guns at each other? The insights into the real people, what they experience, what they are thinking, forces one to think how it really must have been …
>   (footnote: the most moving WW1 image I have ever seen still remains the final scenes of Blackadder 4)[69]

'This is the most complete and gripping story I have ever read, for the first time the writer has made the first war relevant and real to me, in my life, now.'[70] Or as another reader had it: 'People should read this book … to be aware, without reading a dull, factual history book, how dreadful things were in the Great War.'[71]

Readers were not buying *Birdsong* because they knew about their family's involvement in the First World War (although it might inspire them to try to find out more). Where that knowledge did exist, however, it increased their engagement with the text and encouraged them to reconstruct imaginatively the experience of the war in their own minds: 'I picked up this book because it promised to be a war novel but I was surprised to find it was much better constructed than that … I couldn't help trying to put myself in my own grandads [sic] mind to try and understand what he must have gone through in those trenches. It felt like an extremely personal journey to me.'[72]

Knowledge of direct family involvement in the war affected only a minority of readers: 'Living only eighty years after the end of the First World War this book made me realise, just what our forfathers [sic] (Grandfather and Great Uncle and Great Grandfather in my case) went through in the trenches.'[73] For another reader, 'the war years were some of the best descriptions of WW1 I have ever read. Having a relative wounded on 1 July 1916 at the Somme made it all the more realistic and interesting.'[74]

Even those readers who were aware of their ancestors' participation in the war had a very limited stock of knowledge about it. They knew that relatives had served, or been at a specific battle, but they had no access to detailed myths about their wartime experiences. These readers made use of *Birdsong* to create a mental image of what the war had been like. There was a double appropriation going on here: of a relative's involvement as another reason for enjoying the book, and of the text itself as a basis for re-imagining what their experiences had actually been.[75]

The construction of *Birdsong* made this imaginative recreation easy. One of the principal strands of the book is the attempt by the heroine, Elizabeth, to uncover the facts of her grandfather's experiences in the First World War. She is able to do this because she finds his notebooks in her mother's attic – notebooks which have to be carefully decoded. Attractive though this is as a narrative device, how typical it actually was of how Britons were able to relate to their family's participation in the war must be questioned.

Faulks made much of his research in the archives of the Imperial War Museum in London. 'Here was the actual stuff: postcards written from the front, diaries and letters ... Here at last was food for the imagination unmediated by the selection and comment of another writer. The raw material gave a view of a world I was sure had been forgotten.'[76] In fact, Faulks's material can often clearly be seen to have come from published sources, most obviously Alexander Barrie's *War Underground*, published in 1962. Faulks's use of Barrie's work included not only the names of key characters, but the entire claustrophobic episode involving retrieving a wounded canary underground. He also made use of Stuart Cloete's memoir, *A Victorian Son*, and the letters of Wilfred Owen.[77]

Many of those who set out to retrace their family's involvement in the 1990s were in fact frustrated by the lack of significant evidence. The war had left a tide-mark of physical artefacts in families across the land, but the reality was that, once those who lived through the war had died, little remained for the majority of families from which to reconstruct the past. For example, Chris Moore's search for his maternal grandfather's part in the war began with the realisation of just how little survived: 'The hard facts consisted of two campaign medals, a miniature leather purse containing a 10-ore coin dated 1901, and a faded photograph of a soldier in uniform. These comprised the entirety of the Walter Butterworth Great War Archive. There were no letters, no diaries, no documents of any sort.'[78] Rather than a typical story, *Birdsong* offered an ideal model of what anyone interested in their family and the First World War would hope for.

This is not to discount completely the idea that writers and readers were interested because of their forefathers' participation in the war. Their interest was, however, often based on sparse information. Although it might be rekindled by reading a bestselling novel, it was generally not the reason for writing or buying one. There was a tension between a widespread belief in the possibility of recovering family history and the actual difficulty in doing so. Pat Barker was exceptional in her family life, which put her in remarkably direct contact with a veteran of the war in a way perhaps more typical of the inter-war years.

By the time these books were written, of course, there existed in British popular culture a unified mythology of the First World War that depicted it

in terms of mud, horror, stupidity and futility. Unsurprisingly, novels reflected many of these assumptions. A recognisable set of icons pervades them:
poets, men shot at dawn, asinine generals, doomed attacks, universal
bereavement.[79] Interestingly, this reproduction of negative myths took place
despite the fact that many novelists were not writing within an overall framework of embittered irony or in a modernist style. Instead, the war was
incorporated into stories from which courage, heroism and romantic love
emerged triumphant.

If this was a continuity with earlier writing, there was also a marked
change: the degree to which these books incorporated women into the First
World War. In the course of a wide-ranging literary boom, authors found
ways to set every popular genre during the war, but the area which expanded
most rapidly in the 1980s and 1990s was the popular romance with major
female characters.[80] Indeed, these novels made up the bulk of books published in this period. This was a major departure from what had, in fiction,
been largely a male preserve. For example, although the early 1970s saw two
critically acclaimed literary novels about the First World War by women,
Susan Hill's *Strange Meeting* and Jennifer Johnston's *How Many Miles to
Bablyon?*, both these books took as their subject relationships between men
before and during combat. They played heavily on what Fussell termed the
homoerotic.[81]

In contrast, many of the novels of the 1980s and 1990s were written by
women, for women, with women as central characters. Some of these works
enjoyed phenomenally large readerships – particularly since authors like
Catherine Cookson and Teresa Crane had loyal fans who would borrow
every book they wrote from local libraries.[82] In writing women back into the
war, these novels incorporated a further myth that we have not yet examined. They based their representation of the First World War on the belief
that it had brought positive change in the lives of women.

The dustjacket for Jean Saunders's *The Bannister Girls* made plain that the
war was an occasion for both liberation and romance. In 1914:

> little had altered since the days of Queen Victoria. All women, regardless of
> their status, had well defined roles in life – a life whose strict boundaries were
> rarely overstepped. But the advent of the war, which stole the lives of a gener-
> ation of young men, slowly began to erode such man-made barriers to equality
> and fulfilment ...
>
>   The horror of war comes hard to the Bannisters, forcing them to come to
> terms with a range of experience far outside their former sheltered horizons.
> Lady Bannister brings surprising comfort to the shattered minds and bodies of
> returning front line soldiers; Ellen endeavours to find a love that will not

compromise her feminist ideals; Louise loses a husband to find a soulmate among the wounded; and Angel is liberated by a love that comes out of a dark and rainy London night, taking her by surprise, and unleashing a dangerous passion that proves hard to quell.[83]

Kate Saunders put it more bluntly:

Years of careful upbringing and young ladyhood were blasted away into oblivion. The same Rory who had blushed to see Tom naked could now hold the penis of a strange man while he urinated into a bottle, without a tremor of embarrassment. She could hold a bowl filled with blood, and wipe vomit off the floor. It was a nightmare, but curiously liberating.[84]

Analysing the popularity of this myth not only gives us another example of the development and persistence of ideas about the war over time, but also allows us to speculate about the uses to which these modern novels were put.

Before the war, there had been a highly charged debate about women's social role and rights. As a result, when the war began there was already the foundation for its portrayal as a moment of transformation, although commentators at the time were divided as to whether or not any changes were for the better. Total war did indeed affect women's lives in a variety of different ways.

Contrary to popular mythology, the war did not give women the opportunity to get jobs: millions of working class women worked before the war as a necessity. But for many of them it did alter, albeit temporarily, their working lives. Initially, the principal experience for working women was unemployment, as the upper classes cut back on luxury goods and household staff. By the end of the war, however, women had entered a variety of fields of employment and national service. The most dramatic influx was in industry, with the number of women employed as labour increasing by one and a half million by 1918. The vast majority of these women moved into munitions factories for the duration. About half a million of them had formerly been domestic servants. Women also came into areas where they had been almost unrepresented before the war, with over half a million in total going into banking, commerce, the civil service and transport. Women served their country more directly in a number of ways. Farmers were assisted by a women's Land Army 23,000 strong. 40,000 women served as auxiliaries to the armed forces, 8500 of them overseas. By 1917 there were approximately 100,000 extra volunteer nurses, 5000 of whom served overseas.[85]

To what degree these changes transformed the women who experienced them is open to question. Levels of health and domestic service were more permanent changes, but actual forms of employment and attitudes were not. Most heavy industrial jobs disappeared with the end of the war or were handed back to returning soldiers. Although some women had taken on roles that were traditionally male preserves, men themselves had been doing something even more extremely masculine: fighting, killing and protecting home and hearth. The end of the war saw a backlash against transgressions of traditional gender expectations and most women went, not necessarily unhappily, back to their pre-war roles.[86]

The repetitive, dangerous jobs of many women working in the munitions industry were hardly empowering, even if their increased pay packets may have been. At work, few women replaced men directly, as a result of trade union intransigence. Instead they undertook roles which were perceived or portrayed as less skilled. Hierarchical attitudes and pay differentials persisted. Our mental image of women in the First World War may be dominated by grinning female munitions workers manhandling enormous shells, but many of these images were created by the government at the point when it wanted to tempt women into factories in order to sustain the war effort. The statistics for women's employment are themselves untrustworthy: they could vary dramatically depending on whether those gathering them wanted to demonstrate that women had been successfully mobilised or that they were not taking men's jobs.[87]

Most women over thirty did, of course, get the vote in 1918. But it is hard to argue that wartime service led directly to enfranchisement for women. Pre-war suffrage debates had been complex and there had been a widespread assumption – but not a universal acceptance – that eventual female enfranchisement was an inevitability. That it had not already arrived was the result as much of party political calculation as of ideological opposition. Similar short-term political calculations, not least a fear of the rising appeal of the extreme left after the Russian Revolution, seem to have encouraged the granting of the vote to women over thirty in 1918 – it being correctly assumed that this was the social group least likely to vote for radical upheaval. Women's wartime service was widely used shortly afterwards as a post-facto justification by those who had previously opposed female suffrage. If service to the war effort was really a key factor in enfranchisement, it is curious that those young women who had contributed most directly by their work in munitions factories were denied representation.[88]

There were also less tangible changes in attitudes and perception of self. For some women, the experience of higher wages, greater independence from family and participation in a shared cause increased their confidence and led them to think of themselves in new ways. On the other hand, some Britons placed increased emphasis on traditionally feminine behaviour as a reassurance against the shock of the war. Just as with men, whose different versions of the war we have already encountered, women's wartime experiences were complicated.

How complicated is in fact hard to know. Whether or not they have agreed with it, most historians of the period have positioned themselves in relation to the idea that there was positive change in women's employment and political participation. In seeking to prove or disprove that thesis, they have ignored other areas. The result has been that the full breadth and depth of women's experience of the war has remained unexplored. Where are the studies that focus on elderly women, or those married to men at the front, or those who lived outside industrial Britain? These groups – largely unphotographed and absent from the literary record except as a target for combatants' wrath for their incomprehension – are surely also part of the story of what the First World War meant for British women.[89] In particular, little systematic work has been done on the day to day effect – on men and women – of long-term separation from loved ones and of anxiety for their fate.

But these groups were almost absent from public discussion even as the war was being fought. Women's experience of the war was described in terms of change as it was happening. Their transformation could be used in different ways by different groups. If the government wanted to tempt women into the factories, it would stress the degree to which war work had empowered and remunerated them. For social conservatives, the war was seen to have resulted in a tidal wave of sexual misbehaviour and illegitimacy. Neither interpretation was completely divorced from what was actually happening, but neither represented it fully or accurately.[90] All sides focused on the idea that the war had transformed women.

Formed from a variety of motivations – mobilisation, social control, self-justification – it took longer for the myth to develop into an idea that the war had meant change for the better. Whilst its origin lay in a change of the popular media's discussion of suffrage, however, the linkage between wartime service and post-war enfranchisement was so evident to contemporaries that it required no explanation.[91]

In 1934, when Sir John Hammerton compiled his *Popular History of the Great War*, he included, in the final volume, a chapter on 'Women's Activities', which opened by suggesting that:

The scale ... upon which women's services were ultimately utilised in the four years of conflict was entirely without precedent and the record stands as an

astonishing indication of the change wrought by the Great War in the life of
the nation. Work in innumerable trades and professions ... was left in the
hands of the womenfolk, and as their successful encroachment on men's fields
of labour proceeded, forced by the urgent necessity of the times, old barriers
of prejudice and tradition were swept away.

Hammerton's chapter continued by describing women's service in the
VAD, the Auxiliary Army Corps, the WRNS and the Land Army, and by
munitions and public transport workers. He concluded that 'through the
mass demonstration of their abilities in the wide field of their wartime
activities women proved convincingly their fitness for an equal share with
men in public life'. He then moved on to his next chapter, on 'The
Employment of Animals', which suggests that some of the old prejudices
remained.[92]

As with other aspects of the First World War, interest in women's role
was overwhelmed by more immediate concerns through the late 1930s
and 1940s, although the government's handling of women workers in the
Second World War was influenced by the lessons it drew from its predecessor. In popular history the war continued to be constructed as an essentially
masculine event until the late 1960s. *The Great War* television series, broadcast in the mid 1960s, devoted only minutes of its total running time of over
seventeen hours to recounting the experiences of women.[93] Arguably, for all
that it achieved a majestic overview of the war in its twenty-six episodes, it
obscured at least half the story.

The same period, however, saw the production of a number of books
that placed more emphasis on women and the war. In 1965, Arthur Marwick published his social history of Britain and the First World War, *The
Deluge*. Marwick chose to argue a case that remains controversial amongst
historians: that the demands of total war could lead to social change, from
which previously disadvantaged groups – including women – might benefit.
Marwick revelled in the paradox that war might prove a positive force, but
although his argument was new, the beliefs on which it was based fitted
into the prevalent mythology of what the war had meant for women. Unsurprisingly, given that it had been a subject of extensive discussion at the
time, he was able to quote from a variety of wartime sources that supported
his interpretation. What he did not do was to question the context in which
they were created, the motivation of their authors, or how representative
they were of what had actually happened to women. *The Deluge* was typical of the 1960s in that it reflected the period's ambiguities; the continuing
interest in the First World War of the generation which grew up in its aftermath; and the writing of history which, although it might offer new

opinions, was based largely on existing published sources rather than archival research.[94]

Marwick's work became the first point of reference for many of those who wrote about the military, political or cultural history of the war. It was easily accessible, conveyed its author's historical passion, and seemed to provide scholarly backing for widely held beliefs. Indeed, it has become a sort of ur-text, its version of the war accepted and cited uncritically by generations of historians and students.[95]

But *The Deluge* was also symptomatic of a developing academic interest in social history, which, combined with a growth of women's history, resulted in the first serious studies of the female experience of the war. Some of these books sought to challenge the dominant mythology of the war as a moment of decisive change for the better. It is indicative of the strength of that mythology that they were still arguing within its terms – chiefly employment and enfranchisement – rather than moving beyond it to research new interpretations.

Nevertheless, by the time the wave of romantic novels burst over the heads of the reading public in the late 1980s, historians were beginning to recover the variety of ways in which the war affected women. Although they were part of the same overall movement – an increase of interest in women and war – it was not, however, to these new historical texts that novelists turned. Rather, they were influenced by a more popular historical source: literature, and in particular the recently republished (and adapted for television) memoir, *Testament of Youth*. Written by Vera Brittain and first published in 1933, *Testament of Youth* tells the story of her service as a VAD nurse and the tragic loss of her entire circle of male friends, including her fiancé and her brother. The social historian Janet Watson has analysed the diaries and memoirs of Brittain and other female writers of the early 1930s and placed them in the context of the wider remembrance of the war at that time. She suggests that *Testament of* Youth was originally usually read either as a disillusioned war book in the same genre as those produced by male subalterns, or as an example of grief-stricken mourning. Although it was popular, it was not originally a feminist tract.[96]

Testament of Youth was republished in paperback by Virago in 1978 and swiftly became a bestseller, assisted by its adaptation into a BBC drama series, broadcast the following year. Its influence over subsequent novelists is apparent in their choice of occupations for their heroines. In two thirds of the novels produced in the period from 1978 to 1998, the principal activity for the main female characters was nursing, usually in France as a VAD. In fact, of course, this was the role of a tiny minority of women; perhaps 0.00025 per cent of the female population. Writers were not rehearsing

inherited family myths of wartime service, nor representing a historiographical shift: they were making use of a literary trope which was easily
accessible to them and to their readers.

In so doing, however, they developed the meaning of the original text.
Vera Brittain's original intention in writing *Testament of Youth* was not to
celebrate female empowerment but to warn a younger generation of the
horrific impact of modern war. Closely involved with the League of Nations
Union in the early 1930s, she was desperate that no one else should have to
suffer as she had done. Sorrow is the prevalent emotion in her memoirs.[97]
This emphasis survived the translation to the screen. The television adaptation stuck closely to Brittain's original text, unsurprisingly given the strength
of the demands for 'accuracy' of her literary executors and her daughter, the
politician Shirley Williams.[98] Although beautifully performed and designed,
in the best traditions of television literary adaptations, it is dark and depressing viewing. Many reviewers wrote of their emotional reaction. For some
this seems to have been the appropriate reaction for any First World War
drama: 'Even as the opening title of *Testament of Youth* appeared ... I could
feel the tears welling up in my eyes.'[99] Letters written in to the Radio Times
stressed the 'moving' aspect of the series.[100] BBC audience reaction surveys
reveal that the series gained a larger audience as it progressed, growing from
1.9 million to 2.6 million viewers, and coming to dominate the Sunday
evening schedules ahead of programmes on BBC 1 and ITV. Viewers' comments emphasised the *Testament of Youth*'s position as prestige drama,
'moving and memorable', and consistently stressed positively its perceived
'realism' – despite adult actors playing the roles of schoolboys to what now
seems almost comical effect.[101]

The combination of book and television series were enough to establish
Testament of Youth as a central text for the appreciation of women and the
war, and a direct line is traceable between incidents recorded by Brittain –
for example the episode where a nurse sings to wounded Germans – and
more modern fictional texts. Contrary to contemporary predictions,
however, *Testament of Youth* did not introduce a whole new generation of
young women to the war.[102] There is strong anecdotal evidence for it spark-
ing the interest of young women in a way that other television series
connected with the war might not have done, but the statistical evidence is
that the majority of its viewers were older. Although 70 per cent of the audience for the series was female, it was concentrated in the age group above
thirty years old, with the largest proportion of the viewers aged fifty and
above. This was also, of course, a key market for the authors and publishers
of popular romantic fiction.

Can we position the revivification of *Testament of Youth* and the boom in war romances as part of a wider social development? Given the way in which modern novels appropriated Brittain's text in order to emphasise female empowerment, it is tempting to suggest that this was symptomatic of the impact of feminism on popular mythology. *Testament of Youth* was, after all, republished by a feminist publishing house. Were women finally reclaiming their part in the First World War?

Yet examining the contexts in which these myths were reused calls into question their feminist credentials. The social politics of popular romantic fiction were overwhelmingly conservative. The morals these novels drew were traditional: nice girls would find fulfilment through love and marriage, however much penis-holding and vomit-wiping went on in the meantime. Bad girls would come to an even stickier end. However much they mythologised the past in terms of change in women's lives, the expectations they encouraged were far from radical. The most successful romance of the period was *Birdsong*, in many ways just a more explicit version of an old-fashioned 'bodice ripper', which paid very little attention to myths of female empowerment in wartime. Even the image which dominates so many of these novels – voluntary nursing – was used to suggest that 'equality and fulfilment' came through the performance of a traditionally feminine caring role.

On the other hand, we do not have to implicate a radical feminist agenda in order to suggest that these texts did indicate a change in the way women perceived themselves. In the end, how accurately they reflected historical events made little difference to those who were reading them. Whether or not the First World War had a positive effect on women's lives, many Britons came to believe it did. As a result, it has become a milestone in a popular understanding of the twentieth century in terms of continual improvement in women's status and rights. That myth tells those who believe it something about their own identity and social position. Notwithstanding their treacherous tendency to reinforce social traditions, these stories could be used to create an identity involving a struggle for equality. Reading about empowerment was itself empowering.

It is also noticeable that the surge in popular history of the First World War has been driven by women as much as by men. Despite the perception that the war is predominantly a male interest, in fact women play a significant role in the activities of organisations which study and commemorate it, such as the Western Front Association. It might be suggested that the emplacement of the war as a cornerstone of family history has encouraged and legitimised women's involvement in military history as a pastime in a way that was not previously the case. Another area which is ripe for research is the degree to which women's memories of the war

were encouraged to surface in this period because their longevity meant
that it was they, rather than their menfolk, who were the last surviving
participants in the war.

The continuing British relationship with the literature of the First World
War deserves a massive study in its own right – far more so than the works
of the soldier poets themselves, which have been studied to death. The
reduction and concentration of literary representation of the war demonstrate two key processes of popular mythologisation at work. As time went
on, both authors and audiences grew further from the war, feeling less
immediate connection because of their lack of personal knowledge of events
or participants. The difference between the audience for *The Great War*, sitting down in the hope of catching sight of Dad or Grandad, and that for
Birdsong, only inspired to look back at their family's involvement as a result
of reading the book, makes clear a generational shift in the relationship to
the war. At the same time, myths about the war became more coherent and
consistent. The war became more of a symbol – easily shared and commonly
understood – than a multi-faceted, personally remembered event. Even
Owen's poetry, for all that it gained post-Second World War popularity
because of its continued applicability to the sad circumstances of other
conflicts, had lost some of its resonance by the end of the period. It had been
reduced to a unit on the school syllabus marked 'Pity of War'. And yet,
amongst a population which had largely lost any personal knowledge even
of those who had fought in the First World War, a desire existed to recapture its experience. It was this desire that would stimulate the current British
fascination with the war.

6

Veterans

In the last quarter of the twentieth century, as the First World War was reduced to a single set of easily communicated myths, it also became increasingly personalised. As the war grew further away, a central element of its representation became the testimony of a steadily dwindling band of eyewitnesses. Despite frequent predictions of their demise, not an anniversary went by but the last remaining veterans were pursued by television cameras and newspaper journalists as they thought of their fallen comrades or tried to pass on the torch of remembrance to a younger generation. Documentaries on the war could not survive without a veteran on screen as a talking head, stamping their approval on the producers' version of history.

Those who experienced the First World War looked back on it as an important event in their lives. It was their moment of participation in a great historical event. To find them remembering it was nothing new. What was distinctive was the degree to which their memories of the war took centre stage. Ironically, the point at which veterans of the First World War began to die in large numbers coincided almost exactly with the moment at which their testimony, as process as much as content, began to take a significant place in national mythology. This had significant implications for how their accounts were presented and for the memories rehearsed by veterans themselves.

Like anybody else, veterans had always remembered their experiences partially, depending on the context in which they rehearsed their memories. The development of a dominant mythology about the war might not initially affect what a veteran was capable of recalling, but it did alter what he was likely to rehearse in public. Memories grow stronger with repetition and weaker without it, so over time veterans' versions of the war were reconciled with the way the war was being talked about around them.[1] The result was sometimes that veterans might change what they remembered – or even make it up. We cannot assume that because a man was there at the time he is giving us a version of the war which is reliable, accurate or useful.

This can be a difficult subject for the non-combatant historian to tackle. There is a temptation, meeting surviving veterans in person, on screen or on the page, to grant them an aura of instant credibility. They have seen and done things most of us have not and they are very, very old. To question the veracity of their accounts can seem like disrespect. No insult is intended to these men when their testimony is treated critically. To do otherwise, to elevate them to a special status as keepers of a 'truth' which cannot be judged by those who were not there, does a disservice to what they achieved.

Like all their compatriots, British veterans reacted to the war in many different ways. Some could not forget the terrible experiences it had inflicted on them. There were numerous soldiers who returned from the war determined to consign it to history and never think about the whole dreary, monotonous, time-wasting and horrific business again. There were others who were eager to remember actively aspects of what they had experienced. Important elements of ex-servicemen's experience were obscured in public remembrance of the war from the mid 1920s. Veterans who wanted to celebrate wartime comradeship, excitement and loyalty could not do so in the midst of public mourning on 11 November. Those who thought to record these emotions in books, plays or monuments often found that their work was being interpreted in terms of protest against the war. One comfortable space where these versions of the war could be recalled was in the company of fellow soldiers. Sometimes these groups were formalised as Old Comrades' Associations, which allowed the recreation of the camaraderie that had meant so much to many men.[2] These groups participated in public ceremony – as on Armistice Sunday – but also commemorated the war privately in ways that seemed more appropriate to them: nostalgia and beer. Their numbers were never large compared to the total number of soldiers, but there were many who, while they maintained no formal membership, participated in ceremonial or social occasions. Those veterans who belonged to Old Comrades' Associations were not separated from the majority who chose to be less active in their remembrance of the war. Rather, they represented one end of a spectrum, taking part regularly in activities that other veterans might participate in often. Their behaviour might not have been typical, but nor was it completely unrepresentative.[3] Former officers may have had the experience and the social status to organise more formal associations and dinners, but the local basis for recruitment at the start of the war helped to ensure that other ranks continued to encounter each other in the pub, on the street or around the dinner table for years to come.

These Old Comrades' Associations encouraged veterans to rehearse more positive memories of the war. Although there was a place for recalling the awfulness of the trenches, in the company of friends and alcohol it was tempered by a concentration on the better times. Remembering humour, victories and friendships obscured more problematic memories. By their nature, many of their activities were exclusive and ephemeral. They have left

little trace on the historical record. Occasionally in the inter-war years, however, we can catch sight of these veterans: finding a bond of shared wartime
experience, contributing to or buying copies of regimental histories, or
appearing in the memories of their children as they held mysterious
conversations across allotment fences or over a pipe after Christmas dinner.

That many old soldiers continued to value their military service and the
country they had fought for was apparent in the dark days of early summer 1940. When the appeal for volunteers to join the nascent Home
Guard, the Local Defence Volunteers (LDV), was put out by Anthony Eden
on 14 May, Great War veterans were amongst the first to respond. By the
end of June, there were nearly one and a half million volunteers. Numbers
in individual platoons varied, but it has been estimated that approximately
30 per cent were veterans. Some local estimates at the time went as high as
fifty per cent.

As the crisis passed and the duties of the Home Guard became physically more demanding, First World War veterans tended to be sidelined.
But in that first summer of the war, they demonstrated that the patriotism which had seen them join up in 1914 could still be roused when their
nation was under threat. The result – at least in the first months – was an
enormous memory club in a context which encouraged reminiscence.
Night patrols and sentry duties often placed veterans in small groups of
male comradeship where it was easy and appropriate to recall previous
military experiences. Charles Graves, the Home Guard's own historian,
remarked at the time that a striking feature of the Lincoln Area group in
1940 was

> the wide range and diversity of experience amongst the members. One night
> guard (containing about twelve men) included, for instance, a Marine who had
> been on the mole at Zeebrugge; a Heavy Artilleryman, an ex-Cavalryman ...
> who was prepared to take apart and then to reassemble and fire any known
> make of machine gun of British, French, German or Italian make; men who
> had been through the Somme, Ypres and Gallipoli. One secured an epitome of
> the whole of the last war by talking to these men in the Guard Room at night
> when they were off duty.[4]

Another Home Guard veteran suggested that

> none of us will forget our first LDV route march. On it a quarter of a century
> slipped away in a flash. There came memories of the Menin Road, of loose,
> shifting, exasperating cobbles, or the smell of cordite and the scream of shrap-
> nel, of the mud and stench and misery of Flanders, of hopes and fears of battles
> long ago ... There were few youngsters in that first platoon of ours.[5]

Veterans were particularly visible in the Home Guard because they often took leading roles. Many retired senior officers became local area organisers, and other ex-officers took up more junior command roles. This did not necessarily make things easier for the authorities; veterans were not shy about using their experience to claim a right to take charge or to criticise military arrangements and training. Frequent disagreements took place between the military, who saw the Home Guard's role in the event of invasion as one of reconnaissance, and veterans who were keen to attack vigorously any enemy who might come within range, despite the paucity of their weapons. These men thought they knew their jobs and sometimes had the connections to complain about poor equipment.[6] There is a temptation to regard their enthusiasm with ridicule – as *Dad's Army*'s Corporal Jones would have had it: 'They don't like it up 'em!' – but they could lay claim to a better record in combat than their younger counterparts.

The British regular army that fought the Second World War contained a number of men who had seen service twenty-five years before. For the most part, they were long-service NCOs or senior officers. Again, as the war went on the number of First World War veterans playing active roles decreased as they were judged too elderly, but Britain's most senior officers throughout the war were men who had been subalterns in the last great conflict. Most of them had seen front-line service on the Western Front. Their warlike return to the European mainland gave them cause to reflect on their previous experiences.[7]

For example, on 14 December 1939, General Sir Alan Brooke, who had been an artillery officer on the Western Front, went out to reconnoitre a possible flank defence for his II Corps of the British Expeditionary Force. The journey took him past some familiar sites:

> I also went past the first billet I ever occupied near the front in 1914 in the vicinity of Vielle Chapelle. I saw the old ditch into which the trench ambulance had fallen on that first night and out of which my Farrier extracted a silver communion set and a new pole for our water cart. The former we had to return to a French priest who came to reclaim it, but the pole we kept! I also went past where the billet had been when the ration tobacco made us feel ill, another where we lost most of our horses to shellfire, and finally the one where my Colonel Asquith grumbled that the soup would never come up the stairs warm! It was just a mass of memories which were given a bitter tinge through the fact that I was again starting again [*sic*] what I thought at the time I was finishing for good and all.[8]

Notwithstanding the stimuli to memory which came from the Second

World War, these recollections remained privately rehearsed. The creation of a new generation of veterans, with their own reminiscences, might have threatened to overwhelm their forebears. In fact, veterans of the First World War remained passionately interested in their war and became, if anything, more vocal as time went on.

One place where veterans' involvement had always been visible was the letters pages of the national press around anniversaries of the great battles of the war. For example, following the publication of the volume of the *Official History* in 1948 which dealt with the Third Ypres campaign, newspaper letters columns became the forum for a lengthy discussion between former soldiers of all ranks, including senior officers, about the state of the ground and of systems of command during the battle.[9]

Veterans' continuing interest was apparent as younger historians restarted the controversies surrounding the war in the early 1960s. At the centenary of Haig's birth, in 1961, the British Legion's chairman, General Sir Roy Bucher, spoke out against critics of the Field Marshal at the Legion's London conference. Eight hundred veterans applauded loudly.

'I find it ridiculous that young men who know nothing about grand strategy should set themselves up to blot the fame of the great Field Marshal.' Sir Roy, who served under Haig in 1914, said later: 'It's very easy to look back and say what went wrong. But it is ridiculous to lay all the blame on Douglas Haig, who did his damnedest for his country.'[10]

The next week, two letters appeared simultaneously in the *Daily Telegraph*:

Sir, I was pleased to read of the defence of 'the great Field Marshal' Earl Haig by Gen. Sir Roy Bucher at the annual conference of the British Legion. I was a subaltern with the 1st Dorsets in 1916 and the Commander-in-Chief had posted to us as transport officer his elder brother, too old for front-line service in the ordinary way. I remember Earl Haig coming down to see how he was getting on. He spoke very kindly to those of us he met, and we all thought the world of him. We were on the Somme at the time and it was shortly before the battle. Those who criticize Earl Haig have little idea of conditions obtaining at that time, and it is only too true that it is easy to be wise after the event.

Yours faithfully, J. W. Hunt, Captain.

Sir, Haig's formation of the British Legion was the best thing he ever did. But to talk of his 'grand strategy' makes one gasp. He decimated a generation of splendid British volunteers, in 1916, '17 and '18, without showing any appreciable military advantage. On the Somme he ordered division after division to march up to the German concrete machine gun posts, to be wiped out in tens of thousands. The casualties amounted to nearly half a million!

...

T. H. Arundell, late 47th Division, BEF.[11]

These letters demonstrated that veterans continued to hold differing views on the quality of command, and that they based their opinions on personal experience. They claimed authority because of their wartime service and believed that their opinions were not only valid but should be shared with the wider public. Veterans had a powerful sense of ownership of 'their' war and resented any efforts to alter their long held views about it. Four years later, John Brophy, another veteran of the war, remarked of younger writers that 'they have the further advantage, which historians almost always lack, that there are living survivors of the period who can check, and if necessary correct, the factual records from which history proceeds, or ought to proceed'.[12]

Veterans tried to undertake this process of checking and correction as they took part in the great wave of public interest in the war during the 1960s. There were still plenty of them alive: in 1961 it was estimated that there were some two million men still alive in Britain who had fought in the First World War.[13] We have already encountered some influential examples. Captain Basil Liddell Hart was well established as Britain's foremost military commentator and, although the focus of his research had moved elsewhere, remained fascinated by his own war. The huge amount of information he had gathered in the files at his home in Medmenham made it a remarkable military history database, a first port of call for new researchers. He continued to revel in controversy and correspondence and engaged with a range of thought on the First World War throughout the 1960s.[14] In a different sphere, Edmund Blunden exercised a major influence on works of literary criticism and anthologies of war poetry in the same period.

The 1960s also saw an increase in the number of published memoirs by former servicemen. Some of these new books can be accounted for in terms of a renewed willingness on the part of publishers to tackle the war because of the publicity attendant on the fiftieth anniversaries. Others were written in part in reaction to perceived misrepresentations of the war.[15] The most important factor in their production, however, was veterans' own experience of ageing.

Across Britain, the generation of men who had fought the First World War reached an age where they retired from their jobs; in practical terms, this gave them more time to write their memoirs. Being older meant that there was a social expectation that they would remember in public: it had become their role to tell stories about the past. It also increased their awareness of their own mortality, encouraging them to look back and try to make sense of their lives. Some wanted to set down their experiences for the historical record.[16] For members of the social and political elite, it was clearly anticipated that memoirs should be written and published. For the ruling class that retired from British public life in the 1960s, the First World War had been a formative experience. Britain's first four post-Second World War Prime Ministers had all seen service with infantry regiments in the front line. Figures as diverse as Maurice Bowra, John Reith and Alec Waugh all looked back on their war in the 1960s.[17]

These books did not contain a single, monolithic view of the war. Rather, they continued to reflect the variety of veterans' experiences and subsequent reactions. Some had loathed military service, others had loved it. They often displayed an awareness of ongoing controversies about the war and were in part conceived in terms of participation in continuing debates. For example, while Alec Waugh and R. C. Sherriff both stressed that incompetent generals had been unaware of the suffering of the infantry, George Duncan and Charles Carrington argued for their dedication and ability.[18]

Most of these works were not immediately successful or influential. They were seldom heavily reviewed and few made the transition to paperback (the key sign of a book's popularity). They did not offer exciting new interpretations of the war, few were well written, and they had to perform in competition with the host of reissued memoirs and novels that had been popular thirty years before. As a result, their publication passed almost unnoticed. For subsequent writers about the experience of war, however, they were to form a significant resource.[19]

Whilst no comprehensive register of Old Comrades' Associations exists, many of them continued to function into the 1960s. Indeed, as with the writing of memoirs, they may have gained strength from the increased amount of time available to retired veterans. In 1966, for example, the Arras and District Branch of the British Legion produced a pamphlet to mark the fiftieth anniversary of the Battle of the Somme. Although it had a section devoted to 'The Hell of the Somme', its main emphasis was on comradeship. It told its readers: 'above all you'll have paid attention to the beautifully kept "silent cities", the war cemeteries of the Somme where so many of your comrades are sleeping their "sacred sleep" … Today they certainly lived again for you and no doubt they also will have recognised the once well-known tread of a friend.' The pamphlet also described the Branch's innovative approach to fund-raising through the reconstruction of wartime good cheer:

> This was the all-time record breaker which was the 'Dugout'. A large number
> of Legionaires [sic] who happened to be on tour in Arras, were invited to

partake of an original bully-beef supper with pickles, in the setting of a mock-up dugout, with a decor of war souvenirs and badges. This has been repeated and it is hoped that this year it will bring the same success to the branch as it did last year.[20]

A number of former soldiers did indeed return to the Somme for the fiftieth anniversary. One of them wrote to a former comrade: 'it was an extraordinarily good commemoration at Thiepval last Friday, you would not have recognised Albert. All civic buildings were beflagged, the streets were full of bunting and flags, and the town was full of British soldiers, most of them, of course, in civilian clothes ... The *estaminets* were crowded with English people, which was very much like old times.'[21] The vitality of these veterans (as well as their interest in current sporting affairs) is apparent in a contemporary photograph of veterans relaxing after the Thiepval memorial ceremony.

The determination of some veterans to commemorate their more positive version of the war persisted from the inter-war years through to the 1960s. By their nature, however, such events were not accessible or attractive to subsequent generations. Those with experience of a war that had been memorialised in popular culture as the most awful Britain had ever fought were members of an exclusive club: they might fascinate younger men and women, but to participate in their activities was much harder. At the same time as veterans were gathering around Arras, the Commonwealth War Graves Commission was noting a reduction in enquiries about the location of First World War graves, and new visitors to the battlefields found them unnavigable: unsignposted, without amenities and seemingly abandoned.[22]

All these visible activities were symptomatic of remembering which was occurring more privately. Veterans who would not have dreamed of writing their memoirs for public consumption experienced the same ruminating effects of old age and retirement as politicians and philosophers. They began to talk to members of their families about what had happened to them in the First World War. A range of external stimuli, including the growth in public interest in the war, encouraged them to rehearse their memories. In particular, *The Great War* stimulated a wave of family reminiscence in the mid 1960s. The combination of a long-running and highly popular series, authentic-seeming footage and the appearance of numerous eyewitnesses brought home to veterans and others that their experiences had value and were still available for recall.[23]

During the making of the series, the BBC placed an advertisement in the national press asking for eyewitnesses to the war up to the middle of 1915. Veterans wrote to the production team in their tens of thousands. The new assistant appointed to research these contributions found herself confronted with a room full of sacks containing some 50,000 letters. These ranged in length from a few lines to 165 pages, and many veterans sent not just letters but mementoes – badges, photographs and keepsakes – as well.[24] As the series was broadcast, many more veterans wrote in to share their memories. Their letters encompassed a huge range of different attitudes to the war. Whilst some had found the war horrific, and many had clearly been influenced by subsequent representations, others retained positive memories of wartime experience. These letters had little to do with specific images on the screen or points in the script. Rather, old soldiers had been stimulated to an act of memory by the series.

The Great War functioned as a trigger for the rehearsal of memories, not just in writing, but within individual families. It is clear that the series was, in modern terms, event television. People rushed home to make sure they saw it. Families gathered around the screen to watch. Specifically, *The Great War* encouraged an interaction between younger Britons and their grandparents about what they had done during the war. For many veterans the broadcasting of the series encouraged a cathartic reaction, stimulating a discussion which helped to ensure continued interest in the family history of the war and extended the 'shelf-life' of family mythologies.

There were also changes in environment and veterans' social position within families that encouraged them to rehearse their memories for their grandchildren. A common feature of veterans' reminiscences of modern war is a willingness to talk to grandchildren about experiences they have not discussed with their children.[25] One of the roles that societies have traditionally given the elderly is the rehearsal of memories. They are recognised as a repository of the stories that bind individuals and groups to their pasts and allow us to locate ourselves socially and culturally. For the elderly there is an understandable desire not to be forgotten, to pass on memorable information and perhaps, as short-term memory becomes less reliable, greater ease of access to more distant recollections. Wrapped up in this is identification with the young: a recognition that the elderly once stood where their descendants are and a desire to pass on hard-won experience. Grandparents' rehearsals of memories were the equivalent of memoir-writing for a much more specific audience.

As important to consider may be the position that grandchildren occupy relative to their grandparents. They are emotionally closely connected, but not necessarily geographically collocated: indeed, with the growth of the nuclear family, it has become less common for grandparents and grandchildren to live together. This may make it easier for information to be passed on without the consequences of disclosure having to be faced. Potentially difficult memories can be recalled to be preserved for the future, without the need to confront those memories and their impact every day for the rest of a long life. This works both ways, since grandchildren may value their grandparents' memories above those of their own parents, with whom their emotional relationship may be more fraught, or whose experience may seem closer to their own.[26]

We have to be careful before constructing the 1960s as a period of perfect memory transmission. No matter what memories Grandad (and sometimes even Grandma) chose to rehearse, their audience placed them in context and illustrated them with the benefit of a wider set of texts about the war. There was no guarantee that veterans would find an audience. Stanley Holloway, in a narration for the 1916 episode of the ABC series *Time to Remember*, broadcast on ITV in the late 1950s, contrasted the way his two veteran 'uncles' remembered the war. The first, Uncle Ernie, who had been on the Western Front, wouldn't talk about it at all. The second, Uncle Charles, who had been at Salonika, wouldn't stop talking about it, even though nobody wanted to listen. These uncles were fictional, but Holloway (or his writers) had caught the contradiction inherent in veterans' reminiscences: if they don't talk, they must know something fascinating; if they do talk, they can be hard to stop.

C. P. Blacker had been a young officer on the Western Front in the First World War, where his brother was killed. After the war, Blacker had a long and distinguished medical career. He began to write his memoirs for his family in 1963, when he was sixty-seven. Beginning with a short chapter on his schooldays, he moved swiftly on to the war years:

> as his account of the war became longer and longer, members of his family expressed the hope that his 'autobiography' would not be confined to this relatively short period of his life. His war experiences, we pointed out, were far from unique, and such as had already been vividly described by others, notably Robert Graves and Siegfried Sassoon. On the other hand his later life had held much of unusual interest: he had qualified in medicine and then specialized in psychiatry ... he had also played a pioneer role in the birth control movement, which had ... undergone enormous changes during his lifetime. But these suggestions were met with a firm refusal: his 'autobiography' would go no further than November 1918. Eventually it took him longer to write than the war had lasted, and when finished it ran to some 900 pages of typescript.[27]

It was only twenty-five years later that his family realised the importance of the document he had created and published it for public consumption.

From the end of the 1960s, however, veterans' active participation in remembrance of the war declined. Old age caught up with the generation that had fought the First World War, rendering them frailer before finally killing them off. Veterans' independent contributions to debates about strategy and tactics dropped off in the late 1960s. The fiftieth anniversary of Passchendaele was the last to fill newspaper letter columns with veterans' correspondence.[28] Although individual veterans did still contribute letters, there was no longer a sense of an ongoing debate between them. Although, as we will see, veterans would continue to be utilised to represent the war in books and documentaries, it was no longer at their own instigation.

The decline in veterans' participation can also be seen in the fate of the Old Comrades' Associations to which they belonged. Age meant not immediate disappearance but an initial decrease in visibility as a result of illness and falling numbers, before an eventual extinction. For example, the last organised parades of the 'Old Contemptibles' (an association which restricted itself to those regular soldiers who had served throughout the war) took place in London in 1964, and in Ypres in 1966 and 1975. There were no longer sufficient numbers of veterans fit enough to march.[29] The 18th Division's Officers' Dining Club is another example. The club was active for many years after the war, its social occasions raising money for the upkeep of the division's Battlefield Exploit Memorials – marking its victories – which were not maintained by the War Graves Commission. Even in the early 1950s, the club had to downgrade its standard of maintenance on three memorials because declining membership numbers meant that revenue had decreased. Despite this, the club remained active throughout the 1960s, organising celebratory dinners for the anniversary of the division's founding and encouraging public interest in the memorials. By 1978, however, the membership was down to single figures, and the organisation had to be wound up. The list of members, with more and more names crossed through with red ink, forms a sad picture of a passing generation.[30] Other Old Comrades' Association suffered the same fate.[31]

Tracking numbers of ex-servicemen after the end of the war is extremely difficult. Neither the government nor veterans' organisations kept track of the total numbers of surviving veterans. However, it is possible to make use of information from the decennial census and from the Ministry of Pensions to suggest how the population of veterans fell over time. Taken together, what these sources indicate is that there was a specific sharp drop in that population from the end of the 1960s. The rate of decline amongst veterans being paid pensions by the government doubled between the 1960s and the 1970s. By the early 1980s it had tripled.[32] The sheer number of deaths is one explanation for veterans' declining participation in remembrance, but it was not that they had become extinct. Some veterans outlasted the associations they had created. Rather, a 'tipping point' of mortality had been reached.

The deaths of veterans who occupied key nodal roles meant that comradeship groups broke down, convinced them that they were dying out, and made them appear rare in society. Networks of remembrance were broken. Indeed, the effects of old age and illness began this process before the impact of rapidly increasing rates of death took effect.

In the short term, veterans' awareness of their own mortality could act as a stimulant to remembrance. In the early 1970s, C. E. Crutchley was inspired to compile a collection of personal accounts of the Machine Gun Corps by a fear of losing veterans' memories forever. In these circumstances, it was not surprising that works like Crutchley's placed a heavy emphasis on comradeship and heroism. Within individual families, the death of a veteran could lead to a reconsideration of his life and the discovery of artefacts hidden away in attics or cupboards when the deceased's home was cleared out. It does not do to romanticise this process: before the 'heritaging' of the First World War in the 1980s, veterans' mementoes were just as likely to be thrown out as kept.

In the long term, the result of this extinction of veterans was that the war stopped being publicly remembered by those who had experienced the war at first hand. Even where individual artefacts were kept and valued within families, their place in the process of remembrance and mythology had changed: they were hallowed relics of the imagined past, rather than stimuli for acts of memory about wartime experience.

Beyond this, the breakdown in those networks which had encouraged veterans to meet together and repeat positive myths about the war affected their processes of recollection and rehearsal. It moved what individual veterans remembered of the war away from nostalgia and towards denigration. They were encouraged to reproduce old memories in different forms, or to create new rehearsals which would match the expectations of a changed audience. It also left the collection and presentation of veterans' memories in the hands of a younger generation who inevitably recast them for their own purposes. In the public sphere, veterans were no longer in control of their own recollections. The dying out of veterans and the decline of the organisations they had created played a significant role in the establishment of negative myths in an overwhelmingly dominant position. Veterans did not preserve a 'correct' version of the war, but when they remembered it together they could rehearse memories which differed from more widespread myths. Whilst they survived, veterans encouraged each other to commemorate more positive aspects of the war.

Ironically, it was at the same moment that veterans began to die off that they began to be placed centre-stage in new representations of the war. From the mid 1960s, works of popular history in print and on television placed veterans' own accounts of their experiences increasingly in the foreground: to the point where the few veterans still capable of speaking coherently to camera became recurrent stars of remembrance programming. How and why did this happen?

As part of a growing interest in what the war had been like, journalists, writers and television producers all began to pay more attention to veterans' testimony. Many continued to rely on documents written at the time, but others began to base their work more heavily on the accounts of veterans who were still alive. Television programmes, in particular, came increasingly to depend on footage of old men remembering their youth. Published collections of such memories, created by writers who had tracked down surviving veterans, also became popular. In both cases, the standards of the material thus created could vary dramatically.

In televisual terms, it is clear that *The Great War* established a powerful set of conventions about the depiction of veterans. The series used a number of veterans to talk to camera about their experiences. Their accounts were intercut with the archive footage which made up the bulk of each programme, a process rendered less disjointed than it might have been by the fact that all the film stock was in black and white. It was the policy of the series that veterans should be anonymous during their screen appearances: no captions appear to identify them to the audience. This was itself a major departure. Former combatants had appeared in previous representations of the war (for example, Bud Flanagan and J. B. Priestley had both reminisced about their wars on radio in the early 1960s). These men, however, were celebrities first and foremost, who had also happened to see wartime service. In contrast, *The Great War* granted veterans status because of what they had seen and done. In employing them in this way, the series producers were making use of an established news documentary style which emphasised the inclusion of eyewitness accounts of events. *The Great War* was produced by a team which came out of the BBC's *Tonight* current affairs programme. It was therefore not surprising that they should have made greater use of these 'news' conventions than a more contemplative 'arts' approach.[33]

Given the huge number of veterans who responded to the series appeal for information, the makers of *The Great War* were able carefully to select those who would appear on camera. Their criteria were historical as well as presentational. Whilst it was important to them to have veterans who could speak coherently and confidently in front of the rostrum camera, they were also able to choose those who had witnessed key events they wished to illustrate: for example, the landings at Gallipoli or the first German gas attack at

Ypres. In the footage selected for broadcast, veterans were not encouraged
to offer opinions about the war. Their purpose was to describe for viewers
what the war had been like, not what it had meant.

The broadcast of *The Great War* initiated a wave of reminiscence in families across the country. The clarity and vividness of some of its veterans'
accounts also seems to have sparked a realisation in some viewers that their
memories were an underused resource with a limited lifespan. In concrete
terms, the material generated by the series became the basis of archival collections which facilitated future study of the individual experience of the
war. The letters written to the BBC before *The Great War* was broadcast were
deposited in the Imperial War Museum, London, where they became the
basis of the Department of Documents. Staff in the Department used these
letters as the basis for follow up work collecting contemporary materials and
later recollections. Similarly, the initial recordings made when selecting
veterans for inclusion in the series formed the first holdings in the Museum's
Sound Archive. The collection of further material was given added impetus
in the early 1970s by a realisation that veterans were rapidly dying out.

This increased interest in veterans also fitted into a wider growth of interest in the individual's experience of the past. When it came to the recent
past, the collection of material for such studies was greatly facilitated by
the development of the cheap, portable audio-tape recorder. The end of the
1960s saw the beginnings of an oral history movement which aimed to
capture individuals' participation.

By its nature, this nascent branch of historical studies suffered some
severe methodological problems, not all of which were fully realised by participants at the time. The context in which veterans are encouraged to
remember has a major effect on which memories they rehearse. The interviewer's questions, attitudes and responses can therefore have a significant
'observer-effect' on the material which is gathered. For example, for many
(but by no means all) veterans, the question 'Tell me how awful your war
was' will elicit an answer in terms of awfulness and horror. Similarly, beginning by asking questions about specific events tends to result in a small
range of stock answers: particularly from those veterans who have an inclination to remember in anecdotal form. Contemporary oral historians would
suggest that best practice involves the creation of a neutral interviewing
environment, in which veterans are encouraged to take themselves back and
to remember their experiences as they lived them at the time, rather than
through the lens of hindsight. Subsequent interviews might then explore
more specific areas of interest. This was not a model much followed in
the early 1970s with First World War veterans. For example, the first
interviewers sent out by the Imperial War Museum sound archive were

interested in Victoria Cross winners, the horrific nature of trench warfare and soldiers' attitudes to generals and executions. The archive contains a wonderful interview with Philip Neame (a Royal Engineer officer, VC winner and Second World War general), in which he is increasingly baffled by the interviewer's insistence that he should criticise staff officers and the High Command. To the interviewer's evident frustration, Neame insists they were doing the best they could in difficult circumstances.[34]

Such teething difficulties do not mean that we should write off oral history as 'old men drooling', in A. J. P. Taylor's famous condemnation. Some people have an ability to recall in almost infinite detail – in the process bringing to the historian's attention a host of information about everyday life during wartime that might otherwise pass unnoticed. This sort of detail has, in fact, often not been used by documentaries because it is not of immediate interest to non-specialist historians, although in recent years it has become more popular, perhaps because of the increasing foreignness of all these veterans' experiences to modern Britons. Some incidents burn such deep memory traces that they can be recalled sharply years after the event. Not every veteran reacts to popular myths by accepting them. Those who have built an identity around being curmudgeonly can wilfully oppose them: perhaps moving to be more strongly positive about the High Command than they ever were during the war, for example. But we do need to be aware of the importance of *process* in the gathering of such information.

Those who chose to write about the war through research with veterans were largely left to develop their own methods. One of the most distinctive was that employed by Martin Middlebrook, the author of two studies of days of battle in the First World War, 1 July 1916 (*The First Day on the Somme*, published in 1971) and 21 March 1918 (*The Kaiser's Battle*, published in 1978). Middlebrook is a Lincolnshire farmer who grew up with stories about the First World War. His two uncles both served, one being killed and the other wounded and captured. His father was too young to serve, but one of his boyhood friends was shot down and killed flying with the RAF in 1918. Middlebrook visited the battlefields for the first time in 1967. Whilst his family connections were with more northerly sites – Ypres and Arras – it was the huge cemeteries and memorials of the Somme (at that point almost empty of visitors) which impressed him the most and formed the starting point for his book, *The First Day on the Somme.*[35]

Middlebrook's research technique was individual but extremely thorough. He assembled a detailed historical framework from painstaking research in contemporary documents, regimental and official histories. This framework was then fleshed out by a mass of eyewitness accounts, compiled from letters and interviews, resulting from newspaper appeals for information.

When interviewing veterans, Middlebrook first gave them a detailed briefing about what their unit had done on that day to encourage them to give him a description of that battle and no other and to dissuade them from fabrication. He did not record their responses on tape, in the belief that the production of a tape recorder encouraged men to declaim into it. Rather, he took notes and then wrote up their accounts before making use of them. All the veterans involved were asked to approve the use he had made of their testimony: he never had a complaint of misrepresentation.[36]

There are obviously a host of potential risks in this method, but it did acknowledge and confront the problems of fabrication and anecdotage. It is a testament to Middlebrook's scrupulous approach that its results were historically as well as popularly successful. In both *The First Day of the Somme* and *The Kaiser's Battle*, he produced highly accurate and detailed accounts of battles that achieved balanced views about controversial command decisions and casualties, and conveyed a great deal of what the experience had been like for veterans. The books are not only engagingly written: sometimes the depth of Middlebrook's research allowed him to refute established interpretations. Most obviously, in *The Kaiser's Battle* he pointed out the frequency with which British soldiers surrendered in early 1918. Units which were reported 'destroyed' had seldom fought to the last man.[37]

Middlebrook treated veterans' testimony analytically. He used it as another source of evidence for an interpretation, subject to the same critical treatment as other texts.[38] His honesty was apparent in his acknowledgement of the variety of attitudes which veterans still had to their wartime service even in the early 1970s. The last page of *The First Day of the Somme* stresses the breadth of meanings that veterans took from their experience:

'One's revulsion to the ghastly horrors of war was submerged in the belief that this war was to end all wars and Utopia would arise. What an illusion!' (Corporal J. H. Tansley, 9th Yorks and Lancs)

'July 1st 1916 was the most interesting day of my life.' (Lieutenant P. Howe, MC, 10th West Yorks)

'It was pure bloody murder. Douglas Haig should have been hung, drawn and quartered for what he did on the Somme. The cream of British manhood was shattered in less than six hours.' (Private P. Smith, 1st Border)

'As I was one of the lucky ones, I still say I am glad I was there.' (Lance Corporal C. F. T. Townsend, 12th Middlesex).[39]

But this was not 'oral history' in the sense that it was principally based on the testament of those who were there at the time. Rather, Middlebrook can be located in a proud antiquarian line which included many of those officers who wrote wartime histories of their units in the 1920s. Going and talking to the people who had been there and done the business was not a brand new departure in the 1970s.[40] What was different was a greater willingness to talk to ordinary soldiers as well as officers, not least because veterans from specific units were becoming rarer and rarer.

It was not just his research method, but sometimes his writing which harked back to an earlier (but no less well informed) age. There was little room, in Middlebrook's interpretation, for the irony and cynicism which dominate many modern attitudes to the war. He argued that: 'The only good to emerge from that terrible day was the display of patriotism, courage and self-sacrifice shown by the British soldiers. Theirs is a memory that their country should always cherish.'[41] This was a celebration of traditional martial values that would not have been out of place in the inter-war years. Even when writing about the generals with, as one reviewer put it, 'a certain dry tang', Middlebrook's comments were balanced and well argued.[42]

Nevertheless, Middlebrook can be seen to have been influenced by, and contributed to, the dominance of mythical interpretations of the war that emphasise mud, blood and incompetence. Notwithstanding the traditionalism of his language, he selected for study days of disaster for the British army. Courage and patriotism might have been evident in abundance on 1 July 1916 and 21 March 1918, but strategic and tactical ability were not. He did not examine other exceptions (the dramatic victory of 8 August 1918, for example) or more typical days which featured assaults from neither side. His version of 'deep' history did not lend itself to the study of long campaigns. This meant that Middlebrook did not place his subjects in context. He could not point out the learning process gone through by Britain's New Armies on the Somme after 1 July, nor the way in which the conscripts defeated in March 1918 managed to recover and force back the Germans four months later. *The First Day on the Somme*, in particular, grew out of and sustained a focus on 1 July 1916 as symbolic of Britain's whole war.

The First Day on the Somme was the starting point for a television documentary, Brian Duffy's *Lions Led by Donkeys*, broadcast on Channel Four in November 1985. Duffy's programme was typical of the way that veterans' experiences were represented on British television after *The Great War*.[43] The hour long programme focused on the experiences of the Pals' Battalions destroyed on the first day of the Somme and made use of veterans' testimonies, archive footage and computer graphics.

Lions Led by Donkeys was at pains to point out the relevance of its subject to a contemporary audience from a standpoint that was left wing and pacifist. It opened with a modern shot of a young man looking at adverts in a job centre, before turning away to look at a recruiting office. His reflection in the glass lined up with that of cardboard cut-out of a modern soldier. The reflection then changed so that he was dressed in First World War uniform. In the final moments of the programme, a shot of Accrington War Memorial with its myriad names from the First World War was also shown to bear the names of two soldiers who died in the Falklands. As its title (mistaken when Clark applied it to 1915, it is perhaps even less accurately applied to 1916) implied, *Lions Led by Donkeys* was explicitly critical of the senior commanders on the Somme, Haig and Rawlinson. Although it produced an 'expert', Norman Dixon, author of the popular *On the Psychology of Military Incompetence*, to argue that Haig's personality was at fault, it relied on a number of veterans to validate this view. Russell Bradshaw said that 'they made a huge mistake, a terrible mistake, no doubt about that'. Towards the end of the programme, Frank Lindley declared that 'Haig were a butcher, and 'e wanted shooting'.

Lions led by Donkeys highlighted two problems with the use of veterans in television documentaries. During the war, ordinary soldiers held a variety of views about the quality of their leaders. Most of them would not have expressed such extreme views about Haig in particular: they were far more concerned with the quality of their platoon and company commanders. That the veterans portrayed in *Lions Led by Donkeys* were so ready to 'blame the vain, incompetent leadership which sent their comrades to their deaths', in the words of one reviewer, did not necessarily reflect their views at the time. Rather, it was indicative of the degree to which the attitudes some veterans were willing to rehearse had been affected by seventy years in which condemnation of the 'Donkeys' had grown relentlessly stronger. Any such tendency was, of course, strengthened by the programme's editing team, who selected footage of veterans to fit their own agenda. This was a self-reinforcing process, of course, since any veterans watching the programme would have had made it clear to them which memories it was publicly acceptable to rehearse.

There was a second problem, which was to do with the worth of assessment which any veteran was capable of giving purely on the basis of their military service. Just because they were there at the bottom of the heap does not mean that they had the breadth of understanding to come to an assessment of their commanders. Almost by definition, modern total war seen from the bottom looks chaotic, ill-planned and tragic. The planning for the Somme battle contains some notable examples of apparent incompetence; what is remarkable to the modern historian is the degree to which those who had experienced 1 July did *not* lose faith in their commanders straight away.

That the first day of the Somme was in places a disaster does not mean that the whole battle should not have been fought or that Haig and Rawlinson were necessarily murderous idiots, as opposed to capable men struggling with the circumstances in which they found themselves.

The distortions occasioned by this interaction of veterans' recollections with modern commentators' attitudes was apparent in the construction of the 1986 BBC drama series *The Monocled Mutineer*. The programme contains a distressing sequence in which a young officer is reduced to the ranks before being shot at dawn for desertion. The series hero, Percy Toplis, is assigned as a medical orderly to keep him company on the night before his execution. This episode did not occur in the book on which *The Monocled Mutineer* was based, a fanciful account of Toplis's life by the journalists William Allison and John Fairley. It seems to have come instead from the testimony of the BBC star band leader and dancer Victor Silvester. At the time of *The Monocled Mutineer*'s broadcast, it was suggested that these scenes were a direct incorporation of his memories of participation in a wartime execution at Étaples.[44] Discerning what may actually have happened is rather more complicated.

Shortly after Silvester's death in 1978, newspaper stories appeared claiming that, after seeing confidential documents relating to those shot at dawn at Étaples in 1917, he had been punished by being forced to be part of the firing squad for the next five executions. The stories featured direct quotations from Silvester with graphic details of the horrific aftermath of the shootings.[45] The 1978 stories were at variance with Silvester's own memoirs, published in 1958. In these, he wrote that he was only at Étaples very briefly before being posted to Italy. There, he claimed he had seen Italian officers shooting deserters during the retreat from Caporetto.[46]

As the historians of British military discipline, Catherine Corns and John Hughes-Wilson have pointed out, however, Silvester's army records, released in 2000, tell another story. On 4 September 1916, he enlisted in the Argyll and Sutherland Highlanders, claiming to be twenty years old. In fact, he was only sixteen: a week later he was discharged from the regiment when it was discovered that he was under age. Silvester then joined the First Aid Service and served with them as a non-combatant in France from October 1916 to June 1917. When he turned eighteen in January 1918 he re-enlisted in Britain with the Argyll and Sutherlands, but did not serve overseas with them.[47]

Although it is therefore remotely possible that Silvester witnessed executions whilst in France, it is highly unlikely that he participated in them. It is more likely that, as did most soldiers, he heard about them in routine orders or secondhand from his comrades. His fabrication of his military service in his memoirs has to cast doubt on his credibility as a witness. There is no case, moreover, of any British officer being reduced to the ranks before being shot for desertion.[48] Only two British officers were executed for this offence during the war. The senior officers who confirmed these sentences placed particular emphasis on the guilty men's rank: it was necessary to treat officers in the same way as enlisted men. In the case of the first, Eric Skeffington Poole, the Adjutant General of Second Army specifically noted to those responsible for the execution that an officer did not lose that status because a death sentence had been passed. Skeffington Poole should therefore not be stripped of his badges of rank before being shot.[49] It seems probable that Silvester also fabricated his participation in these executions, almost certainly under the influence of the growing interest in the issue of those shot at dawn after the publication of William Moore's *The Thin Yellow Line* in 1974.[50] Allison, Fairley and Alan Bleasdale were, however, happy to incorporate his memories because they fitted well with their preconceptions about the brutality and victimisation inherent in the First World War.

The strength of controversy about some aspects of the war could dissuade the collector of veterans' memories from taking sides. An apparent example of this is the work of Lyn Macdonald. Macdonald's interest in the First World War began when, as a BBC Radio 4 reporter and producer, she accompanied a group of veterans on a visit to the battlefields in 1972. The next year, she left the BBC and began the assembly of information that led to *They Called it Passchendaele*, her first book, published in 1978. Six subsequent volumes have covered nearly every other aspect of Britain's war.[51]

In some ways, Macdonald's achievement is remarkable. Her hard work located and recorded the testimony of numerous veterans which might otherwise have been lost. Her books have stimulated the interest of numerous readers and raised the public profile of the First World War. Macdonald's journalistic background shows, however, in her approach, which was much less detailed and analytic than Middlebrook's. Her writing exists primarily to set out a narrative framework of the war, campaign or battle within which to situate quotations from veterans. The absence of footnotes or referencing makes it difficult to source the quotations she uses from veterans. This problem is exacerbated by Macdonald's (commercially understandable) refusal to allow other researchers access to her files.

To give one example: writing about the landings at V Beach during the Gallipoli campaign, she quotes from the notebook of 'Lieutenant-Colonel Williams of the General Headquarters Staff', who made a minute by minute record of the progress of the landing. Macdonald writes that Williams, 'could hardly believe their good fortune' at the initial lack of opposition, but was then 'appalled, and his hand shook as he scrawled ...' 'Somehow, despite his own horror, Colonel Williams managed to carry on recording the calamity.'[52] In fact, this minute by minute account comes direct from a footnote in the Official History of the campaign.[53] Here the same notebook record of Colonel Weir de Lacy Williams is quoted in its entirety, although without details of his emotional state.

Macdonald identifies with the veterans she encounters to a remarkable degree. She has organised trips back to the battlefields and campaigned for honours on their behalf. She argues that in writing: 'As always, my aim (and in a sense my obligation) has been to stand in their boots – regardless of rank, position or nationality – and ... to see things through their eyes, to try to understand, and above all not to be judgmental.' This lack of judgement has been a continued theme in her introductions. She explicitly wishes to avoid the debates about how the war was fought: 'It is not my intention to enter the lists. This book does not set out to draw political conclusions and, although it is the story of a battle, it is more concerned with the experience of war than with the war itself.'[54]

Co-opting veterans' experience may be an obligation, but it is also a validation: Macdonald's claim to status as an expert on the First World War is based on her knowledge of a large number of veterans. In her most recent book, Macdonald has rejected modern interpretations of the war: 'The word "horror" has become inseparable from contemporary judgement of the First World War, but it is too glib an appraisal. In many years of conversing with older soldiers I can say with perfect honesty that I have never heard the word "horror" on their lips, though many of the experiences they spoke of were indeed horrific.'[55] This forms an interesting comparison to her suppositions about de Lacy Williams' emotions at V Beach, and the introduction to her first book, in which she stressed breathlessly that: 'If this book reads ... at times like a horror story, please do not blame me. It is all true, or rather, it is compiled from more than 600 true stories and eyewitness accounts of men and women who were there in the mudbath of Ypres.'[56]

It is the second half of that statement, however, which is revealing of Macdonald's attitude towards the testimony that she collects and the problem of her refusal to exercise judgement. Just because a veteran said it does not mean that it is true. As we have seen, there can be real value in the testimony of those who experienced an event at first hand. But they are no less subject to the vagaries of memory, cultural influence and fabrication, both at the time and subsequently, than anybody else. If the reader is provided with no information about the nature of the source and the context in which it was gathered, there is no basis for a judgement about its validity. More-over, 'truth' is a tricky concept when it comes to representing a historical event. Whose truth? The veterans' or Macdonald's? By their nature, Mac-donald's books favour one version of 'truth' over another. Constrained by space and by the need to develop a coherent narrative, there was a natural tendency to include the testimony of veterans who were able to compose their memories in the form of self-contained anecdotes with their own beginning, middle and end, in what has been termed a 'stand-up comedian' style of recollection.[57] It is notable how often veterans' testimony in Mac-donald's books ends with an exclamation mark. This may indicate a veteran who is comfortable with certain memories and has frequently rehearsed them, but it is not a comprehensive or necessarily accurate form of remem-bering. One example is that of a veteran remembering with great clarity a disastrous cavalry charge on the Somme, quoted at length by Macdonald. It is a great story, confirming many popular beliefs about the uselessness of mounted soldiers on the Western Front. But military errors in the descrip-tion and the unit diaries of the cavalry units involved, as the historian Richard Holmes has pointed out, make it clear that the event recounted with such emotion never in fact took place.[58]

As time has gone on, of course, the effect of this sort of qualitative selec-tion has interacted with a quantitative selection imposed by death and infirmity. The number of veterans still alive and capable of rehearsing their memories coherently has grown smaller and smaller, although, at the time of writing, they have not yet completely died out. Again, this has tended to promote certain sorts of memory rehearsal: not least the recollections of the youngest soldiers and of the most junior ranks. Those veterans who were identified by historians or by television networks as having particularly good stories which they could recount well found themselves interviewed and filmed time and time again. Unsurprisingly, their recollections became more clearly composed and better articulated with each rehearsal. We might ask ourselves, however, whether they are remembering their wartime experi-ences or the version of them which has been previously condoned and validated.

The difficulties which derived from this combination of credulity and a dwindling number of veterans were apparent in the 1998 BBC series *Veter-ans: Last Survivors of the Great War*. The two episodes of *Veterans* formed the centrepiece of the BBC's coverage of the end of the war's eightieth anniversary. The series' producer, Steve Humphries, had, with the assistance of the historian Richard Van Emden, scoured the country for those old sol-diers who were still alive and capable of telling their stories. The result was two hours which mixed archive photographs and footage with surviving veterans recalling their experiences on camera. Rather than examining single battles, the series described soldiers' lives, bringing out more mundane aspects such as the stultifying effects of boredom and routine, the importance of food and drink for maintaining morale, and the roles of singing and swearing. By concentrating on such details of everyday life, the series seemed to make the best use of veterans' recollections to evoke the past rather than to pass judgement.

It received a great deal of newspaper coverage. Most of this focused on the remarkable longevity of the veterans, a small number of whom were also very active in the eightieth anniversary commemorations in London and Ypres. Both journalists and critics were stunned by the discovery of such coherent geriatrics. More detailed analysis of what they were actually saying was overtaken by astonishment, much as the first glimpse of archival footage in *The Great War* had stunned audiences thirty-four years before. Reviewers tended to concentrate on those aspects of the veterans' stories which fitted best with a model of futile mismanagement, quoting George Littlefair's verdict on the death of his best friend on the Somme: 'All this, and it was for no bloody purpose after all's said and done', and Fred Tayler's conviction that he was wounded because of 'mistakes at the highest level'.[59] Viewers, as well as eyewitnesses and editors, could be selective in the testimony they chose to listen to.

Many of the soldiers' tales were indeed well told and extremely moving. Arthur Wagstaff's surprise at his survival on 1 July 1916, George Littlefair's distress at having to abandon a friend, and Fred Tayler's shock at discovering his leg had been amputated were all still palpable and affecting. They brought home to the audience some of the human components of war. The series script emphasised the value of the veterans' testimony: 'Eighty years on, their stories have become the most eloquent possible account of the tragedy of war.'

Almost too eloquent in fact. These men were not consciously distorting what they recalled, but their memories had been affected by the huge quantity of public discussion of the war over the eighty years since its end. For example, Bill Cotsgrove gave a moving account of the way he would play his harmonica to cheer up the troops – including 'Waltzing Matilda' for any Australians – before taking it out and playing for the camera. Although Banjo Patterson wrote the poem 'Waltzing Matilda' in 1895, it did not arrive as a piece of popular music in Britain until the mid 1920s. It was unknown to British soldiers of the First World War. On the other hand, it has been a staple piece of background music to dramas and documentaries about the war, used to suggest the presence of Australians, much to the disgust of purists, since the 1950s.[60] Perhaps this sort of distortion – hardly the massive fabrication of which Silvester seems to have been guilty – does not matter, but it does indicate the cultural pressures veterans were under.

It should not surprise us that these men should appear so coherent in describing their memories for the camera: they had had eighty years of practise. Some had even more specific experience of historians and television documentary teams. Fred Francis, although severely wounded, survived the attack of the Lonsdale battalion of the Border Regiment on Beaumont Hamel on 1 July 1916. By the 1980s, he was the only survivor of this bloody assault on an iconic day. As a result, he appeared repeatedly on television and in books. The accident of his survival, first of a particularly disastrous action, then of the intervening eighty-two years, had left him with a remarkable influence on the public mythology of the Somme. This was hardly a position he could have suspected when being read the last rites on 1 July 1916. Men like Francis became minor celebrities by the achievement of long-term survival. That achievement had earned them the right for their testimony to go unchallenged.

Yet there was a paradox here. Even as their rarity gave these men potentially more control over what was remembered, so their relative isolation made them more vulnerable to influences which distorted what they remembered. More than that, these veterans had lost power over their own memories. They no longer represented them to the public on their own behalf. Rather, their memories had become commodified: units of historical 'truth' that were passed on for younger generations by producers and writers who edited them for their own purposes, whether political, polemical or for purposes of entertainment. So willing was the public suspension of disbelief at veterans' testimony that it was possible to pass almost anything off as representing the 'real story' of the First World War.

Nowhere is this more apparent than in the recent success of Max Arthur's *Forgotten Voices of the Great War*. The book is a collection of excerpts from taped interviews in the Imperial War Museum's Sound Archive. In total, 146 interviewees are quoted, although their testimonies are divided up and arranged chronologically with reference to different campaigns and battles. Arthur introduces each section with a brief description of the year's action, but for the most part the transcripts are left to speak for themselves. There is no indication of the context in which the interview was made, the age of the speaker or the distance from events, their own intervening life story or the questions to which they were responding. As with other collections of veterans' recollections, it is extremely difficult to assess the value of these men as witnesses. In fact, although this is nowhere indicated in the book, the majority of the interviews on which Arthur relies were conducted as preliminaries for *The Great War* in 1964. These veterans were interviewed because they were eyewitnesses to key events, but also because they were able to compose their stories into coherent narratives. They were interviewed by a junior researcher from the BBC, not by the sort of expert implied by the book's proud trumpeting of its connection with the Imperial War Museum. The interviewees included numerous men who had already written extensively on the war, including Edmund Blunden, Charles Carrington, Graham Greenwell and the German Stefan Westmann. Many of those interviewed by the BBC subsequently made it into the broadcast version of *The Great War*, where they recalled the same events which are detailed in *Forgotten Voices* in the same words.[61]

These tapes from *The Great War* are certainly useful to anyone wanting to construct a book quickly, since they are much briefer than a carefully conducted oral history interview, they already by their nature cover the major events of the war, and they contain the sort of anecdotal remembering that makes good entertainment. Quite what they add to the reader's understanding is less apparent. Arthur's contributions to the volume indicate that he is au fait with current historiography on the war, but this is not fully reflected in the subjects his veterans talk about. Rather, their interviews clearly reflect the concerns either of the BBC researchers in the 1960s or the Imperial War Museum's researchers in the early 1970s. Unsurprisingly, then, there is much repetition of stories about the mud and horror of the trenches and a surprisingly high number of veterans remembering executions, with no explanation of why this might be. The reader is left to assume that the veterans quoted are representative of the wider whole of the army.

There are, of course, elements of these recollections which are useful and faithfully reflect experiences beyond that of the individual who recorded them. Unusual experiences (if they can be identified as such) are also of use. But to what degree any of these voices is 'forgotten' is debatable. Leaving aside the fact that many of these testimonies appeared in the most popular series about the First World War ever shown on British television, men like Carrington (author of two books on his experiences, both of which have been quoted ad nauseam by later writers) have had their voices pretty well preserved by posterity.

But the *idea* that these were rediscovered voices carrying a previously hidden truth about the war was obviously very attractive. *Forgotten Voices* not only made it onto the *Sunday Times* bestseller list, but also garnered critical appreciation from such experts on the First World War as Andrew Motion and Stephen Fry. The *Times Educational Supplement* made it a book of the week and commented that it was 'tailor made for classroom use as well as maximum impact on the general reader'. That this impact consisted of the soft thump of previously held assumptions being comfortably reinforced seems to have been lost on the reviewer.[62]

How are we to understand the popularity of works which described the experience of soldiers in the First World War? One explanation was that, in commercial terms, writing about individual experience offered a useful new approach to the First World War. So much of the material produced in the 1960s had been mired in the same old debates about the quality of generalship or the utility of the war that to further rehash these controversies did not seem a profitable line for the new writer. In contrast, as soon became apparent to those involved, accounts of personal experience could be financially as well as personally rewarding. As the (seemingly unexpected) success of Arthur's *Forgotten Voices* makes clear, these books are still potent commercial propositions.

There was also, in the aftermath of the 1960s, an awareness of veterans' existence and the realisation that they offered a dwindling resource of personal evidence. As we have seen, one of the key innovations introduced by *The Great War* television series was the use of unidentified veterans talking to camera about the episode's events. This not only encouraged Britons to think of their grandparents' memories as of more than personal interest, it also made use of news documentary approach to establish a televisual convention that eyewitnesses should appear on screen wherever possible.

Another explanation is an academic change. The more intrepid historians began to venture outside their ivory towers. The early 1970s did see the acceptance in some academic circles of individual experience of the past as a valid field of historical study. Since the beginning of the twentieth century, political, social and cultural change had encouraged historians to look beyond the traditional areas of study, the activities of politicians, generals, kings and queens, and to examine instead what historical events had meant for those involved at the sharp end. This trend was further encouraged by the increasing democratisation of the educational system after 1945. For historians of the recent past, a key source for such studies was the recollections of those who had experienced events at first hand. The growing interest in such studies encouraged the development of oral history as a recognised branch of wider historical study.[63]

How much influence such academic developments actually had on the study of the experience of the First World War is unclear. Few if any of those who wrote about what the war had been like in the 1970s came from within the university system. Rather, they came from a longer standing tradition: magnificent obsessives who had developed such a fascination with the war that they had to research and write about it. Their inspiration for doing so was often personal; the memory of a father or uncle who had fought in the war and not returned or who had never spoken of his experiences. Simultaneously, the generation of writers who began to examine personal testimonies in the 1970s had been too young to experience combat in the Second World War. Before and after 1939, they had grown up in a society in which military service was a constant reference point, but they had never faced the challenges, trauma or triumphs of war at the sharp end. Its enigma continued to fascinate them.

In this absence of experience they were typical of many of their readers and a growing number of the population. For generations which had not fought, but who were repeatedly reminded of the significance of the world wars, these accounts provided something to fill that experiential gap. As one book trade buyer had it in 1998: 'The First World War is sexy ... Young people want to know why. They want to know what it was like – they find it through poetry and fiction and then want the real history.'[64]

Yet this history was 'real' only in the sense that it fitted with the big myths of what the war had been like. The enormous problems of relying on much-rehearsed memories of events long ago seriously challenge the status of these books. Those which combine a reliance on such individual recollections with an absence of analysis may be entertaining, but readers are deceiving themselves if they think that through them they come to a greater understanding of the past. Entertaining the reader is – or at least should be – one of the uses of history, but if it is the only one what is there to distinguish such texts from works of fiction?

Of course, this is part of what makes the bestselling narratives of personal experience so attractive. They are easy reads which do not force readers to think. Indeed, Macdonald's abdication of historical responsibility allows her readers to use her books to flesh out their own myths. For example, Kate Saunders, in her review of 1915, found plentiful evidence for her view of the generals of the First World War as château-bound idiots, blundering in the mud: 'Through repeated disasters and spectacular casualties, they went on assuming that they could send in the cavalry as soon as the rain stopped.' This is a view that Macdonald herself would reject as inadequate. Reviewing the same book a month before, John Terraine interpreted it as backing up his understanding of 1915 in terms of British heroism and pragmatic ability to overcome logistic disadvantages.[65]

It is not enough, however, to argue that these books were just literary chewing-gum – something to keep the eyes working without any sense of engagement or satisfaction. The key reasons for their success were that they were produced in a context in which the rediscovery of the war became a popular topic and that they personalised a historical event. In doing so, they facilitated the imaginative reconstruction of the past.

It is important to recognise that these texts did not exist in isolation. Instead, they were part of a burgeoning sub-culture of fascination with the war. Collections of personal testimony went alongside newly discovered and published memoirs, novels, films and guidebooks. It was the same readers who were revelling in *Birdsong* or *Regeneration* who were buying collections of eyewitness testimony. As one reader of *Birdsong* explained:

> Since reading this book, I cannot view the Remembrance Day programs [sic] or services without shedding a tear. It has lead [sic] me on to read diaries and other non-fiction works regarding the first world war horrendous trench war-fare [sic]. I encouraged my children to read the book and think that thereby they could more easily empathise with their ancestors who suffered under very similar circumstances ... My sister-in-law subsequently used an extract from it as a reading in her school's Remembrance Day service.[66]

The construction of the First World War as an event in family history was a central part of this fascination with the war. For much of the twentieth century, family history was the interest of a small group of antiquarians and genealogists, primarily concerned with tracing bloodlines and coats of arms. In the 1980s, the subject became much more democratic: a larger number of people studied families from a wider range of social backgrounds. These newer participants were more likely to study the branches of their own family trees. Their pursuit had the nature of a hobby, rather than the full-time occupation of their predecessors, and they learned its techniques as they went along. The explanations for this boom range from the uncertainty attendant on modernisation through to changes in leisure culture.

The war was a natural starting point for these enthusiastic amateurs: not least because they were regularly being told that every family had partici-pated. For many families, it was indeed where 'history' had begun, both because it had slipped beyond the edge of living memory and because some artefacts or family myths had been preserved. Although, until the late 1990s, recovering soldiers' service details was complicated, there were a host of other locations in which information about them could be found, including rolls of honour from parishes, counties and businesses, county record offices, regimental museums and numerous published sources.[67] In itself, this was indicative of what a massive human and bureaucratic effort mobil-isation for a modern industrial war had been.

It was not only the case that official documentation of various sorts still existed, but also that some individuals had recorded and preserved their memories for the future. The growth in house-ownership over the

twentieth century after the end of the First World War had encouraged
the storage of items which might otherwise have been discarded.[68] The
First World War was the starting point for many family archives because
it coincided with an explosion of popular photography.[69] Changes in
property possession and literacy meant that it was possible for artefacts
to survive. But the survival of such physical reminders of the war should
not be overemphasised. Few families had vast collections of letters, photographs or meticulously recorded myths on which to draw. Rather, they
possessed, if anything, a small number of artefacts uncertainly attached to
half-remembered narratives.

For example, John Wright wrote of his fascination with a childhood
memory of a photograph:

> Around six at the time, I remember being passed the khaki coloured postcard
> taken in an indistinct room with a tiled floor, of four young soldiers ... awk-
> wardly posed in attempts at nonchalance on and around a wooden bench. The
> picture had a hole through it.
>
> Later I asked my father why the hole was there and he simply said 'bullet
> hole'. The picture was of my Uncle Bernard and three comrades. It had been
> in the breast pocket of his battledress when the sniper's bullet passed through
> his own face in the picture into him.

Later in life, Wright sought out his aunt to confirm that this had not been
a confabulation of his memory. She not only gave him the photograph,
along with an undamaged copy, but also told him that Bernard had died
close to 'Pullcapple'. Wright was able to research the history of the Yorkshire regiment Bernard had been attached to and pinpoint his involvement
in an action around Poelcappelle in October 1917. Subsequently, Wright
visited the area with his son, attempting to recapture in his mind's eye what
his uncle would have seen.[70] Whilst the preservation of artefacts could help
to ensure that knowledge of participation was passed down within a family,
it was unlikely to carry with it a detailed narrative of experience.

In this context, collections of veterans' testimony in print or on screen
acted as a reservoir for those who knew that their family had been involved
in the First World War, but had none of the more complex narratives of
experience they desired. They could be appropriated and used for an act
of imaginative recreation: *this is what my grandfather went through*. This
act of appropriation was clear in a review of *Veterans: Last Survivors of
the Great War*: 'My own grandfather would never talk about his experiences.
I still have the piece of shrapnel that went into his foot during the Battle
of the Somme, and which brought him home safe, if slightly lame. I have
no idea what he was doing when he was wounded. Fortunately for us, the

men on last night's programme were ready to talk. Their memories have remained extraordinarily sharp, as though indelibly etched on metal plates.'[71] The accident of longevity had given these men the chance to play the role of elderly family members to the nation: they had become universal veterans.

John Wright was just one of numerous visitors to the battlefields of the Western Front. In the 1960s and 1970s, such visitors wrote with the assumption that they were all but forgotten. From the mid 1970s, in a process that paralleled the development of interest in veterans' testimony, journeys to the battlefields and cemeteries of the First World War became popular once more. Numerous guidebooks were published for such tourists, covering both the war as a whole and individual battlefields.[72] At the same time, a number of British men wrote books detailing their experiences as they travelled to France and Belgium to investigate their forefathers' war.[73] All of these books described a degree of re-enactment: walking the front line, following a line of advance, crouching in a preserved trench and imagining what it had been like.

The desire to recreate wartime experience can be traced in other representations of the First World War at the same time. Prior to the 1980s, the depiction of the war in museums was broadly similar, based on the artefacts associated with combat, grouped together in large numbers and placed in cabinets, accompanied by information panels and guarded by occasional mannequins in uniform. The better provided for might have featured displays of medals and accounts of how they had been won.

This continues to be one mode of exhibiting the war, but from the early 1980s new approaches towards display began to gain popularity, which emphasised the importance of 'experiential learning'. In 1990, the Imperial War Museum opened its 'Trench Experience' exhibit. Constructed during the major refit and renovation of the museum in the late 1980s, the Experience rapidly became one of its most popular exhibits, particularly with parties of schoolchildren. The exhibit consists of a dugout and two firebays, modelled on those held by 1/10 Lancashire Fusiliers on the Somme in autumn 1916. A number of mannequins are positioned at different points and the visitor 'overhears' the organisation and launching of a trench raid. A specially developed 'trench smell' pervades the air. Today, if you visit the museum on a weekday, you will still find the Experience surrounded by children on school visits, making faces at the smell and attempting to peer over the top of the darkened trench. Some will almost certainly be making machine gun noises through their teeth.

The development of the 'Trench Experience' saw competition between the desire of many of the museum's staff to represent the trench as accurately as possible and the requirements of space, accessibility and public taste. The result is an exhibit which is painstakingly accurate in detail – one of the project's designers acquired a plastic bag of Somme mud to ensure accurate consistency and colour, and museum staff agonised over the accents and subjects of the tape-recorded conversations – but inaccurate in more basic areas – the 'Trench Experience' had to be wide enough to allow wheelchair access and adequate fire escape routes, and chloride of lime is emphasised over human excrement and decaying flesh in the aroma which fills the exhibit.[74]

Reviewing the opening, the *Museums Journal* stated that: 'The installation invites the public to relive a moment of history ...'[75] Another journalist suggested that: 'The Trench Experience looked and sounded real ...'[76] Yet those veterans whom the museum involved in the opening of the exhibit could not help by note the dissonance from what they remembered: 'It is very well done, but we were always soaking wet, and always lousy', was one reaction. Another said simply: 'Much safer than any trench I've ever been in.'[77]

Like other museums, the Imperial War Museum felt pressure to offer more than traditional exhibits in an effort to involve visitors in the past. The resulting tensions between the need to interest those with no immediate emotional connection with a historical event and a nervousness at their tendency to take inappropriate pleasure – to be entertained – by a version of the past which cannot be allowed to be accurate, has frequently been remarked on. Certainly the way the Trench is 'experienced' by many young visitors offers evidence of a continuing 'pleasure culture of war'. One commentator has noted disapprovingly that 'most schoolchildren seem to see the experiences as a bit of fun, a spectacle that *has* to be seen'.[78] Such enjoyment is, of course, particularly disturbing for a culture whose mental map of the First World War is dominated by horror and disaster.[79]

Two of the greatest modern historians of war and memory, Jay Winter and Emmanuel Sivan, have suggested that museums of modern conflict are popular because they allow families to locate their own myths within a shared national past. Museums are a site where we are taught about why grandad's or grandma's war mattered. Winter and Sivan point to the frequency with which they are visited by grandparents and grandchildren together.[80] Whilst this remains true of the Second World War (indeed, my own first experience of the Imperial War Museum was when I was taken by my father's parents, both soldiers in that second conflict), for the First World War it implies a degree of preservation of family myths that has not actually occurred. Instead, as not only the combatants but those who knew them have died off, families have preserved very limited amounts of information about their participation in that earlier war. Just enough information has been preserved to stimulate further interest. The leisure culture which grew up around the First World War in the 1990s offered the chance not just to locate family stories but to construct and re-enact myths of individual experience that had all but disappeared.

These tensions and desires came to the fore again in 2002 when the BBC screened a three-part series which pitched modern volunteers back into a First World War environment. *The Trench* made use of many of the same veterans located by Richard Van Emden for *Veterans* four years previously, but used them to validate a piece of experiential history. Twenty-four modern volunteers were trained for three weeks, then sent out to France, where they spent twelve days living in and behind a reconstructed set of trench lines. These days were modelled on the experiences of a platoon of 1/10 East Yorkshires (The 1st Hull Pals) over the same period. Again, some aspects of the experience – clothing, food, latrine arrangements – were meticulously authentic. Others – the absence of Germans – were not. The purpose of the series was to explore the very aspects of trench life that were so often omitted from popular mythology: the humdrum toil, the absence of privacy and the importance of small comforts and comrades. In this light, the inability to reproduce the fear of death in those who had volunteered was not an important issue. As an exercise in furthering historical understanding, *The Trench* seems to have succeeded for those that took part in it. As a piece of television it was less successful. The concept was not easily explained or sold and appeared grotesque to many who reviewed it.[81] Editing choices made it hard for viewers to understand the development of close ties between the volunteers, and the BBC itself seemed to be unsure whether to market *The Trench* as history or 'reality' television.

Given what most Britons 'knew' about the First World War by 2001, when the volunteers were selected, why did anybody want to take part? For some, of course, there was the desire to appear on television or to escape everyday life, however briefly. Many chose to emphasise their familial link to the war (if not to the Hull Pals themselves, despite the programme makers' best efforts). Volunteer Carl Jackson's comments on his own motivation suggest some of the reasons for participation and the emotional satisfaction that could be derived:

> My grandfather and my great-grandfather both fought in the First World War and my motive for coming here was to see if I could put up with a little bit of what my relatives went through. At the end, when we walked through the gates at the billet and everyone from the BBC and local people, too, stood there clapping us, I had tears in my eyes. I felt so proud that I had done my best by my grandfather and my great grandfather. I didn't do it for money and I

didn't do it for fame and I didn't do it for anything other than to prove to those people from my life, who are dead now, that given a go I could carry their name forward with pride.[82]

Jackson's statement points us back towards the veterans of the war themselves. They too had sought to recreate certain aspects of the war. Up until the end of the 1960s, they had retained a variety of memories about the war, not least because their informal organisations encouraged them to rehearse more positive recollections. From the 1970s, however, a combination of rapidly declining numbers of veterans, the increasing dominance of negative myths about the war, and the loss of active participation by veterans in public discussion, all exercised a reductive effect on what was remembered. Jackson's words also make clear the degree to which a generational fracture had taken place. The war had passed out of the memory of living Britons. Although a legacy of pride in individual accomplishment remained, it fitted awkwardly with the negative mythology of the war as a whole. The complex emotions that those involved had felt at the time could not be brought back. What were the implications of this for the future of the myths and memory of the First World War?

Modern Memory

A war which involved the whole of British society as it was being fought has fascinated the country ever since. Throughout the rest of the twentieth century, a persistent undercurrent of emotional involvement has dragged Britons back to the war, to revisit, reconsider and refight its battles, whether they experienced them at first hand or not. Yet attitudes towards the war underwent a profound change. A war often entered into in a spirit of hope, enthusiasm and willing sacrifice, and won with resolution, determination and even fury, is now looked back on with a sense of regret, betrayal and failure. How and why did this change occur?

We have to understand the way we now think about the war as a point on a continuum. The modern myth of the war has its origins in events and emotions at the time. It is a distortion, not a fabrication. The British response to the war at the time was multi–vocal: over time, some voices have disappeared and others have grown stronger. The tune we now hear uses the same notes, but it sounds very different to that of 1918. A single melody has emerged and all the voices now audible sing along to it.

For those who study the history of the First World War, it has become a matter of orthodoxy that the 1960s were the key moment for the formation of the modern myth of the war. Fifty years after the war, it is suggested, Britons recast it to fit a set of contemporary concerns. In the context of nuclear war and cultural radicalism, they made use of the war as an example of official stupidity, futility and slaughter. This interpretation is inadequate not only because it misrepresents the 1960s, but also because it imposes a moment of cataclysmic change on a process that was in fact far more gradual. These myths were not created from scratch in the 1960s. The scale of casualties and the horror of war, how the war had been fought, and whether it had been worth it were of prime concern to Britons from the day it broke out. Representations of the war have always been judged in terms of horror, death, generalship and utility, although the conclusions that creators and audiences have come to have differed widely. These elements were not interdependent: there were always those who would argue, for example, that the war had been badly fought but that the sacrifice had been worthwhile. Ambiguities, contradictions and differences of opinion characterised British responses to the war from 1914 onwards. By the 1970s, however, many of these different views had died out or been hushed, as a set of myths which depicted the First World War in purely negative terms achieved universal dominance.

The extremity of views at either end of these spectra of opinion, and how acceptable it was to express them, both changed over time. Anyone putting forward in public the idea that the war had been an incompetently run and colossally futile waste of life, unmitigated by any redeeming heroism, would have been chased from the street in the early 1920s. By 1998, to say anything else was to arouse ridicule and anger. Rather than a sudden shift of perspective, however, these changes took place over a long period. It was only over this longer duration that myths could be recycled and reincorporated into new texts not as statements of opinion but as uncontested facts. Along the way, texts like *The Great War, Oh What a Lovely War* and *The Monocled Mutineer* themselves became the subject of myths.

Changes in the popular mythology of the war were influenced by three factors. The first was the cultural and political context in which they were produced and consumed. This context altered what it was publicly acceptable to say about the war. It was affected not only by superficial changes in policy or fashion – like the liberalisation and experimentation of the late 1960s – but also by deeper-lying developments like the shifts in population which saw the extinction, first of bereaved parents and then of First World War veterans. These generations played key roles in deciding what could be said about the war and how far new interpretations were contested. This cultural context also included a set of traditions and long running myths which predated 1914. Even before the First World War broke out, a model existed in popular culture for mocking senior officers as aristocratic dinosaurs. Faced with the terrible implications of total war, it was little surprise that Britons returned to this interpretation during and after the conflict.

The second factor influencing the popular mythology of the war was that combination of human behaviour and chance which the great military philosopher Clausewitz labelled 'friction'. Accident, confusion and avarice all affected which myths rose to the top. For example, Alan Clark's selection of an evocative phrase 'Lions led by Donkeys', despite his knowledge of its historical inaccuracy, was motivated not by a political agenda but by the desire to make a profit from his writing. Yet this phrase more than any other has come to dominate discussion of British generalship in the First World War. The eventual format of *The Great War*, the series which was influential in so many ways on subsequent representations of the war, owed as much to the inexperience of those involved in its creation as to the cultural climate in which it was broadcast.

The third and most important factor, however, which ensured the survival and triumph of a set of negative myths about the First World War, was that they remained useful throughout the twentieth century. The war did not create a modern mode of artistic expression or cause a total break with tradition. It did, however, confront Britons with many of the archetypal tensions of the modern world. At a time of rapid technological change, was status defined by age, wealth or ability? What was the relationship of individuals to the vast, faceless organisations of which they were part? Could individuals control their fates or were they just cogs in the machine? With the advent of greater democracy, how did the citizen relate to the government? If, through new media and bureaucracy, nations could mobilise their whole population, who should benefit from wartime sacrifice? The negative mythology of the First World War enjoyed a much better fit with the changing circumstances in which these tensions were considered than did more positive interpretations. It therefore retained an explanatory power which ensured its survival and eventual dominance.

We would do ourselves a disservice, however, if we assumed that myths which we perceive as historically inaccurate had an adverse impact on behaviour. Just because people have mistaken beliefs about the past does not mean that the effect of those beliefs was itself negative. Even if we accept an argument which suggests that a concentration on the 'literary' experience of the First World War discouraged Britons from standing up militarily to Hitler in the 1930s, we should also recognise that other 'negative' myths about the First World played an important role in mobilising the population to fight Nazism during the Second World War. The army had to make use of new technology; it must not 'waste' men. This war would not be futile like the last one: the entire population would participate but they must in turn have a share in the spoils of victory. The myths on which these ideas were based were bad history, but they played a part in sustaining Britain through her finest hour. If this helped to confirm them as the dominant mythology, it was perhaps a minor price to pay.

Jay Winter has suggested that national myths are what is left behind by the attempts of a host of individual 'agents of remembrance' to make sense of the trauma of the war. As they cease to be active, only the scaffolding of larger-scale myths, erected to contain this mass of individual efforts, remains.[1] Winter is surely correct to point out that popular myths about the war initially arose from below, rather than being imposed from above. But this model of individual agency does not account for the changes in national mythology during and after the Second World War. The rise to dominance of a set of largely negative myths about the First World War in the 1970s derived less from rehearsed narratives of family experience than from the selective recasting and recycling of national myths to fit a new cultural, political, demographic and emotional context. This selection took place through a series of texts – in particular television programmes and books – which had a national distribution.

At least five generations have now been involved in creating, passing on, developing and forgetting myths about the war. First were the parents of those who fought and died in the war. Unprepared to be predeceased by their sons, many in this group suffered chronic grief. Much lip service was paid to their emotional needs between the wars, but in fact they were not so numerous as to make mourning universal, nor so influential that they could exercise complete control over how the war should be remembered. On the other hand, a perception of their need for respect to be paid to the dead did exert a powerful limiting factor on what could be said about the war in public. Suggestions that the war was futile, ill-fought or mistaken were much more difficult to make when they were seen to strike at the hearts of grieving fathers and mothers. The passing away of this generation in the 1950s played a part in allowing the more violently critical assessments of the war in the subsequent decade.

Second was the generation that experienced the war as young adults and in particular those men who saw military service. One of the most striking points about this generation is just how long it has lasted. Through to the 1960s, significant numbers were still alive and the dramatic decline of the 1970s has still not totally wiped them out. Despite the widespread assumption that those men who had seen military service preserved some special shared memory of the war, veterans' reactions were extremely varied, not only at the time but afterwards. This variety may itself have contributed to their relative lack of influence over the way the war should be remembered and represented. Between the wars an understandable desire on the part of many of them to get on with their lives, combined with a public focus on the needs of the bereaved, discouraged many veterans from communicating their experiences. Ironically, by the time that historians became really interested in the voice of individual experience, the rate of mortality amongst veterans had shot up, and many of the networks which had sustained alternative interpretations of the war had broken down. As a result, the cultural dominance of the modern myth of the war both affected and was reinforced by veterans' public recollections.

The 1970s saw a fracture in terms of personal experience. Those who had lived through the war as adults died off in large numbers. It was not the case that these individuals had been ceaseless fonts of perfectly recalled knowledge, nor that families ceased to pass on myths of their deceased forebears' wartime exploits, but simply that a potential link to the past had gone. Dead veterans told no tales. The number of occasions of which myths were rehearsed fell: although still important to some members of the family, they were no longer significant parts of an individual's life story. They had become the memory of a memory.

The third generation, and perhaps the most important for this book, was made up of the children of those who saw service in 1914–18. It was members of this third generation who created the books, plays and television programmes which underpin the way modern Britons think about the First World War. It included not only those born in the immediate aftermath of the war, such as John Terraine and Charles Chilton, but also those born in the early 1930s, Martin Middlebrook, Lyn Macdonald and Malcolm Brown amongst them. Brought up in the long shadow of the war, fascinated by a conflict which had killed or shaped fathers and uncles, this generation was initially inculcated with the ambivalence of a period when the war's reputation hung between triumph and disaster. Their obsession, unresolved by their own experience of a second global conflict, led them back to the First World War as they reached middle age. Of all those born after the war's end, it was the children of the generation which fought it who retained the most developed personal connection to it for the longest period of time. Yet even whilst they retained some of the nostalgia and pride they had learned as children, it was whilst they were adults that the modern myth of the war became dominant.

The fourth generation bound up with the First World War were the grandchildren of those who had fought. They shared less of their parents' visceral emotional fascination with the war, but they were still aware of it. It remained a reference point for them in popular culture: but beyond that this generation still had contact with those who had experienced the war at first hand. In the 1960s in particular, an interaction took place between those who had fought and their grandchildren in a context that stimulated acts of memory. In the long run, it may be that what made the 1960s important for the future representation of the war was not a radical new expression of disgust with generals or wars, but this intersection of different generations and the preservation of sufficient family myths to maintain interest in the war at the level of individual experience.

It was from this fourth generation that new versions of the war came in the late 1980s and early 1990s. The grandchildren of those who had fought also made up much of the audience for these works. By this point, a difference was apparent between those families that had maintained and preserved a myth of war experience and those that had not. For some, like Alan Bleasdale, a grandparent's participation in the war had become a key element in a family's identity. For others, the myths or artefacts that had come down through the family were less detailed, or deemed less important. The potential existed for them to be discarded or forgotten, yet any vague awareness of family involvement could later form an impetus to research into a family's history.

The position of the fifth generation, the great grandchildren of those who fought, may be more problematic. They have grown up with well established myths of the Great War, but no personal connection to it. They remain aware of the war, if only because they had to read its poetry at school. They were part of the enthusiastic audience for *Birdsong* in the early 1990s, and they laughed at the jokes in *Blackadder Goes Forth*. Whether they still cared deeply about it as the twenty-first century began is doubtful. Within families, even though mementoes or stories of ancestors' involvement may have been passed down, their impact has inevitably been reduced. These stories have lost detail and nuance in the telling, but more importantly, the war has passed over the boundary of lived experience. More important than this fracture of experience, however, may be the end of relevance. It has been argued that modern beliefs about the war were shaped by those myths which remained useful through the twentieth century. If the issues which the myths of the First World War were used to illuminate – global war, military service, and national identity – are no longer relevant, then younger Britons will not refer back to it. They will not consciously abandon the war, but simply fail to preserve it through lack of use.

What implications does this have for the future of the First World War in British culture? Julian Barnes wrote his short story 'EVERMORE', first published in 1996, from the point of view of the elderly sister of Sammy Moss, a soldier killed on the Somme. Miss Moss visits her brother's grave and contemplates the future of commemoration of the First World War:

> EVERMORE, they said, and she wanted to hear: for all future time ... She didn't believe them. Soon – in fifty years or so – everyone who had served in the war would be dead; and at some point after that, everyone who had known anyone who served would also be dead ...
>
> Then the great forgetting could begin, the fading into the landscape. The war would be levelled to a couple of museums, a set of demonstration trenches, and a few names, shorthand for pointless sacrifice.
>
> Might there be one last fiery glow of remembering? ... Might there not be, at some point in the first decades of the twenty-first century, one final moment, lit by evening sun, before the whole thing was handed back to the archivists? ...

Then, in the space of a wet blink, the gap in the trees would close and the mown grass disappear, a violent indigo cloud would cover the sun, and history, gross history, daily history, would forget. Is this how it would be?[2]

Looking at the leisure culture of the First World War in 1998, with demonstration trenches and a shared shorthand of myths about the war both in existence, this process of levelling and forgetting seemed already well under way.

For those who retain a close personal connection to the past, this sort of simplification and commodification, the transformation of historical experience into 'heritage', is without doubt distressing. For some it seemed, worse still, a prelude to forgetting about the past: enjoying it as leisure experience rather than being aware of its importance.[3] Once reduced to this status it could be abandoned as easily as last year's fashion. Yet this is a calamitous view of the future of remembrance. There is not much point bemoaning a process which is inevitable. It also fails to consider what elements might make remembrance of this war different from those which have gone before.

Viewed in the longer term, is there good reason for distress? One of the central tenets of this book has been that myths about the past are reductive. That is their social function. By establishing an unspoken convention about what is meant by 'the First World War', 'Haig' or 'the trenches', we avoid the need to enter into a lengthy dissection of what exactly is implied by those terms each time they are used. Such simplifications, painful as they can be to veterans, relatives or historians, are a crucial part of an event finding a place in popular culture. It is that place which will ensure that some myths about it, at various levels, continue to be rehearsed. It may even be the basis for eventual reassessment by individuals, albeit that this revisionism may have little impact. There does not seem to be evidence that myths about a past that remains controversial are more likely to be rehearsed than those which have been simplified and widely accepted. Reductionism and inaccuracy may be the price that has to be paid for remembrance. Few now care whether the battle of Hastings was well fought or not, but everyone knows Harold got hit in the eye.

Common sense suggests that Miss Moss (and, by implication, Julian Barnes) was right to assume that British remembrance of the First World War will have a shelf life of some sort. Many of the most distinctive representations of the war have been produced by those with a close link to the war: either they experienced it or they knew someone who had. Eventually, all of these people will die. When they have done so, the nature of how the war is 'remembered' will change, even if it does not disappear. If we are

talking in terms of shelf-life, remembrance may have a 'best before' before
it has a definite expiry date.

Given a looming fracture with those for whom the war really mattered, we
can suggest that representations of the war will fade from British culture
because their core audience will disappear. Certainly some of the hype surrounding the eightieth anniversary of the war's end was based on the belief
that this was one of the last ceremonial commemorations of the war. It
would be easy to suggest that with the deaths of the last veterans, the last
veterans' widows and eventually the last veterans' children, giant steps will
have been taken towards the point where the war is purely a symbol, without any emotional significance. Family myths will be found elsewhere, and
no one will have reason to care about the way the war is represented. Looking at other great national events – the French and American Revolutions,
the battles of the Napoleonic Wars – we can see that centenaries, and even
bicentenaries, are sometimes marked by dramatic celebrations, but tend not
to be understood in terms of family involvement. Nor do these great events
play a significant role in popular culture outside those anniversaries. They
become symbols to which most people feel little understanding or concern.
Perhaps the First World War inevitably faces the same future. If this is the
case, the process may be regretted, but it cannot be opposed – forgetting
the First World War is an historical inevitability.

Yet there are things which are different about Britain's First World War
that may extend the period in which it remains a subject of popular interest. Three things make remembrance of this war distinct from those that
have gone before.

The first is the unique nature of Britain's involvement. The responsibility
which the country took on from 1917 in particular, fighting the mass of a
great power opponent's army in a land campaign in continental Europe,
made huge demands on the country in terms of the development of military power and the mobilisation of people, economy and state. The level of
mobilisation was unprecedented. The intensity of military commitment
remained unequalled even during the Second World War. It is little wonder
that the war has been a touchstone of British culture ever since. Comparisons with the length of time it took for Trafalgar or Waterloo to pass from
the list of significant dates may not be relevant. Important though they were
for the future of the country, the levels of real commitment and involvement they demanded from the state and the bulk of the population were
relatively small. In contrast, its scale not only meant that the First World
War would come to be commemorated as an important historical event at
a national level, but also that most families were touched by the war, even
if only a minority of households were bereaved at the time.

Secondly, modern total war demanded a bureaucratic effort that recorded individual involvement. Despite the degradations which British soldiers' service records from the First World War have suffered, numerous documentary sources remain which catalogue participation. At the most basic level, even those who do not know of any familial involvement with the war can search a database of the dead with the likelihood – given the scale of participation – that they will find a namesake amongst the fallen. The advent of the internet has revolutionised access to these sources, making it more likely that those who encounter the war for the first time will be encouraged to understand it in terms of individual experience.

Thirdly, social and cultural changes at the start of the twentieth century meant that artefacts that marked individuals' involvement in the war were created and preserved on a large scale for the first time. Newly joined up soldiers went to the photographers. They wrote letters home from the front. They retained souvenirs from their wartime service. Widespread possession of private property meant that there was a place to preserve much of this material, at least so long as veterans were alive. At the point at which they began to die out in large numbers, many Britons were already being encouraged to retain any links they had to their own heritage. In themselves, these artefacts did not preserve any detailed account of the war, but they did serve to stimulate the rehearsal of myths and the creation of interest. Again, access to many of these objects has become more widespread as a result of technological developments and the birth of specific collections aimed at preserving them, some at least of which also attempted to locate veterans and record their recollections. As a result, their testimony may outlast their family's ability to retain it.

Taken together these factors both stimulate interest in family involvement in the past and permit the location of that involvement in a formative event in British history. They have encouraged, and will go on encouraging, the creation of imaginative links with the past which, whether or not they have a basis in fact or personal experience, are a prerequisite if remembrance of the war is to continue. It is unlikely that, in the very longest term, these elements can prevent the inevitable passage of the war into an event of history, devoid of emotional interest or attachment for the bulk of the population. What they may do, however, is to delay the moment at which this takes place; extending remembrance's expiry date. In the short term, Britons will still be convinced that they should care about the First World War. Interest will be renewed around the centenary of the war. Remembrance of the First World War in popular culture will outlast not only those that experienced the war, but those who knew them too.

One of the things 'everyone knows' about the First World War is that it was different from what had gone before. That may well prove to be as true of the way the war is remembered as of events on the fields of France and Flanders. It is marked out both by the longevity of familial myths and by the continued sense of personal involvement which comes from them. These in turn come from a social and cultural setting distinct to Britain in the twentieth century. The war was a new sort of event for the country and its myths have been preserved in new ways. When Paul Fussell wrote about *The Great War and Modern Memory* he did not have in mind such prosaic items as the card-index filing system, the photographic plate, the tape recorder and the loft. Yet it was these developments that may eventually prove the distinctive characteristics of British remembrance of the First World War.

Notes

Notes to Introduction

1. See, for example, Leading article, 'The Few and the Many', *Times*, 7 November 1998, 23; A. Gilligan, 'Tears as France Honours Last Thirteen British Heroes' and A. Alderson, 'Actors Go AWOL after a Taste of the Trenches', *Sunday Telegraph*, 8 November 1998, 5; J. Treays, '"To Our Dear Boys"', *Sunday Telegraph Review*, 8 November 1998, 4; I. Jack, 'As I Paid Tribute to Great Uncle Jack, I Thought of Something Else …', *Independent*, 7 November 1998, 1; S. Moss, 'Oh, for a Lovely War', *Guardian*, 10 November 1998, 6; J. Lichfield, 'The Echoing Voices of a Land where Folly and Courage Lie Side by Side', *Independent*, 12 November 1998, 3. Successful efforts to reintroduce the two minutes' silence at 11 a.m. on 11 November itself should also be considered, although this act of remembrance was inevitably also bound up with the Second World War as well as the First; A. Lee and J. Young, 'Millions Observe the Two Minute Silence', *Times*, 12 November 1998, 4.
2. A. Motion, 'Lest We Forget', *New Statesman*, 18 September 1998, 38.
3. For a similar statement of this myth, see S. Hynes, *A War Imagined: The First World War and English Culture* (London, 1990), xii.
4. The book which best sums up the range of British experience of war, at home and on the front line, remains Trevor Wilson's *The Myriad Faces of War: Britain and the Great War, 1914–18* (Cambridge, 1986).
5. W. C. Sellar and R. J. Yeatman, *1066 and All That* (Harmondsworth, 1960, first published 1930), 5.
6. This section draws in particular on the seminal work of Roland Barthes, *Mythologies* (Paris, 1957), 236–37.
7. Discerning the truth about the war – from a variety of viewpoints – has been a perennial concern of historians, critics and commentators. See, just for example, B. H. Liddell Hart, *The Real War* (London, 1930); D. Jerrold, *The Lie about the War* (London, 1930); G. Sheffield, *Forgotten Victory: The First World War, Myths and Realities* (London, 2001); J. Terraine, *The Smoke and the Fire: Myths and Anti-Myths of War* (London, 1985). On the Second World War, see C. Ponting, *1940: Myth and Reality* (London, 1990).

Notes to Chapter 1: Mud

1. Imperial War Museum, London (IWM), E(AUS) 1220 1911–0.

2. IWM, Q5935.

3. J. Masefield to C. Masefield, 22 October 1916, in P. Vansittart, ed., *John Masefield's Letters from the Front, 1915–1917* (London, 1984), 194.

4. E. Campion Vaughan, *Some Desperate Glory: The Diary of a Young Officer, 1917* (London, 1985), 223–25.

5. Some of the implications for nations and individuals of this global war are seen in H. Strachan, *The Oxford History of the First World War*, i, *The Call to Arms* (Oxford, 2000), 441–94 (the war in the Pacific), 495–643 (the war in Africa) and 993–1113 (industrial mobilisation). On Britain and total war see T. Wilson, *The Myriad Faces of War: Britain and the Great War, 1914–1918* (Cambridge, 1986), 389–407, 507–40, 705–30. Although Wilson argues that this was not a 'total war' (705), he certainly produces evidence that it tended towards totality.

6. R. Holmes, *Tommy: The British Soldier on the Western Front* (London, 2004), 191, 273; I. M. Brown, *British Logistics on the Western Front* (London, 1998).

7. C. Edmonds (C. Carrington), *A Subaltern's War* (London, 1929), 120–21. Junior subalterns enjoyed the shortest life expectancy of any rank in the infantry, since it was their job, alongside their NCOs, to attempt to control the battle at the tactical level. Doing so meant exposing themselves to enemy fire.

8. Janet Watson has argued that different Britons defined their wartime activities as either service or as work, and that their experience and memory of the war were shaped by these definitions. J. Watson, *Fighting Different Wars: Experience, Memory and the First World War in Britain* (Cambridge, 2004).

9. G. Craig and H. Scott, *An Outline History of the Great War for Use in Schools* (Cambridge, 1929), 260–62.

10. Holmes, *Tommy*, 590.

11. B. Neville to family, 16 March 1916, published in R. E. Harris, *Billie: The Neville Letters, 1914–1916* (Uckfield, 1991), 165.

12. E. Belfield and H. Essame, *The Battle for Normandy* (London, 1975), 145

13. G. Sheffield, 'The Shadow of the Somme: The Influence of the First World War on British Soldiers' Perception and Behaviour in the Second World War', in P. Addison and A. Calder, *A Time to Kill: The Soldier's Experience of War in the West, 1939–1945* (London, 1997), 30–39.

14. C. Barnett, *The Collapse of British Power* (London, 1972), 422–35.

15. N. Ferguson, *The Pity of War: Explaining World War I* (London, 1998), 342.

16. A. Carton de Wiart, *Happy Odyssey* (London, 1950), 85.

17. M. Bloch trans. C. Fink, *Memoirs of War* (Ithaca, New York, 1980), 89.

18. E. Leed, *No Man's Land: Combat and Identity in World War I* (Cambridge, 1979), 193–204; G. Mosse, 'Two World Wars and the Myth of the War

Experience', *Journal of Contemporary History*, 21 (1986), 491–513; G. Mosse, *Fallen Soldiers: Reshaping the Memory of the Two World Wars* (Oxford, 1990), 5–9; S. Hynes, *A War Imagined: The First World War and English Culture* (London, 1991), x.

19. This discussion of the theoretical basis of memory and recollection draws heavily on E. Sivan and J. Winter, 'Setting the Framework', in Sivan and Winter, eds, *War and Remembrance in the Twentieth Century* (Cambridge,), 6–39, the best recent summary of ongoing work in this field across a number of disciplines.

20. R. Graves, *Goodbye to All That* (London, 1957), 237; V. Brome, *J. B. Priestley* (London, 1988), 53.

21. T. F. Main, 'Clinical Problems of Repatriates', *Journal of Mental Science*, 92 (1947), 354, 363, quoted in B. Turner and T. Rendell, *When Daddy Came Home: How Family Life Changed Forever in 1945* (London, 1995), 124–25.

22. R. McKibbin, *Classes and Cultures: England, 1918–1951* (Oxford, 1998), 166. See also Watson, *Fighting Different Wars*, 20–29, for a discussion of the degree to which the war was perceived as a job. Deborah Cohen has also recently highlighted the degree to which a combination of a reliance on voluntarist care and a widely shared belief in the traditional tenets of silent male virtue discouraged disabled British veterans from expressing their frustration and anger through political conflict. D. Cohen, *The War Come Home: Disabled Veterans in Britain and Germany, 1914–1939* (Berkeley, California, 2001), 144.

23. Jones's epic poem, one of the greatest to come out of the war, describes his service on the Somme. D. Jones, *In Parenthesis* (London, 1937).

24. S. Hynes, *The Soldiers' Tale: Bearing Witness to Modern War* (London, 1998), 1–30.

25. N. Gullace, *'The Blood of Our Sons': Men, Women and the Renegotiation of British Citizenship during the Great War* (Basingstoke, 2002), 17–97.

26. IWM Department of Documents (hereafter, DoD), Martin Hardie Collection, item 7, writing tablet, quoted ibid, 28. See also J. Bourke, *An Intimate History of Killing: Face to Face Killing in Twentieth Century Warfare* (London, 1998).

27. On reactions to the outbreak of war, see A. Gregory, 'British "War Enthusiasm" in 1914: A Reassessment', in G. Braybon, ed., *Evidence, History and the Great War: Historians and the Impact of 1914–18* (Oxford, 2004), 67–85.

28. M. Paris, *Warrior Nation: Images of War in British Popular Culture, 1850–2000* (London, 2000), 13–109, and in particular 64–78. The phrase, 'pleasure culture of war' is Graham Dawson's, from his *Soldier Heroes: British Adventure, Empire and the Imagining of Masculinity* (London, 1994), 233–58. See also J. Mackenzie, ed., *Popular Imperialism and the Military, 1850–1950* (Manchester, 1992) and I. F. Clarke, *Voices Prophesying War: Future Wars, 1763–3749* (Oxford, 2nd edn, 1992).

29. Gullace, '*The Blood of Our Sons*', 18–25. The degree to which complaints of German atrocities were valid is examined in Chapter 4, but has been thoroughly investigated in J. Horne and A. Kramer, *German Atrocities, 1914: A History of Denial* (New Haven, Connecticut, 2001). For the issue of their representation in Britain, see also T. Wilson, 'Lord Bryce's Investigation into Alleged German Atrocities in Belgium, 1914–15', *Journal of Contemporary History* (July 1979), 369–83, and Gullace, '*The Blood of Our Sons*', 18–27.

30. Paris, *Warrior Nation*, 113–14.

31. Ibid.

32. M. Finn, 'The Realities of War', *History Today*, 52 (August 2002), 25–31. See also S. Badsey and P. Taylor, 'Images of the Battle: The Press, Propaganda and Passchendaele', in P. Liddle, ed., *Passchendaele in Perspective: The Third Battle of Ypres* (London, 1997), 371–89.

33. P. MacGill, *The Great Push* (Edinburgh, 2000; first published 1915), 38.

34. N. Reeves, 'Through the Eye of the Camera: Contemporary Cinema Audiences and their "Experience" of War in the Film *Battle of the Somme*', in H. Cecil and P. Liddle, *Facing Armageddon: The First World War Experienced* (London, 1996), 786–87.

35. Paris, *Warrior Nation*, 116.

36. 'Ian Hay' (John Hay Beith), *The First Hundred Thousand* (London and Edinburgh, 1915).

37. R. Smither, '"A Wonderful Idea of the Fighting": The Question of Fakes in *The Battle of the Somme*', *Historical Journal of Film, Radio and Television*, 13 (1993), 151–52.

38. Quoted in R. Cork, *A Bitter Truth: Avant-Garde Art and the Great War* (New Haven, Connecticut, and London, 1994), 220.

39. Hynes, *A War Imagined*, 134.

40. *His Master's Voice: New Records for November 1930* (London, 1930), 4 and cover. My thanks to Dr Peter Martland for pointing out this extremely useful source to me.

41. J. Winter, *Sites of Memory, Sites of Mourning: The Great War in European Cultural History* (Cambridge, 1995); A. Gregory, *The Silence of Memory: Armistice Day, 1919–1946* (Oxford, 1994); D. Lloyd, *Battlefield Tourism: Pilgrimage and the Commemoration of the Great War in Britain, Australia and Canada, 1919–1939* (Oxford, 1998); A. King, *Memorials of the Great War in Britain: The Symbolism and Politics of Remembrance* (Oxford, 1998); A. Gaffney, *Aftermath: Remembering the Great War in Wales* (Cardiff, 1998); M. Connelly, *The Great War, Memory and Ritual: Commemoration in the City and East London, 1916–1939* (Woodbridge, 2002).

42. 18th Division ATNODC papers, IWM DoD, Misc 1208; A. Danchev, *Alchemist of War: The Life of Sir Basil Liddell Hart* (London, 1998), 53 (ironically, the

toast, which was to become a badge of pride, originated in a lengthy silence following a dispute within the unit); D. Todman, '"Sans Peur et Sans Reproche": The Retirement, Death and Mourning of Sir Douglas Haig, 1918–1928', *Journal of Military History*, 67 (October 2003), 1083–106.

43. R. M. Bracco, *Merchants of Hope: British Middlebrow Writers and the First World War, 1919–1939* (Oxford, 1993), 71.

44. G. Frankau, *Peter Jackson, Cigar Merchant: A Romance of Married Life* (London, 1949; first published 1919), 171. See also 201, 221, 234, 257, 289–97, 300–6 and 322–25; H. Cecil, *The Flower of Battle: British Fiction Writers of the First World War* (London, 1995), 185–211.

45. Cecil, *The Flower of Battle*, 206.

46. Frankau, *Peter Jackson*, 9.

47. E. M. Remarque, trans. A. Wheen, *All Quiet on the Western Front* (London, 1991 [1929]), 91.

48. On popular pacifism, see R. Mackay, *The Test of War* (London, 1999), 33–38; Connelly, *The Great War, Ritual and Memory*, 196–231.

49. L. Clark, '"Goodbye to All What?" The Great War Writers, their Truth and the Great War Myth', MA, King's College London (1992); B. Bond, 'Anti-War Writers and their Critics', in Cecil and Liddle, eds, *Facing Armageddon*, 820–21.

50. Edmonds (Carrington), *A Subaltern at War*; C. Carrington, *Soldier from the Wars Returning* (London, 1965), 264.

51. C. Falls, *War Books: A Critical Guide* (London, 1930), ix–xii.

52. D. Jerrold, *The Lie about the War* (London, 1930), 20–25.

53. Graves managed to annoy many of those who had served with him: see Keith Simpson's introduction to J. C. Dunn, *The War the Infantry Knew, 1914–1919* (London, 1989, first published 1938), xxx–xxxi.

54. Bracco, *Merchants of Hope*, 149–86.

55. J. Vance, *Death So Noble: Memory, Meaning and the First World War* (Vancouver, 1997), 82–83.

56. W. A . Darlington, *Daily Telegraph*, 22 January 1929. I am grateful to Professor John Ramsden for drawing my attention to these reviews.

57. Watson, *Fighting Different Wars*, 211–8.

58. V. Robinson, *On Target* (Wakefield, 1991), 3

59. J. Connell, 'Writing about Soldiers', *Journal of the Royal United Services Institute*, 40 (August 1965), 221. See also E. Waugh, *A Little Learning* (London, 1964), 113. For a French colonial parallel, see A. Camus, trans. D. Hapgood, *The First Man* (London, 1995), 118.

60. R. Kee, 'How the Lights Went Out', *Spectator*, 1 June 1962, 723.

61. Paris, *Warrior Nation*, 147; K. Drotner, *English Children and their Magazines, 1751–1945* (New Haven, Connecticut, 1988), 198–201.

62. For a slightly later survey of children's reading habits, see A. Jenkinson, *What*

Do Boys and Girls Read? (London, 1940), 64–75. For memoirists' accounts of their reading, see D. Smith, *Cricket Stumps and Sticklebacks: A Childhood on Teeside* (Penistone, 1989), 165–66; V. Scannell, *The Tiger and the Rose* (London, 1983), 71; P. McVeigh, *Look after the Bairns: A Childhood in East Lothian* (East Linton, 1999), 108.

63. H. Macrae, 'Pals of the Great War', *Champion*, 9 May 1925, 423–28, which opened with: 'Fighting Mac and Co don't care an Army biscuit for peril, chaps! They're in the thick of it to get to the Front – and they're waiting for you to join them! If you want to experience the biggest batch of thrills imaginable, pack up your kit and accompany the – PALS OF THE GREAT WAR!'

64. See, for example, 'Good Stuff Coming Over', *Triumph*, 13 August 1927, 243. These cards were positioned as war souvenirs to rank with those brought back by veterans. See D. Todman, 'Representations of the First World War in British Popular Culture, 1918–1998', PhD, University of Cambridge (2003), 57–59.

65. J. Richards, 'Popular Imperialism and the Image of the Army in Juvenile Literature', in J. Mackenzie, ed., *Popular Imperialism and the Military, 1850–1950* (Manchester, 1992), 80–108.

66. See biographies assembled in B. Doyle, *Who's Who of Boys' Writers and Illustrators* (London, 1964), 13, 24, 42, 47, 63, 51.

67. H. Macrae, 'The Dauntless Gunners of the Somme!', *Champion*, 9 February 1929, 50.

68. H. Macrae, 'The Battlefield Mystery', *Triumph*, 9 November 1929, 75, 76, 77.

69. R. Hall, 'To Victory with the Tanks', *Triumph*, 15 March 1930, 524.

70. H. Macrae, 'The Fighting Freelance', *Triumph*, 15 April 1933, 15.

71. Watson, *Fighting Different Wars*, 306, 219–61.

72. A. Rhodes, *Sword of Bone* (London, 1943), 8.

73. J. A. Crang, *The British Army and the People's War, 1939–45* (Manchester, 2000), 64.

74. The 'military participation ratio', and its development as an idea, is described in M. Shaw, 'The Rise and Fall of the Military Democratic State: Britain, 1940–1985', in C. Creighton and M. Shaw, eds, *The Sociology of War and Peace* (Basingstoke, 1987), 145.

75. P. Ryder as told to G. Bennett, *Guns Have Eyes: One Man's Story of the Normandy Landings* (London, 1984), 165–66, 36–37, 63.

76. Sheffield, 'The Shadow of the Somme', 29–35; H. Strachan, 'The Soldier's Experience in Two World Wars: Some Historiographical Comparisons', in Addison and Calder, *A Time to Kill*, 369–78; D. French, *Raising Churchill's Army: The British Army and the War against Germany, 1919–1945* (Oxford, 2000), 126.

77. A. McKee, *Vimy Ridge* (London, 1966), 10.

78. G. Blaxland, *Amiens: 1918* (London, 1981, first published 1968), ix.

79. Sheffield, 'The Shadow of the Somme', 37.

80. G. Enser, *A Subject Bibliography of the First World War in English, 1914–1987* (London, 1990). 135 books were published between 1939–1958, 198 between 1959–1968. John Ramsden suggests over 300 books were published in the 1960s, but this seems to take into account books published in America as well as those in Britain. J. Ramsden, '*The Great War*: The Making of the Series', *Historical Journal of Film, Radio and Television*, 22 (March 2002), 8. Enser's bibliography does contain some repetition and omissions – most obviously the absence of texts other than history, but it is a useful point of reference. Even more works were published in the periods 1969 to 1978 and 1979 to 1987 (254 and 167 respectively), although this may be accounted for by the growth of the history publishing trade as a whole.

81. On the 1960s, see A. Danchev, '"Bunking" and Debunking: The Controversies of the 1960s', in B. Bond, ed., *The First World War and British Military History* (Oxford, 1991); B. Bond, *The Unquiet Western Front* (Cambridge, 2002), chapter 3.

82. See, for example, the forewords of R. Rhodes James, *Gallipoli* (London, 1965), iv; J. Baynes, *Morale: A Study of Men and Courage* (London, 1967),v; R. Woollcombe, *The First Tank Battle: Cambrai, 1917* (London, 1967), 13.

83. A process examined in more depth in Chapter 6 below, 'Veterans'.

84. Danchev, '"Bunking" and Debunking', 279–81.

85. BBC Audience Research Reports, BBC Written Archives Centre, Caversham, (hereafter, WAC), VR/64/483, VR/64/624, VR/64/461.

86. Ramsden, '*The Great War*: The Making of the Series', 12.

87. See *Radio Times*, 30 July 1964, 26. Other programmes included *The Life of Wilfred Owen, Songs of the Trenches, Britten's War Requiem* and war tunes in *Music from the Guildhall*.

88. Anonymous BBC insider, 'The Great Failure', *Daily Mirror*, 29 May 1964, Liddell Hart Centre for Military Archives, Kings College London (hereafter LHCMA), LH 13/62. This book makes extensive use of the press-cuttings archives kept by Sir Basil Liddell Hart and preserved at the LHCMA. Although wide-ranging, they seldom include the page numbers of the newspapers from which they are taken. For this reason, where I have used them, I have indicated the file in which they can be found.

89. N. Frankland, *History at War: The Campaigns of a Historian* (London, 1998), 160–61.

90. See, for example, John Terraine's tribute to Essex in his introduction to *The First World War* (London, 1984), vii.

91. J. Haworth, 'Producing the Great War', *Guardian*, 11 February 1965, LHCMA, LH 13/62.

92. Essex to Milne, 27 May 1963, WAC, T32/1, 158/1, emphasis in original.

93. S. Badsey, 'The Great War since *The Great War*', *Historical Journal of Film, Radio and Television*, 22 (March 2002), 40.

94. Essex to Milne, 15 July 1964, 1–2, WAC, T32/1, 158/1, emphases in original.

95. As he himself was to write to a viewer: 'Your suggestion of a "pink" tendency comes as somewhat amusing to one who, amongst his colleagues, is so "blue" as to be regarded as a "fascist".' Essex to Ferrier, 28 December 1964, WAC, T32/1, 145/2.

96. Horne to Liddell Hart, 4 September 1964, LHCMA, LH 1/380. Horne did end his letter by pointing out how impressed he had been with the achievement of the series as a whole despite these failings.

97. Cataloguer's Notes Episode 1 (compiled by Stephen Badsey), IWM Department of Film, *The Great War* File A.

98. Ibid. See also Smither, 'A Wonderful Idea of the Fighting', and S. Badsey, 'The IWM Series: A Guide to the IWM Collection of Archive Film of the First World War', both in *Historical Journal of Film, Radio and Television*, 13 (1993), 151–52, 160, 208.

99. Roads to Watkins, 14 February 1964, Frankland to Greene, 24 September 1964, cutting from *Daily Telegraph*, 14 January 1965, IWM Department of Film, *The Great War*, file D. This researcher was Peter Simkins, later to become a major historian of the British army in the First World War in his own right.

100. Essex to James, 22 April 1965, WAC, T32/1, 145/2.

101. *The Great War*, episode 10.

102. Gillard to Essex, 8 April 1965, WAC, T32/1, 145/2, emphasis in original.

103. Most footage from the First World War was filmed on hand-cranked cameras operating at around sixteen frames a second. Run at modern film speed of twenty-four frames a second, images can appear jerky and people move in an apparently ill coordinated way. The footage used in *The Great War* was 'stretch-printed' – every second frame was copied and cut into the film – so that it could be run at modern speed without this problem. I am grateful to Mr Eric Davidson for an explanation of this process (Davidson to Todman, 21 April 1999). See also K. Brownlow, *The War, the West and the Wilderness* (London, 1979), 60–61, 67. It is stimulating to compare this process to the closing credits of the 1989 series *Blackadder Goes Forth*, where modern footage was deliberately treated to make it look like archival film.

104. For an example of the stunned reaction of 1960s audiences to fifty-year-old film, see C. H. Roads, 'A View of the Use of Film by the Universities', *University Vision*, 1 (1968), 11. Roads was the IWM's film curator at the time; when touring with early films he found it difficult to persuade audiences to shed their 'reverence' for archival film in order to analyse it as a historical source.

105. Hynes, *The Soldiers' Tale*, 30.

106. Chandos, *From Peace to War: A Study in Contrasts, 1857–1918* (London, 1968), 83.

107. C. Carrington, 'Some Soldiers', in G. Panichas, ed., *Promise of Greatness* (London, 1968), 157.

108. See Essex form letter for refusing requests, WAC, T32/1, 145/1; on other documentaries, A. Rosenthal, *The Documentary Conscience: A Casebook in Film Making* (Berkeley, California, 1980), 38.

109. British Film Institute, London (hereafter BFI), Bound Script no. 141, reels 3/7, 4/3, 8/1, 9/9. Bogarde himself played an important part in the construction of the film, and wrote some scenes. Losey was happy to involve him because of Bogarde's family's experience of the First World War, and his own service in the Second World War. M. Ciment, *Conversations with Losey* (London, 1985), 242. Bogarde's father suffered nightmares and continued illness as a result of his service on the Western Front and in Italy. Bogarde himself claimed in rather hysterical terms to have become obsessed with the war in his mid teens. D. Bogarde, *The Complete Autobiography* (London, 1988), 127, 593, 597. His scripts, preserved in the BFI, show some changes to scenes as well as numerous doodles of shellbursts, guns and soldiers. BFI Script Catalogue no. 1238, in particular reverse page 6.

110. M. Thornton, 'War in the Mud – But this Time There are No Heroes', *Sunday Express*, 6 December 1964; C. Wilson, 'If You Can Stand It, Go to See Private Hamp', *Daily Mail*, 1 December 1964, BFI *King and Country* Press Cuttings Microjacket.

111. A. Walker, 'King and Country', *Evening Standard Hot Tickets Magazine*, 6 August 1998, 16.

112. W. Allison and J. Fairley, *The Monocled Mutineer* (London, 1978).

113. I. Williams, 'From Giro Fodder to Gun Fodder', *New Statesman*, 5 September 1986, 12.

114. See, for example, the full-page advertisements taken out in the national press. 'More Black Stuff from Bleasdale', *Sun* and others, 30 August 1986, 8.

115. H. Lee and G. Eskyn, 'Errors in Mutineers TV series', *Daily Telegraph*, 13 September 1986, 40.

116. M. Leapman, 'Cries of Rage about Toplis', *New Statesman*, 26 September 1986, 16. There is a comparison to be made with the outrage prompted by the depiction the following year of the Falklands War in *Tumbledown*, a television drama about the wounding of Lieutenant Robert Lawrence and his subsequent treatment by the establishment. K. Foster, *Fighting Fictions: War, Narrative and National Identity* (London, 1999), 106–15.

117. C. Clover, 'Going Over the Top', *Daily Telegraph*, 1 September 1986, 19.

118. Unsigned article, 'A Monocle that Magnifies the Truth of War', *Daily Mail*, 10 September 1986, WAC, *Monocled Mutineer* press cutting file.

119. BBC Audience Reaction Report, WAC, TV/86/109, 1–3.

120. Letter from L. Gray, 'Letters', *Radio Times*, 11 October 1986, WAC, *Monocled Mutineer* press cutting file.

121. Letter from P. Gooch, *Sunday Times*, 21 September 1986, 34.

122. A. Rusbridger, 'A Dog in the Deep Freeze', *Guardian*, 14 September 1986, 30.

123. J. Saunders, *The Bannister Girls* (London, 1990), 76.

124. E. Stirling, *A Field of Bright Poppies* (London, 1990), 46–47.

Notes to Chapter 2: Death

1. J. Winter, *The Great War and the British People* (Cambridge, 1986), 66–72.

2. Ibid., 81–83.

3. Ibid., 73, 75.

4. Ibid., 244–45.

5. Quoted in C. Corns and J. Hughes-Wilson, *Blindfold and Alone: British Military Executions in the Great War* (London, 2001), 469.

6. A. Gregory, *The Silence of Memory: Armistice Day, 1919–1946* (Oxford, 1994); 19.

7. Quoted in J. E. Lewis, ed., *The Mammoth Book of War Diaries and Letters* (London, 1998), 327.

8. Quoted in M. Brown, *The Imperial War Museum Book of the Western Front* (London, 1996), 213.

9. B. Cartland, *We Danced All Night: A Dazzling Memoir of the Glittering Twenties* (London, 1994), 34–35.

10. P. Jalland, *Death in the Victorian Family* (Oxford, 1996), 358–81.

11. For example, J. Winter, *Sites of Memory, Sites of Mourning: The Great War in European Cultural History* (Cambridge, 1995), 58–63; J. Winter and B. Baggett, *The Great War and the Shaping of the Twentieth Century* (New York, 1996), 382–84; T. and V. Holt, '*My Boy Jack?*': *The Search for Kipling's Only Son* (London, 1998).

12. H. Lauder, *A Minstrel in France* (New York, 1918), 72.

13. P. Liddle, 'Britons Overseas', in P. Liddle and H. Cecil, eds, *At the Eleventh Hour: Reflections, Hopes and Anxieties at the Closing of the Great War, 1918* (London, 1998), 52–67.

14. Brown, *Imperial War Museum Book of the Western Front*, 343.

15. Liddle, 'Britons Overseas', 54–56; P. Liddle, 'Britons on the Home Front', in Liddle and Cecil, eds, *At the Eleventh Hour*, 68–83.

16. Diary of Robert Saunders, 11 November 1918, quoted in T. Wilson, *The Myriad Faces of War* (Cambridge, 1986), 755. See also Liddle, 'Britons on the Home Front', in particular 69, 73, 77.

17. D. Lloyd, *Battlefield Tourism: Pilgrimage and the Commemoration of the Great War in Britain, Australia and Canada, 1919–1939* (Oxford, 1998),

18. Ibid., 70.

19. This section draws heavily on Adrian Gregory's *The Silence of Memory*, 22–165.

20. It is worth comparing ex-servicemen's participation in Armistice Day in Britain with that around Anzac Day in Australia, where dawn parades and remembrance were often followed by afternoons of drinking, unregulated gambling and affirmations of 'mateship' – the crucial constituent in the legend of Anzac martial brilliance.

21. A. King, *Memorials of the Great War in Britain* (Oxford, 1998), 216.

22. Sheppard to Editor, *Times*, 20 October 1925, 15.

23. Durno-Steele to Editor, *Times*, 15 October 1925, 10.

24. Gregory, *Silence of Memory*, 36.

25. Whether we can take this as an indicator of their support for its aims is an issue tackled in N. Barr, '"Service not Self": The British Legion, 1921–1939', PhD Thesis, University of St Andrews (1994), 113–14.

26. Gregory, *Silence of Memory*, 83.

27. C. Carrington, *Soldier from the Wars Returning* (London, 1965), 258.

28. S. Humphries and R. van Emden, *Veterans: The Last Survivors of the Great War* (London, 1998), 142.

29. Gregory, *Silence of Memory*, 39.

30. H. Lauder, *Roamin' in the Gloamin'* (London, 1928), 189–212, 193.

31. Lauder, *A Minstrel in France*, 71–79.

32. Lauder, *Roamin' in the Gloamin'*, 188, 220, 217.

33. *22nd Annual Report of the Ministry of Pensions, from 1st April 1938 to 31st March 1939*, (London, 1939) 232.

34. A. Gregory, 'Demobilising the Nation, Remobilising the Dead: The Persistent Mythology of British Commemoration', paper at 'Demobilising the Nation' Conference, Dublin, September 2001.

35. J. Bourke, *Dismembering the Male: Men's Bodies, Britain and the Great War* (London, 1996), 237–48.

36. Lloyd, *Battlefield Tourism*, 85.

37. M. Connelly, *The Great War, Memory and Ritual: Commemoration in the City and East London, 1916–1939* (Woodbridge, 2002), 196–231.

38. Gregory, *Silence of Memory*, 165–166. Connelly, *The Great War, Memory and Ritual*, 182–83, 196.

39. Lloyd, *Battlefield Tourism*, 87.

40. R. Bryson, 'The Once and Future Army', in B. Bond et al, eds, '*Look to Your Front': Studies in the First World War* (Staplehurst, 1999), p. 28, using figures from J. Terraine, *The Smoke and the Fire, Myths and Anti-Myths of War, 1861 to 1945* (London, 1992), chapters 3–5 and 8 and table F.

41. See, for example, figures in C. d'Este, *Decision in Normandy* (London, 2001 [1983]), 252–70, 280.

42. P. Calvocoressi, G. Wint and J. Pritchard, *Total War: Causes and Courses of the Second World War* (2nd edn, New York and Harmondsworth, 1989), 577.

43. P. Orr, *The Road to the Somme: Men of the Ulster Division Tell Their Story*, (Belfast, 1987), vii, 218.

44. Details of Chilton's life from interviews with Dan Todman, 14 May 2000, and Alex Danchev, 8 August 1988.

45. Winter, *Sites of Memory, Sites of Mourning*, chapter 2, and particularly 30, 53, 225.

46. *Oh! What a Lovely War* Programme, Theatre Royal Stratford, 19 March 1963, LHCMA, LH 13/61.

47. C. Chilton, *The Long Long Trail*, as broadcast script, 27 December 1961, 21 February and 11 November 1962, 22, WAC. The radio play enjoyed a long life. Reproduced as a resource for schools by BBC Education in the 1970s, it was still in use in the late 1980s (personal knowledge). Bud Flanagan's wartime experiences are detailed in B. Flanagan, *My Crazy Life* (London, 1962), 52–60.

48. Theatre Workshop, *Oh What a Lovely War* (London, 2001), 74, 78, 82.

49. P. Lewis, 'I'm with you Mr Levin ... raving!', *Daily Mail*, 21 June 1963, LHCMA, LH 13/61.

50. In the transition from stage to screen, the film acquired an exclamation mark. Here, *Oh What a Lovely War* is a play, *Oh! What a Lovely War* the film. Deighton's name was removed from the film after a disagreement with his co-producer, Brian Duffy.

51. M. Hinxman, 'A Lovely War for British Film', *Sunday Telegraph*, 6 April 1969, 6.

52. This scene bears similarities to images in Rex Ingram's *Four Horsemen of the Apocalypse* (1921) and Abel Gance's *J'accuse* (1918 and 1937). I have not been able to determine if either of these influenced Attenborough, Winter, *Sites of memory*, 15–17. Incidentally, Jack's daughter was played by Richard Attenborough's daughter, Charlotte, Official Synopsis, BFI, OWGA107, 17.

53. P. French, 'Oh! What a Lovely War', *Sight and Sound*, 38, 2 (Spring 1969), 94.

54. M. Hinxman, 'An Exhilarating Sadness', *Sunday Telegraph*, 6 April 1969, 12.

55. A. Dougan, *The Actor's Director: Richard Attenborough Behind the Camera* (Edinburgh, 1994), 17.

56. T. Bolas, 'Oh! What a Lovely War', *Screen*, 10, 3 (May/June 1969), 84–90.

57. BBC as broadcast script for programme thirteen of *The Great War*, 1, LHCMA, LH 13/62. The images are cropped from the following: 'Mourning a Fallen Comrade, August 1917' (IWM, Q2756), 'Remains of a German Soldier, November 1916' (IWM, Q2041) and 'Ration Party of the Royal Irish Rifles Resting in a Communication Trench, Battle of the Somme, 1 July 1916' (IWM, Q1).

58. Farrall to Essex, 22 April 1965, Dyer to Essex, 9 April 1965, Close to Essex, 14 April 1965, WAC, T32/1, 145/1–2.

59. Essex to Redmayne, 22 December 1964, WAC, T32/1, 145/4, emphases in original. The soldier was identified as Private Joseph Bailey, after his daughter wrote in to the programme. If this is the case, it may be that the picture has a particular resonance, since Bailey was killed on 1 July 1916. However, there remains some doubt – Bailey's daughter was the first of a number of viewers who wrote in to claim the forlorn soldier, and her subsequent attempts to claim compensation from the BBC may arouse suspicion. There is a divergence between Bailey's unit – 1/12 Yorkshire and Lancashire Regiment – and the unit identified by the photographer, the Royal Irish Rifles, although it is possible the caption may be in error. Shepherd to Essex, 20 October 1964, WAC, T32/1, 145/4; R. Gibson, 'Somme Soldier', *Stand To! The Journal of the Western Front Association*, 54 (January 1999), 38–39.

60. *Royal Gardeners*, BBC2, 10 December 2003, 8.30–9.00 p. m.

61. 'Queen Honours Australian War Dead', BBC News, 11 November 2003, http://news.bbc.co.uk/1/hi/uk/325907. stm, accessed 1335 4 August 2004.

62. Winter, *The Great War and the British People*, 75.

63. Dyer, *Missing of the Somme*, 27.

64. R. Kee, 'How the Lights Went Out', *Spectator*, 1 June 1962, 723; A. Quinn, 'What Sassoon Could Never Resolve', *Daily Telegraph*, 2 September 1995, A4.

65. R. Stummer, 'The War We Can't Forget', *Guardian*, 5 November 1998, 12.

66. C. Moore, *Trench Fever* (London, 1998), 136.

67. T. Walter, 'War Grave Pilgrimage', in I. Reader and T. Walter, eds, *Pilgrimage in Popular Culture* (Basingstoke, 1993), 76–84.

68. P. Barker, 'How Did Uncle Edmund Die?', *Observer Review*, 7 November 1999, 2. See also S. O'Shea, *Back to the Front: An Accidental Historian Walks the Trenches of World War One* (London, 1997), 113.

69. Walter, 'War Grave Pilgrimage', 72.

70. In terms of identifying and understanding the 'heritage boom', a good survey is provided by N. Merriman, *Beyond the Glass Case: The Past, the Heritage and the Public in Britain* (Leicester, 1991), 8–10. See also R. Weight, *Patriots: National Identity in Britain, 1940–2000* (London, 2002), 579–85; D. Lowenthal, *The Past is a Foreign Country* (Cambridge, 1999), 4–10; P. Wright, 'Falling Back Together in the Nineteen Eighties', in his *On Living in an Old Country: The National Past in Contemporary Britain* (London, 1985), 161–92; J. Richards, *Films and British National Identity: From Dickens to Dad's Army* (Manchester, 1997), 169. On academic interest in the boom, see J. Winter, 'The Generation of Memory: Reflections on the "Memory Boom" in Contemporary Historical Studies', *Bulletin of the German Historical Institute Washington*, 27 (2000), 86–90; S. Radstone, 'Working with Memory: An Introduction', in S. Radstone, ed., *Memory and Methodology* (Oxford, 1999), 2–8.

71. See for example, J. Treays, 'To Our Dear Boys', *Sunday Telegraph*, review section, 8 November 1998, 4.

72. C. Moore, 'Is Wanting a Relic from Ground Zero Morbid ? No, It's a Way of Understanding Human History on a Personal Level', *Guardian*, 31 January 2002, section 2, 7.

73. For example, L. Milner, *Leeds Pals: A History of the 15th (Service) Battalion (1st Leeds), the Prince of Wales's Own (West Yorkshire Regiment), 1914–1918* (London, 1991); W. Turner, *The 'Accrington Pals': The 11th (Service) Battalion, (Accrington), East Lancashire Regiment. A Pictorial History* (Preston, 1986); J. Garwood, *Chorley Pals: 'Y' Company, 11th (Service) Battalion, East Lancashire Regiment: A Short History of the Company in the Great War, 1914–1919* (Radcliffe, 1989).

74. Moore, *Trench Fever*, 237–38.

75. C. Moriarty, 'Review Article: The Material Culture of Great War Remembrance', *Journal of Contemporary History*, 34, 4 (1999), 653.

Notes to Chapter 3: Donkeys

1. Pierson to Haig, 2 February 1928, Haig Papers, National Library of Scotland (HPNLS), Acc 3155/249. See also Dickson to Haig, 16 February 1928, HPNLS, Acc 3155/249.

2. J. Laffin, *British Butchers and Bunglers of World War One* (Stroud, 1988); A. Clark, *The Donkeys* (London, 1961).

3. M. Hastings, 'I Do Not Believe Our Generation Could Have Borne the Martyrdom of World War One', *Evening Standard*, 2 November 1998, 8.

4. G. Sheffield, *Forgotten Victory: The First World War, Myths and Realities* (London, 2001), 21–40, 64; M. Howard, *The Continental Commitment: The Dilemma of British Defence Policy in the Era of Two World Wars* (London, 1972), 53–59.

5. D. French, 'Allies, Rivals and Enemies: British Strategy and War Aims during the First World War', in J. Turner, ed., *Britain and the First World War* (London, 1988), 24–25; Sheffield, *Forgotten Victory*, 67–70.

6. R. Prior and T. Wilson, *Passchendaele: The Untold Story* (New Haven and London, 1996), 8–10; Sheffield, *Forgotten Victory*, 90–94

7. Sheffield, *Forgotten Victory*, 98–99, 103.

8. Ibid., 99–102, Prior and Wilson, *Passchendaele*, 11–13, 15–24.

9. A point made to me repeatedly by Chris Pugsley and re-emphasised in his *New Zealand, Australia and Empire, 1914–1918: Reflections on the ANZAC Experience in the First World War* (Birkenhead, New Zealand, 2004). I am grateful to Dr Pugsley for letting me read his manuscript in advance of publication.

10. Sheffield, *Forgotten Victory*, 116–21, 147–48. On the British army's ability to

create and adopt technical solutions, see A. Palazzo, *Seeking Victory on the Western Front: The British Army and Chemical Warfare in World War I* (Lincoln, Nebraska, and London, 2000).

11. Sheffield, *Forgotten Victory*, 77–80.

12. Ibid., 83–86. On British strategy throughout the war, see French, 'Allies, Rivals and Enemies', 28–35.

13. Sheffield, *Forgotten Victory*, 115–16, 230–31.

14. Sheffield, *Forgotten Victory*, 95–97.

15. I. Malcolm Brown, *British Logistics on the Western Front, 1914–19* (Westport, Connecticut, and London, 1998), 17–73; B. Bond, *The Victorian Army and the Staff College, 1854–1914* (London, 1972), 230–306. On the British Army at all levels and the changes it went through during the war, see R. Holmes, *Tommy: The British Soldier on the Western Front, 1914–18* (London, 2004); G. Sheffield and D. Todman, eds, *Command and Control on the Western Front: The British Experience, 1914–18* (Staplehurst, 2004); T. Travers, *The Killing Ground: The British Army, the Western Front and the Emergence of Modern Warfare, 1900–1918* (London, 1987).

16. Bond, *The Victorian Army and the Staff College*, 306–26; R. Holmes, *The Little Field Marshal* (London, 1981), 197–251.

17. Sheffield, *Forgotten Victory*, 110.

18. N. Barr, 'Command in the Transition from Mobile to Static Warfare', in Sheffield and Todman, eds, *Command and Control*.

19. Sheffield, *Forgotten Victory*, 103–10; Malcolm Brown, *British Logistics*, 75–108.

20. Sheffield, *Forgotten Victory*, 133–57; P. Griffith, *Battle Tactics of the Western Front: The British Army's Art of Attack, 1916–18* (New Haven and London, 1994), 56–83. On the impact of the Somme on the German army, see I. Passingham, *All the Kaiser's Men* (Stroud, 2004), 97–126.

21. Sheffield, *Forgotten Victory*, 116–29, 159–84; Malcolm Brown, *British Logistics*, 139–78; Griffith, *Battle Tactics*, 83–90; B. Rawling, *Surviving Trench Warfare: Technology and the Canadian Corps, 1914–18* (Toronto, 1992); J. Walker, *The Blood Tub: General Gough and the Battle of Bullecourt, 1917* (Staplehurst, 1998); and I. Passingham, *Pillars of Fire: The Battle of Messines Ridge, June 1917* (Stroud, 1998).

22. Sheffield, *Forgotten Victory*, 137–38, 171–72; Prior and Wilson, *Passchendaele*, 45–53; P. Liddle, ed., *Passchendaele in Perspective: The Third Battle of Ypres* (London, 1997).

23. Sheffield, *Forgotten Victory*, 171–81; Prior and Wilson, *Passchendaele*, 86–181.

24. B. Bond, 'Passchendaele: Verdicts Past and Present', in Liddle, ed., *Passchendaele in Perspective*, 482–83.

25. Prior and Wilson, *Passchendaele*, 195–200.

26. Sheffield, *Forgotten Victory*, 187–96; Griffith, *Battle Tactics*, 90–92.

27. Griffith, *Battle Tactics*, passim and particularly 93–100, 135–75; Sheffield, *Forgotten Victory*, 197–200; Malcolm Brown, *British Logistics*, 179–209.

28. Sheffield, *Forgotten Victory*, 221–23.

29. Ibid., 220.

30. See G. Sheffield and D. Todman, 'Introduction', and D. Todman, 'The Grand Lamasery Revisited: GHQ, 1914–1918', in Sheffield and Todman, eds, *Command and Control*.

31. Including, since 1945 and in no order of merit: J. Davidson, *Haig: Master of the Field* (London, 1953); Clark, *The Donkeys*; J. Terraine, *Douglas Haig: The Educated Soldier* (London, 1963); G. Duncan, *Douglas Haig As I Knew Him* (London, 1966); E. K. G. Sixsmith, *Douglas Haig* (London, 1976); G. De Groot, *Douglas Haig, 1861–1928* (London, 1988); D. Winter, *Haig's Command: A Reassessment* (London, 1991); B. Bond and N. Cave, *Haig: A Reappraisal Seventy Years On* (Barnsley, 1999).

32. My thanks to Dr Chris Pugsley for this point.

33. Holmes, *Tommy*, 170–72.

34. J. Bourne, 'British Generals in the First World War', in G. Sheffield, ed., *Leadership and Command: The Anglo-American Experience since 1861* (London, 1997), 109–10.

35. M. Howard, 'Leadership in the British Army in the Second World War: Some Personal Observations', ibid., 120.

36. Lord Moran (C. Wilson), *Anatomy of Courage* (London, 1945), 203–4.

37. *Henry IV, Part I*, Act I, Scene iii, 29–52.

38. R. Fielding, *War Letters to a Wife* (Staplehurst, 2001, first published 1929), 173, asterisks in original.

39. GSO (Sir Frank Fox), *GHQ (Montreuil-sur-Mer)* (London, 1920), 29.

40. Quoted in Terraine, *Douglas Haig*, 433.

41. V. Brittain, *Testament of Youth* (London, 1988), 420. I am grateful to Phylomena Badsey for bringing this quote to my attention.

42. S. Badsey, 'Haig and the Press', in Bond and Cave, eds, *Haig: A Reappraisal Seventy Years On*, 176–95.

43. D. Todman, '"Sans Peur et Sans Reproche": The Retirement, Death and Mourning of Sir Douglas Haig, 1918–1928', *Journal of Military History*, 67, 4 (October 2003), 1083–106.

44. *Times*, leader, 23 December 1854, quoted in K. Chesney, *Crimean War Reader* (London, 1960), 180–81.

45. G. Egerton, 'The Lloyd George *War Memoirs*: A Study in the Politics of Memory', *Journal of Modern History*, 60 (March 1988), 58.

46. D. French, 'Sir Douglas Haig's Reputation, 1918–1928: A Note', *Historical Journal*, 28, 4 (1985), 953–60; J. Boraston and G. Dewar, *Sir Douglas Haig's Command, 1915–1918* (London, 1922).

47. W. Churchill, *The World Crisis, 1911–1918* (London, 1931, abridged and revised), 640–41.

48. R. Prior, *Churchill's 'The World Crisis' as History* (Beckenham, 1983), 261–71.

49. 'Churchill and World War', *Daily Herald*, 3 March 1927, 7.

50. *Times*, 31 January 1927, 12; 1 February, 12; 2 February, 12; 3 February, 12; 4 February, 14; 5 February, 10; 12 February, 13–14; 16 February, 15–16; February 24, 15–16.

51. 'C.S.', 'The Best Story of the War', *New Statesman*, 5 March 1927, 636.

52. F. Maurice, 'Marshal Haig: A Memoir', *Daily Mirror*, 31 January 1928, 4.

53. 'Earl Haig', *Daily Sketch*, 31 January 1928, 7.

54. Picture caption, ibid., 1.

55. 'Earl Haig', *Daily Herald*, 31 January 1928, 1.

56. Cited in G. Wooton, *The Official History of the British Legion* (London, 1956), 66.

57. This section draws heavily on my article, '"Sans Peur et Sans Reproche": The Retirement, Death and Mourning of Sir Douglas Haig, 1918–1928', 1083–106.

58. H. Strachan, 'Liddell Hart, Cruttwell and Falls', in B. Bond, ed., *The First World War and British Military History* (Oxford, 1991), 53.

59. Egerton, 'The Lloyd George *War Memoirs*', particularly 66–67.

60. B. Bond, *The Unquiet Western Front* (Cambridge, 2002), 47–48.

61. Egerton, 'The Lloyd George *War Memoirs*', 79–80.

62. Lloyd George Papers, G/236, quoted ibid., 80.

63. C. Forester, *The General* (London, 1936), 173.

64. Ibid., 207.

65. R. van Gelder, 'Author of *Captain Horatio Hornblower*', *New York Times Review of Books*, 23 February 1941, 2, quoted in S. Stemlicht, *C. S. Forester* (Boston, 1981), 87. Stemlicht notes that Hitler greatly enjoyed *The General* and gave copies to Göring and Keitel. William Joyce, Lord Haw Haw, broadcast passages from the book into Britain during the Second World War.

66. D. Todman, 'A Statue for Earl Haig', *The Douglas Haig Fellowship Records*, 8 (December 2002), 6–13.

67. B. H. Liddell Hart, *Through the Fog of War* (London, 1938), 40–41.

68. Sheffield, *Forgotten Victory*, 230.

69. D. French, *Raising Churchill's Army: The British Army and the War against Germany, 1919–1945* (Oxford, 2000), 81–88

70. On the concerns of Churchill and others and the use of the First World War as a comparator, see C. d'Este, *Decision in Normandy* (London, 2004, first published 1983), 108, 302

71. Although in individual campaigns the quantity of manpower available for infantry replacements remained an issue of vital concern. See D'Este, *Decision in Normandy*, 252–70.

72. This is not to suggest that the relationship between Churchill and his senior generals was ever harmonious. But it never approached the rivalry, discord and downright hatred that existed between Lloyd George and Haig.

73. Quoted in D. Haig, *My Father's Son: The Memoirs of Major the Earl Haig* (London, 2000), 175.

74. On the development of Blimp see C. Seymour-Ure, 'Introduction' to M. Bryant, ed, *The Complete Colonel Blimp* (London, 1991), 13–29; J. Richards, *Films and British National Identity: From Dickens to Dad's Army* (Manchester, 1997), 92, 165. For the modern watcher, a further layer of connections binds *Blimp* into the representation of war in British popular culture. Candy's batman and driver in the First World War, who stays with him afterwards and joins the Home Guard with him, is played by John Laurie. Laurie is now best known for his role as the doom prophesying undertaker, Private Fraser, in the BBC TV series *Dad's Army*: again, a member of the Home Guard. When he disappears from *Blimp*, apparently killed by a bomb, it is hard not to imagine that he has in fact left for a new life in Walmington-on-Sea.

75. J. Chapman, '*The Life and Death of Colonel Blimp* Reconsidered', *Historical Journal of Film, Radio and Television*, 15, 1 (March 1995), 19–36.

76. D. Graham, ed., *Keith Douglas: The Complete Poems* (Oxford, 1987), 110, 139.

77. Those influences continue through the cinematic representation of the Second World War. Anyone who, watching a Saturday afternoon television repeat of *A Bridge Too Far* (1977), has cheered at the moment when an umbrella-wielding British subaltern discusses surrender terms with the German troops who surround him, and declares 'I'm afraid we haven't got room for you all', knows exactly what is meant. The concept of officership in British popular culture in the twentieth century is an area I intend to research in a future project.

78. J. Edmonds, *Military Operations France and Belgium, 1917* (London, 1949); R. Blake, *The Private Papers of Sir Douglas Haig* (London, 1952), and see newspaper reviews of both collected in LHCMA, LH 15/21.

79. Clark, *The Donkeys*, 180, see notes. I am grateful for Dr Gary Sheffield, whose co-edited version, with Dr John Bourne, of Haig's wartime diaries is in the process of publication as I write, for advice about the selective uses that have been made of Blake's version of the diaries.

80. J. Baynes, *Far from a Donkey: The Life of General Sir Ivor Maxse* (London, 1995), frontpages.

81. Clark, *The Donkeys*, 12.

82. Clark to Liddell Hart, 21 Oct 1958, LHCMA, LH 1/172/3.

83. Liddell Hart sent a 'rocket' to Clark after his corrections on the proofs of *The Donkeys* were ignored: 'As the "white hope" of the new generation of military historians in combatting [sic] the latest batch of "myth embroiderers", it is of

the greatest importance, not only to yourself, that you should be as careful as possible in dealing with facts and leave no flanks open to counter-attack.' (Liddell Hart to Clark, 22 June 1961, LHCMA, LH 13/34). However, Liddell Hart still provided ammunition for Clark against hostile reviews. Liddell Hart to Clark, 14 and 16 July 1961, LHCMA, LH 13/34.

84. Clark to Blake, 16 July 1961, LHCMA, LH 1/172/222.

85. Clark to Liddell Hart, 21 January 1959, Liddell Hart to Clark, 29 January 1959, LHCMA, LH 1/172/15–16.

86. Clark to Liddell Hart, 8 February 1961, LHCMA, LH 1/172/90, emphases in original.

87. Clark to Liddell Hart, 11 June 1961, LHCMA, LH 1/172/111.

88. B. Fergusson, 'Sniping at the 1914 Generals', *Daily Telegraph*, 21 July 1961; A. J. P. Taylor, 'Diaries Bring Doom', Observer, 23 July 1961; M. Howard, 'The Donkeys', *Listener*, 3 August 1961, 180–81. See also '1914–18 in Retrospect', *Economist*, 5 August 1961; J. Cameron, 'Lord of the Shambles', *Spectator*, 28 July 1961, 145. All reviews in LHCMA, D546 C54.

89. C. Douglas Home, 'The Donkeys', *Daily Express*, 15 July 1961, LHCMA, D546 C54.

90. See notes.

91. P. Johnson, 'Durable Brasshats', *New Statesman*, 4 August 1961, 158.

92. '1914–18 in Retrospect', *Economist*, 5 August 1961.

93. D. Paget, 'Popularising Popular History: "Oh! What a Lovely War" and the Sixties', *Critical Query and Survey*, 2, 2 (1990), 122–26.

94. A. Danchev, '"Bunking" and Debunking: The Controversies of the 1960s', in Bond, ed., *The First World War and British Military History*, 282.

95. Theatre Workshop, *Oh What a Lovely War Playscript* (London, 2000).

96. 'Joan Littlewood', *Tribune*, 19 April 1963, 9.

97. *Oh What a Lovely War*, 35.

98. Ibid., 66.

99. Ibid., 77.

100. M. Howard, 'The Demand for Military History', *Times Literary Supplement*, 13 November 1969, 1293–295.

101. Paget, 'Popularising Popular History', 118.

102. Clark threatened to sue Theatre Workshop for breach of copyright on *The Donkeys*: the case was settled out of court. Barbara Tuchman acquiesced to the thefts from her book. Allan sued because he claimed that his script, which Raffles and Littlewood had rejected as being too realistic, was the basis for the final production. He was unsuccessful. See cuttings in LHCMA, LH 13/61.

103. *Radio Times*, 2 July 1964, 47.

104. P. Larkin, *Collected Poems* (London, 1988), 167.

105. Bond, *The Unquiet Western Front*, 52.

106. On this mythologisation, see Peter York's comments quoted in R. Hewison, *Too Much: Art and Society in the Sixties, 1960–1975* (London, 1986), xi.

107. On all these changes in the 1960s, see R Weight, *Patriots: National Identity in Britain, 1940–2000* (London, 2002), 252–53, 322–23; P. Clarke, *Hope and Glory: Britain, 1900–1990* (London, 1996), 248–82, 290–93, 307–8; K. Morgan, *The People's Peace: British History, 1945–1990* (Oxford, 1992), 184–85; A. Marwick, *British Society since 1945* (London, 1996), 110–19. On the hostile attitudes of the bulk of the population to the elite who took part in the mythical 1960s, see M. Farren, *Give the Anarchist a Cigarette* (London, 2001), 42–44, 94–95, 121–22.

108. A. Sked, *An Intelligent Person's Guide to Post-War Britain* (London, 1997), 136.

109. S. Wagg, 'You've Never Had it So Silly: The Politics of British Satirical Comedy from *Beyond the Fringe* to *Spitting Image*', in D. Strinati and S. Wagg, eds, *Come On Down? Popular Culture in Post-War Britain* (London, 1992), 256–79, Morgan, *The People's Peace*, 209.

110. My thanks to Dr Peter Martland for supplying me with these examples.

111. Hewison, *Too Much*, xiii.

112. H. Goorney, *The Theatre Workshop Story* (London, 1981), 120, 127.

113. R. Hastings, 'Sketches Aid 1914–18 War Songs', *Daily Telegraph*, 20 March 1963, LHCMA, LH 13/61.

114. *Oh! What a Lovely War* programme LHCMA, LH 13/61.

115. P. Hope Wallace, 'Review', *Guardian*, 21 June 1963, LHCMA, LH 13/61.

116. 'Gone West', *Sunday Telegraph*, 23 June 1963, LHCMA, LH 13/61.

117. J. Ardagh, 'OWALW', *Observer*, 23 June 1963, LHCMA, LH 13/61. Liddell Hart's copy of the programme from his first visit to the play has been preserved in the same file. Even he, no great fan of Haig, noted 'Haig as villain' with a characteristically disapproving exclamation mark.

118. Untitled article, *Times*, 21 March 1963, LHCMA, LH 13/61.

119. A. Brien, 'Looking for Enemies', *Sunday Telegraph*, 24 March 1963, LHCMA, LH 13/61.

120. D. Pryce-Jones, 'Shot in the Arm', *Spectator*, 28 June 1963, LHCMA, LH 13/61

121. J. Lambert, untitled article, *Sunday Times*, 23 June 1963, LHCMA, LH 13/61.

122. R. Gellert, 'General Joan', *New Statesman*, 28 June 1963, LHCMA, LH 13/61.

123. Hastings, 'Sketches Aid 1914–18 War Songs', LHCMA, LH 13/61.

124. E. Swinton, ed., *Twenty Years After: The Battlefields of 1914–18 Then and Now* (London, 1936–37); J. Hammerton, ed., *World War, 1914–1918: A Pictured History* (London, 1934–35); *I Was There: Undying Memories of 1914–18* (London, 1938–39). Restrictions of time have only allowed a brief survey of these remarkable part works, the production and reception of which have not yet been the subject of academic study. The written material in them is often ambiguous in its attitude to the war, in line with the suggestions made in Chapter 1, but the

photographs that were reproduced were sometimes shocking to modern eyes. A detailed attempt to trace the history of reproduction and reuse of these images would be a fruitful field of research.

125. J. Littlewood, *Joan's Book: Joan Littlewood's Peculiar History as She Tells It* (London, 1994), 676.

126. J. Littlewood, 'Introduction', and V. Spinetti, 'Afterword', *Oh What a Lovely War*, ix, 89.

127. H. Neill, 'When Did You Last See Your Father Cry?', *Times*, 18 March 1998, 41.

128. Goorney, *The Theatre Workshop Story*, 127–29. Goorney also cites MacColl's irritation at the 'rosy glow of nostalgia' created by the production.

129. D. Pryce-Jones, 'Theatre Review', *Spectator*, 3 July 1964, LHCMA, LH 13/61.

130. Liddell Hart to Chapman, 21 June 1961, LHCMA, LH 13/34.

131. Todman interview with John Terraine, 14 January 1999. See also his footnote on wounded soldiers having to return to the front because Lloyd George was starving Haig of manpower: 'The author's father was one of these' (*Douglas Haig*, 324 note 1).

132. J. Terraine, *The Smoke and the Fire: Myths and Anti-Myths of War* (London, 1982), 13–14; W. Moodie, ed., *The Crown of Honour: Being Stories of Heroism, Gallantry, Magnanimity and Devotion from the Great War of 1914–18* (London, 1931), 7.

133. Information on Terraine's career from Brian Bond's obituary of him in *Guardian*, 1 January 2004, 17.

134. Terraine to Essex, July 1964, WAC, T32/827/1, quoted in M. Connelly, 'The Great War, Part 13', *Historical Journal of Film, Radio and Television*, 22, 1 (2002), 23.

135. Ibid., 24.

136. Ibid.

137. BBC Audience Research Report, VR/64/461.

138. I. Williams, 'From Giro Fodder to Gun Fodder', *New Statesman*, 5 September 1986, 12.

139. A. Bleasdale, *The Monocled Mutineer* (London, 1986), 14, 20.

140. More generally, Bleasdale may be seen to have recycled source material produced in the 1960s in his drama. A scene in the second episode where Toplis entertains his comrades with a 'circus showman' act is taken verbatim from J. Brophy and E. Partridge, *The Long Trail: What the British Soldier Sang and Said in the Great War of 1914–18* (London, 1965), a volume originally published in the 1930s, and reproduced in the 1960s, at least in part to counter what its authors saw as faults in *Oh What a Lovely War*.

141. 'A Monocle That Magnifies the Truth of War', *Daily Mail*, 10 September 1986, WACMM.

142. Weight, *Patriots*, 550–73.

143. S. Donaldson, 'Filmmakers on Film: Stephen Fry', http://www.portal.tele-graph.co.uk/arts/main.jhtml;$sessionid$RXSH12XIM1H3RQFIQMFSFFWAVC BQoIVo?xml=/arts/2003/09/27/bffmof27.xml&sSheet=/arts/2003/09/27/ixar-tright.html, accessed 4 August 2004, 1103.

144. R. Curtis et al., *Blackadder: The Whole Damn Dynasty, 1485–1917* (London, 1998), 354.

145. Ibid., 449–50.

146. Conversation with Helen Bettinson (producer of the programme), 29 May 2002. I am extremely grateful to Dr Bettinson for providing me with a video-tape of this programme, and making a range of press cuttings from the time available to me.

147. S. Day Lewis, 'History, Haig and Human Sacrifice', *Daily Telegraph*, 4 July 1996, (Bettinson press cutting).

148. T. Sutcliffe, 'Review', *Independent*, 4 July 1996, section two, 28.

149. S. Jeffries, 'Somme Leader', *Guardian*, 4 July 1996 (Bettinson press cutting).

150. P. Paterson, 'Pinning It On the Donkey', *Daily Mail*, 4 July 1996, 57. See also S. Hildred, 'What I Watched Last Night', *Sun*, 4 July 1996, 27; M. Bond, 'Nei-ther a Butcher Nor a Donkey, but a Man', *Times*, 4 July 1996, 47; R. Hattersley, 'Television Last Night', *Daily Express*, 4 July 1996, 49.

151. Sheffield to Todman (email), 14 February 2003.

Notes to Chapter 4: Futility

1. http://amazon.co.uk/exec/obidos/tg/...sr=1–1/ref=sr_sp_re/202–0151039–9361411, accessed 11 September 2001, 0941.

2. R. Prior and T. Wilson, *The First World War* (London, 1999), 16–28; D. Steven-son, *The First World War and International Politics* (Oxford, 1988), 38–40.

3. Stevenson, *First World War and International Politics*, 34–38; G. Sheffield, *Forgotten Victory: The First World War, Myths and Realities* (London, 2001), 33–40.

4. Sheffield, *Forgotten Victory*, 23–34.

5. Ibid., 48–50.

6. H. Strachan, *The First World War*, i, *To Arms*, (Oxford, 2001), 103–62, 114–39.

7. Sheffield, *Forgotten Victory*, 23–24.

8. A. Horne and G. Kramer, *German Atrocities 1914: A History of Denial* (New Haven and London, 2001); Sheffield, *Forgotten Victory*, 50–51.

9. C. Townshend, *Britain's Civil Wars: Counterinsurgency in the Twentieth Century* (London, 1986).

10. Sheffield, *Forgotten Victory*, 63–64.

11. D. French, 'The Meaning of Attrition, 1914–1916', *English Historical Review*, 103, (April 1988), 385–405.

12. N. Ferguson, *The Pity of War: Explaining World War I* (London, 1998), 290–317.

13. Stevenson, *First World War and International Politics*, 310–24; Sheffield, *Forgotten Victory*, 223–29, 234.

14. J. M. Wilson, *Siegfried Sassoon: The Making of a War Poet, 1886–1918*, (London, 1998), 373–74.

15. H. G. Wells, *Mr Britling Sees It Through* (London, 1916), 351. For an excellent discussion of Wells, see S. Hynes, *A War Imagined: The First World War and English Culture* (London, 1991), 130–34.

16. E. Lucas of the 1st Devons, writing in the scrapbook of Dorothy Scholes, 'Papers' Wigan Archives Service D/DZ EHC, quoted by J. Bourke, 'Effeminacy, Ethnicity and the End of Trauma: The Sufferings of "Shell-Shocked" Men in Great Britain and Ireland, 1914–39', *Journal of Contemporary History*, 35, 1 (2000), 58.

17. J. McRae, 'In Flanders Fields', B. Gardner, *Up the Line to Death* (London, 1964), 49.

18. M. Connelly, *The Great War, Memory and Ritual: Commemoration in the City and East London, 1916–1939* (Woodbridge, 2002), 108. Thorne later became a Labour MP.

19. Listener, *100 Years of Economic Statistics*, 44–45, cited in P. Hennessy, *Never Again: Britain, 1945–51* (London, 1992), 450. In comparison, the figures for the five years after the Second World War were between 1.7 and 1.1. per cent.

20. P. Clarke, *Hope and Glory: Britain, 1900–2000* (London, 2004), 152.

21. P. Leese, 'Problems Returning Home: British Psychological Casualties of the Great War', *Historical Journal*, 40, 4 (1997), 1058.

22. P. Gibbs, *The Realities of War* (London, 1920).

23. A. G. Macdonell, *England, Their England* (London, 1983, first published 1933), 164.

24. J. Winter, *Sites of Memory, Sites of Mourning: The Great War in European Cultural History* (Cambridge, 1995); R. M. Bracco, *Merchants of Hope: British Middlebrow Writers and the First World War, 1919–1939* (Oxford, 1993); A. Gregory, *The Silence of Memory: Armistice Day, 1919–1946* (Oxford, 1994); D. Lloyd, *Battlefield Tourism, Pilgrimage and the Commemoration of the Great War in Britain, Australia and Canada, 1919–1939* (Oxford, 1998); A. King, *Memorials of the Great War in Britain: The Symbolism and Politics of Remembrance* (Oxford, 1998); A. Gaffney, *Aftermath: Remembering the Great War in Wales* (Cardiff, 1998); Connelly, *The Great War, Memory and Ritual*.

25. D. Boorman, *At the Going Down of the Sun: British First World War Memorials* (York, 1988), 111, 93.

26. Quoted in Connelly, *The Great War, Memory and Ritual*, 157.

27. Quoted ibid., 190.

28. *Morning Post*, 12 November 1921, 8, quoted in Gregory, *The Silence of Memory*, 37.

29. J. Richards, *Visions of Yesterday* (London, 1973), 153–54.

30. E. Raymond, *Tell England: A Study in a Generation* (London, 1928, first published 1922), 299.

31. Bracco, *Merchants of Hope*, 29.

32. G. Carey and H. Scott, *An Outline History of the Great War for Use in Schools* (Cambridge, 1929), 108.

33. Even Churchill's most vituperative comment on the generals, that they 'fought machine guns with the breasts of brave men', explicitly validated the war in heroic terms. See Churchill, *The World Crisis*, (London, 1938, first published 1927), 1091–92 and Lloyd George, *War Memoirs*, i (London, 1936), 321, 514, and ii, 1247.

34. C. B. Firth, *From James I to George V* (London, 1936), 95–96.

35. Connelly, *The Great War, Memory and Ritual*, 182–83.

36. 'A Correspondent', 'Martinmas: The Soldier's Service', *Times*, 12 November 1932, 15.

37. Connelly, *The Great War, Memory and Ritual*, 8.

38. A. J. P. Taylor, *English History, 1914–1945* (Oxford, 1965), 600.

39. The following is written in a spirit of speculation: the topic of the First World War in the Second is one that deserves sustained research in its own right.

40. Quoted in A. Calder, *The People's War* (London, 1992, first published 1969), 53.

41. Ibid., 570.

42. M. Connelly, *We Can Take It: Britain and the Memory of the Second World War* (London, 2004), 128–97; M. Donnelly, *Britain in the Second World War* (London, 1999), 33–53.

43. Hennessy, *Never Again*, 2.

44. Unsigned article, 'Joan Littlewood', 9.

45. *Oh! What a Lovely War*, 15.

46. 'Notes from the Authors – Theatre Workshop', *Oh! What a Lovely War* Programme, LHCMA, LH 13/61. I have been able to find no evidence that this computer or this operation actually existed.

47. A. Sisman, *A. J. P. Taylor: A Biography* (London, 1995), 15–19; A. J. P. Taylor, *A Personal History* (London, 1983), 242–43.

48. Sisman, *A. J. P. Taylor*, 306–7.

49. Taylor, *The First World War: An Illustrated History* (Harmondsworth, 1967, first published 1963), 28, 83.

50. Taylor, *Illustrated History*, 62, 194, 11.

51. A. J. P. Taylor, 'Dead Men's Battle Orders', *Observer*, 23 November 1958, 3–4.

52. A. Danchev, '"Bunking" and Debunking: The Controversies of the 1960s', in

B. Bond, ed., *The First World War and British Military History* (Oxford, 1991), 272.

53. Ibid., 264.

54. N. Dixon, *On the Psychology of Military Incompetence* (London, 1976), 80–85.

55. Ibid., 80.

56. P. Johnson, 'Bloody Ships', *New Statesman*, 15 November 1963, 711.

57. 'Remembrance Day', note by Robert Beloe for Archbishop of Canterbury, 5 September 1967, Lambeth Palace Library, London, Ramsey 119, fol. 278.

58. Ibid.

59. B. Priestley, 'Lest We Forget to Remember', *Times*, 13 November 1967, 8. For the genesis of this survey, see Chester to Beloe, 20 October 1967, LPL, Ramsey 119, fol. 301.

60. Jenkins to Ramsey, 23 May 1967, and Robert Beloe note for Archbishop of Canterbury, 15 November 1967, LPL, Ramsey 119, fos 263–64, 313

61. 'Remembrance Day Service Drops 6 Old Hymns', *Times*, 28 September 1968, 14.

62. BBC audience research reports VR/64/483, VR/64/624, VR/64/461, WAC, emphasis in original.

63. K. Morgan, *The People's Peace: Britain, 1945–1990* (Oxford, 1992), 180–83.

64. R. Weight, *Patriots: British National Identity, 1940–2000* (London, 2002), 286–87; P. Hennessy, *The Secret State: Whitehall and the Cold War* (London, 2003), xvii, 6, 123.

65. My thanks to Mr Matthew Grant, of Queen Mary University of London, for these figures.

66. There is possibly an interesting comparison to be made between the reception of Stanley Kubrick's *Paths of Glory* in France and Britain in the late 1950s. The film depicts the execution, during the First World War, of three French soldiers for cowardice after an unfair trial. Released late in 1957, it was banned in France because of its negative depiction of the military. Kubrick's anti-war message seemed to have an immediate relevance in a France whose continued involvement in Algeria had led to an extension in the power of military courts in the 1950s. The film was not shown there until 1975. In contrast the film seems to have made relatively little impact in Britain. It was acknowledged as a powerful piece by a new director, but not one that would necessarily reach a large audience. Although it coincided with long-standing beliefs about the horror of the First World War, its depiction of French soldiers and generals did not encourage a discourse on executions or incompetence in the British army. Although British forces were involved in conflicts as a result of the retreat from Empire, they were not sufficiently large or traumatic to encourage a prolonged anti-war movement or social fracture. N. Offenstadt, *Les fusillés de la Grande Guerre et la mémoire collective, 1914–1999* (Paris, 1999), 124–28.

67. J. Richards, *Films and British National Identity: From Dickens to Dad's Army* (Manchester, 1997), 160.

68. Ibid., 164.

69. Personal knowledge. Weight, *Patriots*, 340–47. On *Victor* and later comics, see E. MacCallum Stewart, 'Comics and the War', accessed 5 February 2003, 1016.

70. D. Todman, 'Representations of the First World War in British Popular Culture, 1918–1998', PhD thesis, University of Cambridge (2003), 232–42; Ministry of Pensions, *Reports on War Pensions* (London, 1926–76); Department of Health and Social Security, *Reports on War Pensions* (London, 1977–81); figures from 31 March 1981 provided by War Pensions Agency.

71. R. Curtis et al., *Blackadder: The Whole Damn Dynasty, 1485–1917* (London, 1998), 412.

72. Poll carried out by the *Observer* in 1999, and televised by Channel Four, broadcast 31 April 2000.

73. Curtis, *Blackadder: The Whole Damn Dynasty*, 452.

74. Leader, 'Come Back Blackadder', *Sun*, 4 November 1989, BBC Written Archives Centre *Blackadder Goes Forth* Press Cuttings File.

75. P. Stoddart, 'Caught by Candid Cameras', *Sunday Times (C)*, 5 November 1989, 16.

76. P. Jackson and R. Curtis, 'Call Me Mr Comedy', *Independent on Sunday*, 16 April 2000, 16.

77. P. Barker, *The Ghost Road* (London, 1994), 273–75.

78. V. Vitaliev, 'Foreign Fields', *Sunday Telegraph*, 11 November 2001, Travel Section, 2.

79. http://amazon.co.uk/exec/obidos/tg/...sr=1–1/ref=sr_sp_re/202–0151039–9361411, accessed 11 September 2001, 0941.

80. Ferguson, *The Pity of War*, xxi.

81. 'The Gift of Remembrance', *Sunday Telegraph*, 11 November 2001, 26.

82. *1914–18*, weekly from 11 November 1996, BBC 2, 7–7.50 p.m. I am grateful to Dr Peter Martland for providing me with a videotape of this series.

83. I have been unable to find a surviving copy of this education pack.

84. A. Gill, 'Oh What a Luvvie War', *Sunday Times Culture*, 17 November 1996, 2.

85. C. Barnett, 'Oh What a Whingeing War!', *Spectator*, 18 January 1997, 18–19.

86. J. Winter and B. Baggett, *The Great War and the Shaping of the Twentieth Century* (New York, 1996), 11.

87. Ibid.

88. *1914–18*, episode 1, 'Explosion'.

89. Audiences varied from 2.6 to 1.6 million, averaging just under 2.5 million. However the audience reaction index for those who did watch was consistently high, between eighty-three and eighty-seven points. Figures from BBC

audience research, provided by Eileen Inkson (Inkson to Todman, email, 8 August 2002).

90. See also P. Hoggart, 'Bombarded with Memories', *Times, Vision*, 21 November 1998, 2.

91. A. Macaulay, 'How to Survive in the Post-War Era', *Financial Times Arts*, 25 August 1998, 9.

92. M. Billington, 'Laugh? I Really Cried', *Guardian, The Week*, 4 April 1998, 24.

93. E. J. Dickson, 'Oh What a Lovely Tour', *Daily Telegraph*, 7 March 1998, 6.

94. R. Morrison, 'Marriage of Daring and Imagination', *Times*, 26 May 1998, 18.

Notes to Chapter 5: Poets

1. Episode 4, 'Private Plane', R. Curtis et al., *Blackadder: The Whole Damn Dynasty, 1485–1917* (London, 1998), 416; emphasis in original.

2. M. Gray, 'Lyrics of the First World War: Some Comments', in Gray, ed., *British Poetry, 1900–1950: Aspects of Tradition* (Basingstoke and London, 1992), 46.

3. For example, consider the huge amount of poetry produced, publicly and privately, to mark the death of Field Marshal Sir Douglas Haig in 1928. D. Todman, '"Sans Peur et Sans Reproche": The Retirement, Death and Mourning of Sir Douglas Haig, 1918–1928', *Journal of Military History*, 67, 4 (October 2003), 1083–106.

4. On the growth in demand for reading during and after the war, see J. McAleer, *Popular Reading and Publishing* (Oxford, 1992), 43.

5. Samuel Hynes has based his study of personal recollections of war on the notion of an irrecoverable whole, which he calls 'The Soldiers' Tale'. To truly grasp the widest impact of the First World War, we would have to go further, or change our definition of soldiering to match the mobilisation of the population in time of total war. Hynes, *The Soldiers' Tale: Bearing Witness to Modern War* (London, 1998), xii–xiii.

6. Anonymous author, quoted in 'Poetry', *Stand To! The Journal of the Western Front Association*, 70 (April 2004), 29. See also the poems from the *Ilkeston Advertiser* and *Ilkeston Pioneer* collected by Simon Featherstone in his *War Poetry: An Introductory Reader* (London, 1995), 135–41.

7. M. Stephen, *The Price of Pity: Poetry, History and Myth in the Great War* (London, 1996), 138–39.

8. H. Cecil, 'British War Novelists', in H. Cecil and P. Liddle, eds, *Facing Armageddon: The First World War Experienced* (London, 1996), 801.

9. See above Chapter 1.

10. A. Macdonell, *England, Their England* (London, 1933), 7–8.

11. Quoted in McAleer, *Popular Reading and Publishing in Britain*, 95. Emphasis in original.

12. S. Chibnall, 'Pulp versus Penguins: Paperbacks Go to War', in P. Kirkham and D. Thoms, eds, *War Culture: Social Change and Changing Experience in World War Two Britain* (London, 1995), 140.

13. Hynes, *The Soldiers' Tale*, 125.

14. With the exception of John Harris's novel *Covenant with Death*. There was, however, a limited and dispersed rise in poems written by the children of the wartime generation. See, for example, Ted Hughes, 'Six Young Men' and 'Griefs for Dead Soldiers', *The Hawk in the Rain* (London, 1957), 54–55, 52–53, and John Berger's 'Self-Portrait, 1914–18', *The White Bird: Writings by John Berger* (London, 1985), 21.

15. Unsigned review, 'Poets in Hell', *Times Literary Supplement*, 1 April 1965, 251.

16. L. Smith, 'Paul Fussell's *The Great War and Modern Memory*: Twenty-Five Years Later', *History and Theory*, 40 (May 2001), 244.

17. P. Fussell, *The Great War and Modern Memory* (London, 1975), 204–7.

18. R. Prior and T. Wilson, 'Paul Fussell at War', *War in History*, 1, 1 (1994), 63–80.

19. The basis for his military historical research was Liddell Hart's *History of the First World War*. Fussell, *Great War and Modern Memory*, x.

20. An excellent counterpoint to Fussell's work is Jay Winter's *Sites of Memory, Sites of Mourning: The Great War in European Cultural History* (Cambridge, 1995), which makes clear the variety of possible responses to the war.

21. See, for example, his comments on the story of Kiggell crying in the mud. Fussell, *Great War and Modern Memory*, 84.

22. Its landmark status is recalled by Martin Stephen: 'I cannot remember where I was when Kennedy was assassinated, but I can remember where I was when I first read ... Paul Fussell's *The Great War and Modern Memory* (for over an hour, in the long suffering Heffers bookshop in Cambridge!).' Stephen, *Price of Pity*, 230.

23. G. Dyer, *The Missing of the Somme* (London, 1994), 29.

24. D. Hibberd, *Owen the Poet* (London, 1986), 36, 43–44, 49–50, 75–77, 182–83; idem, *Wilfred Owen: The Last Year, 1917–18* (London, 1992), 1, 8, 10, 157–94

25. A. Caesar, *Taking It Like a Man: Suffering, Sexuality and the War Poets* (Manchester, 1993), 157, 166–67; C. Coker, *War and the Twentieth Century: A Study of War and Modern Consciousness* (London, 1994), 131–37.

26. H. Owen and J. Bell, eds, *Wilfred Owen: Collected Letters* (Oxford, 1967), 385, 422, 427–28, 431–32, 452–53, 458; quote 461.

27. Some useful notes on Owen's early editors are provided by S. Cloutier, 'Wilfred Owen and his Early Editors', http://www.firstworldwar.com/poetsand prose/owen_editors.htm, accessed 6 July 2004, 0905, but Cloutier is rather dogmatic in his assertion of motives to Sassoon and Blunden, and errs in ascribing the rise in Owen's popularity to the period 1931–63 as a whole.

28. Hynes, *A War Imagined*, 302.

29. W. B. Yeats, ed., 'Introduction' to his *The Oxford Book of Modern Verse* (Oxford, 1936), xxxiv.

30. B. Uttenthal, *Wilfred Owen: Selected Poems* (Harlow, 1986), 5.

31. My thanks to Dr Gary Sheffield for this point.

32. D. S. R. Welland, *Wilfred Owen* (London, 1960), 9–10; idem, 'Sassoon on Owen', *Times Literary Supplement*, 31 May 1974, 589.

33. Review in the *Listener*, collected in P. Larkin, *Required Writing: Miscellaneous Pieces, 1955–1982* (New York, 1984), 162–63.

34. Unsigned review, 'Requiem for a Dead Soldier', *Times Literary Supplement*, 7 November 1963.

35. Arthur Bliss's *Morning Heroes* (1930) was an earlier work which incorporated Owen's poem 'Spring Offensive' into a symphony which also made reference to other conflicts. Bliss dedicated *Morning Heroes* to his brother, Francis, who was killed in the First World War. See 'H.G.', '"Morning Heroes": A New Symphony by Arthur Bliss', *Musical Times and Singing-Class Circular*, 1 October 1930, 881–86. I am grateful to Dr Peter Martland for pointing out this comparison to me.

36. H. Carpenter, *Benjamin Britten: A Biography* (London, 1992), 6, 9, 405–8. Carpenter suggests that in some photographs – for example the one in a book Christopher Isherwood sent to Britten in the summer of 1961 – Owen bears a resemblance to Britten's fourth dead friend, Piers Dunkerley.

37. Letter to Dietrich Fischer-Dieskau, 1961, quoted ibid., 405.

38. Winter, *Sites of Memory, Sites of Mourning*, 204–5.

39. D. Shaw-Taylor, 'Britten's Requiem', *Sunday Times*, 9 December 1962, 34; D. Shaw-Taylor, 'Britten's Craft and Vision', *Sunday Times*, 13 January 1963, 34; P. Heyworth, 'The Two Worlds of Modernism', *Observer*, 3 June 1962, 26; C. Mason, 'Britten's War Requiem', *Guardian*, 31 May 1962, 9.

40. H. King, 'Britten's War Requiem', and M. Gowers, 'The Life of Wilfred Owen', *Radio Times*, 30 July 1964, 26.

41. Information from former head of secondary school English department.

42. Stephen, *Price of Pity*, 204, Caesar, *Taking It Like a Man*, 233.

43. R. Jeffcoate, 'Teaching Poetry of the First World War in the Secondary School', *Critical Survey*, 2, 2 (1990), 158. For a survey of literature aimed at children which describes similar attitudes to those identified by Jeffcoate, see K. Agnew and G. Fox, *Children at War: From the First World War to the Gulf* (London, 2001).

44. W. J. Essex, ed., *Poems on the First World War, Form 3E, 1977–1978, St John's College, Southsea* (Portsmouth, 1980), 5.

45. Note in particular H. Wallace, 'Death on the Front'; H. Jackson, 'Maniac'; P. Matley, 'Death in the Trenches'; S. Wellington, 'War' in Essex, *Poems on the First World War*, 26, 19, 24, 12.

46. A. Epps, 'Over the Top', in Essex, *Poems on the First World War*, 21.

47. On the other hand, it is worth pointing out that other sources have suggested a more nuanced approach to the war. See, for example, M. Marland, ed., *The Times Authors Number Five: The War Poets* (London, 1971), cover sheet, 'Trench Warfare' booklet and 'Owen' broadsheets 1–4. The pack also included a copy of a recruiting poster 'for ironic comparison', and a reading list which suggested the works of both A. J. P. Taylor and John Terraine.

48. C. Moore, *Trench Fever* (London, 1998), 4–5.

49. R. Samuel, *Theatres of Memory: Island Stories, Unravelling Britain*, ii (London, 1998), 215–19.

50. R. Hoare, *World War One: An Illustrated History in Colour, 1914–1918* (London, 1973), 61.

51. J. Fines and T. Hopkins, *Teaching for Attainment Target One in National Curriculum History (Using a First World War Project)* (London, 1994), 13.

52. G. Minikin, 'Pride and Delight: Motivating Pupils Through Poetic Writing about the First World War', *Teaching History*, 95 (May 1999), 37.

53. Ibid., 39.

54. It is also worth noting the influence of the comic book evident in the drawn out speech bubble of 'Cha-a-a-arge!'.

55. J. Radway, *Reading the Romance: Women, Patriarchy and Popular Literature* (London, 1987, first published 1984), 20, 34–35. Although Radway's work is based on patterns of reading amongst American women, her suggestions of the structural developments which affected the American market – manufacture, distribution and takeovers by multinational conglomerates – all applied to Britain as well.

56. J. Cowley, 'Was the Pity All in the Poetry?', *Sunday Times Culture Magazine*, 8 November 1998, 2–3.

57. S. Faulks, *Charlotte Gray* (London, 1998), 383–84, in which Colonel Gray passes on his memory of the massacre of prisoners to his daughter.

58. B. Shephard, *A War of Nerves: Soldiers and Psychiatrists, 1914–1994* (London, 2000), 355–68, 385–99.

59. S. Hill, *Strange Meeting* (London, 1984, first published 1971), vi, emphasis in original.

60. D. Reeman, *The Horizon* (London, 1993), unnumbered frontpages.

61. J. Harris, *Covenant with Death* (London, 1969, first published 1961), 5; M. Hennessy (Harris's pseudonym), *Blunted Lance* (London, Arrow, 1981), unnumbered frontpages, 219–21. In fact, the well known 'disaster' with which this charge is supposed to have ended seems not in fact to have occurred, R. Holmes, *Tommy: The British Soldier on the Western Front, 1914–18* (London, 2004), 441.

62. J. Hamilton, *The Idle Hill of Summer* (London, 1988), 5.

63. B. Morrison, 'War Stories', *New Yorker*, 22 January 1996, 79.

64. Ibid., 78–79.

65. P. Barker, *Union Street* (London, 1982); idem, *Blow Your House Down* (London, 1984); idem, *The Century's Daughter* (London, 1986); idem, *The Man Who Wasn't There* (London, 1989).

66. 'And the Week They ...', *Observer*, 12 November 1995, 2.

67. For a French example of an author making use of family mythology, see M. Dugain, *La chambre des officiers* (Paris, 1998). An interesting line for further investigation would be the degree to which male writers made more use of specific myths about combat experience than their female counterparts, and whether this related to gender differences in their role as agents of memory rehearsal.

68. A reader from Bexley, Kent, http://www.amazon.co.uk/exec/obidos/tg/... sr= 1–1/ref=sr_ sp_re/202–0151039–9361411, accessed 11 September 2001, 0941.

69. A reader from Upminster, Essex, 19 October 2000, ibid.

70. A reader from London, 13 September 2000, ibid.

71. A reader from Kent, 13 October 2000, ibid.

72. Anonymous reader, 10 March 2000, ibid.

73. A reader from Stoke on Trent, 21 November 1999, ibid.

74. A reader from Carnmoney, Northern Ireland, ibid.

75. That this could affect an older generation as well is suggested by Robert Dinnage's review of Pat Barker's *The Ghost Road*: 'My father won medals in that war, but never told me anything about it. Barker has now done it for him'. R. Dinnage, 'Death's Grey Land', *New York Review of Books*, 43, 4 (15 February 1996), 21.

76. S. Faulks, 'Back to the Front with Tommy', *Guardian 2*, 15 September 1993, 3.

77. A. Barrie, *War Underground* (London, 1981, first published 1962), 114; Faulks, *Birdsong*, 300–7; Barrie, *War Underground*, 165. See also Barrie, *War Underground*, 108–9, 113, 217. Despite its somewhat breathless tone, Barrie's book is highly evocative and occasionally moving. It was based on the testimony of surviving miners – sixty-eight of them questioned, twenty-six interviewed face to face – as well as original texts and research in British and German military archives. (ibid., 9–10). Faulks, *Birdsong*, 351; S. Cloete, *A Victorian Son: An Autobiography* (London, 1972), 237; Faulks, *Birdsong*, 294; Dyer, *The Missing of the Somme*, 80.

78. Moore, *Trench Fever*, 11. See also Geoff Dyer's comments at the beginning of his *Missing of the Somme*, 2–3.

79. For example, J. Saunders, *The Bannister Girls* (London, 1990), 76; E. Stirling, *A Field of Bright Poppies* (London, 1990), 46–47; M. Hardwick, *The War to End Wars* (London, 1975), 129; K. Saunders, *Night Shall Overcome Us* (London, 1993), 594; Rock, *Passing Bells*, 324; Hennessy, *Blunted Lance*, 256; Reeman, *The Horizon*, 136; R. Hill, *The Wood Beyond* (London, 1996), 129. A particular

recurrent theme was that of the soldier executed for desertion despite suffering from shell shock. For example, Stirling, *A Field of Bright Poppies*, 265;
Reeman, *The Horizon*, 200; J. Thynne, *Patrimony* (London, 1997), 179–80,
207–8. There was also evidence of the persistence of other myths. For example,
Jay Winter has pointed out the popularity of narratives of returning soldiers in
the years after the war – based on the desperate hope of many of the bereaved
that, in the absence of a body, soldiers had been reported dead but were in fact
alive but lost or insane (Winter, *Sites of Memory*, 22–44). Despite the fact that
it had lost its emotional significance, this narrative remained popular in the
1990s. For example, K. Haig, *Apple Blossom Time* (London, 1997); Hill, *The
Wood Beyond*; Thynne, *Patrimony*. For a French equivalent, see S. Japrisot, *Un
Longue Dimanche de Fiançailles* (Paris, 1991).

80. Of the thirty-two novels I have identified set in the war in the period 1978 to
1998, seventeen were romances. I have probably underestimated the total number of publications, but I am more likely to have missed romantic texts than
any other.

81. C. Tylee, *The Great War and Military Consciousness: Images of Militarism and
Womanhood in Women's Writings, 1914–1964* (Basingstoke, 1990), 14–15.

82. Catherine Cookson's *The Cinder Path* (London, 1978) was on the list of top
hundred books borrowed from British libraries consistently from January 1983
to June 1991. C. Goodwin, *To Be a Lady: The Story of Catherine Cookson* (London, 1994), 311–19.

83. Saunders, *The Bannister Girls*, dustjacket.

84. Saunders, *Night Shall Overcome Us*, 347.

85. G. Braybon and P. Summerfield, *Out of the Cage: Women's Experiences in Two
World Wars* (London, 1987), 38–41, Tylee, *The Great War and Women's Consciousness*, 11.

86. For the variety of women's experiences and responses, see Braybon and Summerfield, *Out of the Cage*, 68–69, 81–83, 117–122, 281–82.

87. D. Thom, *Nice Girls and Rude Girls: Women Workers in World War One* (London, 2000), 1–52, 207.

88. For a powerful counter-argument to the one I put forward here, see N. Gullace, *'Blood of Our Sons': Men, Women and the Renegotiation of British
Citizenship during the Great War* (Basingstoke, 2002), 169–95 and passim.

89. G. Braybon, 'Winners or Losers: Women's Symbolic Role in the War Story', in
G. Braybon, ed., *Evidence, History and the Great War: Historians and the Impact
of 1914–18* (Oxford, 2003), 85–113. My thanks to Dr Braybon for her numerous
useful comments during the preparation of this book.

90. Thom, *Nice Girls and Rude Girls*, 53–77; S. Grayzel, 'Liberating Women? Examining Gender, Morality and Sexuality in First World War France and Britain',
in Braybon, *Evidence, History and the Great War*, 113–34.

91. Gullace, *'Blood of Our Sons'*, 185.

92. J. Hammerton, *A Popular History of the Great War*, vi (London, 1934), 290–300, quotes 290 and 299.

93. See draft scripts in LHCMA, LH 13/61.

94. A. Marwick, *The Deluge: British Society and the First World War* (2nd edn, London, 1991). *The Deluge*, first printed in 1965, was reprinted in the original edition in 1973, 1975, 1978, 1979, 1986 and 1989. For the second edition, Marwick added an extremely useful new preface, which summarises his arguments at the time and since, ibid., 9–31.

95. Braybon, 'Winners and Losers', 89–94.

96. J. Watson, *Fighting Different Wars: Experience, Memory and the First World War in Britain* (Cambridge, 2004), 240–61.

97. It is instructive to compare *Testament of Youth* with the diary Brittain kept during the war (published as *Chronicle of Youth*), which is all the more affecting for being a less mature and considered response.

98. P. Toomey, 'Vera Brittain and the Testament that Came Late to Life', *Times*, 9 August, 1980, WAC *Testament of Youth* News Clippings File (WACTOY); P. Berry and M. Bostridge, *Vera Brittain: A Life* (London, 1996), 1–2.

99. Unsigned article, 'Oh What a Lovely War Story', *Daily Express*, 19 November 1979, WACTOY.

100. 'Letters', *Radio Times*, 5 January 1980, WACTOY.

101. BBC Audience Research reports, WAC, VR/79/497 and VR/79/545.

102. 'I am about to put a lock and chain on my copy of the book, since practically every girl of twenty-five or under whom I know has made an attempt to "borrow" it.', C. Adams, 'War Requiem' WACTOY.

Notes to Chapter 6: Veterans

1. A. Thomson, *ANZAC Memories: Living with the Legend* (Melbourne and Oxford, 1994), 7–11, 213–15 (quotation 215).

2. G. Sheffield, *Leadership in the Trenches: Officer–Man Relations, Morale and Discipline in the British Army in the Era of the First World War* (Basingstoke, 1999), 131.

3. N. Barr, '"Service not Self": The British Legion 1921–1939', unpublished PhD thesis, University of St Andrews (1994) 113–14.

4. C. Graves, *The Home Guard of Britain* (London, 1943), 44.

5. F. H. Lancum, *Press Officer, Please!* (London, 1946), 76, quoted in A. Calder, *The People's War: Britain, 1939–1945* (London, 1992 [1969]), 124.

6. S. Mackenzie, *The Home Guard: A Military and Political History* (Oxford, 1995), 35–38.

7. To what degree their memories actually affected their handling of a second war

is open to debate. See, for example, the comments in R. Macleod, ed., *The Ironside Diaries* (London, 1962), 352, quoted in J. Terraine, *The Smoke and the Fire: Myths and Anti-Myths of War* (London, 1982), 103.

8. A. Danchev and D. Todman, *War Diaries, 1939–1945: Field Marshal Lord Alanbrooke* (London, 2001), 24–25.

9. 'Letters', *Daily Telegraph*, 20, 25, 26, 27, 29 April, 5, 7, 9, 10, 11, 13, 15, 19 May, 13 June 1949, collected in LHCMA, LH 15/21

10. Unsigned article, 'General Fights for Haig', *Daily Herald*, 22 May 1961, LHCMA, LH 15/21.

11. 'Letters – Earl Haig', *Daily Telegraph*, 30 May 1961, LHCMA, LH 15/21.

12. J. Brophy, 'After 50 Years', in J. Brophy and E. Partridge, *The Long Trail: What the British Soldier Sang and Said in the Great War of 1914–18* (London, 1965), 10.

13. A. Bryant, '1914–18', *TV Times*, 24 February 1961, 6.

14. A. Danchev, *Alchemist of War: The Life of Sir Basil Liddell Hart* (London, 1998), Chapters 2, 8, 9; B. Bond, 'Liddell Hart and the First World War', in Bond et al., *Look to your Front!: Studies in the First World War* (Staplehurst, 1999), 14–15; B. Bond, *The Unquiet Western Front* (Cambridge, 2002), 58–59.

15. Chandos, *From Peace to War: A Study in Contrasts, 1857–1918* (London, 1968), 83; C. Carrington, 'Some Soldiers', in G. Panichas, ed., *Promise of Greatness* (London, 1968), 157.

16. For an exploration of this issue in an Australian context, see Thomson, *ANZAC Memories*, 184–87

17. M. Bowra, *Memoirs, 1898–1939* (London, 1966), 91; J. Reith, *Wearing Spurs* (London, 1966); A. Waugh, 'A Light Rain Falling', in Panichas, ed., *Promise of Greatness*, 332–44. The contributors to Panichas's volume – including Vera Brittain, R. C. Sherriff, Liddell Hart and R. H. Mottram – give an idea of how many eminent figures had seen war service and were still alive in the late 1960s. Other memoirs included A. Behrend, *As from Kemmel Hill: An Adjutant in France and Flanders 1917 and 1918* (London, 1963); J. B. Priestley, *Margin Released* (London, 1962) and Lord Boyd Orr, *As I Recall: The 1880s to the 1960s* (London, 1966), 16, 68–74. Although he had won the MC and the DSO as a Medical Officer on the Western Front in 1917, taking over his battalion when all the combatant officers had been killed, Boyd Orr made no mention of this episode, and downplayed the war's significance and his own ability to contribute any interesting memories.

18. Waugh, 'A Light Rain Falling'; R. Sheriff, 'The English Public Schools in the War', in Panichas, ed., *Promise of Greatness*, 340, 150–53; G. Duncan, *Douglas Haig As I Knew Him* (London, 1966); C. Carrington, *Soldier from the Wars Returning* (London, 1965).

19. For example, Denis Winter's book about front line experience in the war,

Death's Men, makes use of 127 published personal testimonies, of which almost a sixth were published in the period 1959–68. (*Death's Men: Soldiers of the Great War* (Harmondsworth, 1979), 269–74.

20. Arras and District Branch, British Legion, 'Fiftieth Anniversary of the Battle of the Somme', 6–7, 28. Harrod Papers, IWMDD, 88/52/1.

21. N. Keen to Welch, 4 July 1966, 18th Division, ATNODC Papers, IWMDD, Misc 1208. Professor Alex Danchev has informed me that Basil Liddell Hart attended performances of *Oh What a Lovely War* with reunion groups of KOYLI in the early 1960s.

22. P. Longworth, *The Unending Vigil* (London, 1967), 237; M. Middlebrook, *The First Day on the Somme: 1 July 1916* (London, 1971), 314; see also Winter, *Death's Men*, 261–62.

23. P. Simkins, 'Everyman at War: Recent Interpretation of the Front Line Experience', in B. Bond, ed., *The First World War and British Military History* (Oxford, 1991), 289–90. See also P. Liddle, 'From Liverpool to Leeds via Sunderland: The Collection's Own History', *The Poppy and the Owl: The Journal of the Friends of the Liddle Collection, the Library, the University of Leeds, Leeds, UK*, 24 (November 1998), 107–8. I am grateful to Dr Gail Braybon for discussing with me her own family's experience of this phenomenon.

24. Unsigned article, 'The Great War', *Radio Times*, 28 May 1964, 6; interview with Julia Cave (production assistant and eyewitness researcher), 22 January 1999.

25. E. Sivan and J. Winter, 'Introduction', in E. Sivan and J. Winter, eds, *War and Remembrance in the Twentieth Century* (Cambridge, 2000), 3.

26. The basis for this suggestion lies in the interviewing experience of Peter Liddle, conversation with Peter Liddle, 1999.

27. J. Blacker, introduction to C. P. Blacker, *Have You Forgotten Yet? The First World War Memoirs of C. P. Blacker* (Barnsley, 2000), vii.

28. R. Macleod, 'Passchendaele Fifty Years On', *Daily Telegraph*, 31 July 1967 and letters 3, 8, 10, 13, 14, 16, 18, 24, 29, 31 August, and 2, 14, 25 September 1967, LHCMA, LH 6/1967/1.

29. Letters from Old Contemptibles to Commissioner of Police for the Metropolis, National Archives, Kew, Surrey (NA), MEPO 2/865; Longworth, *The Unending Vigil*, 238, suggests 1966 for the final Ypres parade; Winter, *Death's Men*, 262, suggests 1975.

30. 18th Division, ATNODC Papers, IWMDD, Misc 1208. As a successful unit with a very strong sense of its identity, the 18th Division may have found it easier to sustain post-war interest from its members.

31. For example, the OCA of the 22nd Royal Fusiliers lasted from 1919–1976, the Ruhleben Association, for civilians interned in that camp in Germany, ceased existence in the mid-1970s (information from Dr Gary Sheffield and Dr Matthew Stibbe).

32. See the analysis in my doctoral thesis, 'Representations of the First World War in British Popular Culture, 1918–1998', University of Cambridge (2003) 232–42. My thanks to the War Pensions Agency for their assistance in compiling the most recent figures on which this analysis is based.

33. S. Badsey, 'The Great War since *The Great War*', *Historical Journal of Film, Radio and Television*, 22, 1 (March 2002), 42.

34. Sound Archive, Imperial War Museum, London, Neame 48/15/5 (1974).

35. M. and M. Middlebrook, *The Somme Battlefields: A Comprehensive Guide from Crecy to the Two World Wars* (London, 1991), 1–2. On the desertion of the battlefields when Middlebrook first wrote, see also *The First Day on the Somme*, 314.

36. Private information.

37. Middlebrook, *The Kaiser's Battle*, 261–71.

38. For Middlebrook's opinion of changing soldiers' views, *The First Day on the Somme*, 50. For his efforts to see the battle without the benefits of hindsight, ibid., 289.

39. Middlebrook, *The First Day on the Somme*.

40. Consider, for example, the construction of the semi-official history of 1/2 Royal Welch Fusiliers by James Dunn, and the interviews conducted by Charles Bean when writing the Australian Official History of the war. J. C. Dunn, *The War the Infantry Knew, 1914–1919* (London, 1989, first published 1938]); J. Macleod, *Reconsidering Gallipoli* (Leicester, 2004). I am grateful to Dr Macleod for letting me see the relevant portions of her work before publication.

41. Middlebrook, *The First Day on the Somme*, 292. See also his description of the British assault, ibid., 129.

42. 'The Butcher's Bill', *Times Literary Supplement*, 27 August 1971, 1037.

43. We might also consider, for example, the 1984 programme *Very Exceptional Soldiers* (BBC North) and the 1986 *Remembrance Sunday* programme, which interspersed veterans with the ceremony at the Cenotaph.

44. P. Stoddart, 'Murder in the Morning', *Sunday Times*, 7 September 1988, 45.

45. C. Corns and J. Hughes-Wilson, *Blindfold and Alone: British Military Executions in the Great War* (London, 2001), 291, citing 'Victor's Deadly Secret', *Daily Express*, 16 August 1978, and 'The Grim Wartime Secret of Victor Sylvester [sic], *Guardian*, 16 August 1978.

46. V. Silvester, *Dancing is My Life: An Autobiography* (London, 1958), 19–22, 27.

47. Corns and Hughes-Wilson, *Blindfold and Alone*, 292.

48. J. Putkowski and J. Sykes, *Shot at Dawn* (Barnsley, 1989), 224.

49. Corns and Hughes-Wilson, *Blindfold and Alone*, 325. Corns and Hughes-Wilson point out that the odds for officers tried for desertion were rather worse than those for enlisted men.

50. Ibid., 441; W. Moore, *The Thin Yellow Line* (London, 1974).

51. L. Macdonald, *They Called it Passchendaele: The Story of the Third Battle of Ypres and of the Men Who Fought in It* (London, 1978); idem, *Somme* (London, 1983); idem, *The Roses of No Man's Land* (London, 1980); idem, *1914* (London, 1987); idem, *1914–1918: Voices and Images of the Great War* (with research by Shirley Seaton) (London, 1988); *1915: The Death of Innocence* (London, 1993); *To the Last Man: Spring 1918* (London, 1998).

52. Macdonald, *1915*, 356–59.

53. Macdonald does not cite 'Williams' or his relatives as providing assistance, but does cite the Official History in her bibliography. Macdonald, *1915*, 603, 610.

54. Macdonald, *1918*, xvi. Macdonald is herself a member of the Machine Gun Corps Old Comrades' Association. C. Campbell, 'Historian Leads her Old Boys Back Up the Line', *Sunday Telegraph*, 25 October 1998, Cambridge University Library CD-ROM of broadsheet newspapers (CULCD).

55. Macdonald, *1918*, xv.

56. Macdonald, *They Called it Passchendaele*, xiii.

57. Thomson, *ANZAC Memories*, 15.

58. R. Holmes, *Tommy: The British Soldier on the Western Front, 1914–18* (London, 2004), 441.

59. J. Ezard, '80 Years On, the Last of the Survivors Relive the Horrors of the First World War', *Guardian*, 16 October 1998, 3; M. Bright, 'No Forgetting for Those Who Survived', *Observer*, 8 November 1998, 15.

60. The tune to which the words were set is a traditional one, which might have been known to troops by its original name. We might also note the frequency with which First World War soldiers mention the iconic poster of Lord Kitchener, when in fact comparatively few of these posters were produced. See N. Hiley, '"KITCHENER WANTS YOU" and "Daddy, What Did YOU Do in the Great War?": The Myth of British Recruiting Posters, *Imperial War Museum Review*, 11 (1997), 53–54.

61. Compare the accounts of gas in Arthur, *Forgotten Voices of the Great War*, 77–88, and *The Great War*, episode 7.

62. Quotations from *Forgotten Voices*, front pages and cover.

63. In a similar way, it seems likely that the collection and availability of veterans' recollections of all conflicts is likely to be revolutionised by digital recording and file sharing.

64. Campbell, 'Historian Leads her Old Boys Back Up the Line', CULCD.

65. K. Saunders, 'Fight the Good Fight', *Sunday Times*, section 4, 19 December 1993, 5; J. Terraine, 'Please Think Before Firing Off a Shell', *Daily Telegraph*, 13 Nov 1993, CULCD

66. Lucy Moore, 4 January 2000, /obidos/tg/ ... sr=1–1/ref=sr_sp_re/202–0151039 –9361411, accessed 11 September 2001, 0941. The same page contains a number

of recommendations of Macdonald's works by readers of *Birdsong* to each other.

67. See, for example, the advice given in N. Holding, *World War One Army Ancestry* (Ramsbottom, 1982, 1986, 1991, 1997); idem, *Location of British Army Records 1914–18* (Ramsbottom, 1984, 1987, 1991, 1999); idem, *More World War One Army Ancestry* (Ramsbottom, 1986, 1991, 1998); and idem, 'Finding the Men Who Fought in the Trenches', *Family Tree Magazine*, 2, 6 (September-October 1986), 22–23; 3, 1 (November 1986), 14–15.

68. On this growth in the 1920s, see P. Clarke, *Hope and Glory: Britain, 1900–2000* (London, 2004), 145–46.

69. M. Smith, 'The War and British Culture', in S. Constantine, M. Kirby and M. Rese, eds, *The First World War in British History* (London, 1995), 170–71. See also C. Moriarty, 'Though in a Picture Only: Portrait Photography and the Commemoration of the First World War', in G. Braybon, ed., *Evidence, History and the Great War: Historians and the Impact of 1914–18* (Oxford, 2004), 30–47.

70. J. Wright, 'No Known Grave', accessed 23 July 2001, 1226.

71. P. Hoggart, 'Veterans: Not So Quiet on the Western Front', *Times*, 9 November 1998, 47.

72. R. Coombs, *Before Endeavours Fade: A Guide to the Battlefields of the First World War* (London, 1994); J. Giles, *Flanders Then and Now: The Ypres Salient and Passchendaele* (London, 1970, 1979, 1987); J. Giles, *The Somme Then and Now* (London, 1977); T. and V. Holt, *Battlefields of the First World War: A Traveller's Guide* (London, 1993). The *Battleground Europe* series, edited by Nigel Cave and published in London by Leo Cooper, comprised nineteen titles by 1998. More have since been published including H. McPhail and P. Guest, *Wilfred Owen: On the Trail of the Poets of the Great War* (London, 1998).

73. N. Jones, *The War Walk: A Journey Along the Western Front* (London, 1983); G. Dyer, *The Missing of the Somme* (London, 1994); Moore, *Trench Fever*. Works by Canadian writers published in Britain might also be considered: S. O'Shea, *Back to the Front: An Accidental Historian Walks the Trenches of World War One* (London, 1997), (O'Shea had British and Irish grandfathers), and D. Macfarlane, *Come From Away* (London, 1991), which describes a journey more spiritual than physical. R. Holmes, *Riding the Retreat: Mons to the Marne 1914 Revisited* (London, 1995), describes an attempt by a military historian and Territorial soldier to ride the route of the BEF's retreat of 1914. On the importance of recreation to pilgrimage, and continuities with inter-war tourism, see D. Lloyd, *Battlefield Tourism: Pilgrimage and the Commemoration of the Great War in Britain, Australia and Canada, 1919–1939* (Oxford, 1998).

74. P. Simkins, 'My Thirty-Five Years at the Imperial War Museum, Part II – Old Curators Never Die ...', *The Western Front Association Bulletin*, 57 (June 2000),

19–20. For comments on the degree of success of the Museum's revamp see unsigned article, 'Out of Battle', *New Statesman*, 30 June 1989, 5.

75. Quoted in K. Walsh, *The Representation of the Past: Museums and Heritage in the Post-Modern World* (London, 1992), 111.

76. M. Kennedy, 'Soldiers Find a Better Hole', *Guardian*, 30 June 1990, 3.

77. Brigadier Harry Hopthrow, Colonel William Taylor, quoted ibid.

78. Walsh, *The Representation of the Past*, 112.

79. Sadly there has not been space in this study to compare the Trench Experience to some of the most high profile museums in France and Belgium, the Historial de la Grande Guerre at Peronne, and the In Flanders Fields Museum at Ypres. The Historial attempts to represent the war in a very different way to the Imperial War Museum, whilst the In Flanders Fields Museum takes a broadly similar, if more sensationalist, approach. I would contend, however, that all three museums have had to deal with similar tensions in terms of the need to engage the public and the potential to encourage re-enactment.

80. Winter and Sivan, 'Introduction', in Winter and Sivan, eds, *War and Remembrance in the Twentieth Century*, 3.

81. It is interesting to compare this to the reaction to a similar piece broadcast to mark the sixtieth anniversary of the liberation of Europe, *D-Day: The Raw Recruits* (BBC, 2004). Although much less academically respectable (the twenty-first century volunteers did not wear authentic uniforms or eat contemporary rations, nor experience the 'live-fire' exercises which were a feature of Second World War training, but they did undertake exercises which mimicked combat), this series attracted far less critical comment. It is unclear whether this was because the myths of the First World War depicted it as an inviolable tragedy, or because viewers had become so jaded with this sort of television in the intervening two years that they could no longer muster a protest.

82. Carl Jackson, Hull Pal 2001, in R. Van Emden, *The Trench: Experiencing Life on the Front Line 1916* (London, 2003), 269.

Notes to Chapter 7: Modern Memory

1. J. Winter, 'Forms of Kinship and Remembrance in the Aftermath of the Great War', in J. Winter and E. Sivan, eds, *War and Remembrance in the Twentieth Century* (Cambridge, 1999), 60.

2. J. Barnes, 'Evermore' in *Cross Channel* (London, 1997), 110–11.

3. It is interesting to note recent developments in the parade past the Cenotaph on Remembrance Sunday in this context. A ceremony once closely defined as a means of representing and mourning the dead of the two world wars has grown to include the relatives of those 'shot at dawn' in the First World War and civilian evacuees of the Second World War.

Bibliography

PRIMARY SOURCES

Archives and Collections

BBC Written Archive Centre, Caversham

As Broadcast Script
C. Chilton, *The Long Long Trail*

Audience Research Reports
VR/64/300
VR/64/381
VR/64/461
VR/64/483
VR/64/545
VR/64/561
VR/64/624
VR/64/661
VR/64/649
VR/79/497
VR/79/545
VR/76/345
TV/86/109
TV/89/M171

Press Cuttings Files
Testament of Youth, press cuttings file (WACTOY)
The Monocled Mutineer, press cuttings file (WACMM)
Blackadder Goes Forth, press cuttings file (WACBGF)

Production and Post-Production Files
T32/1, 158/1
T32/1, 145/1–4
T32/827/1

British Film Institute, London
OWGA107 (*Oh! What a Lovely War* file)
Bound script no. 141, *King and Country*
Script Catalogue no. 1238 (Bogarde script for *King and Country*)
King and Country, Press Cuttings Microjacket

British Newspaper Library, Colindale
Champion, 1920–40
Triumph, 1925–39

Cambridge University Library, Cambridge
CD-ROMs of broadsheet newspapers, 1989–98
Family History: The Journal of the Institute of Heraldic and Genealogical Studies, new
    series, April 1975–90
Family History Monthly, October 1995-December 1998
Ministry of Pensions, *Reports on War Pensions* (London, 1926–76)
Department of Health and Social Security, *Reports on War Pensions* (London,
    1977–81)

Imperial War Museum, London

Department of Documents
Misc 1208, 18th Division ATNODC papers
Harrod Papers, 88/52/1

Department of Film
The Great War, documents files A-D
The Great War, television series episodes 1–26

Sound Archive
D. Lane, *Oral History Project Recordings Western Front, 1914–1918* (catalogue)
Neame 48/15/5 (1974)

Lambeth Palace Library, London
Ramsay 119, fo. 263–313

Liddell Hart Centre for Military Archives, Kings College London
LH 1/380
LH 1/577
LH 1/683
LH 1/172
LH 6/1967/1
LH 13/34
LH 13/61
LH 13/62
LH 13/63
LH 15/21
LH 12/1960/47–62
LH D542/472 W83/4
LH D546 C54

National Archives, Kew, Surrey
MEPO 2/865

National Library of Scotland, Edinburgh
Haig Papers, Acc 3155/249

Broadcast Media

Testament of Youth, Acorn Video, AVO 177
The Monocled Mutineer, Acorn Video, AVO143
The Great War, DD Video, A 548
Time To Remember, 1914–18, Media Resources Centre, Royal Military Academy Sandhurst

Interviews

Alex Danchev with Charles Chilton, 8 August 1988
Dan Todman with Charles Chilton, 14 May 2000
Dan Todman with John Terraine, 14 January 1999
Dan Todman with Julia Cave, 22 January 1999

Books

W. Allison and J. Fairley, *The Monocled Mutineer* (London, 1978).

M. Arthur, *Forgotten Voices of the Great War* (London, 2002).

P. Barker, *The Ghost Road* (London, 1994).

P. Barker, *Union Street* (London, 1982).

P. Barker, *Blow Your House Down* (London, 1984).

P. Barker, *The Century's Daughter* (London, 1986).

P. Barker, *The Man Who Wasn't There* (London, 1989).

J. Barnes, 'Evermore' in *Cross Channel* (London, 1997).

A. Barrie, *War Underground* (London, 1981, first published 1962).

J. Baynes, *Morale: A Study of Men and Courage* (London, 1967).

A. Behrend, *As from Kemmel Hill: An Adjutant in France and Flanders, 1917 and 1918* (London, 1963).

J. Berger, *The White Bird: Writings by John Berger* (London, 1985).

C. P. Blacker, *Have You Forgotten Yet? The First World War Memoirs of C. P. Blacker* (Barnsley, 2000).

M. Bloch (trans. C. Fink), *Memoirs of War* (Ithaca, 1980).

G. Blaxland, *Amiens: 1918* [1968] (London, 1981).

R. Blake, *The Private Papers of Sir Douglas Haig* (London, 1952).

A. Bleasdale, *The Monocled Mutineer* (London, 1986).

D. Bogarde, *The Complete Autobiography* (London, 1988).

J. Boraston and G. Dewar, *Sir Douglas Haig's Command, 1915–1918* (London, 1922).

M. Bowra, *Memoirs, 1898–1939* (London, 1966).

Lord Boyd Orr, *As I Recall: The 1880s to the 1960s* (London, 1966).

V. Brittain, *Testament of Youth* (London, 1988).

J. Brophy and E. Partridge, *The Long Trail: What the British Soldier Sang and Said in the Great War of 1914–18* (London, 1965).

E. Campion Vaughan, *Some Desperate Glory: The Diary of a Young Officer, 1917* (London, 1985).

A. Camus (trans. D. Hapgood), *The First Man* (London, 1995).

C. Carrington, *Soldier from the Wars Returning* (London, 1965).

B. Cartland, *We Danced All Night: A Dazzling Memoir of the Glittering Twenties* (London, 1994).

A. Carton de Wiart, *Happy Odyssey* (London, 1950).

Lord Chandos (O. Lyttelton), *From Peace to War: A Study in Contrasts, 1857–1918* (London, 1968).

W. Churchill, *The World Crisis, 1911–1918* (abridged and revised edn, London, 1931).

M. Ciment, *Conversations with Losey* (London, 1985).

A. Clark, *The Donkeys* (London, 1961).

S. Cloete, *A Victorian Son: An Autobiography* (London, 1972).

C. Cookson, *The Cinder Path* (London, 1978).

R. Coombs, *Before Endeavours Fade: A Guide to the Battlefields of the First World War* (London, 1994).

G. Craig and H. Scott, *An Outline History of the Great War for Use in Schools* (Cambridge, 1929).

R. Curtis et al., *Blackadder: The Whole Damn Dynasty, 1485–1917* (London, 1999).

A. Danchev and D. Todman, eds, *War Diaries, 1939–1945: Field Marshal Lord Alanbrooke* (London, 2001).

J. Davidson, *Haig: Master of the Field* (London, 1953).

N. Dixon, *On the Psychology of Military Incompetence* (London, 1976).

B. Doyle, *Who's Who of Boys' Writers and Illustrators* (London, 1964).

M. Dugain, *La chambre des officiers* (Paris, 1998).

G. Duncan, *Douglas Haig As I Knew Him* (London, 1966).

J. C. Dunn, *The War the Infantry Knew, 1914–1919* (London, 1989, first published 1938).

'C. Edmonds' (C. Carrington), *A Subaltern's War* (London, 1929).

J. Edmonds, *Military Operations France and Belgium 1917* (London, 1949).

W. J. Essex, ed., *Poems on the First World War, Form 3E, 1977–1978, St John's College, Southsea* (Portsmouth, 1980).

M. Farren, *Give the Anarchist a Cigarette* (London, 2001).

S. Faulks, *Birdsong* (London, 1994).

S. Faulks, *Charlotte Gray* (London, 1998).

R. Fielding, *War Letters to a Wife* (Staplehurst, 2001, first published 1929).

J. Fines and T. Hopkins, *Teaching for Attainment Target One in National Curriculum History (using a First World War Project)* (London, 1994).

C. B. Firth, *From James I to George V* (London, 1936).

B. Flanagan, *My Crazy Life* (London, 1962).

C. Forester, *The General* (London, 1936).

'GSO' (Sir Frank Fox), *GHQ (Montreuil-sur-Mer)* (London, 1920).

G. Frankau, *Peter Jackson, Cigar Merchant: A Romance of Married Life* (London, 1949, first published 1919).

N. Frankland, *History at War: The Campaigns of a Historian* (London, 1998).

P. Fussell, *The Great War and Modern Memory* (London, 1975).

B. Gardner, *Up the Line to Death* (London, 1964).

J. Garwood, *Chorley Pals: 'Y' Company, 11th (Service) Battalion, East Lancashire Regiment: A Short History of the Company in the Great War, 1914–1919* (Radcliffe, 1989).

P. Gibbs, *The Realities of War* (London, 1920).

J. Giles, *Flanders Then and Now: The Ypres Salient and Passchendaele* (London, 1987).

J. Giles, *The Somme Then and Now* (London, 1977).

H. Goorney, *The Theatre Workshop Story* (London, 1981).

D. Graham, ed., *Keith Douglas: The Complete Poems* (Oxford, 1987).

C. Graves, *The Home Guard of Britain* (London, 1943).

R. Graves, *Goodbye to All That* (London, 1957).

G. De Groot, *Douglas Haig, 1861–1928* (London, 1988).

D. Haig, *My Father's Son: The Memoirs of Major the Earl Haig* (London, 2000).

K. Haig, *Apple Blossom Time* (London, 1997).

J. Hamilton, *The Idle Hill of Summer* (London, 1988).

J. Hammerton, *A Popular History of the Great War*, vi (London, 1934).

J. Hammerton, ed., *World War 1914–1918: A Pictured History* (London, 1934–35).

J. Hammerton, *I Was There: Undying Memories of 1914–18* (London, 1938–39).

M. Hardwick, *The War to End Wars* (London, 1975).

J. Harris, *Covenant with Death* (London, 1969, first published 1961).

R. E. Harris, ed., *Billie: The Neville Letters, 1914–1916* (Uckfield, 1991).

'Ian Hay' (John Hay Beith), *The First Hundred Thousand* (London and Edinburgh, 1915).

'M. Hennessy' (J. Harris), *Blunted Lance* (London, 1981).

S. Hill, *Strange Meeting* (London, 1984, first published 1971).

R. Hill, *The Wood Beyond* (London, 1996).

HMV, *His Master's Voice New Records for November 1930* (London, 1930).

R. Hoare, *World War One: An Illustrated History in Colour, 1914–1918* (London, 1973).

N. Holding, *World War One Army Ancestry* (Ramsbottom, 1997).

N. Holding, *Location of British Army Records, 1914–18* (Ramsbottom, 1999).

N. Holding, *More World War One Army Ancestry* (Ramsbottom, 1998).

R. Holmes, *Riding the Retreat: Mons to the Marne 1914 Revisited* (London, 1995).

T. and V. Holt, *Battlefields of the First World War: A Traveller's Guide* (London, 1993).

T. Hughes, *The Hawk in the Rain* (London, 1957).

S. Humphries and R. van Emden, *Veterans: The Last Survivors of the Great War* (London, 1998).

S. Japrisot, *Un Longue Dimanche de Fiancialles* (Paris, 1991).

P. Larkin, *Required Writing: Miscellaneous Pieces, 1955–1982* (New York, 1984).

P. Larkin, *Collected Poems* (London, 1988).

H. Lauder, *A Minstrel in France* (New York, 1918).

H. Lauder, *Roamin' in the Gloamin'* (London, 1928).

B. H. Liddell Hart, *The Real War* (London, 1930).

B. H. Liddell Hart, *Through the Fog of War* (London, 1938).

J. Littlewood, *Joan's Book: Joan Littlewood's Peculiar History as She Tells It* (London, 1994).

P. Longworth, *The Unending Vigil* (London, 1967).

N. Jones, *The War Walk: A Journey Along the Western Front* (London, 1983).

A. G. Macdonell, *England, Their England* (London, 1983, first published 1933).

D. Macfarlane, *Come From Away* (London, 1991).

P. MacGill, *The Great Push* (Edinburgh, 2000, first published 1915).

W. Moodie, ed., *The Crown of Honour: Being Stories of Heroism, Gallantry, Magnanimity and Devotion from the Great War of 1914–18* (London, 1931).

A. Jenkinson, *What Do Boys and Girls Read?* (London, 1940).

D. Jerrold, *The Lie about the War* (London, 1930).

D. Jones, *In Parenthesis* (London, 1937).

L. Macdonald, *1914* (London, 1987).

L. Macdonald, *1914–1918: Voices and Images of the Great War* (with research by Shirley Seaton) (London, 1988).

L. Macdonald, *1915: The Death of Innocence* (London, 1993).

L. Macdonald, *Somme* (London, 1983).

L. Macdonald, *The Roses of No Man's Land* (London, 1980).

L. Macdonald, *They Called It Passchendaele: The Story of the Third Battle of Ypres and of the Men Who Fought in It* (London, 1978).

L. Macdonald, *To the Last Man: Spring 1918* (London, 1998).

M. Marland, ed., *The Times Authors Number Five: The War Poets* (London, 1971).

A. Marwick, *The Deluge: British Society and the First World War* (2nd edn, London, 1991).

A. McKee, *Vimy Ridge* (London, 1966).

H. McPhail and P. Guest, *Wilfred Owen: On the Trail of the Poets of the Great War* (London, 1998).

P. McVeigh, *Look After the Bairns: A Childhood in East Lothian* (East Linton, 1999).

M. Middlebrook, *The First Day on the Somme: 1 July 1916* (London, 1971).

M. Middlebrook, *The Kaiser's Battle: 21 March 1918. The First Day of the German Spring Offensive* (London, 1978).

M. and M. Middlebrook, *The Somme Battlefields: A Comprehensive Guide from Crecy to the Two World Wars* (London, 1991).

L. Milner, *Leeds Pals: A History of the 15th (Service) Battalion (1st Leeds), The Prince of Wales's Own (West Yorkshire Regiment), 1914–1918* (London, 1991).

C. Moore, *Trench Fever* (London, 1998).

W. Moore, *The Thin Yellow Line* (London, 1974).

Lord Moran (C. Wilson), *Anatomy of Courage* (London, 1945).

S. O'Shea, *Back to the Front: An Accidental Historian Walks the Trenches of World War One* (London, 1997).

H. Owen and J. Bell, eds, *Wilfred Owen: Collected Letters* (Oxford, 1967).

G. Panichas, ed., *Promise of Greatness* (London, 1968).

J. B. Priestley, *Margin Released* (London, 1962).

E. Raymond, *Tell England: A Study in a Generation* (London, 1928, first published 1922).

D. Reeman, *The Horizon* (London, 1993).

J. Reith, *Wearing Spurs* (London, 1966).

A. Rhodes, *Sword of Bone* (London, 1943).

R. Rhodes James, *Gallipoli* (London, 1965).

V. Robinson, *On Target* (Wakefield, 1991).

A. Rosenthal, *The Documentary Conscience: A Casebook in Film Making* (Berkeley, 1980).

P. Ryder as told to G. Bennett, *Guns Have Eyes: One Man's Story of the Normandy Landings* (London, 1984).

J. Saunders, *The Bannister Girls* (London, 1990).

K. Saunders, *Night Shall Overcome Us* (London, 1993).

V. Scannell, *The Tiger and the Rose* (London, 1983).

W. C. Sellar and R. J. Yeatman, *1066 and All That* (Harmondsworth, 1960, first published 1930).

V. Silvester, *Dancing is My Life: An Autobiography* (London, 1958).

E. K. G. Sixsmith, *Douglas Haig* (London, 1976).

D. Smith, *Cricket Stumps and Sticklebacks: A Childhood on Teeside* (Penistone, 1989).

E. Stirling, *A Field of Bright Poppies* (London, 1990).

E. Swinton, ed., *Twenty Years After: The Battlefields of 1914–18 Then and Now* (London, 1936–37).

J. Terraine, *Douglas Haig: The Educated Soldier* (London, 1963).

J. Terraine, *The First World War* (London, 1984).

A. J. P. Taylor, *English History, 1914–1945* (Oxford, 1965).

A. J. P. Taylor, *The First World War: An Illustrated History* (Harmondsworth, 1967, first published 1963).

A. J. P. Taylor, *A Personal History* (London, 1983).

Theatre Workshop, *Oh! What a Lovely War* (London, 2001).

J. Thynne, *Patrimony* (London, 1997).

W. Turner, *The 'Accrington Pals': The 11th (Service) Battalion (Accrington), East Lancashire Regiment: A Pictorial History* (Preston, 1986).

P. Vansittart, ed., *John Masefield's Letters from the Front, 1915–1917* (London, 1984).

B. Uttenthal, *Wilfred Owen: Selected Poems* (Harlow, 1986).

E. Waugh, *A Little Learning* (London, 1964).

D. S. R. Welland, *Wilfred Owen* (London, 1960).

H. G. Wells, *Mr Britling Sees It Through* (London, 1916).

J. Williams, *Mutiny 1917* (London, 1962).

D. Winter, *Death's Men: Soldiers of the Great War* (Harmondsworth, 1979).

D. Winter, *Haig's Command: A Reassessment* (London, 1991).

R. Woollcombe, *The First Tank Battle: Cambrai 1917* (London, 1967).

W. B. Yeats, 'Introduction' in W. B. Yeats, ed., *The Oxford Book of Modern Verse* (Oxford, 1936).

Newspapers, Journals and Periodicals

Daily Express

Daily Mail

Daily Telegraph

Financial Times

Guardian

Independent

New Statesman

Radio Times

Spectator

Sun

Times

Times Literary Supplement

Today

Tribune

Articles

T. Bolas, 'Oh! What a Lovely War', *Screen*, 10, 3 (May/June 1969).

J. Connell, 'Writing about Soldiers', *Journal of the Royal United Services Institute*, 40, 639 (August 1965).

P. French, 'Oh! What a Lovely War', *Sight and Sound*, 38, 2 (Spring 1969).

R. Jeffcoate, 'Teaching Poetry of the First World War in the Secondary School', *Critical Survey*, 2, 2 (1990).

P. Liddle, 'From Liverpool to Leeds via Sunderland: The Collection's Own History', *The Poppy and the Owl: The Journal of the Friends of the Liddle Collection, the Library, the University of Leeds, Leeds, UK*, 24 (November 1998).

G. Minikin, 'Pride and Delight: Motivating Pupils through Poetic Writing about the First World War', *Teaching History*, 95 (May 1999).

P. Simkins, 'My Thirty-Five Years at the Imperial War Museum, Part II – Old Curators Never Die …', *The Western Front Association Bulletin*, 57 (June 2000).

C. H. Roads, 'A View of the Use of Film by the Universities', *University Vision*, 1, 1 (1968).

Websites

'Queen Honours Australian War Dead' BBC News, 11 November 2003, http://news.bbc.co.uk/1/hi/uk/325907.stm, accessed 4 August 2004, 1335.

S. Donaldson, 'Filmmakers on Film: Stephen Fry', http://www.portal.telegraph.co.uk/arts/main.jhtml;$sessionid$RXSH12XIM1H3RQFIQMFSFFWAVCBQoIV0?xml=/arts/2003/09/27/bffmof27.xml&sSheet=/arts/2003/09/27/ixartright.html, accessed 4 August 2004, 1103.

http://amazon.co.uk/exec/obidos/tg/ … sr=1–1/ref=sr_sp_re/202–0151039–9361411, accessed 11 September 2001, 0941.

J. Wright, 'No Known Grave', accessed 23 July 2001, 1226.

SECONDARY SOURCES

Books

P. Addison and A. Calder, eds, *A Time To Kill: The Soldier's Experience of War in the West, 1939–1945* (London, 1997).

K. Agnew and G. Fox, *Children at War: From the First World War to the Gulf* (London, 2001).

C. Barnett, *The Collapse of British Power* (London, 1972).

R. Barthes, *Mythologies* (Paris, 1957).

J. Baynes, *Far from a Donkey: The Life of General Sir Ivor Maxse* (London, 1995).

E. Belfield and H. Essame, *The Battle for Normandy* (London, 1975).

P. Berry and M. Bostridge, *Vera Brittain: A Life* (London, 1996).

B. Bond, *The Unquiet Western Front* (Cambridge, 2002).

B. Bond, ed., *The First World War and British Military History* (Oxford, 1991).

B. Bond, *The Victorian Army and the Staff College, 1854–1914* (London, 1972).

B. Bond et al., *Look to Your Front! Studies in the First World War* (Staplehurst, 1999).

B. Bond and N. Cave, eds, *Haig: A Reappraisal Seventy Years On* (Barnsley, 1999).

D. Boorman, *At the Going Down of the Sun: British First World War Memorials* (York, 1988).

J. Bourke, *An Intimate History of Killing: Face to Face Killing in Twentieth Century Warfare* (London, 1998).

J. Bourke, *Dismembering the Male: Men's Bodies, Britain and the Great War* (London, 1996).

R. M. Bracco, *Merchants of Hope: British Middlebrow Writers and the First World War, 1919–39* (Oxford, 1993).

G. Braybon and P. Summerfield, *Out of the Cage: Women's Experiences in Two World Wars* (London, 1987).

G. Braybon, ed., *Evidence, History and the Great War: Historians and the Impact of 1914–18* (Oxford, 2004).

I. M. Brown, *British Logistics on the Western Front* (London, 1998).

M. Brown, *The Imperial War Museum Book of the Western Front* (London, 1996).

K. Brownlow, *The War, the West and the Wilderness* (London, 1979)

V. Brome, *J. B. Priestley* (London, 1988).

M. Bryant, ed., *The Complete Colonel Blimp* (London, 1991).

A. Caesar, *Taking It Like a Man: Suffering, Sexuality and the War Poets* (Manchester, 1993).

A. Calder, *The Myth of the Blitz* (London, 1991).

A. Calder, *The People's War*, (London, 1992 [1969]).

P. Calvocoressi, G. Wint and J. Pritchard, *Total War: Causes and Courses of the Second World War* (2nd edn, New York and Harmondsworth, 1989).

H. Carpenter, *Benjamin Britten: A Biography* (London, 1992) .

H. Cecil and P. Liddle, eds, *Facing Armageddon: The First World War Experienced* (London, 1996).

H. Cecil, *The Flower of Battle: British Fiction Writers of the First World War* (London, 1995).

I. F. Clarke, *Voices Prophesying War: Future Wars, 1763–3749* (2nd edn, Oxford, 1992).

P. Clarke, *Hope and Glory: Britain, 1900–1990* (London, 1996).

D. Cohen, *The War Come Home: Disabled Veterans in Britain and Germany, 1914–1939* (Berkeley, California, 2001).

C. Coker, *War and the Twentieth Century: A Study of War and Modern Consciousness* (London, 1994).

M. Connelly, *We Can Take It! Britain and the Memory of the Second World War* (London, 2004).

M. Connelly, *The Great War, Memory and Ritual: Commemoration in the City and East London, 1916–1939* (Woodbridge, 2002).

S. Constantine, M. Kirby and M. Rese, eds, *The First World War in British History* (London, 1995).

C. Goodwin, *To Be a Lady: The Story of Catherine Cookson* (London, 1994).

R. Cork, *A Bitter Truth: Avant-Garde Art and the Great War* (New Haven, Connecticut and London, 1994).

C. Corns and J. Hughes-Wilson, *Blindfold and Alone: British Military Executions in the Great War* (London, 2001).

J. A. Crang, *The British Army and the People's War, 1939–45* (Manchester, 2000).

C. Creighton and M. Shaw, eds, *The Sociology of War and Peace* (Basingstoke, 1987).

A. Danchev, *Alchemist of War: The Life of Sir Basil Liddell Hart* (London, 1998).

G. Dawson, *Soldier Heroes: British Adventure, Empire and the Imagining of Masculinity* (London, 1994).

G. Day, ed., *British Poetry, 1900–1950: Aspects of Tradition* (Basingstoke and London, 1992).

M. Donnelly, *Britain in the Second World War* (London, 1999).

A. Dougan, *The Actor's Director: Richard Attenborough Behind the Camera* (Edinburgh, 1994).

K. Drotner, *English Children and Their Magazines, 1751–1945* (New Haven, Connecticut, 1988).

G. Dyer, *The Missing of the Somme* (London, 1994).

G. Enser, *A Subject Bibliography of the First World War in English, 1914–1987* (London, 1990).

C. d'Este, *Decision in Normandy* (London, 2001, first published 1983).

C. Falls, *War Books: A Critical Guide* (London, 1930).

S. Featherstone, *War Poetry: An Introductory Reader* (London, 1995).

N. Ferguson, *The Pity of War: Explaining World War I* (London, 1998).

K. Foster, *Fighting Fictions: War, Narrative and National Identity* (London, 1999).

D. French, *Raising Churchill's Army: The British Army and the War against Germany, 1919–1945* (Oxford, 2000).

A. Gaffney, *Aftermath: Remembering the Great War in Wales* (Cardiff, 1998).

A. Gregory, *The Silence of Memory: Armistice Day, 1919–1946* (Oxford, 1994).

N. Gullace, 'The Blood of Our Sons': Men, Women and the Renegotiation of British Citizenship during the Great War* (Basingstoke, 2002).

P. Griffith, *Battle Tactics of the Western Front: The British Army's Art of Attack, 1916–18* (New Haven, Connecticut and London, 1994).

P. Hennessy, *The Secret State: Whitehall and the Cold War* (London, 2003).

P. Hennessy, *Never Again: Britain, 1945–51* (London, 1992).

R. Hewison, *Too Much: Art and Society in the Sixties, 1960–1975* (London, 1986).

D. Hibberd, *Wilfred Owen: The Last Year, 1917–18* (London, 1992).

D. Hibberd, *Owen the Poet* (London, 1986).

R. Holmes, *Tommy: The British Soldier on the Western Front, 1914–18* (London, 2004).

R. Holmes, *The Little Field Marshal* (London, 1981).

T. and V. Holt, 'My Boy Jack?': The Search for Kipling's Only Son* (London, 1998).

J. Horne and A. Kramer, *German Atrocities, 1914: A History of Denial* (New Haven, Connecticut, 2001).

M. Howard, *The Continental Commitment: The Dilemma of British Defence Policy in the Era of Two World Wars* (London, 1972).

S. Hynes, *The Soldiers' Tale: Bearing Witness to Modern War* (London, 1998).

S. Hynes, *A War Imagined: The First World War and English Culture* (London, 1990).

S. Hynes, *The Auden Generation: Literature and Politics in England in the 1930s* (London, 1976).

P. Jalland, *Death in the Victorian Family* (Oxford, 1996).

A. King, *Memorials of the Great War in Britain: The Symbolism and Politics of Remembrance* (Oxford, 1998).

P. Kirkham and D. Thoms, eds, *War Culture: Social Change and Changing Experience in World War Two Britain* (London, 1995).

J. Laffin, *British Butchers and Bunglers of World War One* (Stroud, 1988).

E. Leed, *No Man's Land: Combat and Identity in World War I* (Cambridge, 1979).

J. E. Lewis, ed., *The Mammoth Book of War Diaries and Letters* (London, 1998).

P. Liddle, ed., *Passchendaele in Perspective: The Third Battle of Ypres* (London, 1997).

P. Liddle and H. Cecil, eds, *At the Eleventh Hour: Reflections, Hopes and Anxieties at the Closing of the Great War, 1918* (London, 1998).

D. Lloyd, *Battlefield Tourism: Pilgrimage and the Commemoration of the Great War in Britain, Australia and Canada, 1919–1939* (Oxford, 1998).

D. Lowenthal, *The Past is a Foreign Country* (Cambridge, 1999).

J. Mackenzie, ed., *Popular Imperialism and the Military, 1850–1950* (Manchester, 1992).

R. Mackay, *The Test of War* (London, 1999).

S. Mackenzie, *The Home Guard: A Military and Political History* (Oxford, 1995).

J. Macleod, *Reconsidering Gallipoli* (Leicester, 2004).

A. Marwick, *British Society since 1945* (London, 1996).

J. McAleer, *Popular Reading and Publishing* (Oxford, 1992).

R. McKibbin, *Classes and Cultures: England, 1918–1951* (Oxford, 1998).

N. Merriman, *Beyond the Glass Case: The Past, the Heritage and the Public in Britain* (Leicester, 1991).

K. Morgan, *The People's Peace: British History, 1945–1990* (Oxford, 1992).

G. Moorhouse, *Hell's Foundations: A Town, its Myths and Gallipoli* (London, 1992).

G. Mosse, *Fallen Soldiers: Reshaping the Memory of the Two World Wars* (Oxford, 1990).

N. Offenstadt, *Les Fusillés de la Grande Guerre et la Mémoire Collective, 1914–1999* (Paris, 1999).

P. Orr, *The Road to the Somme: Men of the Ulster Division Tell Their Story* (Belfast, 1987).

A. Palazzo, *Seeking Victory on the Western Front: The British Army and Chemical Warfare in World War I* (Lincoln, Nebraska, and London, 2000).

M. Paris, *Warrior Nation: Images of War in British Popular Culture, 1850–2000* (London, 2000).

I. Passingham, *All the Kaiser's Men* (Stroud, 2004).

I. Passingham, *Pillars of Fire: The Battle of Messines Ridge, June 1917* (Stroud, 1998).

C. Ponting, *1940: Myth and Reality* (London, 1990).

R. Prior, *Churchill's 'The World Crisis' as History* (Beckenham, 1983).

R. Prior and T. Wilson, *The First World War* (London, 1999).

R. Prior and T. Wilson, *Passchendaele: The Untold Story* (New Haven, Connecticut, and London, 1996).

C. Pugsley, *New Zealand. Australia and Empire, 1914–1918: Reflections on the ANZAC Experience in the First World War* (Oxford, 2004).

J. Putkowski and J. Sykes, *Shot at Dawn* (Barnsley, 1989).

S. Radstone, ed., *Memory and Methodology* (Oxford, 1999).

J. Radway, *Reading the Romance: Women, Patriarchy and Popular Literature* (London, 1987, first published 1984).

B. Rawling, *Surviving Trench Warfare: Technology and the Canadian Corps, 1914–18* (Toronto, 1992).

I. Reader and T. Walter, eds, *Pilgrimage in Popular Culture* (Basingstoke, 1993).

J. Richards, *Visions of Yesterday* (London, 1973).

J. Richards, *Films and British National Identity: From Dickens to Dad's Army* (Manchester, 1997).

K. Robbins, *The First World War* (Oxford, 1994).

R. Samuel, *Theatres of Memory*, ii, *Island Stories, Unravelling Britain* (London, 1998).

G. Sheffield, *Forgotten Victory: The First World War, Myths and Realities* (London, 2001).

G. Sheffield, *Leadership in the Trenches: Officer–Man Relations, Morale and Discipline in the British Army in the Era of the First World War* (Basingstoke, 1999).

G. Sheffield, ed., *Leadership and Command: The Anglo-American Experience since 1861* (London, 1997).

G. Sheffield and D. Todman, eds, *Command and Control on the Western Front: The British Experience, 1914–18* (Staplehurst, 2004).

B. Shephard, *A War of Nerves: Soldiers and Psychiatrists, 1914–1994* (London, 2000).

A. Sisman, *A. J. P. Taylor: A Biography* (London, 1995).

E. Sivan and J. Winter, eds, *War and Remembrance in the Twentieth Century* (Cambridge, 1999).

A. Sked, *An Intelligent Person's Guide to Post-War Britain* (London, 1997).

M. Smith, *Britain and 1940: History, Myth and Popular Memory* (London, 2000).

S. Stemlicht, *C. S. Forester* (Boston, 1981).

M. Stephen, *The Price of Pity: Poetry, History and Myth in the Great War* (London, 1996).

D. Stevenson, *The First World War and International Politics* (Oxford, 1988).

H. Strachan, *The Oxford History of the First World War*, i, *The Call to Arms* (Oxford, 2000).

D. Strinati and S. Wagg, eds, *Come On Down? Popular Culture in Post-War Britain* (London, 1992).

J. Terraine, *The Smoke and the Fire: Myths and Anti-Myths of War* (London, 1985).

D. Thom, *Nice Girls and Rude Girls: Women Workers in World War One* (London, 2000).

A. Thomson, *ANZAC Memories: Living with the Legend* (Melbourne and Oxford, 1994).

C. Townshend, *Britain's Civil Wars: Counterinsurgency in the Twentieth Century* (London, 1986).

B. Turner and T. Rendell, *When Daddy Came Home: How Family Life Changed Forever in 1945* (London, 1995).

T. Travers, *The Killing Ground: The British Army, the Western Front and the Emergence of Modern Warfare, 1900–1918* (London, 1987).

J. Turner, ed., *Britain and the First World War* (London, 1988).

C. Tylee, *The Great War and Military Consciousness: Images of Militarism and Womanhood in Women's Writings, 1914–1964* (Basingstoke, 1990).

J. Vance, *Death So Noble: Memory, Meaning and the First World War* (Vancouver, 1997).

R. Van Emden, *The Trench: Experiencing Life on the Front Line, 1916* (London, 2003).

J. Walker, *The Blood Tub: General Gough and the Battle of Bullecourt, 1917* (Staplehurst, 1998).

K. Walsh, *The Representation of the Past: Museums and Heritage in the Post-Modern World* (London, 1992).

J. Watson, *Fighting Different Wars: Experience, Memory and the First World War in Britain* (Cambridge, 2004).

R. Weight, *Patriots: National Identity in Britain, 1940–2000* (London, 2002).

J. M. Wilson, *Siegfried Sassoon: The Making of a War Poet, 1886–1918* (London, 1998).

T. Wilson, *The Myriad Faces of War: Britain and the Great War, 1914–18* (Cambridge, 1986).

J. Winter, *Sites of Memory, Sites of Mourning: The Great War in European Cultural History* (Cambridge, 1995).

J. Winter, *The Great War and the British People* (Cambridge, 1986).

J. Winter and B. Baggett, *The Great War and the Shaping of the Twentieth Century* (New York, 1996).

G. Wooton, *The Official History of the British Legion* (London, 1956).

P. Wright, *On Living in an Old Country: The National Past in Contemporary Britain* (London, 1985).

Articles

S. Badsey, 'The Great War since *The Great War*', *Historical Journal of Film, Radio and Television*, 22, 1 (March 2002).

S. Badsey, 'The IWM Series: A Guide to the IWM Collection of Archive Film of the First World War', *Historical Journal of Film, Radio and Television*, 13, 2 (1993).

J. Bourke, 'Effeminacy, Ethnicity and the End of Trauma: The Sufferings of "Shell-Shocked" Men in Great Britain and Ireland, 1914–39', *Journal of Contemporary History*, 35, 1 (2000).

J. Chapman, '*The Life and Death of Colonel Blimp* Reconsidered', *Historical Journal of Film, Radio and Television*, 15, 1 (March 1995).

M. Connelly, 'The Great War, Part 13', *Historical Journal of Film, Radio and Television*, 22, 1 (2002).

G. Egerton, 'The Lloyd George *War Memoirs*: A Study in the Politics of Memory', *Journal of Modern History*, 60 (March 1988).

M. Finn, 'The Realities of War', *History Today*, 52, 8 (August 2002).

D. French, 'Sir Douglas Haig's Reputation, 1918–1928: A Note', *Historical Journal*, 28, 4 (1985).

D. French, 'The Meaning of Attrition, 1914–1916', *English Historical Review*, 103, 407 (April 1988).

N. Gedi and Y. Elam, 'Collective Memory: What Is It?', *History and Memory*, 8, 1 (Spring/Summer 1996).

R. Gibson, 'Somme Soldier', *Stand To! The Journal of the Western Front Association*, 54 (January 1999).

A. Gregory, 'Demobilising the Nation, Remobilising the Dead: The Persistent Mythology of British Commemoration', paper at 'Demobilising the Nation' Conference, Dublin, September 2001.

N. Hiley, '"KITCHENER WANTS YOU" and "Daddy, What did YOU do in the Great War?": The Myth of British Recruiting Posters', *Imperial War Museum Review*, 11 (1997).

P. Leese, 'Problems Returning Home: The British Psychological Casualties of the Great War', *Historical Journal*, 40, 4 (1997).

C. Moriarty, 'Review Article: The Material Culture of Great War Remembrance', *Journal of Contemporary History*, 34, 4 (1999).

G. Mosse, 'Two World Wars and the Myth of the War Experience', *Journal of Contemporary History*, 21 (1986).

D. Paget, 'Popularising Popular History: "Oh What a Lovely War" and the Sixties', *Critical Query and Survey*, 2, 2 (1990).

R. Prior and T. Wilson, 'Paul Fussell at War', *War in History*, 1, 1 (1994).

J. Ramsden, '*The Great War*: The Making of the Series', *Historical Journal of Film, Radio and Television*, 22, 1 (March 2002).

L. Smith, 'Paul Fussell's *The Great War and Modern Memory*: Twenty-Five Years Later', *History and Theory*, 40 (May 2001).

R. Smither, '"A Wonderful Idea of the Fighting": The Question of Fakes in *The Battle of the Somme*', *Historical Journal of Film, Radio and Television*, 13, 2 (1993).

D. Todman, 'A Statue for Earl Haig', *Douglas Haig Fellowship Records*, 8 (December 2002).

D. Todman, '"Sans Peur et Sans Reproche": The Retirement, Death and Mourning of Sir Douglas Haig, 1918–1928', *Journal of Military History*, 67, 4 (October 2003).

J. Winter, 'The Generation of Memory: Reflections on the "Memory Boom" in Contemporary Historical Studies', *Bulletin of the German Historical Institute Washington*, 27 (2000).

T. Wilson, 'Lord Bryce's Investigation into Alleged German Atrocities in Belgium, 1914–15', *Journal of Contemporary History* (July 1979).

Unpublished Theses

L. Clark, '"Goodbye to All What?" The Great War Writers, their Truth and the Great War Myth', MA, Kings College London (1992).

N. Barr, '"Service not Self": The British Legion, 1921–1939', PhD, University of St Andrews (1994).

D. Todman, 'Representations of the First World War in British Popular Culture, 1918–1998', PhD, University of Cambridge (2003).

Websites

S. Cloutier, 'Wilfred Owen and his Early Editors', http://www.firstworldwar.com/poetsandprose/owen_editors.htm, accessed 6 July 2004, 0905.

E. MacCallum Stewart, 'Comics and the War', accessed 5 February 2003, 1016.

Index